Why I Love Vienna

By Catherine Le Nevez, Writer

With its rambling palaces, winding cobbled lanes, elegant *Kaffeehäuser* (coffee houses) and cosy wood-panelled *Beisln*, Vienna is steeped in history. Yet it's also at the cutting edge of design, architecture, contemporary art, and new directions in drinking and dining. What I love most about the city is that not only does it hold on to its traditions, it incorporates them in everything from high-fashion *Dirndls* (women's traditional dress) with pop-art motifs or punk conical studs to handmade *Sacher Torte*–flavoured doughnuts and inspired neo-retro cafes. Vienna's past is alive in its present, and, by extension, its future.

For more about our writers, see p264

Top: Café Griensteidl (p71)

Vienna's Top 10

1

lonely planet

Vienna

"All you've got to do is decide to go and the hardest part is over.

So go!"

TONY WHEELER, COFOUNDER – LONELY PLANET

Contents

(left) **Schloss Belvedere p141** Art collection in a baroque palace.

(above) **The Hofburg p60** Dome of the former imperial palace.

(right) ***Sacher Torte*** **p70** Vienna's favourite cake.

Welcome to Vienna

Baroque streetscapes and imperial palaces set the stage for artistic and musical masterpieces alongside vibrant epicurean and design scenes.

Imperial Architecture

Vienna's imperial grandeur is the legacy of the powerful Habsburg monarchy. Their home for more than six centuries, the Hofburg palace complex, incorporates the Burgkapelle (Imperial Chapel) and the famed Spanish Riding School, along with a trove of museums, including the chandeliered Kaiserappartements (Imperial Apartments). Other immense palaces include the baroque Schloss Belvedere and Schloss Schönbrunn, while 19th-century splendours such as the neo-Gothic Rathaus (City Hall) line the magnificent Ringstrasse encircling the Innere Stadt (inner city).

Masterpiece-Filled Museums

One of the Habsburgs' most dazzling palaces, the Kunsthistorisches Museum, houses the imperial art collection. It's packed with priceless works by Old Masters, and treasures including one of the world's richest coin collections. Behind the Hofburg, the innovative MuseumsQuartier has a diverse ensemble of museums, from 19th- and 20th-century Austrian art at the Leopold Museum to often-shocking avant-garde works at the contemporary MUMOK. Meteorites, fossils and prehistoric finds fill the Naturhistorisches Museum, while exquisite furnishings at the applied-arts Museum für Angewandte Kunst are also among the artistic feasts in store.

Soul-Stirring Music

With a musical heritage that includes composers Wolfgang Amadeus Mozart, Joseph Haydn, Ludwig van Beethoven, Franz Schubert, Johann Strauss (father and son), Johannes Brahms and Gustav Mahler, among countless others, Vienna is known as the City of Music. Incredible venues where you can catch performances today include the acoustically renowned Musikverein, used by the Vienna Philharmonic Orchestra, the gold-and-crystal main opera house, the Staatsoper, and the multistage Konzerthaus. Music comes to life through interactive exhibits at the captivating Haus der Musik museum.

Drinking & Dining

The Viennese appreciation of the finer things in life extends to its opulent coffee-house 'living rooms' serving spectacular cakes; its beloved pub-like *Beisln* dishing up hearty portions of Wiener Schnitzel and goulash; elegant restaurants; and its fine Austrian wines served in vaulted *Vinothek* (wine bar) cellars, and in rustic vine-draped *Heurigen* (wine taverns) in the vineyards fringing the city. Local and international delicacies fill the heady Naschmarkt stalls, and creative chefs are experimenting with local produce and fresh new flavour combinations in innovative, often repurposed venues.

Schloss Schönbrunn *(p167)*

1 The magnificent rococo former summer palace and gardens of the Habsburgs are a perfect place to experience the pomp, circumstance and gracious legacy of Austria's erstwhile monarchs. A visit to 40 of the palace's lavishly appointed rooms reveals the lifestyle and the eccentricities of Europe's most powerful family. Beyond the palace, Schloss Schönbrunn Gardens invite a stroll past pseudo-Roman ruins, along bucolic paths winding through leafy woods and a stopover in the gardens' highlight, the Gloriette, with mesmerising views of the palace and city beyond.

Schloss Schönbrunn & Around

Kunsthistorisches Museum *(p109)*

2 The jewel in Vienna's artistic crown is its Kunsthistorisches Museum. As well as accumulating vassal lands, the Habsburgs assembled one of Europe's finest collections of art and artefacts. Housed inside a majestic neoclassical building, the highlight of this incredible cache is the Picture Gallery, an encounter with a vast and emotionally powerful collection of works by grand masters, such as Pieter Bruegel the Elder's evocative and 'industrial' *Tower of Babel* from the 16th century or the bright plenitude of Giuseppe Arcimboldo's *Summer.*

The Museum District & Neubau

© SCHLOSS SCHÖNBRUNN KULTUR- UND BETRIEBSGES.M.B.H. / KOLLER

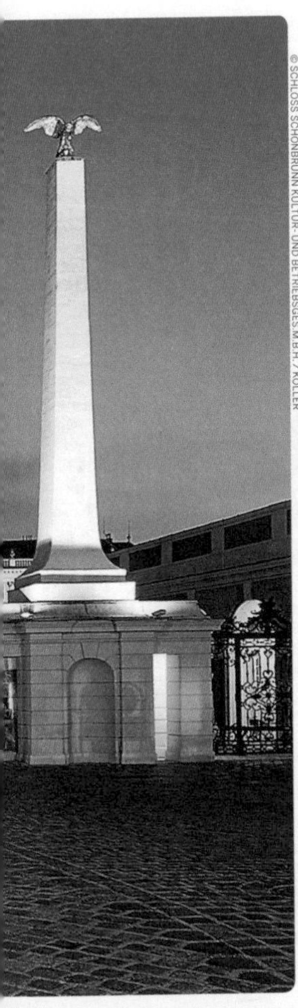

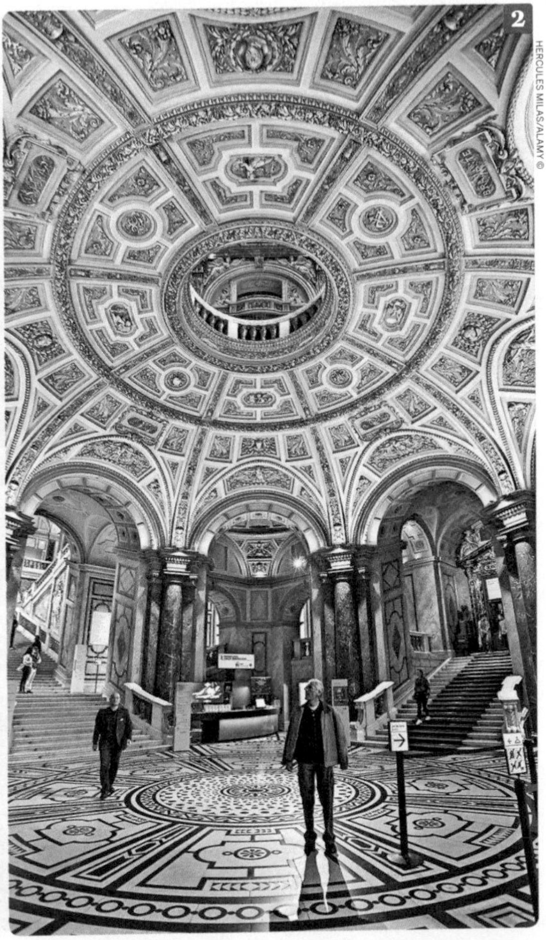

2

HERCULES MILAS/ALAMY ©

3

4

Schloss Belvedere

(p141)

3 Living up to its Italianesque name 'beautiful view', this 18th-century palace and garden ensemble is deceptively close to Vienna's city centre while still creating a feeling of being worlds apart. Symmetrical, finely sculpted and manicured gardens overlooking Vienna's unfolding skyline connect two exquisite palaces dedicated to a who's who of Austrian art. Gustav Klimt's painting *The Kiss* is a highlight. The masterpieces on display are complemented by interiors so stately that they're worthy of a visit in their own right.

Schloss Belvedere to the Canal

Prater & Ferris Wheel *(p157)*

4 Rising above the beautiful green open spaces of the Prater, the 1897-built Riesenrad Ferris wheel, where Graham Greene sent his fictional character Harry Lime for a slow rotation in the 1949 film *The Third Man*, is a Viennese icon. A ride takes you high above the Prater, giving you a bird's-eye view of the city and the expanse of wooded parkland and meadows, which you can explore on inline skates, by bicycle or on a walk after hitting ground level.

Prater & East of the Danube

Ringstrasse Tram Tour *(p29)*

5 For a spin around Vienna's architectural highlights, jump on a tram and travel along the Ringstrasse, one of Europe's most magnificent streets. This circular boulevard of imposing state buildings, palaces and majestic hotels was carved out of the space once occupied by fortifications protecting Vienna from Ottoman Turk attack in the 16th century. The monumental 19th-century masterpieces now rise up along the flanks, encircling most of the central Innere Stadt and separating the centre from the character-laden *Vorstädte* (inner suburbs).

Guided Walks & Tours

Hofburg Palace *(p60)*

6 The imposing former wintering ground of the Habsburg monarchs for over 700 years not only has a fine collection of museums, it's also a living palace that today is home to the Austrian president, Austria's National Library and public offices (and is the temporary home of the Austrian Parlament). A leisurely stroll through the palace complex is an encounter with one gracious building, statue and square after another, taking in highlights such as the Swiss Courtyard, the grotesquely proportioned Heldenplatz, and diminutive arches of the Outer Palace Gate. BELOW: VOLKSGARTEN (P64)

The Hofburg & Around

Coffee Houses *(p35)*

7 Great works of art have been created in these 'living rooms' of the Viennese. Patronised by luminaries such as Mahler, Klimt, Freud, Trotsky and Otto Wagner in their day, Vienna's *Kaffeehäuser* (coffee houses) were added to the Unesco list of Intangible Cultural Heritage in 2011. Many retain their opulent original decor, and often specialise in a particular cake, such as the *Sacher Torte*, an iced-chocolate cake with apricot jam once favoured by Emperor Franz Josef, at Café Sacher. New-wave coffee houses are putting their own twist on the tradition. RIGHT: CAFÉ CENTRAL (P135)

Coffee Houses & Cake Shops

7

Beisln *(p31)*

8 A Viennese tradition, a *Beisl* is akin to a bistro pub, dishing up heaping portions of goulash, *Wiener Schnitzel, Tafelspitz* (prime boiled beef) and other favourites along with wine and/or beer on unadorned tables in wood-panelled surrounds. In the warmer months, many *Beisln* open onto terraces or lantern-lit cobbled courtyards. Linger over a drink, enjoy the classic Austrian fare and soak up the unique atmosphere at stalwarts such as Griechenbeisl (pictured left; p85). These institutions have inspired a new breed of neo-*Beisln*, with a slightly upmarket edge and often organic produce.

Eating

Vienna Boys' Choir *(p46)*

9 When Maximilian I founded the Wiener Sängerknaben (Vienna Boys' Choir) in 1498 he replaced castrati with young boys whose voices had not broken, creating the world's most celebrated choir. Today the celestial tones of this choir echo through the Burgkapelle (Imperial Chapel) of the Hofburg, where the choir performs classical music from Schubert, Mozart and other musical greats during Sunday Mass; it also stages an eclectic program of classical and contemporary music across town in MuTh, its own dedicated performing space.

☆ ***Entertainment***

Stephansdom *(p76)*

10 A Gothic reminder of another age, the Stephansdom is Vienna's heart and soul. The awe-inspiring cathedral lords over the city, topped by an intricately tiled roof, with its distinctive row of chevrons and Austrian eagle. Below the cathedral are the *Katakomben* (catacombs), with their eerie collection of the deceased; inside, a magnificent Gothic stone pulpit presides over the main nave; and rising above it to dizzying heights is the South Tower with its viewing stage offering dazzling views over town.

⊙ ***Stephansdom & the Historic Centre***

What's New

Hip, Happening Hotels

Innovative new hotel openings include the Grätzlhotel (p196), in previously abandoned shops where electricians, lamp makers and bakers once plied a trade, overhauled by some of Vienna's top architects; the multibudget Grand Ferdinand (p194), with parquet-floored, mahogany-bunk dorms, swish designer rooms with chaises longues, and chandeliered suites with private champagne bars; mid-20th-century eyesore-turned-designer digs Hotel Capricorno (p193); and Magdas (p196), a funky boutique hotel run by refugees, with one-off murals and upcycled furniture.

Arriving in Style

Unveiled in 2015, Vienna's new main train station and premier rail hub, the Wien Hauptbahnhof, is topped by a diamond-shaped glass-and-steel roof and incorporates 84 shops, bars and restaurants. (p221)

Literary Luminaries

Books, manuscripts, letters, photos, illustrations and personal effects from seminal authors, playwrights and poets from the 18th century onwards are displayed in the Biedermeier building housing the 2015-opened Literaturmuseum. (p81)

Vintage Cinema

Cinematic exhibitions spread over two levels of the Austrian Film Archive's 2015-opened Metro Kinokulturhaus. Below, the restored wood-panelled cinema screens historic and art-house Austrian films. (p89)

Hot Rod Highlights

Zoom around the Ringstrasse and past iconic sights such as the Ferris-wheel-crowned Prater in a single-driver mini hot rod on day and night convoy circuits run by Hot Rod City Tour. (p29)

A Walk on the Wild Side

Get a completely different perspective of the elegant Austrian capital with Space and Place, whose alternative tours include 'Vienna Ugly' and the olfactory-driven 'Smells Like Wien Spirit'. (p29)

Vegetarian Heaven

A cornucopia of new veggie and/or vegan openings in the city includes Tian Bistro (p121), run by Michelin-starred restaurant Tian, and bohemian haven Harvest (p160).

Reinvented Institutions

New spins on old Viennese favourites include retro-grand cafe–concept store Supersense (p161), with locally roasted coffee, and *Würstelstand*-style Yppenplatz 4 (p132), in the old Ottakringer brewery offices, matching beers with local sausages.

Craft Beer Craze

Vienna's hopping on-board with the craft-beer trend: try dozens on tap or by the bottle at the Brickmakers Pub & Kitchen (p122), or pick up takeaway brews at emporium Beer Lovers (p105).

Paired Cocktails

Red-hot new bar-restaurant Blue Mustard, with backlit wood hand-carvings of Stephansdom's Gothic windows, a wall-to-wall neon-lit map of Vienna and in-foyer street-food truck, is making a splash with its cocktail pairings. (p69)

For more recommendations and reviews, see **lonelyplanet.com/austria/vienna**

Need to Know

For more information, see Survival Guide (p219)

Currency
Euro (€)

Language
German

Visas
Generally not required for stays of up to 90 days (or at all for EU nationals); some nationalities need a Schengen visa.

Money
ATMs are widely available. Credit cards are not always accepted in budget hotels or budget to midrange restaurants. Bars and cafes usually only accept cash.

Mobile Phones
You can use your mobile phone (*Handy* in German) in Austria provided it is GSM and tri-band or quad-band. Check with your service provider about using your phone in Austria, but beware of roaming costs, especially for data.

Time
Central European Time (GMT/UTC plus one hour)

Tourist Information
Tourist Info Wien (p226) Vienna's main tourist office, with a ticket agency, hotel booking service, free maps and brochures.

Daily Costs

Budget: Less than €100
- Dorm bed: €25–30
- Cheap double per person: €40–65
- Self-catering or lunchtime specials: €6–12
- Free sights and cheap museums: to €7
- Happy hour: beer/wine €2–4, cocktails €4.50–6.50

Midrange: €100–180
- Hotel double per person: €65–105
- Two-course midrange meal with glass of wine: €25–35
- High-profile museums: €13

Top end: More than €180
- Upmarket hotel double per person: from €105
- Multicourse meal with wine: from €70
- Opera and theatre: from €40

Advance Planning

Three months before Reserve tickets for Staatsoper seating, Vienna Boys' Choir, the Spanish Riding School and major events.

One month before Make reservations for top-shelf restaurants; check upcoming events at www.wien.info and venue websites. Book accommodation in summer.

One week before Check Falter (www.falter.at) for drinking and dining tips and reserve a table in popular restaurants for weekend nights.

Useful Websites

Tourist Info Wien (www.wien.info) Information, hotel bookings, events, special interest.

Falter (www.falter.at) Eating, drinking and entertainment listings and advice.

Lonely Planet (www.lonelyplanet.com/austria/vienna) Destination information, hotel bookings, traveller forum and more.

Vienna Webservice (www.wien.gv.at) Official Vienna city council website.

WHEN TO GO

July and August are busy. April–June and September–October are ideal times to visit. November can be drizzly, while December–March often brings snow.

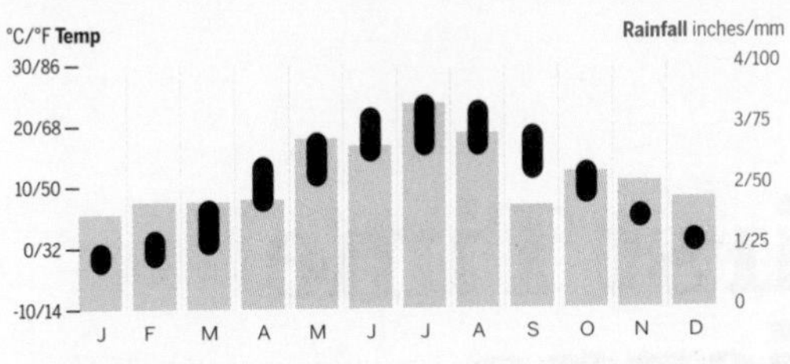

Arriving in Vienna

Vienna International Airport The City Airport Train (CAT; €11, 15 minutes) leaves the airport every 30 minutes from 6.09am till 11.39pm 365 days. The cheaper but slower S7 suburban train (€4.40, 25 minutes) also runs every 30 minutes from 4.48am to 12.18am from the airport to Wien-Mitte. Expect to pay €25 to €50 for a taxi.

Wien Hauptbahnhof Situated 3km south of Stephansdom, Vienna's gleaming-new main train station handles all international trains as well as trains from all of Austria's provincial capitals, and many local and regional trains. It's linked to the centre by U-Bahn line 1, trams D and O, and buses 13A and 69A. A taxi to the centre costs about €10. All stations are generally safe late at night and have good connections with the centre and suburbs.

For much more on **arrival** see p220

Getting Around

U-Bahn Fast, comfortable and safe. Trains run from 5am to midnight Monday to Thursday and continuously from 5am Friday through to midnight Sunday. Tickets are sold at machines or windows at stations. Validate tickets prior to boarding.

Tram Slower but more enjoyable. Depending on route, trams run from around 5.15am to about 11.45pm. Buy tickets at kiosks or from the driver (more expensive). Validate tickets when boarding.

Bus Reliable, punctual, with several very useful routes for visitors. Most run from 5am to midnight; services can be sporadic or nonexistent on weekends. Tickets can bought from the driver or from a *Tabakladen* (tobacconist). Validate tickets on boarding.

Night Bus Especially useful for outer areas; runs every 30 minutes from 12.30am to 5am. Main stops are located at Schwedenplatz, Schottentor and Kärntner Ring/Oper.

For much more on **getting around** see p222

Sleeping

Vienna has a huge range of lodgings, from luxury establishments with chandeliers and antique furniture to inexpensive youth hostels. In between are cutting-edge design hotels, cosy family-run *Pensionen* (guesthouses) and traditional hotels, plus a smart range of apartments.

Useful Websites

Lonely Planet (www.lonelyplanet.com/austria/vienna/hotels) Reviews of Lonely Planet's top choices.

Hostelling International (www.hihostels.com) Global youth hostel organisation.

Tourist Info Wien (www.wien.info/en/hotels) Vienna's tourist office.

For much more on **sleeping** see p190

First Time Vienna

For more information, see Survival Guide (p219)

Checklist

➡ Make sure your passport is valid for at least six months past your arrival date.

➡ Arrange travel insurance and/or medical insurance.

➡ Inform your bank/credit-card company of your travel.

➡ Make copies of all important documents and cards and store separately.

➡ Contact your mobile provider to enquire about roaming charges or getting an international plan.

What to Pack

➡ Comfortable walking shoes for exploration (with profile for ice in winter)

➡ Umbrella or rain jacket

➡ Decent shoes and jacket for going out – the Viennese dress up

➡ Day pack

➡ Electrical adaptor if needed

Top Tips for Your Trip

➡ Sightsee on foot in central Vienna. The Innere Stadt is deceptively small and most places are a short walk from Stephansplatz. Save time outside the centre by taking public transport, and save money by using a public transport pass. It's easy to cross town on a U-Bahn or tram to explore outer neighbourhoods.

➡ Linger over coffee and cake at one of 'Vienna's living rooms', its resplendent coffee houses, and over specialities such as schnitzels, with a local wine or beer, in its cosy *Beisln* (bistro pubs). These institutions are as much a part of Vienna as its palaces and museums.

➡ Catch a classical-music or opera performance for a quintessential City of Music experience. Standing-room tickets start from just a few euros.

What to Wear

Winter can be cold and the ground icy, so several layers of warm clothing and good shoes are essential, along with gloves, a scarf and a woollen cap or a hat. In spring and summer the weather can be very changeable, so wear layers you can peel off and make sure you have a waterproof jacket (or umbrella) for rain showers. The Viennese tend to dress up well in the evening or at good restaurants, but smart jeans are usually fine even for upmarket clubs and restaurants if combined with a good shirt or blouse. Pack a dress/suit if you're attending the opera or similar high-end venues.

Be Forewarned

Vienna is a very safe city and in general women and men will have no trouble walking around at night.

➡ Karlsplatz station and Gumpendorfer Strasse can be boisterous late in the evening.

➡ The Prater and Praterstern can get dodgy at night. Ausstellungsstrasse is best avoided due to street walkers and kerb-crawlers.

➡ The Gürtel has a sprinkling of red-light clubs: north of Westbahnhof along the Neubaugürtel has a high concentration (with fewer around Thaliastrasse), and south to Gumpendorfer Strasse can be seedy.

➡ S-Bahn and tram stops along Margareten and Wiedner Gürtel can be edgy.

Money

ATMs are widely available. Credit cards are not always accepted in budget hotels or budget to midrange restaurants. Bars and cafes usually only accept cash.

For more information, see p225.

Taxes & Refunds

Austria has a *Mehrwertsteuer* (MWST; value-added tax) of 20% on most items. This is always included in the price but almost always listed separately on a formal receipt. Visitors from outside the EU can claim back around 13% for individual purchases over €75.01; see www.globalrefund.com for instructions. Vienna International Airport has refund desks.

Tipping

- **Restaurants and cafes** Tips are generally expected; round up smaller bills (to the nearest 50 cents or euro) when buying coffee or beer, and add 5% to 10% to the bill for full meals. Tip at the time of payment as one lump sum with the bill.
- **Taxis** Drivers will expect around 10% extra.
- **Hotel porters and cloakroom attendants** Tip a euro or two.

DZIEWUL/SHUTTERSTOCK ©

Stephansdom (p76)

Etiquette

The Viennese are fairly formal and use irony to alleviate social rules and constraints.

- **Greetings** *Grüss Gott* or the less formal *Servus!* are the usual forms of greeting; *Guten Tag* is also common. Stick to the polite *Sie* (you) form unless you know someone well or are of a similar age in a young-ish scene. Never use *du* with shop assistants or waiters.
- **Acknowledgements** When entering a breakfast room, it's usual to acknowledge others by saying *'Guten Morgen'* when you walk in and *'Auf Wiedersehen'* on leaving.
- **Telephone** Give your name at the start of a telephone call, especially when making reservations. When completing the call, say *'Auf Wiederhören'* ('goodbye'; customary form on phone).

Top Itineraries

Day One

Stephansdom & the Historic Centre (p74)

Start your day at Vienna's heart, the **Stephansdom**, being awed by the cathedral's cavernous interior, Gothic stone pulpit and baroque high altar. For a bird's-eye view of Vienna, climb the **cathedral south tower** to the viewing platform. Or delve below ground into its ossuary, the **Katakomben** (catacombs). Spend the rest of the morning strolling the atmospheric narrow streets around the cathedral.

Lunch Deli food and a glass of wine at Zum Schwarzen Kameel (p86).

The Hofburg & Around (p58)

Make your way along **Graben** and Kohlmarkt to the **Hofburg**, where one of the ultimate pleasures is simply to wander through and soak up the grandeur of this Habsburg architectural masterpiece. Narrow it down to one or two of the museums here, such as the **Kaiserappartements**.

Dinner Restaurant Herrlich (p70): traditional but classy Viennese cuisine.

The Museum District & Neubau (p107)

Head into the cobblestoned Spittelberg district to enduring favourites such as old-school brewery **Sebensternbräu** and hip new bars like the **Brickmakers Pub & Kitchen** for craft beers and ciders or **Le Troquet** for cocktails.

Day Two

The Museum District & Neubau (p107)

Enjoy one of the city's best breakfasts at **Figar** before making your way to the **Kunsthistorisches Museum**, where you can plan on spending at least a whole morning in the thrall of its Old Masters.

Lunch Duck behind the MuseumsQuartier to hidden Glacis Beisl (p122).

The Museum District & Neubau (p107)

The afternoon is a good time to change artistic direction and explore at least one of the museums in the MuseumsQuartier. The light, bright **Leopold Museum** has splendid Austrian art. **MUMOK** makes a complete contrast, with contemporary, often controversial works. The MuseumsQuartier has plenty of bars if you need a break, such as laid-back **Kantine**.

Dinner Motto am Fluss (p86); a hip lounge ambience on the Danube Canal.

Stephansdom & the Historic Centre (p74)

Explore the Innere Stadt's streets and bar scene in the evening in the centre, sipping Austrian wines at **Vinothek W-Einkehr**, deliberating over dozens of varieties of gin at **Vinogin** or hitting architectural treasures such as **Zwölf Apostelkeller** or **Kruger's American Bar**.

Day Three

Schloss Belvedere to the Canal (p139)

Divide your morning between Schloss Belvedere's magnificently landscaped French-style formal **gardens** and its galleries. The **Unteres Belvedere** (Lower Belvedere) has baroque state apartments and ceremonial rooms, and hosts some superb temporary exhibitions in its orangery, while a walk through **Oberes Belvedere** (Upper Belvedere) takes you through a who's who of Austrian art.

Lunch Meierei im Stadtpark (p151) for possibly Austria's best goulash.

Prater & East of the Danube (p155)

Make your way to the Prater, Vienna's playground of woods, meadows and sideshow attractions at the **Würstelprater**. The highlight here is the 19th-century **Riesenrad** Ferris wheel, famed for its role in 1949 film *The Third Man,* as well as the James Bond instalment *The Living Daylights* and art-house favourite *Before Sunrise.*

Dinner Fabulous vegan fare at Harvest (p160) in Leopoldstadt.

Prater & East of the Danube (p155)

Leopoldstadt is fast becoming one of Vienna's hippest districts, and there are an increasing number of cafes and bars popping up. Finish the evening at 18th-storey **Le Loft** for a cocktail accompanied by a sweeping panorama of the city.

Day Four

Schloss Schönbrunn & Around (p165)

Take an eye-popping tour of baroque extravaganza **Schloss Schönbrunn**, and stroll the French formal gardens, detouring to the **Gloriette**, with breathtaking views of the palace and city skyline beyond.

Lunch Eat at the Naschmarkt (p96) or just browse for picnic supplies.

Karlsplatz & Around Naschmarkt (p92)

Continue to another baroque jewel, the **Karlskirche**, and ride the lift (elevator) into the dome for an up-close view of its stunning fresco by Johann Michael Rottmayr. Take a break at the upbeat, design-driven **Café Drechsler**. Then head to **Secession** to see seminal works by members of the Vienna Secession including Klimt's 34m-long *Beethoven Frieze.*

Dinner Dine on local and/or organic produce at neo-*Beisl* Silberwirt (p100).

Karlsplatz & Around Naschmarkt (p92)

The Margareten (the 5th district) and Mariahilf (the 6th), both flanking the trickling Wien River, offer plenty of drinking and nightlife opportunities. Sip *Sekt* (sparkling wine) at **Sekt Comptoir**, enjoy a pint at **Café Rüdigerhof**, and hit the dance floor at **Club U**.

If You Like...

Great Works of Art

Kunsthistorisches Museum Masterpieces in every room at Vienna's finest museum. (p109)

Leopold Museum Stunning collection of works with a strong focus on expressionists. (p115)

MUMOK The Museum of Modern Art covers virtually all 20th- and 21st-century movements. (p116)

Schloss Belvedere The galleries here focus on the pantheon of Austrian artists from the Middle Ages to the present. (p141)

Kunsthalle Wien Showcases local and international artists in changing exhibitions. (p116)

Albertina Striking state apartments with the outstanding Batliner Collection. (p66)

Classical Music

Musikverein Used by the Vienna Philharmonic Orchestra, this concert hall has some of the world's best acoustics. (p103)

Staatsoper A performance at Vienna's famous opera house is unforgettable. (p103)

Konzerthaus Top-flight classical concerts are staged at this multistage venue. (p154)

MuTh Listen to the angelic voices of the Vienna Boys' Choir at its dedicated home venue. (p163)

Haus der Musik The Museum of the Vienna Philharmonic and interactive exhibitions. (p80)

Live Music & Clubs

Porgy & Bess Vienna's most popular jazz club has a velvety, grown-up vibe. (p90)

Naschmarkt (p96)

Arena Rock, reggae, metal and more plays at this former slaughterhouse's outdoor and indoor stages. (p46)

Volksgarten ClubDiskothek Pavillon-housed venue with wide-ranging gigs, DJs and theme nights. (p70)

Flex Local and international DJs on the Danube Canal. (p136)

Getting Active

Donauinsel This artificial island is a favourite for swimming, boating and waterskiing. (p163)

Wienerwald These woods are a paradise for walkers and cyclists, and home to plenty of *Heurigen* (wine taverns). (p160)

Prater Forest trails lead through this central Viennese oasis. (p157)

Flakturm In summer the *Flakturm* (flak tower) housing the Haus des Meeres has a climbing wall on one side. (p106)

Oberlaa Therme Wien Thermal baths with whirlpools, waterfalls and grotto-like pools. (p154)

Wiener Eistraum In winter, twirl on the ice outside the magnificent Rathaus at this picture-book-pretty rink. (p126)

Grand Architecture

Hofburg The Habsburgs' home from 1279 to 1918 exemplifies imperial splendour. (p60)

Schloss Belvedere Built for military strategist Prince Eugene of Savoy, the Belvedere now incorporates an art gallery. (p141)

Ringstrasse Ride a tram past this magnificent parade of 19th-century masterpieces. (p29)

Schloss Schönbrunn Of the palace's 1441 rooms, 40 are open to the public. (p167)

Churches

Stephansdom Vienna's landmark Gothic cathedral soars above the city's rooftops. (p76)

Karlskirche Head up into the cupola for fresco close-ups at this baroque wonder. (p94)

Peterskirche This sublime church invites contemplation beneath a dome fresco by Rottmayr. (p78)

Franziskanerkirche The beauty of this church is its deceptive *trompe-l'oeil* dome. (p81)

Ruprechtskirche Believed to date from 740, this is Vienna's oldest church. (p80)

Habsburg Heritage

Kaiserappartements In the Hofburg's former apartments, the Sisi Museum relates the story of Empress Elisabeth. (p60)

Schloss Schönbrunn Tours through the palace shed light on its former residents. (p167)

Kapuzinerkirche The crypt contains the remains of almost every royal Habsburg. (p66)

Augustinerkirche The Habsburgs' hearts are stored in urns here. (p67)

Markets

Naschmarkt Vienna's largest and most famous market is a feast for the senses. (p96)

Brunnenmarkt This fruit, vegetable and foodstuff market reflects its location in the Turkish district. (p132)

Karmelitermarkt Leopoldstadt's local flavour is in full swing at this ethnically diverse market. (p162)

Bio-Markt Freyung Pick up organic picnic ingredients at this Innere Stadt market. (p138)

For more top Vienna spots, see the following:

- Eating (p31)
- Drinking & Nightlife (p40)
- Entertainment (p44)
- Shopping (p48)
- Sports & Activities (p51)

Rochusmarkt A hive of activity in the Landstrasse district. (p153)

Flohmarkt Browse for bargains at one of Europe's best flea markets. (p99)

Panoramas

Riesenrad Take in the quintessential Viennese panorama from the top of this historic Ferris wheel. (p157)

Gloriette Vienna shimmers in the distance from this viewpoint overlooking Schloss Schönbrunn. (p169)

Belvedere Gardens These baroque gardens provide skyline, Stephansdom and Hofburg views. (p143)

Le Loft Views unfurl across the Danube canal and over the Innere Stadt from this 18th-floor restaurant. (p161)

Stephansdom South Tower Hiking up 343 steps rewards with an incredible view over the Innere Stadt's rooftops. (p77)

DO & CO This design hotel's 5th-floor restaurant and 6th-floor bar have rare, direct views onto Stephansdom's roof. (p194)

Naturhistorisches Museum Rooftop tours offer architectural close-ups and city panoramas. (p118)

Sky Bar Ride the glass lift (elevator) to the Steffl department store's bar and terrace. (p88)

Month By Month

TOP EVENTS

Wiener Festwochen, May to mid-June

OsterKlang Festival, around Easter

Donauinselfest, June

Jazz Fest Wien, July

Christkindlmärkte, mid-November to late December

January

One of the coldest months but also the least expensive, with a lively winter cultural scene.

Wiener Eistraum

From January to about mid-March the square in front of Vienna's Rathaus turns into a massive ice rink (p126).

February

Days remain short, dark and often snowy, but key attractions have few-to-no crowds and coffee houses make wonderful refuges from the elements.

Fasching

This carnival time of costumes and parties runs from November to Ash Wednesday but things peak in February (www.wien.info).

Opernball

Of the 300 or so balls held in January and February, the Opernball (Opera Ball; www.wiener-staatsoper.at) is by far Vienna's most lavish.

March

Days start getting longer, especially when daylight saving starts on the last Sunday of the month.

Frühlingsfestival

Alternating each year between the Musikverein and Konzerthaus concert halls, this festival of classical concerts begins in late March or early April and runs into May (www.wien.info).

April

Greenery emerges, flowers bloom and Easter heralds the start of Vienna's tourist season. Weather is changeable.

OsterKlang Festival

Orchestral and chamber-music recitals fill music halls during the OsterKlang Festival, around Easter each year (www.osterklang.at).

May

Cycling is possible, Danube cruises are frequent and it's warm enough to consider an excursion to the Wachau.

Life Ball

The AIDS charity Life Ball (p225) is a highlight of the Viennese social calendar. It's held in the Rathaus around the middle of May or as late as July.

June

Warm days segue into lingering, balmy nights. Festivals take place Vienna-wide, and visitors start flocking to the city.

Wiener Festwochen

A wide-ranging program of theatre, concerts, dance and visual arts from around the world, the month-long festival (www.festwochen.at).

Identities: Queer Film Festival

In odd-numbered years, Identities (p225) showcases

queer movies from around the world over a week at the Filmcasino.

Donauinselfest

Held over three days in late June, the free Donauinselfest on Donauinsel (Danube Island) features rock, pop, folk and country performers, attracting three million onlookers (www.donauinselfest.at).

Regenbogen Parade

Mid-June sees the Regenbogen Parade (Rainbow Parade; p225), a predominantly gay and lesbian festival attracting some 150,000 people, take over the Ringstrasse. Colourful floats, flamboyant costumes and lots of bare skin.

July

School holidays start. Temperatures – and visitor numbers – soar and Vienna's pavement cafes and courtyard gardens come into their own.

Jazz Fest Wien

During Jazz Fest Wien, Vienna swings to jazz, blues and soul flowing from the Staatsoper and a number of clubs. (www.viennajazz.org)

August

Locals leave the city, and smaller shops, restaurants and bars close for the *Sommerpause* (summer break). Major museums and attractions stay open.

ImPulsTanz

Vienna's premiere avant-garde dance festival attracts troupes between mid-July and mid-August at theatres across Vienna (www.impulstanz.com).

Musikfilm Festival

Free screenings of operettas, operas and concerts outside the Rathaus in July and August during the Musikfilm Festival (p46).

September

Autumn is in the air. Temperatures fall, schools go back, businesses reopen after the *Sommerpause*, and crowds tail off at museums.

Vienna Fair

Held at the Messe Wien (trade fair grounds), just east of Prater, the Vienna Fair in September or October is Austria's prime contemporary art fair (www.viennacontemporary.at).

October

***Goldener Oktober;* in a good year you can sit outside, but nights can get chilly. Daylight saving ends on the last Sunday of the month.**

Lange Nacht der Museen

On the first Saturday of October, 80-plus museums in Vienna open their doors to visitors between 6pm and 1am (http://langenacht.orf.at). One ticket (adult/child €15/12) allows entry and includes public transport.

Viennale

Austria's best film fest, the Viennale Film Festival (p46), features fringe and independent films from around the world, with screenings across the city.

November

Vienna can be grey and wet; it's an ideal time to embrace the restaurant, coffee-house and cultural scenes.

Wien Modern Festival

The Wien Modern festival features modern classical and avant-garde music from late October to late November at 16 venues Vienna-wide (http://wienmodern.at).

December

An enchanting month. Festive lights twinkle, decorations garland the city, and magical *Christkindlmärkte* (Christmas markets) sell toys and other quality gifts along with warming *Glühwein* (mulled wine).

Christkindlmärkte

Vienna's much-loved Christmas market season (p48) runs from around mid-November to Christmas Eve, when magical *Christkindlmärkte* set up in streets and squares. The centrepiece is the Rathausplatz Christkindlmarkt.

Silvester

The Innere Stadt becomes one big party zone for Silvester (New Year's Eve), with outdoor concerts and loads of fireworks in the crowded streets.

Le Grand Bal

Held on New Year's Eve at the Hofburg, Le Grand Bal is the ultimate opportunity to ring in the new year in style (www.hofburgsilvesterball.com).

With Kids

Vienna is a wonderfully kid-friendly city. Children are welcomed in all aspects of everyday life, and many of the city's museums go out of their way to gear exhibitions towards children. Children's servings are typically available in restaurants, and, when kids need to burn off energy, playgrounds are plentiful.

Museums

Exhibits especially well suited to children include the following:

Haus der Musik (p80) Has lots of practical exhibits for almost all ages to promote an understanding of music.

Naturhistorisches Museum (p118) Has a superb anthropology section where you can have a photo of yourself taken as a prehistoric human and delve into forensics. Check schedules for its *Nacht im Museum* (Night at the Museum) program, where kids (who must be accompanied by adults) can get a torch (flashlight) tour and bed down overnight (BYO sleeping bags).

Technisches Museum (p171) Has lots of hands-on exhibits to promote the understanding of science and technology.

The MuseumsQuartier has a couple of spaces created especially for kids:

Zoom (p117) Exhibition sections and programs of hands-on arts and crafts (from eight months to 14 years old).

Dschungel Wien (p116) Children's theatre with dance and occasional English performances.

Playgrounds & Open Space

Playgrounds are everywhere, but the **Jesuitenwiese** in the Prater – along Hauptallee, about 1.5km east of Praterstern – has a good one with a Wild West theme, while on the Donauinsel (p163) there's the **Wasserspielplatz Donauinsel** where toddlers can paddle and kids can dart across water on flying foxes and cross suspension bridges. Take the U-Bahn to Donauinsel, then walk seven minutes downriver. Inside the MuseumsQuartier (p115) there's a sand pit from about May to September, as well as various events. Open-air winter ice rink Wiener Eistraum (p126) has a special area for children.

Schloss Schönbrunn

The splendid Schloss Schönbrunn palace will enchant children, who can dress up as princes and princesses at its Kindermuseum (Children's Museum; p170), and check out exhibitions of natural science, archaeology and toys. Guided tours (in English by reservation) lasting 1½ hours let them discover the lives of the Habsburg children.

Performances of *The Magic Flute* (2½ hours) and *Aladdin* (1¼ hours) take place at the palace's puppet theatre, the Marionetten Theater (p174).

The **maze** at Schloss Schönbrunn is good fun for everyone, and the **Labyrinthikon** playground is designed for kids, with 14 playing stops for climbing, crawling and educational exploration.

Kids will also love visiting the world's oldest zoo, Schönbrunn Tiergarten (p168), which is home to some 750 animals including giant pandas and Siberian tigers.

Need to Know

Public Transport Free for children under six years; half-price on single tickets under 15 years.

Restaurants Nappy (diaper) changing facilities are rare. Dedicated kids' menus are also uncommon but children's servings are usually on offer.

Hotels Cots (cribs) usually available. Children under 12 often stay free in their parents' room.

Breastfeeding in Public Fine.

Babysitters Best arranged through your hotel.

Like a Local

With its monumental palaces and horse-drawn Fiaker carriages, Vienna could be a film set. But behind the scenes you'll find locals hanging out in up-and-coming neighbourhoods, lingering at cool cafes, canalside beaches and Schanigärten (pavement terraces), and hiking in the woods and vineyards that fringe the city.

TARTALJA/SHUTTERSTOCK ©

)pen-air cafe, Stephansplatz

Navigating

The 23 Wiener *Bezirke* (Vienna districts) spiral out clockwise from the centre like a snail shell (although in some instances leapfrog position). The Innere Stadt (01) sits at the centre, encircled by the Ringstrasse. Roughly between the Ringstrasse and the Gürtel ring road are the Vorstädte (inner suburbs): 02 (Leopoldstadt), 03 (Landstrasse), 04 (Wieden), 05 (Margareten), 06 (Mariahilf), 07 (Neubau), 08 (Josefstadt) and 09 (Alsergrund). Outside the Gürtel are the Vororte (outer suburbs): 10 (Favoriten), 11 (Simmering), 12 (Meidling), 13 (Hietzing), 14 (Penzing), 15 (Fünfhaus), 16 (Ottakring), 17 (Hernals), 18 (Währing), 19 (Döbling), then 20 (Brigittenau). Districts 21 (Floridsdorf) and 22 (Donaustadt) are on the city's northeastern flank, while 23 (Liesing) sits on the southwestern edge.

Every address in Vienna begins with the district number, starting with 01 for the Innere Stadt (inner city), with street numbers starting closest to the city. The district number is easily identifiable by the middle two digits of its four-digit post code, so for example 1010 is the 01 (Innere Stadt).

Each of the *Bezirke* has its own style and character. Within or straddling these districts, you'll often find smaller neighbourhoods, such as the romantic, cobblestoned Spittelberg, 07, behind the MuseumsQuartier, and the foodie favourite Freihausviertel on the edge of the 04 and 05 districts.

Drinking & Dining

In the chilly winter months, the city's famous *Kaffeehäuser* (coffee houses) come into their own as Vienna's 'living rooms', and cosy wood-panelled *Beisln* (bistro pubs) and wine bars (many with candlelit vaulted cellars) are favourite places to retreat.

When the weather warms up, everything spills outdoors to the *Schanigärten*. Unlike *Gastgärten* (beer gardens), *Schanigärten* set up on public property such as pavements and sometimes parking areas and squares according to inexpensive permits issued by authorities, which are valid from 1 March to 15 November. Actual opening dates depend on the weather each season.

Beach bars pop up along the waterfront in summer, such as the positively hopping

Strandbar Herrmann (p152). They're a great alternative for Viennese who don't join their fellow citizens decamping from the city to the Austrian lakes during the July/August *Sommerpause* (summer break), when many of the city's restaurants, bars and smaller shops shut down.

Heurigen (wine taverns) at vineyards within the greater city limits are also wonderful places to experience the local wines as well as hearty Viennese hospitality. Two of the best are Wieninger (p42), with a lantern- and candlelit vine-draped garden, wood-panelled interior and outstanding Austrian cuisine; and Zahel (p42), in a 250-year-old farmhouse with panoramic vineyard and city skyline views and a heated garden house for winter.

Hanging Out

A fantastic introduction to local Viennese life is to take a local-led tour with Space and Place (p29). These edgy city walks are run by Brit-turned-Viennese Eugene Quinn, who'll reveal everything from Vienna's ugly side to covering its coffee-house conversations, and even offers a 'smell' tour (named Smells Like Wien Spirit).

Great neighbourhoods away from the big-hitting tourist sights to start exploring include Leopoldstadt, 02, which is becoming increasingly hip. Independent boutiques, galleries and retro cafes have all popped up in recent years, especially around Praterstrasse. The stretch of the Danube Canal here has been given a push with new graffiti art (now legal, so the quality is up).

Another hotspot-of-the-moment is Yppenplatz, 16, which is loaded with delis and boutiques. The square is at its liveliest during the Saturday morning Bauernmarkt. Look out for Yppenplatz 4 (p132), in the old Ottakringer brewery offices, with handmade organic *Würstel* (sausages) and the brewery's Brauwerk-label craft beers.

In Neubau (07), Kirchengasse, Lindengasse, Neubaugasse and Zollergasse are filled with art, design and fashion ateliers and boutiques. And near the chaotic, colourful Naschmarkt, artisan producers, delis, design stores and one-of-a-kind boutiques make for a tantalising wander in the Freihausviertel (04 and 05).

NEED TO KNOW

Cycling Cycle like a local with wheels from city-wide share-bike scheme Citybike Wien (p221).

Brunch Forgo breakfast at your hotel: the brunch scene is big in Vienna. Favourite brunch hang-outs include the multigenerational Vollpension (p98), and muralled Figar (p120).

Dress Dress up to blend in with the stylish Viennese. Smart clothes are best for midrange venues. Bring your finery if you're heading to the opera.

Celebrating

A favourite local festival is the **Summer Stage** (Map p254; ☎01-315 52 02; www.summerstage.at; 09, Rossauer Lände; ⏰5pm-1am Mon-Sat, 3pm-1am Sun May-Sep; Ⓤ Schottenring, Rossauer Lände), with concerts, food stalls and activities on Rossauer Lände on the Danube Canal, which takes place between May and September.

Come winter, some of the more local village-like *Christkindlmärkte* (Christmas markets) include the Spittelberg Christkindlmarkt (p48) and the Schönbrunn Christkindlmarkt (p48).

Woodland Escapes

Wandern (walking) is a favourite local pastime. Places like the Prater (p157) are popular but to really get off the beaten track, join the Viennese heading to the Wienerwald, a 45km swath of forested hills bordering the capital from the north-west to the southeast.

Walks covered on the city council website (www.wien.gv.at/umwelt/wald/freizeit/wandern/wege) include some that lead into the forest. One of the best is Trail No 1, an 11km loop, which starts in Nussdorf (take tram D from the Ring) and climbs the vineyard-ribboned hill Kahlenberg (484m), with fantastic city panoramas. Afterwards, back in Nussdorf, rejuvenate at a *Heuriger* such as **Mayer am Pfarrplatz** (☎01-370 12 87; www.pfarrplatz.at; 19, Pfarrplatz 2, Nussdorf; ⏰4pm-midnight Mon-Sat, noon-midnight Sun; 👪; 🚋D), where Beethoven lived in 1817. Regular live music includes traditional Austrian tunes; the atmosphere is especially local of an evening.

For Free

Vienna offers a wealth of opportunities to experience the city for free, from strolls through the city streets soaking up the spectacular architecture to a number of free museums, exhibitions, public buildings, parks and churches, as well as fabulous free entertainment.

Free Museums & Exhibitions

Some museums are free for those under 19 years, and permanent exhibitions at the municipal museums run by the City of Vienna are free on the first Sunday of the month. If you're interested in modern or contemporary art, drop into any of the free private art galleries scattered throughout the Innere Stadt. The following are free:

Dorotheum (p73) Sensational auction house packed with everything from paintings to furnishings and household objects.

Archiv des Österreichischen Widerstands (p79) Exhibition documenting the antifascist resistance movement under Nazi rule.

Neidhart-Fresken (p79) Frescoes surviving from the 14th century.

Schloss Belvedere Gardens (p143) Exquisitely laid out gardens between the Upper and Lower Belvedere palaces.

Schloss Schönbrunn Gardens (p169) Expansive gardens, manicured and adorned in some parts, but also with pleasant wooded parkland.

Museum für Angewandte Kunst (p149) Tuesday from 6pm to 10pm. Vienna's best collection of applied arts.

Hundertwasserhaus (p150) A building designed by the eccentric architect Friedensreich Hundertwasser (the interior is closed to the public).

Free Public Buildings, Parks & Churches

The Ringstrasse is home to many spectacular buildings, including the Hofburg (p60) palace complex, which is free to wander (individual museums and attractions within incur admission fees). Other Ringstrasse highlights include the University Main Building (p129) and the Justizpalast (p119; supreme court).

Rathaus (p120) Vienna's splendid City Hall has free guided tours.

Zentralfriedhof (p151) Beethoven, Brahms, Strauss and Schubert are among the luminaries buried at this cemetery.

Servitenkirche & Servitenviertel (Map p254; 09, Servitengasse 9; ⏲Mass only; Ⓤ Rossauer Lände) Wonderfully quiet church grounds and quarter around it.

Prater (p157) Vienna's park and woodland across the Danube Canal.

Donauinsel (p163) An island and recreation area in the middle of the Danube River.

Augarten (p159) Eighteenth-century parkland with paths and meadows.

Hietzinger Friedhof (p171) Burial place of Gustav Klimt, Otto Wagner and other notables.

Free Entertainment

Free festivals and events abound during summer, including rock, pop, folk and country performances at the Donauinselfest (p164), opera, operettas and concerts at the Musikfilm Festival (p46), and films at outdoor cinemas including the Kino Unter Sternen (p46). The spectacle of Vienna's pride parade, the Regenbogen Parade (p225; Rainbow Parade), is also free.

In April, May, June and September and on Silvester (New Year's Eve), an open-air LED video wall sets up outside the Staatsoper (p103), screening operatic performances, with 180 chairs set up for each broadcast.

You can often hear DJs spinning for free in bars, and sometimes at open-air spaces such as the MuseumsQuartier (p115).

Guided Tours & Walks

Vienna offers some great opportunities for guided exploration. Join a tour by bus, boat or on foot (perhaps on a specific theme), hop in a mini hot rod or aboard a Fiaker (horse-drawn carriage), jump on a tram tour, or tour a wine region outside town.

MIKECPHOTO/SHUTTERSTOCK ©

A *Fiaker*, a traditional horse-drawn carriage

Guided Walks

Vienna Tour Guides (www.wienguide.at; adult/child €16/8) Vienna Tour Guides is an organisation of highly knowledgeable guides who conduct over 60 different guided walking tours (some in English) covering everything from art nouveau architecture to Jewish traditions in Vienna. Tours last roughly 1½ to two hours; some require a valid public transport pass and extra euros for entrance fees into sights. The monthly *Wiener Spaziergänge* (Vienna's Walking Tours) leaflet from tourist offices details all tours, gives the various departure points and also indicates which tours are conducted in English.

Vienna Walks & Talks (01-774 89 01; www.viennawalks.com) Offers the excellent 1½-hour Third Man Tour (adult/child €19/16.50) based on the film, and many other options in both English and German.

Bus Tours

Vienna Sightseeing Tours (01-712 468 30; www.viennasightseeingtours.com; 04, Rainergasse 1; Hop On Hop Off tour €17-25, other tours €39-119; 6.30am-6.30pm; D, U Südtiroler Platz/Wien Hauptbahnhof) Runs the Hop On Hop Off city tours and the tours by the affiliated Cityrama. These take in Schönbrunn, plus some thematic (mostly music) tours in Vienna, but also tours to Bratislava, Budapest, Prague and Salzburg. The latter include hotel pick-ups and entrance fees.

Hop On Hop Off (Vienna Sightseeing Tours; Map p248; 01-712 46 83; www.viennasightseeing.com; 01, Opernring; 24/48/72-hr ticket €25/29/33; 9.30am-8pm; D, 1, 2, 71 Kärntner Ring/Oper, U Karlsplatz) Covers six routes with over 50 stops around Vienna. Popular routes include one that follows the Ringstrasse and makes a detour to Stephansplatz; Hundertwasserhaus and sights east of the Danube Canal, such as the Prater and UNO City; and Schönbrunn and Belvedere. All buses depart from directly outside the Staatsoper. The website has route maps.

Oldtimer Bus Tours (Map p246; 01-503 74 43 12; www.oldtimertours.at; 01, departure from Heldenplatz; tours adult/child €19/12; May–mid-Oct; D, 1, 2, 71 Burgring, U Museumsquartier) Vintage open-top (closed if rainy) coaches trundle around the city centre and occasionally up to the Wienerwald (Vienna Woods). Tours last one hour and leave from in front of the Hofburg at Heldenplatz from Tuesday to Sunday at 11.15am, 12.45pm, 2.15pm and 4pm.

Redbus City Tours (Map p246; ☎01-512 40 30; www.redbuscitytours.at; 01, Kärntner Strasse 25; 24hr adult/child €24/12, 48hr €30/15; ⊙9am-7pm; 🚊D, 1, 2 Kärntner Ring/Oper, UKarlsplatz) These hop-on, hop-off tours include a 1½-hour route covering the main sights around the Innere Stadt and two-hour tours hitting all of the city's big sights. Buses leave from outside the Albertina.

Boat Tours

DDSG Blue Danube (Map p244; ☎01-588 80; www.ddsg-blue-danube.at; 01, Schwedenbrücke; 1½-hour tours adult/child €22/11; ⊙10.30am-6.20pm Easter-Oct; USchwedenplatz) Boats cover a variety of cruise routes; some of the most popular include circumnavigating Leopoldstadt and Brigittenau districts using the Danube Canal and the Danube as their thoroughfare. Select tours include passing through the Nussdorf locks (built by Otto Wagner around 1900) or to the Wachau.

Wine Tours

Vienna Explorer (Map p244; ☎01-890 96 82; www.viennaexplorer.com; 01, Franz-Josefs-Kai 45; ⊙tours Easter-Oct, bike rental 8.30am-6pm year-round; 🚊1, USchwedenplatz) This longstanding outfit is excellent for bike tours in Vienna itself (three hours; adult/child $29/14.50) and further afield through the Wachau vineyards (10½ hours; €64/39), and also has Vienna city walking tours (2½ hours; €16/8). There's a bike rental service (per hour/day from €5/15) if you want to head out on your own.

Other Tours

Fiaker (20min/40min/1hr tour €55/80/110) One of the most romantic ways to see Vienna is aboard a *Fiaker*, a traditional-style open carriage drawn by a pair of horses. Drivers generally speak English and point out places of interest. Lines of horses, carriages and bowler-hatted drivers can be found at Stephansplatz, Albertinaplatz and Heldenplatz at the Hofburg. Short tours take you through the old town, while long tours include the Ringstrasse.

Ring Tram (Map p244; ☎01-790 91 00; www.wienerlinien.at; 01, Schwedenplatz, Platform C; adult/child €9/4; ⊙10am-5.30pm; 🚊1, 2, USchwedenplatz) You can do a DIY tour of the Ringstrasse (p29) by public tram but if you prefer a seamless tour with video screens and multilingual commentary, hop on the Ring Tram tour, which operates a continuous 30-minute loop around the Ringstrasse (no stops). Tour tickets are valid for one unbroken trip, meaning you can't hop on and off.

Hot Rod City Tour (Map p244; ☎01-660 87 73; www.hotrod-citytour-wien.com; 01, Judengasse 4; 2hr tour per person €99-119; ⊙10am-8pm Oct-May, 8am-10pm Jun-Sep; USchweden-platz) If you've ever wanted to get behind the wheel of a mini hot rod, this is your chance. The low-to-the-ground one-person vehicles set off in convoy and cover a circuit of the city in 1½ hours, with Vienna's landmarks as a backdrop. Helmets, walkie-talkies and insurance are included in the price; you'll need a valid driver's licence (foreign-issued licences accepted).

Space and Place (http://spaceandplace.at) For the inside scoop on Vienna, join Eugene on one of his fun, quirky tours. The alternative line-up keeps growing: from Vienna Ugly tours, homing in on the capital's ugly side, to Smells Like Wien Spirit, a playful exploration of the city through smell, and the sociable Coffeehouse Conversations. See the website for dates and details.

Ringstrasse Tram Tour: Do-It-Yourself

Public trams are a cheap way to see the sights and enjoy a slice of everyday life in Vienna at the same time. This quintessential Vienna tram experience takes you past the city's palatial monuments.

Board tram 1 at Schwedenplatz (platform B) heading towards Stefan-Fadinger-Platz and immediately look out on the left for the **Monument to the Victims of Fascism** at the former Gestapo headquarters site.

On your left on the Ringstrasse will emerge Vienna's **Börse Palais** (Stock Exchange), a handsome structure bedecked in dusty brick with white trimmings, designed by renowned Ringstrasse architect Theophil von Hansen.

Pulling into Schottentor station you'll be accosted on your right by two stone-carved steeples reaching for the sky – the marvellous neo-Gothic Votivkirche (p129) is quite reminiscent of France's Chartres Cathedral. When the spires of an arresting Flemish-Gothic edifice beck on your gaze on the right, you will have reached the Rathaus (p120) and Rathausplatz.

The neoclassical facade of **Parlament**, Austria's parliament, with its majestic Greek pillars, will spill into view on the

Ringstrasse Tram Tour

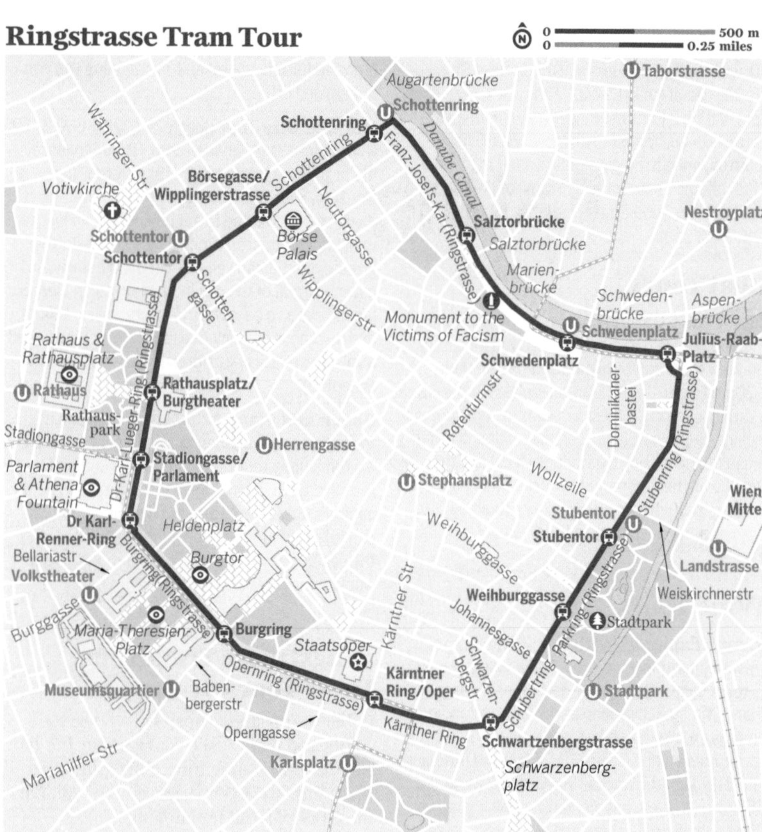

right, flanked by the **Athena Fountain** – the four figures lying at her feet represent the Danube, Inn, Elbe and Vltava, the four key rivers of the Austro-Hungarian Empire. The Parlament itself is closed for major renovations until at least 2024 (parliament temporarily sits in the Hofburg complex but it's not accessible to the public).

A majestic testament to Austria's 1813 triumph over Napoleon in Leipzig, the **Äusseres Burgtor** (Outer Palace Gate) will loom into view on the left – the Roman gate leads the way to the Hofburg (Imperial Palace). Directly opposite the Burgtor is **Maria-Theresien-Platz**, anchored by a statue of Empress Maria Theresia, the only female to ascend to the Austrian throne. Note the bundle of papers clasped in her left hand – these are the Pragmatic Sanctions of 1713, which made it possible for women to rule the empire.

The marvellous neo-Renaissance Staatsoper (p103; State Opera House) impresses the masses today, but when it was originally built the Viennese dubbed it 'the *Königgrätz* of architecture', likening it to the 1866 military disaster of the same name.

The final stretch of the tram route (tram 2) continues past Stadtpark (p152) back to the Danube Canal and Schwedenplatz.

RINGSTRASSE TRAM PRACTICALITIES

You can tour the Ringstrasse on the tourist Ring Tram (p29), but it's much cheaper to catch regular city trams (without commentaries).

Trams Tram 1 heading northwest from Schwedenplatz, changing to tram 2 at Stadiongasse/Parlament, Dr-Karl-Renner-Ring, Burgring or Kärntner Ring-Oper to finish at Schwedenplatz.

Cost Use your normal transport ticket; 24-hour tickets are best (€7.60).

Eating

Dining in Vienna gives you a taste of the city's history, at its street stands sizzling up sausages, candlelit vaulted-cellar wine bars and earthy, wood-panelled Beisln (bistro pubs) serving goulash and Wiener Schnitzel; its present, at hip cafes, multiethnic markets and international eateries; and its future, at innovative spaces with a wave of exciting chefs pushing in new directions.

The Dining Scene

Vienna has a lively and changing culinary scene. Traditional Austrian cuisine is taking on a lighter note, and new generations of chefs are turning to high-quality seasonal and local ingredients, coupled with the rapid uptake of new food ideas locally and from abroad.

Brunch is another red-hot trend in the Austrian capital, with retro-styled cafes serving breakfast until late into the afternoon. And craft cocktail pairings and craft beer pairings are emerging in venues that blur the line between a restaurant and bar.

The Viennese have also reaffirmed their love for traditional-style eateries, in particular *Beisln,* dishing up heaping portions of Austrian favourites like *Wiener Schnitzel, Tafelspitz* (prime boiled beef, served with radish) and *Gulasch* (goulash).

Today, eating out in Vienna lets you enjoy the best of both traditional and contemporary dining, with many places crossing effortlessly between the two.

HISTORY

Historically, classic Viennese cuisine has always thrived on foreign influences and change. *Wiener Schnitzel* (a true *Wiener Schnitzel* is made with veal) is rumoured – though hotly disputed today – to have originated from the recipe for Milanese crumbed veal cutlet brought back by Field Marshal Radtetzky in 1857. *Gulasch* comes from Hungary, but the dumplings served with it come from Czech regions. Interestingly, *Tafelspitz* was the favourite dish of Kaiser Franz Josef, but when foreign guests visited Schönbrunn Palace, he fed them French delights. Once they had left, he ate his *Wiener Schnitzel* and *Tafelspitz* again.

The fastidious Viennese approach to coffee and the tradition of the *Kaffeehaus* (coffee house, where you can also eat a light meal) owes much to Ottoman Turks who brought their exotic elixir into Vienna's *Vorstadt* in 1683. This approach captures the essence of *die klassische Wiener Küche* (classic Viennese cuisine): pilfered by the Habsburgs wherever they reigned, localised at home, shoehorned into the imperial tradition, and given new blood by the great culinary capitals abroad, like Paris – in this case, one of the relatively few places where the Habsburgs didn't actually rule – before being stylised in all its rich features for the contemporary table.

Beisln

Originating in the 18th century as inns offering local specialities, these cosy, down-to-earth, uniquely Viennese eateries are simple bistro pubs featuring wood-panelling, plain tables, perhaps a ceramic oven, and hearty local cuisine. Many have tables in cobbled courtyards or on pavement terraces in summer. The name *Beisl* is thought to be Jewish, from the Yiddish word *Bajiss,* meaning 'house'. In recent years, marginally more expensive neo-*Beisln* have emerged, offering new takes on old recipes.

NEED TO KNOW

Price Ranges

Prices refer to a two-course meal, excluding drinks.

€	under €15
€€	€15-30
€€€	over €30

Opening Hours

Restaurants Generally 11am to 2pm and 6pm to 10pm or 11pm. Kitchens may stay open all day. Some places close on Sunday or Monday.

Cafes From 8am to midnight.

Beisln From 11am or noon to 11pm or midnight.

Lunch Menu

Most restaurants have an inexpensive lunch special (*Mittagsmenü* or *Tagesteller*) for around €7 to €11.

Mobile Phones

Switch off your phone, or at least the sound, in restaurants. Take calls away from your table.

Tipping

If the bill has been presented in a folder, you can leave the tip in the folder when you depart. It's also common to round up verbally by simply stating the amount and adding *'danke!'* or by saying *'das stimmt so'* (keep the change).

Booking Tables

Advance reservations are recommended for midrange restaurants and essential for high-end and/or popular places (several weeks for the most sought-after tables). Remember to state your last name at the start of a phone call.

Gedeck

Some restaurants charge €2 to €3 extra for the *Gedeck* (table setting), which includes bread and various sundries.

Online Resources

Falter (www.falter.at) is Vienna's quintessential foodie guide.

Street Food & Markets

The humble *Wurst* (sausage) is sold in up to a dozen varieties at *Würstelstände* (sausage stands) throughout the city. Sausages are served inside a bread roll hot dog-style or sliced and accompanied by cut bread, and weighed down with sweet *(süss)* or hot *(scharf)* mustard *(Senf)*. As well as *Bratwurst* (fried sausage), you could try *Burenwurst* (the boiled equivalent), *Debreziner* (spicy) or *Käsekrainer* (infused with cheese).

The largest and best-known of Vienna's markets is the aromatic Naschmarkt (p96), which is laden with produce from all over Austria and the world and lined with food 'stalls', including many fully fledged restaurants. Other fantastic markets include the Brunnenmarkt (p132), leading to Yppenplatz in Ottakring, and the Karmelitermarkt (p162), east of the Danube Canal.

Vegetarians & Vegans

Vegetarians will have no problem in Vienna, with generally at least one dish available at even the most tradition *Beisln*. Spurred by the locavore trend towards organic produce, vegetarian cuisine is now popular all over the city and numerous cafes and restaurants have extensive offerings. There are also many exclusively vegetarian places in all price ranges, including Michelin-starred Tian (p87).

Vegan cuisine is also rapidly gaining a following, and plenty of places have at least some vegan options.

The Naschmarkt and other farmers markets offer lots of choices for vegetarian picnics, takeaway or sit-down meals.

How to Eat & Drink Like a Local

Meals A typical breakfast for the Viennese consists of a *Semmel* (bread roll) with jam, ham and/or cheese. Lunch is often the largest meal. In the evening, bread with cheese or ham and a beer or wine is usually eaten at home, although many Viennese enjoy a more substantial meal.

Where to Eat The main choices for a sit-down meal are a restaurant, *Beisl,* cafe or coffee house or *Heuriger* (p41; wine tavern) on the outskirts of the city, with overflowing buffets of salads and pork, along with new wine.

Arriving In better establishments, a waiter will greet you and take your coat before showing you to a table. Once you're seated you'll have the chance to order a drink right away. The waiter is unlikely to return to take your order until you've closed your menu. In midrange and less formal places, it's usually fine to place your jacket over the back of your chair if you don't want to use the cloakroom.

Eating & Toasting Before starting to eat say *'Guten appetit!'* Before starting to drink, toast by clinking glasses while looking the person in the eye. Not to have eye contact is said to bring seven years of bad sex (you've been warned!). *'Zum Wohl'* (to well-being) is the generic toast if you're drinking wine; *'Prost!'* ('Cheers!') if you're drinking beer.

Paying the Bill Many places don't accept credit cards. Tip 5% to 10% (or don't bother coming back) by rounding up the bill. If several of you are eating together, you will be asked *'Geht das zusammen oder getrennt?'* (Together or separately?). If paying separately, there's no need to pool the money: each diner pays the waiter and tips individually.

Cooking Courses

Pick up cooking tips from old hands and rising stars at the following:

Babettes (www.babettes.at; 04, Schleifmühlgasse 17; ⏲10am-7pm Mon- Fri, to 5pm Sat; Ⓤ Kettenbrückengasse) From breads and pastries to burgers, hotpots, risotto and curries; in German.

Vestibül (p122) Offers one-day Austrian cooking courses in English and German.

Wrenkh (☎01-533 15 26; www.wrenkh-wien.at; 01, Bauernmarkt 10; ⏲per person from €48; Ⓤ Stephansplatz) Austrian classics, international cuisines and vegetarian and vegan classes; in English and German.

Eating by Neighbourhood

➡ **Stephansdom & the Historic Centre** Packed with options, especially around Stephansplatz and streets leading down towards the Danube Canal.

➡ **Karlsplatz & Around Naschmarkt** Myriad food stalls and restaurants on Naschmarkt, and lots of options in Margareten and Mariahilf districts.

➡ **The Museum District & Neubau** Some of the best eating in Vienna's *Vorstadt* districts, especially in and behind MuseumsQuartier.

➡ **Alsergrund & the University District** Great markets, local eateries and student places close to the university campuses.

➡ **Schloss Belvedere to the Canal** A handful of gems, otherwise limited; plenty of summer picnic spots.

➡ **Prater & East of the Danube** Burgeoning dining scene, especially west of Karmeliterplatz and Taborstrasse, extending north towards Augarten.

VIENNESE SPECIALITIES

Vienna has a strong repertoire of traditional dishes. One or two are variations on dishes from other regions. Classics include:

Schnitzel *Wiener Schnitzel* should always be crumbed veal, but pork is gaining ground in some places.

Goulash *Rindsgulasch* (beef goulash) is everywhere in Vienna but attains exquisite heights at Meierei im Stadtpark (p151).

Tafelspitz Traditionally this boiled prime beef swims in the juices of locally produced *Suppengrün* (fresh soup vegetables), before being served with *Kren* (horseradish) sauce.

Beuschel Offal, usually sliced lung and heart with a slightly creamy sauce.

Backhendl Fried, breaded chicken, often called *steirischer Backhendl* (Styrian fried chicken).

Zwiebelrostbraten Slices of roast beef smothered in gravy and fried onions.

Schinkenfleckerln Oven-baked ham and noodle casserole.

Bauernschmaus Platter of cold meats.

The undeniable monarchs of all desserts are *Kaiserschmarrn* (sweet pancake with raisins) and *Apfelstrudel* (apple strudel), but also look out for *Marillenknödel* (apricot dumplings) in summer.

Lonely Planet's Top Choices

Steirereck im Stadtpark (p152) Vienna's class act by the Wien River.

Punks (p134) Refreshing 'no concept' concept where it's all about the locally sourced food.

Lingenhel (p150) Deli-shop-bar-restaurant in a 200-year-old house serving seasonal treats.

Plachutta (p87) The ultimate place for Viennese *Tafelspitz*.

Blue Mustard (p69) Incredible Vienna-inspired decor, adventurous cooking, a permanent food truck and cocktail pairings.

Griechenbeisl (p85) The history-soaked *Beisl* of your dreams.

Best by Budget

€

Bitzinger Würstelstand am Albertinaplatz (p69) Sausage stand opposite the opera.

Pure Living Bakery (p172) NYC-style deli with a laid-back garden near Schönbrunn.

Naschmarkt (p96) A snacker's fantasyland, Vienna's largest market teems with eateries.

Eis Greissler (p98) Organic ice cream with vegan options.

€€

Motto am Fluss (p86) Ultimate restaurant, bar and cafe on the canal.

Said the Butcher to the Cow (p98) Phenomenal burgers and a hip gin bar.

Brezl Gwölb (p85) *Beisl* big on Gothic charm and Austrian home cooking.

Flein (p132) Exquisitely simple, atmospheric space with a daily changing handwritten menu.

€€€

Steirereck im Stadtpark (p152) Seasonal taste sensations at a two-Michelin-starred restaurant in Stadtpark.

Schnattl (p135) Elegant wood-panelled interior, seasonally changing menus and courtyard dining.

Meinl's Restaurant (p69) Exceptional quality through the seasons.

Best Beisln

Rustic

Beim Czaak (p86) Traditional as it gets.

Steman (p100) Friendly, high-ceilinged *Beisl*.

Zum Alten Fassl (p100) Falco once lived above this woody *Beisl*, which has a regionally focused menu.

Haas Beisl (p100) Meaty menu and a genuinely local vibe.

Schank zum Reichsapfel (p160) Warm, wooden wine-tavern-style favourite.

Figlmüller (p86) Ever popular for its enormous schnitzels.

Contemporary Atmosphere

Silberwirt (p100) Atmospheric with an accent on organic and local grub.

Tancredi (p100) Pared-down interior, seasonal menu and garden for summer dining.

Amerlingbeisl (p122) Courtyard dining in the Biedermeier heart of Spittelberg.

Huth Gastwirtschaft (p86) Local favourite in an under-the-radar location.

Best Schnitzels

Figlmüller (p86) Bills itself as the home of the schnitzel.

Gasthaus Wickerl (p135) Warm wooden *Beisl* decor and sizzling schnitzels.

Huth Gastwirtschaft (p86) Serves a superb *Wiener Schnitzel* with cranberry sauce and parsley potatoes.

Zum Alten Fassl (p100) Residential setting with private garden.

Ubl (p98) *Beisl* dishing up four types of schnitzel, all cooked to thin, golden perfection.

Best Goulash

Meierei im Stadtpark (p151) Some speak of the world's best.

Café Drechsler (p102) DJs, Terence Conran cool with accomplished goulash.

Soupkultur (p132) Soup specialist.

Haas Beisl (p100) Like Oma (grandma) made it.

Bier & Bierli (p101) The signature dish here is its goulash.

Best Vegetarian

Tian (p87) Michelin-starred vegetarian cuisine.

Harvest (p160) Vintage decor and super-fresh veggie and vegan fare.

Tian Bistro (p121) Tian's laid-back younger sibling.

Hollerei (p173) Convivial veggie bistro near Schloss Schönbrunn.

Café Central (p135)

Coffee Houses & Cake Shops

Vienna's long-standing tradition of coffee houses and cake shops captures the spirit of Gemütlichkeit – that quintessential Austrian quality of cosiness and languid indulgence. Grand or humble, poster-plastered or chandelier-lit, this is where you can join the locals for coffee, cake and a slice of living history.

NEED TO KNOW

Prices Expect to pay between €2 and €5 for a coffee, between €3 and €6 for a slice of cake, and around €9 for a main.

Opening hours Usually open around 8am, and close anywhere between 7pm and midnight (earlier on Sundays).

Meals Many *Kaffeehäuser* also serve *Frühstuck* (breakfast) and a moderately priced lunchtime *Tagesteller* (dish of the day). Dishes are invariably hearty.

Viennese coffee

Coffee Houses

Poet and playwright Bertolt Brecht once described Vienna as a small city built around a few coffee houses where the locals sit together and read papers. It's a simple observation but a perceptive one, for despite the overwhelming variety of coffee on offer, caffeine is secondary to the *Kaffeehaus* experience. In many ways coffee is but an entrance ticket to a world where you can meet friends, browse newspapers, play games, put the world to rights, reflect and linger undisturbed for hours. Many Wiener go misty eyed when you ask them about their favourite *Kaffeehaus,* affectionately dubbed Vienna's 'living rooms'.

HISTORY

It all started with some mystery beans. Back at the Battle of Vienna in 1683, when Polish-Habsburg allies sent the Ottoman invaders packing, the Turks, so the story goes, left sacks of precious coffee beans at the city gates as they beat a hasty retreat. There was much speculation as to what these beans were, with most surmising camel feed or dung. King Jan III Sobieski handed over the beans to his military officer, Jerzy Franciszek Kulczycki, who recognised their value, having encountered coffee during time spent in captivity in Turkey. Adding a dash of milk and sweetening the aromatic blend to Viennese tastes, he soon opened Vienna's first coffee house: the Hof zur Blauen Flasche. In coffee-house circles to this day, Kulczycki is considered something of a patron saint.

The Viennese were hooked and soon coffee houses began to pop up all over the city. By the late 18th century *Kaffeehäuser* were in vogue in high society, with composers such as Mozart and Beethoven giving public performances. They became places to meet, socialise and, on a practical level, warm up.

This boom continued in the 19th century thanks to the Habsburgs' insatiable appetite for coffee, cake and palatial surrounds. *Sacher Torte* was created for Prince Klemens Wenzel von Metternich in 1832 and swiftly became an imperial favourite. In the latter half of the century, grand coffee houses such as Landtmann, Central and Sperl opened their doors, setting a precedent with grand interiors adorned with chandeliers, Thonet chairs and marble-topped tables.

At the turn of the century, coffee houses attracted the greatest artists, musicians, writers and radical thinkers of the age – Mahler, Klimt, Freud, Trotsky and Otto Wagner. The 1950s signalled the end of an era for many *Kaffeehäuser* – a period the Viennese call the *Kaffeehaussterben* (coffee house death). Postwar, a new generation of Viennese had grown tired of the coffee house, which they saw as being antiquated and/or elitist. TVs and espresso bars also played a part in their closure, as did the scattering of Jews, many of whom were pivotal to making the coffee house a cultural institution. Luckily many of the best coffee houses survived and the tradition later revived.

COFFEE-HOUSE CULTURE

In 2011 Vienna's coffee houses were added to the Unesco list of Intangible Cultural Heritage, which defines them as 'places

Above: Kleines Café (p89)
Right: *Apfelstrudel*

JAROMIR KLEIN/SHUTTERSTOCK ©

where time and space are consumed, but only the coffee is found on the bill'. Indeed, life may rush ahead outside, but the clocks are stuck in 1910 in the *Kaffeehaus,* where the spirit of unhurried gentility remains sacrosanct. Neither time nor trend obsessed, coffee houses are like a nostalgic balm for the stresses of modern life; they are places where life dissolves into the warm simplicity of a good cup of coffee, impromptu conversation and nostalgic daydreaming.

While the echoes of the past can still be felt keenly in the marble splendour of stalwarts such as Central and Sperl, a growing number of coffee houses are ushering in a new age of creativity, from pretty cupcake shops to feline-focused cat cafes imported from Japan.

Another nod to the social importance of *Kaffeehäuser* is the Kaffeesiederball, staged by the coffee-house owners at the Hofburg in February, one of the most glittering events on the ball calendar.

COFFEE DECODER

Ask for 'a coffee, please' and you may get a puzzled look. The following are fixtures on most menus:

Brauner Black but served with a tiny splash of cream; comes in *gross* (large) or *klein* (small).

Einspänner Strong coffee with whipped cream, served in a glass.

Verlängerter *Brauner* lengthened with hot water.

Mocca Sometimes spelled *Mokka* or *Schwarzer* – black coffee.

Melange The Viennese classic, half-coffee, half-milk and topped with milk froth or whipped cream, similar to a cappuccino.

Kapuziner With more milk than coffee and perhaps a sprinkling of grated chocolate.

Eiskaffee Cold coffee with vanilla ice cream and whipped cream.

Maria Theresia With orange liqueur and whipped cream.

Türkische Comes in a copper pot with coffee grounds and sugar.

ETIQUETTE

- In more formal coffee houses wait to be seated, otherwise take your pick of the tables.
- There's no dress code per se, but smart-casual wear is the norm at posh coffee houses.
- You're generally welcome to linger for as long as you please – waiters present the *Rechnung* (bill) when you ask for it.
- Some coffee houses have English menus, but failing that, you can sometimes choose from the counter.
- Viennese waiters are notoriously brusque, but a polite *Grüss Gott* (good day) and a smattering of German will stand you in good stead.
- Newspapers are freely available, often also in English.

Cake Shops

Forget the schnitzel clichés: if the sweet-toothed Viennese could choose one last meal on earth, most would go straight for dessert. The city brims with *Konditoreien* (cake shops), where buttery aromas lure passers-by to counters brimming with fresh batches of cream-filled, chocolate-glazed, fruit-topped treats. In these mini temples of three o'clock indulgence, pastries, cakes and tortes are elevated to a near art form.

Many cake shops also do a fine line in *Confiserie* (confectionery), producing their own sweets and chocolate. Sumptuous examples include Demel, one-time purveyor to the imperial and royal court, famous for its chocolate-nougat *Annatorte* and fragrant candied violets. The Viennese swear by the feather-light macaroons, chocolates and tortes at Oberlaa, while retro Aïda time warps you back to the 1950s with its delectable cakes and pink-kissed interior.

Top of the charts in Viennese cakes is *Sacher Torte*. Emperor Franz Josef was partial to this rich iced chocolate cake – its sweetness offset by a tangy layer of apricot jam – and it's still a favourite at Café Sacher (p71) today. *Esterházytorte,* a marbled butter-cream and meringue torte, and flaky, quark-filled *Topfenstrudel* would also make the top 10. *Gugelhupf,* a ring-shaped marble cake; *Linzertorte,* a spiced tart filled with redcurrant jam; and good old apple strudel are as popular as ever, too.

Lonely Planet's Top Choices

Café Sperl (p101) The real-deal coffee house: history, good food, games and faded grandeur.

Café Central (p135) A drop of opulence in vaulted, marble surrounds.

Café Leopold Hawelka (p70) Viennese character exudes from the walls of this convivial coffee house.

Demel (p71) Decadent cakes that once pleased the emperor's palate.

Sperlhof (p162) Offbeat and arty 1920s haunt.

Supersense (p161) Retro-grand cafe in an 1898-built Italianate mansion.

Best Historic Coffee Houses

Café Sperl (p101) A blast of nostalgia and a game of billiards in this *Jugendstil* beauty.

Café Central (p135) Trotsky and Lenin once played chess under the soaring vaults here.

Café Landtmann (p136) Mahler and Marlene Dietrich loved this old-world classic near the Burgtheater.

Café Griensteidl (p71) Going strong since 1847, this *Jugendstil* gem was a literary magnet.

Café Leopold Hawelka (p70) Hundertwasser and Warhol once hung out at this warm, wood-panelled cafe.

Café Korb (p85) Freud's old haunt is now part gallery, part cafe.

Best Cakes & Sweets

Demel (p71) Cakes and tortes fit for royalty.

Café Sacher (p71) King of the *Sacher Torte.*

Oberlaa (p73) Beautifully wrapped chocolates and *macarons*.

Bonbons Anzinger (p73) Specialises in the chocolate-covered *Mozartkugel* filled with pistachio marzipan and nougat.

Diglas (p89) Legendary *Apfelstrudel.*

Vollpension (p98) Intergenerational gem with a combined repertoire of 200 cake recipes.

Best Local Coffee Houses

Kaffee Alt Wien (p88) A dimly lit, arty haunt popular with students; located in the centre and has long hours.

Café am Heumarkt (p152) Old-school charmer near the Stadtpark.

Sperlhof (p162) Race back to the 1920s in this cafe with books, billiards and ping-pong.

Café Jelinek (p101) Warm, down to earth and full of regulars.

Kleines Café (p89) Boho flair can be found in this dinky cafe on Franziskanerplatz.

Zur Rezeption (p160) Vintage decor and home cooking.

Best New-Wave Cafes

Supersense (p161) Locally roasted coffee and a cool concept shop.

Cafe Menta (p150) Nouveau-retro hang-out.

Balthasar (p162) Colourful spot serving tip-top espresso.

POC Cafe (p135) Seriously good coffee in lab-like surrounds.

Pure Living Bakery (p172) Boho-flavoured garden cafe near Schönbrunn.

Best Free Live Music

Café Bräunerhof (p72) Classical music from 3pm to 6pm on weekends.

Café Central (p135) A pianist plays from 5pm to 10pm daily.

Café Landtmann (p136) Live piano music tinkles from 8pm to 11pm Sunday to Tuesday.

Café Prückel (p89) Piano music from 7pm to 10pm on Monday, Wednesday and Friday in 1950s surrounds.

Diglas (p89) Bag a cosy booth to hear piano music from 7pm to 10pm Thursday to Saturday.

Drinking & Nightlife

In this city where history often waltzes with the cutting edge, the drinking scene spans vaulted wine cellars here since Mozart's day to boisterous beer gardens, boho student dives and dressy cocktail bars, retro and rooftop bars. And with over 700 hectares of vineyards within its city limits, a visit to a Heuriger (wine tavern) is a quintessential Viennese experience.

Vienna's Nightlife Hotspots

Vienna's wave of repurposed venues have their own distinctive flair and story to tell, such as former pet grooming parlours, electrical shops and ruby-gold brothels that have been born again as bars. Also on the up are rooftop bars where you can take in skyline views while sipping a mojito. Retro cafe/bars with vintage-shop charm are in vogue, too, in a city that loves to time travel to a different era; many serve locally roasted coffee along with local wines. And given the Viennese appreciation of quality, craft beer bars, specialist gin bars and craft cocktail venues are all gaining a stronghold, with numerous new venues.

Your options are limitless, but particularly lively nightlife stretches include Gumpendorferstrasse in Mariahilf, between Naschmarkt and Mariahilferstrasse, Schleifmühlgasse in the Freihausviertel south of Naschmarkt (Wieden district), and the more international *Bermudadreieck* (Bermuda Triangle) in the Innere Stadt's old Jewish quarter. The Gürtel ring road is great for DJs and live music in bar-club hybrids under the railway arches.

Summer in the City

With the advent of summer, many revellers descend on outdoor venues. The bars and shady courtyards at Altes AKH university attract plenty, as does the market square Yppenplatz in Ottakring and the Freihausviertel in Wieden. The reinvention of the Danube Canal as a bar strip has been a huge success; Flex (p136) is a long-established location, but the likes of Strandbar Herrmann (p152) and Badeschiff (p91), pool by day, bar by night, have added an entirely new dimension to the waterway.

As spring ushers in summer, *Schanigärten* (courtyard gardens and pavement terraces) begin to pop up like wildflowers, luring the Viennese outdoors. There were over 1800 at the last count.

Intimate Clubbing

The Austrian capital's relatively small club scene still traverses the entire stylistic and musical spectrum, from chandelier-lit glamour to industrial-style grunge, with playlists skipping from indie through to house, electro, techno, R&B, reggae, metal and '80s pop. Clubs invariably feature excellent DJs, with both home-grown and international talent working the decks.

Bombastic venues are rare creatures here and the vibe is kept intimate and friendly in small clubs, where dress codes and bouncers are often refreshingly relaxed. The borders between bars and clubs are often blurred, with DJs amping up the atmosphere as the night wears on. Indeed, what the clubs here often lack in size, they make up for with alternative flair or unique locations, whether you're partying poolside in a former sauna-turned-club in the Prater, under the arches on the Gürtel or in a 1950s-style pavilion in the Volksgarten.

Microbreweries

Venues where the beer is always fresh, the atmosphere jovial and families are welcome, Vienna's microbreweries make for a great night out. Most offer a healthy selection of beers brewed on the premises (and proudly display the shining, brass brewing equipment), complemented by filling Austrian staples. Punters spill out into their courtyard gardens in summer.

Outside the centre, **Fischer Bräu** (☎01-369 59 49; www.fischerbraeu.at; 19, Billrothstrasse 17; ⏰4pm-12.30am; Ⓤ Nussdorfer Strasse) brews a new beer every four to six weeks, and a *Helles* (light) lager all year round. Live music often plays in the rollicking beer garden on summer Sunday afternoons.

Grape & Grain

While wine is the chosen drink of the Viennese, beer features heavily in the city's cultural make-up. Try the following:

Blauburgunder Complex, fruity Pinot noir red.

Grüner Veltliner Strong, fresh white with hints of citrus and pear.

Riesling Fruity white with strong acidity.

Zweigelt Full-bodied red with intense cherry aromas.

Dunkel Thick dark beer with a very rich flavour.

Helles Lager with a bite – clear and lightly hoppy.

Pils Crisp, strong and often bitter Pilsner beer.

Märzen Red-coloured beer with a strong malt taste.

Zwickel Unfiltered beer with a cloudy complexion.

Schnäpse (schnapps) Fruit brandy; usually consumed after a meal.

Visiting Heurigen

Heurigen are rustic wine taverns mostly on the outskirts of the city serving young wine (invariably serving traditional food), usually in a courtyard setting. *Buschenschenken* are a smaller variation open less often (usually in September), which bloomed after Joseph II decreed in 1784 that producers could sell their own wine from the vineyard without obtaining a licence.

Heuriger Wine The most important feature of any *Heuriger* is the wine, traditionally made by the owner and usually only a year old. *Sturm* (literally 'storm' for its cloudy appearance, perhaps even for its chaotic effects on drinkers) is yeasty because it is still fermenting. It's sold from around early September to the middle of October. A new vintage of bottled *Heuriger* wine is released each year on 11 November.

Heuriger Food & Ordering Traditionally, food is sold by the decagram (dag) in portions of 10 dag (100 grams), but increasingly a buffet meal is offered for a fixed price, from around €7.50 to €14 at simple places to about €17 to €29 at more

NEED TO KNOW

Opening Hours

Opening hours vary greatly and depend on season, with later hours in summer.

Bars & Pubs Generally open around 4pm or 5pm and close anywhere between midnight and 4am.

Clubs Generally open between 6pm and 10pm and close roughly around 4am; many are only open Thursday through to Saturday.

Useful Websites

Falter (www.falter.at) Event and party listings.

Vienna Online (www.vienna.at) Keep track of club nights with this event calendar.

Tourist Info Wien (www.wien.info) Nightlife listings arranged by theme.

Drink Prices

➡ Standard beer prices range from €2 to €5, depending on the venue and location (central Vienna tends to be more expensive).

➡ A decent glass of local wine starts at around €3.

➡ Expect to pay at least €7 for a simple mixed drink and around €9 and up for a cocktail.

Club Entry

Entry prices can and do vary wildly – from nothing to €20 – and depend on who's on the decks. Many small, intimate clubs offer free entry at least once a week.

Tipping

Tipping is standard: for smaller bills (under €10) it is customary to round up and add another euro if need be; for larger tabs, 5% to 10% is customary.

upmarket establishments with greater choice. Typically, you'll find a selection of warm and cold foods, such as roast pork in one or the other variety, blood sausage, meat loaf and a range of cured meats, lard and breads, pickled vegetables and salads such as *Schwarzwurzelsalat* (black salsify salad) and potato salad, as well as strudel for dessert.

Where & When *Heurigen* are concentrated in and around winegrowing regions on Vienna's fringes. Many are only open part of the year or every other month. To avoid disappointment, double-check opening times at www.heuteausgsteckt.at, which shows all *Heurigen* opening hours and maps their locations, or contact the individual establishments before heading out.

Transport & Map Some *Heurigen* are up to 20 minutes' walk from the public transport stop. Download the *Verkehrslinienplan für Wien* transport map (also showing streets in outer suburbs) for free at www.wienerlinien.at, or pick it up from any Wiener Linien service desk for €2.50.

TOP HEURIGEN

Wieninger (☎01-292 41 06; www.heuriger-wieninger.at; 21, Stammersdorfer Strasse 78, Stammersdorf; ⏱3pm-midnight Fri, noon-midnight Sat & Sun mid-Mar–late Apr, 3pm-midnight Thu & Fri, noon-midnight Sat & Sun late Apr–mid-Dec; 🚌30A, 🚋30, 31) A hidden wonderland with a convivial local atmosphere, Wieninger has a magical lantern- and candle-lit garden draped with vines and a cosy, wood-panelled interior. Enjoy its light, fruity wines (mainly whites) alongside an extensive buffet laden with gourmet Austrian dishes, augmented by seasonal specialities or its à la carte menu. Visits outside normal hours can be made by appointment.

Zahel (☎01-889 13 18; www.zahel.at; 23, Maurer Hauptplatz 9; ⏱11.30am-midnight Mon-Sat; 🚋60) One of the oldest *Heurigen* in Vienna, Zahel occupies a 250-year-old farmhouse with panoramic views over the Viennese skyline and vine-ribboned hills to the south. Its whites are considered some of Vienna's best, and Viennese and seasonal cuisine fills the buffet table. In addition to the timber-framed interior and terrace, there's a heated winter garden house. Cash only.

Sirbu (☎01-320 59 28; www.sirbu.at; 19, Kahlenberger Strasse 210; ⏱4-11pm Mon-Fri, 5pm-midnight Sat mid-Apr–mid-Oct; 👪; 🚌38A) Far-reaching views across Vienna's urban expanse extend from the terraces of this peaceful spot, which is marked by a small sign leading to the vine-draped rear garden adjoining the vineyards. Be sure to sample its award-winning Rieslings. A playground keeps kids occupied.

Edlmoser (☎01-889 86 80; www.edlmoser.com; 23, Maurer Lange Gasse, Maurer; ⏱2.30pm-midnight, see website for dates; 🚋60) Run by passionate winemaker Michael Edlmoser, Edlmoser occupies a house that's four centuries old, with a charming, tree-shaded garden centred on a splashing fountain, with varnished pine benches and wine barrels for tables. It's especially renowned for its whites, including Riesling and Grüner Veltliner.

Heuriger Huber (☎01-485 81 80; www.sissi-huber.at; 16, Roterdstrasse 5; ⏱3pm-midnight Tue-Sat, hours can vary; 🚋10, 44) Riesling and Weissburgunder (Pinot blanc) are the main wines produced by this charming *Heuriger*, which has a sprawling Mediterranean garden surrounded by olive groves, citrus orchards and drifts of lavender. Seafood, salads, pastas and grilled meats appear on its select menu. Confirm opening hours before you visit. Take tram 10 or 44 to Dornbach/Güpferlingstrasse.

Drinking by Neighbourhood

➡ **The Hofburg & Around** Old-world wine taverns, intimate cocktail bars and drinks with Hofburg views in the Burggarten and Volksgarten.

➡ **Stephansdom & the Historic Centre** Narrow lanes hide a mix of cellar bars, wine bars, pubs and serious cocktail bars.

➡ **Karlsplatz & Around Naschmarkt** Boho hood crammed with clubs, retro and alternative bars, especially along Gumpendorferstrasse.

➡ **The Museum District & Neubau** Arty bars with a spritz of culture and alfresco seating – hit Spittelberg for *Schanigärten*.

➡ **Alsergrund & the University District** Student pubs and all-night parties under the Gürtel viaduct.

➡ **Schloss Belvedere to the Canal** Bars by the Danube Canal and the odd microbrewery.

➡ **Prater & East of the Danube** Clubbing livewire around Praterstern, rooftop haunts and relaxed cafe-bars around Karmelitermarkt.

➡ **Schloss Schönbrunn & Around** A smattering of cafe-bars and clubs.

Lonely Planet's Top Choices

Vinothek W-Einkehr (p88) Superb Austrian wines.

Le Loft (p161) Map out Vienna from above at this super-sleek lounge bar.

Loos American Bar (p70) Find a cosy alcove for a cocktail at Loos' 1908 classic.

Volksgarten ClubDiskothek (p70) Party in the park at this glam club near the Hofburg.

Brickmakers Pub & Kitchen (p122) Craft beers, ciders and pop-up guest chefs.

Palmenhaus (p71) Cocktail sip in this palm house with great outdoor seating overlooking Burggarten.

Best Riverside Bars

Strandbar Herrmann (p152) Lively 'beach' bar beside the Costa del Danube.

Urania (p152) Slick glass-walled bar overlooking the Danube Canal.

Motto am Fluss (p86) Inside the Wien-City ferry terminal with dazzling canal views.

Best Wine Bars

Vinothek W-Einkehr (p88) Wines from all over Austria.

Achtundzwanzig (p135) Young, edgy but very serious about their wines.

Vis-à-vis (p88) Postage stamp of a wine bar tucked down a narrow passage.

Weinstube Josefstadt (p136) Atmospheric *Stadtheurigen* (city wine tavern) hiding in an oasis of a garden.

Villon (p71) The central district's deepest wine cellar has a light, modern ambience.

Sekt Comptoir (p104) Effervescent bar with Burgenland *Sekt* (sparkling wine) near the Naschmarkt.

Best Microbreweries

Siebensternbräu (p123) Cheery brewpub with hoppy beers and a warm-weather courtyard.

Wieden Bräu (p102) Helles, Märzen and hemp beers, plus summertime garden.

Salm Bräu (p152) Relaxed pick for home brews right by Schloss Belvedere.

Best Cocktail Bars

Loos American Bar (p70) Mixology magic in this minimalist, Adolf Loos–designed bar.

Vinogin (p88) Specialist gin and wine bar.

Le Troquet (p123) Retro cocktails.

Kruger's American Bar (p87) Sip a classic margarita in this 1920s, wood-panelled den.

Barfly's Club (p101) Terrific cocktails in an intimate setting.

Lutz (p102) Club chairs for conversing over a frozen mojito.

Best Gay & Lesbian Hang-outs

Café Berg (p136) Friendly, open and stocks gay books.

Felixx (p101) A class act, complete with chandeliers.

Café Savoy (p102) The atmosphere of a traditional Viennese cafe plus a little pizzazz.

Mango Bar (p103) Perennially popular bar open every night of the week.

Frauencafé (p125) A women-only favourite of Vienna's lesbian scene.

Best Clubs

Volksgarten ClubDiskothek (p70) Popular house-spinning club.

Fluc (p162) Turbo-charged Praterstern club with an alternative edge.

Donau (p123) Tucked-away techno club with a friendly crowd.

Best Rooftop Bars

Le Loft (p161) Knockout skyline views from glass-clad bar on the 18th floor of the Sofitel.

Dachboden (p123) Big-top views of Vienna from the 25hours Hotel's rooftop bar.

Café Oben (p123) Landmark spot from this cafe atop Hauptbücherei Wien.

Sky Bar (p88) Vienna's most spectacular rooftop bar in the Innere Stadt.

Best Schanigärten

Palmenhaus (p71) Slide into summer with DJ beats, barbecues and beers.

Volksgarten ClubDiskothek (p70) Drink in Hofburg views and summer vibes from this pavilion's tree-shaded garden.

Café Leopold (p123) A terrace perfect for lapping up the MuseumsQuartier's cultural buzz.

Strandbar Herrmann (p152) Vienna's best urban beach bar.

Entertainment

From opera, classical music and theatre to live rock or jazz, Vienna offers a wealth of entertainment opportunities. The capital is home to the German-speaking world's oldest theatre, the Burgtheater, as well as the famous Wiener Sängerknaben (Vienna Boys' Choir) and the Vienna Philharmonic Orchestra, which performs in the acoustically superb Musikverein.

Opera

Vienna is a world capital for opera, and a stroll down Kärntner Strasse from Stephansplatz to the Staatsoper will turn up more Mozart lookalikes (costumed ticket sellers) than you can poke a baton at. The two main performance spaces are the Staatsoper, which closes in July and August, and Theater an der Wien (p103), which remains open during these months.

STAATSOPER TICKETS

As one of the world's premier venues, demand for Staatsoper (p103) tickets is high: book up to eight weeks in advance to be sure of getting a seating ticket. For some performances, one month or even in some cases a few days is sufficient. The chances of getting seats on the day at the *Abendkasse* (evening sales desk) or in the opera foyer are quite low for most performances. The best alternative in that case is a standing-room ticket.

The state ticket office, the Bundestheaterkassen, is located on Operngasse, on the west side of the Staatsoper. Tickets are available here for the Staatsoper two months prior to performance dates. Credit-card purchases can be made online or by telephone. The **Info unter den Arkaden** (Map p248; www.bundestheater.at; 01, Herbert von Karajan-Platz 1; ⌚9am-1hr before performance begins Mon-Fri, 9am-5pm Sat) branch is located on the Kärntner Strasse side of the Staatsoper.

Collecting Tickets Pick up tickets from the Bundestheaterkassen office using your ticket code. If you don't do this, the tickets must be collected at the *Abendkasse*, which opens one hour before the performance. If you use the 'print at home' option on the internet, you will be given a certain time period during which you must print your ticket.

Abendkasse Located inside the Staatsoper, it opens one hour prior to performances and sells the leftover contingent. Expect to queue for about 10 minutes here.

Staatsoper Foyer Sells tickets from 9am to two hours before performance Monday to Friday and 9am to noon Saturday.

Standing Room *Stehplätze* (room for 567 people) tickets are sold from an entrance on Operngasse, beginning 80 minutes before the performance (arrive two to three hours ahead). Tickets cost €3 for the *Parterre* (closest to the stage but without a view of the orchestra) and *Balcon* (balcony, but on the sides and sometimes with an obstructed view) to €4 for the *Galerie* (the best option, on the balcony with a full view of the stage). Cash only; limit of one ticket per person.

Cost Varies according to performance popularity and availability.

Binoculurs Rental Costs €2.

Classical Music

Opportunities to listen to classical music in Vienna abound. Churches are a hub for recitals of Bach and Händel especially, but also great venues for all sorts of classical music recitals. Vienna's Philharmonic Orchestra is based in the Musikverein (p103).

Standing Room Costs €5.

Seating Cheapest is directly above the stage, with good views of the hall but not the orchestra. Everything up to €49 has partially obscured views, above €49 is with unimpeded views (ask when booking).

Return Tickets Although tickets are often sold out years ahead, tickets of those who are unable to attend a particular performance are returned and sold for between €15 and €101. Depending on whether the Musikverein or the Wiener Philharmoniker has organised the concert, returned tickets can be bought from the Musikverein itself (seven weeks or less before the concert) or from the **Wiener Philharmoniker Karten- und Ballbüro** (Map p248; ☎01-505 65 25; www.wienerphilharmoniker.at; 01, Kärntner Ring 12; ⏰9am-3.30pm Sep-Jun, 10am-1pm Aug, closed Jul) on the Monday before the performance or, for standing-room tickets, go to the ticket booking office at least one hour before the performance.

Rock & Jazz

Vienna's rock and jazz scene is lively, with a strong local list as well as international acts playing from the smallest bars to the largest arenas. See Falter (www.falter.at) for bands, venues and dates. The biggest bashes are the Donauinselfest (p164) and Jazz Fest Wien (p23).

Theatre

The Burgtheater (p125), Volkstheater (p125), Theater in der Josefstadt (p138) and Akademietheater (p154) are Vienna's prime theatre addresses in an innovative and lively scene. Options for non-German speakers are generally limited to Vienna's English Theatre (p125).

Cinema

Both independent art-house films and Hollywood blockbusters are popular in Vienna. The website www.film.at, Falter (www.falter.at) and the daily Der Standard (http://derstandard.at) newspaper are the best sources for listings. Some cinemas have discounted admission on Monday and/or Tuesday and/or Wednesday.

OF or *OV* following a film title means it will screen in the original language; *OmU* indicates the film is in the original language with German subtitles; and *OmenglU* and *OmeU* signify that it's in the original language with English subtitles.

NEED TO KNOW

Opening Hours

Opera & Theatre Staatsoper (p103) has no performances in July and August. Theater an der Wien (p103) is open during these months.

Live Rock & Jazz Usually starts at 8pm or 9pm.

Advance Booking

Advance bookings are highly advisable for classical cultural offerings, but there are also plenty of opportunities to catch performances at short notice. Bookings for live rock and jazz are rarely required.

Ticket Organisations & Reservations

Bundestheaterkassen (Map p248; ☎01-514 44 7810; www.bundestheater.at; 01, Operngasse 2; ⏰8am-6pm Mon-Fri, 9am-noon Sat & Sun; ⓊStephansplatz) Official ticket office and exclusive outlet for the Staatsoper, Volksoper and Burgtheater.

Wien-Ticket Pavillon (Map p248; ☎01-588 85; www.wien-ticket.at; Kärntner Strasse; ⏰10am-7pm; 🚋D, 1, 2, 71 Kärntner Ring/Oper, ⓊKarlsplatz) Charges anything from no commission up to a 6% levy. Tickets for all venues except the Staatsoper, Burgtheater and Volksoper.

Online Resources

Falter (www.falter.at) Weekly listings of all events.

Tourist Info Wien (http://events.wien.info/en) Lists upcoming events up to 18 months in advance.

THE VIENNALE

Vienna's annual international film festival, the 'fringe-like' **Viennale** (www.viennale.at; ⏲late Oct–early Nov), is the highlight of the city's celluloid calendar. For two weeks from mid-October, public cinemas screen works ranging from documentaries to short and feature films.

Ticket sales commence on the Saturday before the festival begins. You can book by credit card, online or via a special hotline number that is published on the website once sales begin. Tickets can be picked up at any of the booths set up around town, such as the **Viennale main booth** (Map p248; www.viennale.at; 06, MuseumsQuartier, cnr Mariahilfer Strasse; ⏲10am-8pm; UMuseumsquartier).

OPEN-AIR CINEMA

Open-air cinema is hugely popular in Vienna when the weather warms up. The city hosts numerous such cinemas across town, the biggest of which is the **Musikfilm Festival** (http://filmfestival-rathausplatz.at; 01, Rathausplatz; ⏲mid-Jul–early Sep; 🚋D, 1, 2 Rathaus, URathaus). **Kino Unter Sternen** (Cinema Under Stars; www.kinountersternen.at; ⏲late Jun–mid-Jul; UKarlsplatz), a highly popular outdoor cinema on Karlsplatz, hosts films from late June to mid-July. **Arena** (www.arena.co.at; 03, Baumgasse 80; UErdberg, Gasometer) has open-air screenings over three weeks in August, and **Kino wie noch nie** (Map p258; www.kinowienochnie.at; 02, Augarten; tickets €8.50; UTaborstrasse) has open-air screenings in July and August.

VIENNA BOYS' CHOIR

Founded by Maximilian I in 1498 as the imperial choir, the Wiener Sängerknaben (Vienna Boys' Choir) is the most famous of its type in the world. The experience will be very different depending on where you see the performance. The most formal occasions are held in the Burgkapelle, where the focus is obviously on sacral music. Performances at other venues might range from pop through to world music. Regardless of the setting and style of the performance, the beauty and choral harmony of the voices remains the same.

Performances

The choir sings during Sunday mass in the Burgkapelle (p61) in the Hofburg, but occasional concerts are also given during the week at other venues in Vienna and elsewhere. Sunday performances in the Burgkapelle are held from mid-September to June at 9.15am. Other venues where you can hear the choir include MuTh (p163), the choir's dedicated hall in Augarten, which hosts regular Friday afternoon performances.

The Vienna Boys' Choir website (www.wienersaengerknaben.at) has links to the venues alongside each performance date.

Tickets

Book tickets through the individual venue. Tickets for the Sunday performances at Burgkapelle cost €10 to €36 and can be booked through the booking office (p61) by sending an email or fax. It's best to book about six weeks in advance.

For orders under €60, you pay cash when you pick up your tickets, which can be done from 11am to 1pm and 3pm to 5pm at the booking office of the chapel in the Schweizerhof of the Hofburg on the Friday before the performance. You can also pick them up between 8.15am and 8.45am on the Sunday, but this is less advisable as queues are long. If your order amounts to €60 or more, you will be sent the bank details for transferring the money. Credit cards and cheques aren't accepted. Seats costing €10 do not afford a view of the choir itself.

Tickets for a free *Stehplatz* (standing-room space) are available from 8.30am. Uncollected tickets are also resold on the day from 8am. The queues for these and for standing-room tickets are long, so arrive very early – around 7am – and be prepared to wait.

Lonely Planet's Top Choices

Staatsoper (p103) One of the world's foremost opera houses.

Musikverein (p103) Home of the Vienna Philharmonic Orchestra.

Hofburg Concert Halls (p72) The sumptuous Festsaal and Redoutensaal are regularly used for Strauss and Mozart concerts.

Radiokulturhaus (p152) Expect anything from odes to Sinatra and REM to evenings dedicated to Beethoven and Mozart.

MuTh (p163) The new home of the Wiener Sängerknaben (Vienna Boys' Choir).

Konzerthaus (p154) Major venue in classical-music circles.

Best Classical Music

Staatsoper (p103) A sublime setting for opera productions.

Radiokulturhaus (p152) Venues here include the Grosser Sendesaal, home to the Vienna Radio Symphony Orchestra.

MuTh (p163) Catch concerts by the celestial Vienna Boys' Choir.

Burgkapelle (p61) The Vienna Boys' Choir also sings Sunday Mass in this chapel.

Konzerthaus (p154) Up to three simultaneous performances can be staged in the Konzerthaus' halls.

Orangery (p174) Regular classical concerts take place in Schloss Schönbrunn's orangery.

Best Rock & Jazz

Konzerthaus (p154) Ethnic music, rock, pop or jazz can also be heard in the Konzerthaus' hallowed halls.

Jazzland (p89) Long-standing venue covering all jazz styles.

Porgy & Bess (p90) Modern jazz plays at this 350-capacity club.

B72 (p137) Grungy venue with some great alternative acts.

Miles Smiles (p138) Intimate jazz club named after the great Miles Davis.

Café Carina (p138) Local bands play folk, jazz, rock and country at this tiny bar.

Best Theatre

Burgtheater (p125) One of the most important theatres in the German-speaking world.

Volkstheater (p125) Built in 1889, this is one of Vienna's largest and grandest theatres.

Akademietheater (p154) This 1920s-built theatre is the second venue of the highly esteemed Burgtheater.

Theater in der Josefstadt (p138) Ornate interior and traditional productions.

Marionetten Theater (p174) The puppets here delight kids and adults alike.

Best Cinema

Metro Kinokulturhaus (p89) Austria's national film archive has a restored cinema screening home-grown films.

Gartenbaukino (p90) Art-house films play to a 736-capacity crowd at this '60s timewarp.

Filmcasino (p103) Indie films from around the world plus shorts and documentaries from Asia and Europe.

Shopping

With a long-standing history of craftsmanship, in recent years this elegant city has spread its creative wings in the fashion and design world. Whether you're browsing for hand-painted porcelain in the Innere Stadt, new-wave streetwear in Neubau or epicurean treats in the Freihausviertel, you'll find inspiration, a passion for quality and an attentive eye for detail.

Markets

One of the true joys of shopping in Vienna is milling around its markets first thing in the morning and having the chance to chat to the producers.

Almost every district has at least one market selling fresh produce from Monday to Saturday, many reflecting the ethnic diversity of their neighbourhood. Some host *Bauernmärkte* (farmers markets) on Saturday mornings, where growers from the surrounding countryside travel to the big city to sell their wares: fresh vegetables, tree-ripened fruit, cured hams, free-range eggs, homemade schnapps and cut flowers. Do as the laid-back Viennese do and linger for banter and brunch at a market-side cafe or deli.

CHRISTMAS MARKETS

From around mid-November to late December, **Christkindlmärkte** (Christmas markets; www.wien.info/en/shopping-wining-dining/markets/christmas-markets; ⌚mid-Nov–25 Dec) bring festive cheer into the city's squares, courtyards and cobbled lanes. Each has its own flair but all have *Glühwein* (mulled wine), *Maroni* (chestnuts) and twinkling trees. Annual dates and times are listed on www.wien.info.

Favourites include the following:

Rathausplatz (Map p252; www.christkindlmarkt.at; ⌚10am-10pm 13 Nov–26 Dec; 🚋D, 1, 2 Rathaus, Ⓤ Rathaus) A whopper of a tree, 150 stalls and kid-pleasing activities from cookie-baking workshops to pony rides, all set against the atmospheric backdrop of the neo-Gothic Rathaus.

Schönbrunn (Map p262; ⌚10am-9pm daily 3rd week Nov-26 Dec; 🚌1A, Ⓤ Schönbrunn) Shop for nutcrackers, crib figurines and puppets at this handicraft market in the palace courtyard, with loads of events for the kids, and daily classical concerts at 6pm weekdays and 2pm weekends.

Spittelberg (Map p252; www.spittelberg.at; 07, Spittelberggasse; ⌚2-9pm Mon-Thu, 2-9.30pm Fri, 10am-9.30pm Sat, 10am-9pm Sun 13 Nov-23 Dec; Ⓤ Volkstheater, Museumsquartier) The cobbled lanes of this Biedermeier quarter set the scene for this market, beloved of the Viennese, where stalls sell quality arts and crafts.

Trends

The Viennese have a love of life's fine details that extends to the way they shop, prizing quality, eye-catching details and an individual sense of style over identikit high streets and throw-away products. The city is full of ateliers and independent boutiques where regulars are greeted by name and designers can often be seen at work, whether adding the finishing touches to a shift dress, knitting chunky beanies from silky merino wool, or custom-making jewellery.

One of Europe's most dynamic, Vienna's contemporary fashion and design scene is fed by an influx of young up-and-coming creatives. This scene took root in the 7th district and has spread fresh new shoots everywhere from Praterstrasse in the 2nd to Yppenplatz in the 16th today. Social consciousness is key, with many shops placing the accent on fair-trade materials, and locally recycled or upcycled products – one person's junk becoming another's treasure is big.

Shopping Strips

Kärntner Strasse The Innere Stadt's main shopping street and a real crowd-puller.

Kohlmarkt A river of high-end glitz, flowing into a magnificent Hofburg view.

Neubau Track down the city's hottest designers along boutique-clogged streets like Kirchengasse, Lindengasse and Neubaugasse.

Mariahilfer Strasse Vienna's mile of high-street style, with big names and crowds.

Freihausviertel Lanes packed with home-grown fashion, design and speciality food stores, south of Naschmarkt.

Theobaldgasse Hole-in-the-wall shops purvey everything from fair-trade fashion to organic food.

Shopping by Neighbourhood

➡ **The Hofburg & Around** A nostalgic backstreet romp reveals fine porcelain, hat shops and one of Europe's best auction houses.

➡ **Stephansdom & the Historic Centre** Upper-crust Graben and Kohlmarkt fan into side streets hiding Austrian design stores, jewellers and confectioners.

➡ **Karlsplatz & Around Naschmarkt** A picnic-basket banquet at the Naschmarkt and the Freihausviertel's idiosyncratic galleries, boutiques and speciality stores.

➡ **The Museum District & Neubau** Vienna's creative trailblazer – streets ahead of other neighbourhoods when it comes to fashion and design.

➡ **Alsergrund & the University District** Farm-fresh goods at Freyung Market, delis and chocolatiers in the ever-so-grand Palais Ferstel.

➡ **Prater & East of the Danube** Karmelitermarkt and Praterstrasse have a growing crop of future-focused galleries, boutiques and design stores.

NEED TO KNOW

Bargaining

Bargaining is a no-no in shops, although you can certainly haggle when buying secondhand. It's a must at the *Flohmärkte* (flea markets).

Opening Hours

Most shops open between 9am and 6.30pm Monday to Friday and until 5pm on Saturday. Some have extended hours on Thursday (occasionally Friday) until around 8pm or 9pm.

Taxes

➡ *Mehrwertsteuer* (MWST; value-added tax) is 20% for most goods.

➡ Non-EU visitors can claim a MWST refund on purchases over €75.01. Ask shops to fill out a tax-refund cheque at the time of purchase, and get it stamped by border officials when you leave the EU.

➡ Check www.globalblue.com for more details.

Useful Websites

7tm (www.7tm.at) For the lowdown on fashion and design in Neubau.

Guided Vienna (www.guided-vienna.com) Pin down the city's hottest fashion and design by district.

Tourist Info Wien (www.wien.info) Takes a comprehensive look at shopping in Vienna by theme and neighbourhood.

Lonely Planet's Top Choices

Steiff (p72) The original creator of the teddy bear.

Art Up (p91) Where the rising stars of Austria's fashion and design scene shine.

Henzls Ernte (p104) Garden veg and foraged herbs go into delectable spreads, sugars and salts.

Dorotheum (p73) Hammer time at this giant treasure chest of an auction house.

Gabarage Upcycling Design (p106) Reborn cast-offs become cutting-edge design.

Best Antiques & Crafts

Dorotheum (p73) One of Europe's largest auction houses.

feinedinge (p106) Porcelain from the understated to the filigree.

Augarten Wien (p73) Vienna's finest hand-painted porcelain since 1718.

Gmundner (p73) Over half of all Austrian households own at least one piece of Gmundner porcelain.

Best Design

Das Möbel (p124) Furniture on the cusp of cool at a try-before-you-buy cafe.

Österreichische Werkstätten (p73) A showcase for top-quality Austrian design.

Die Werkbank (p124) Design collective showcasing some of Vienna's most innovative creators.

Best Food & Drink

Staud's (p138) Wine jellies, apricot jams and chutneys.

Wiener Rosenmanufaktur (p91) Viennese roses are used to create jams, jellies, liqueurs and more.

Blühendes Konfekt (p105) Say it with a bouquet of chocolate-dipped herbs or candied flowers.

Unger und Klein (p91) The Austrian wine world uncorked.

Wald & Wiese (p87) Honey from Vienna's own rooftop apiaries.

Gegenbauer (p99) Prized oils and vinegars.

Best Fashion & Accessories

Mein Design (p106) Fresh-faced fashion and accessories with a sustainable focus.

Atelier Naske (p90) Elke creates jewellery as delicately beautiful as the materials she uses.

Ina Kent (p125) Silky soft leather bags made from vegetable-tanned leather.

Schau Schau (p90) Handcrafted eyewear beloved by celebs.

Mühlbauer (p126) In the hat business since 1903.

Best Markets

Naschmarkt (p96) Hands-down Vienna's best food market and street food.

Flohmarkt (p99) Fabulous flea market.

Karmelitermarkt (p162) Bag fresh produce and do brunch Viennese-style.

Brunnenmarkt (p132) As buzzing as a Turkish bazaar.

Bio-Markt Freyung (p138) Organic farm goodies.

Sports & Activities

Vienna is a cracking city for outdoor activities. The Wienerwald to the west is criss-crossed with hiking and cycling trails, while the Danube, Alte Donau, Donauinsel and Lobau to the east offer boating, swimming, cycling and inline skating. There are over 1200km of designated cycle paths, and the city is dotted with parks, some big (the Prater), some small (Stadtpark).

Hiking & Walking

The Viennese are into *Wandern* (walking) and their vast backyard is perfect for hiking in woods, through meadows and along riverside trails. The green belt of the Wienerwald (p160), on the western edge of Vienna, attracts walkers and cyclists, but the likes of the Prater, with its lengthy tree-flanked trails, and the Lainzer Tiergarten (p172), a park to the west of Vienna where deer roam freely in woods of beech and oak, attract plenty of locals. Bordering the Danube, the Nationalpark Donau-Auen (p164) is a back-to-nature wilderness for walkers, and offers themed excursions such as birdwatching rambles.

The Vienna Forestry Office maintains a number of local hiking paths, all of which are well signposted and accessible by public transport. Many include children's playgrounds, picnic tables and exceptional views en route. For a comprehensive list of local hiking trails in and around the Greater Vienna area, including detailed route descriptions and printable maps, go to www.wien.gv.at/en and type 'hiking' in the search field.

Cycling

Vienna is easily handled by bicycle. Around 1200km of cycle tracks cover the city, making it a breeze to avoid traffic, but not always pedestrians. Many one-way streets do not apply to cyclists; these are indicated by a bicycle sign with the word *ausgen* alongside it. Cycling routes lead through Vienna's parklands, along its waterways and the 7km path around the Ringstrasse. Popular cycling and inline skating areas include the Donauinsel (Danube Island), the Prater and along the Danube Canal (Donaukanal).

Most bike- and skate-hire places are well informed and give local tips about where to head, including maps. Expect to pay between €25 and €30 per day.

Over 120 Citybike Wien (p221) bike-share-scheme stands are located across the city. A credit card and €1 registration fee is required to hire bikes; just swipe your card in the machine and follow the multilingual instructions. The bikes are intended as an alternative to transport and can only be locked up at a bike station (unless you use your own lock). A lost bike will set you back €600.

Swimming

Swimming is the favoured summer pastime of the Viennese. The Donauinsel, Alte Donau and Lobau are often swamped with urbanites cooling off on hot summer days. Topless sunbathing is common, as is nude sunbathing, but only in designated areas; much of Lobau and both tips of the Donauinsel are FKK (*Freikörperkultur;* free body culture/naked) areas.

There are also lidos run by the city, which open from early May to early September, with open-air pools for swimming laps and lawns for sunbathing. Many also feature picnic areas, volleyball courts and slides for kids. They're open from 9am to around 7pm daily

NEED TO KNOW

Planning Ahead

For most activities in Vienna, just turn up and you're good to go. It's worth pre-booking guided walking and cycling tours a week or two in advance, especially in the high summer season, and the same goes for purchasing tickets for spectator sports.

Online Resources

Wein.at (www.wien.gv.at) A rundown of the main outdoor activities available in Vienna, from inline skating to running, swimming and climbing.

Tourist Info Wien (www.wien.info) The inside scoop on activities in Vienna, from climbing halls to ice rinks, open-air swimming pools to jogging trails.

Fahrrad Wien (www.fahrradwien.at) Helps plan your cycling route.

Sporting Events

Argus Bike Festival (www.bikefestival.at) Trial shows, trick competitions and riders' parties, alongside workshops, exhibitions and other bike-focused fun. Held on Rathausplatz.

Vienna City Marathon (www.vienna-marathon.com) Races through town in mid-April, starting at the Reichsbrücke and finishing at the Burgtheater.

Friday Night Skating (http://wien.gruene.at/skater) Roll along to Heldenplatz at 9pm on Friday from May to September and join the Friday Night Skating team on a 15km to 25km tour of the city. Participation is free.

Wiener Eistraum (p126) From late January to mid-March, you can twirl across the open-air ice rink in front of the Rathaus.

from May to mid-September and entry typically costs €5.50/3 for adults/children. For a full list of pools, visit www.wien.gv.at/english/leisure/bath.

Ice Skating

Most Viennese have ice skates collecting dust at the back of the wardrobe that are dragged out at least once over winter. Along with specialised ice-skating rinks, a number of outdoor basketball courts are turned into rinks during winter. For as little as €1 you can spend the whole day gliding around one of these temporary rinks: 08, Buchfeldgasse 7a; 16, Gallitzinstrasse 4; and 19, Osterleitengasse 14. Expect to pay €7.50/5.50 per adult/child for skate hire. When it's cold enough, the Alte Donau is transformed into an ice-skater's paradise, with miles of natural ice.

Boating

The Alte Donau is the main boating and sailing centre in Vienna, but the Neue Donau, a long stretch of water separated from the Danube by the Donauinsel, also provides opportunities for boating, windsurfing and waterskiing. You can learn to sail or rent a boat at Hofbauer (p164).

Spectator Sports

The **Stadthalle** (Map p252; ☎01-79 99 979; www.stadthalle.com; 15, Roland-Rainer-Platz 1; U Burggasse-Stadthalle) is a major player in hosting sporting events. Tennis tournaments (including the Austrian Open), horse shows and ice-hockey games are just some of the diverse events held here. The swimming pool is a major venue for aquatic events like races, water polo and synchronised swimming.

Krieau (Map p258; ☎01-728 00 46; www.krieau.at; 02, Nordportalstrasse 247; U Krieau, Stadion) is where Vienna's trotting racing events are held, and you can of course watch Lipizzaner stallions perform at the Spanish Riding School (p61).

Sports & Activities by Neighbourhood

- **The Hofburg & Around** Home to the Spanish Riding School and sculpture-dotted parks.
- **Stephansdom & the Historic Centre** Leap into the Badeschiff's pool by the Danube Canal.
- **The Museum District & Neubau** Open-air ice skating in front of the illuminated Rathaus in winter.
- **Schloss Belvedere to the Canal** Park life, ice skating and proximity to Vienna's best day spa.
- **Prater & East of the Danube** Tops for activities in Vienna, with the Danube, lidos and a wildlife-crammed national park.

Lonely Planet's Top Choices

Donauinsel (p163) Walk, cycle, swim, sail, boat or windsurf on this island in the Danube.

Wienerwald (p160) Tiptoe off the beaten trail to hike or mountain bike in these wooded hills.

Therme Wien (p154) Revive in the whirlpools, waterfalls and grotto-like pools of this thermal water wonderland.

Wiener Eislaufverein (p154) Get your skates on at the world's biggest open-air ice rink.

Prater (p157) Join the Wiener to jog, cycle and stroll in their best-loved park.

Best Hiking & Walking

Lobau (p164) Trails weave across this woody, lake-dotted floodplain, nicknamed Vienna's 'jungle'.

Wienerwald (p160) Don a pair of boots and head into Vienna's forested hills for a scenic day hike.

Nationalpark Donau-Auen (p164) Keep your eyes peeled for deer, kites and kingfishers on a back-to-nature ramble through these wetlands.

Prater (p157) Meadows, pockets of woodland and tree-lined boulevards are great for strolling.

Best Cycling

Wienerwald (p160) Roll through dappled woodlands or tear downhill mountain biking on 46 marked trails.

Donauinsel (p163) Pedal gently along the Danube, pausing for picnics, swims and cityscape views.

Prater (p157) The Prater's die-straight, chestnut-fringed Hauptallee is terrific for a city-centre spin.

Pedal Power (p164) Hook onto a cycling tour to cruise past city landmarks.

Best Adrenalin Rushes

Wienerwald (p160) Test your mettle on 1000km of mountain bike trails.

Donauturm (p159) Feel the rush as you bungee jump from 152m, hitting speeds of 90km/h.

Kletteranlage Flakturm (p106) Scale the stark outside walls of the *Flakturm* (flak tower) in Esterházypark.

Best Lidos & Pools

Badeschiff (p91) Splash around with the cool kids in this ship-shape pool on the Danube.

Strandbad Gänsehäufel (p164) Summertime magnet, with a pool, activities and nudist area.

Strandbad Alte Donau (p164) Take a cooling dip in the river at this urban beach.

Oberlaa Therme Wien (p154) Thermal pools, slides, saunas and more.

Ice Rinks

Wiener Eislaufverein (p154) Glide across the ice at this gargantuan open-air skating rink.

Wiener Eistraum (p126) DJ beats put a swing in your skate at this open-air rink on Rathausplatz.

Alte Donau (p164) When it freezes, Viennese skaters head to this arm of the Danube.

Explore Vienna

VIENNA'S TOP SIGHTS

Neighborhoods at a Glance

1 The Hofburg & Around p58

Vienna's imperial splendour peaks in this part of the Innere Stadt (city centre), where horse-drawn carriages prance along curved, cobbled streets. Its centrepiece is the magnificent Hofburg palace complex, which brims with museums and world-famous attractions. Museums also abound in the streets north towards Stephansplatz.

2 Stephansdom & the Historic Centre p74

Vienna's most distinctive landmark is the Gothic cathedral Stephansdom. The oldest part of the city, with a tangle of cobbled lanes and elegant thoroughfares graced, this epicentral neighbourhood takes in the medieval Jewish quarter in the northwest, the stretch down to Danube Canal's southern bank and the areas northeast and east of Stephansplatz.

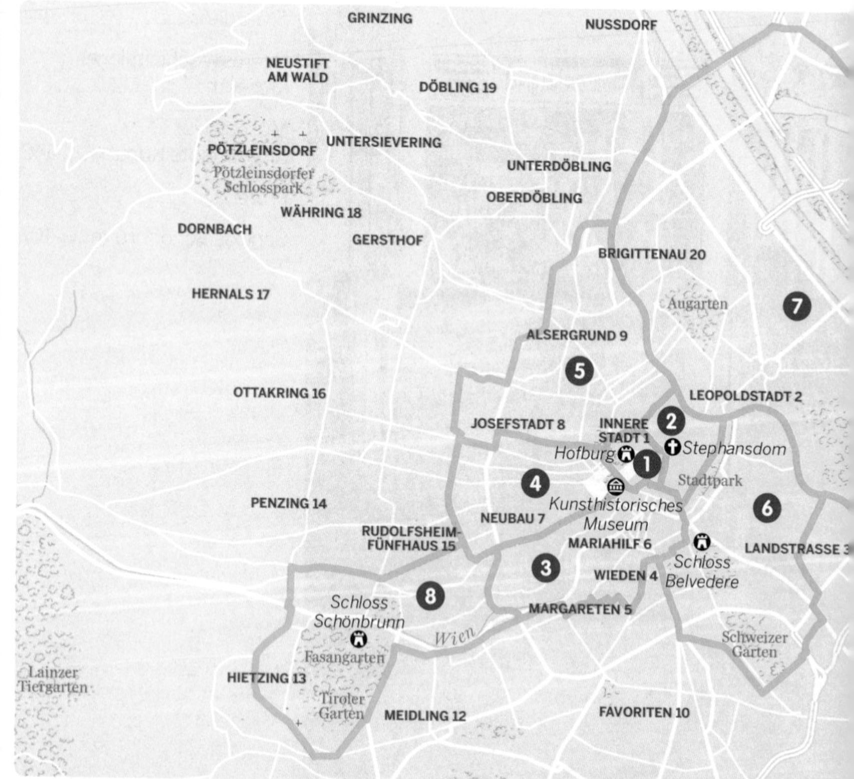

3 Karlsplatz & Around Naschmarkt p92

Fringing the Ringstrasse in the southeast corner of the Innere Stadt, this neighbourhood includes the city's sublime Staatsoper opera house, and extends south beyond Vienna's enormous market and food paradise, Naschmarkt, into some of the city's most interesting *Vorstädte* (inner suburbs): Margareten, Mariahilf and Wieden. There's great eating, drinking and nightlife and a truly Viennese *Vorstadt* character.

4 The Museum District & Neubau p107

Attractions in this cultural neighbourhood include the Kunsthistorisches Museum (Museum of Art History), packed with Old Masters; the MuseumsQuartier's cache of museums, cafes, restaurants, bars and performance spaces; and the Renaissance-style Burgtheater, where premieres have included Mozart's and Beethoven's works. To the west, hip Neubau is an incubator for Vienna's vibrant fashion, art and design scenes.

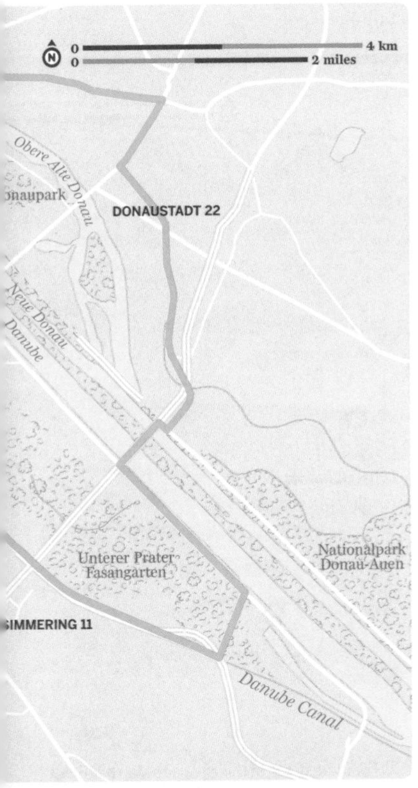

5 Alsergrund & the University District p127

Book-ended by one of Europe's biggest universities, Alsergrund (9th district) spills south into Josefstadt (8th district), which moves to a similar groove and is scattered with low-key restaurants, cafes and shops. Further west lies the ethnically diverse Ottakring (16th district).

6 Schloss Belvedere to the Canal p139

Schloss Belvedere and its gardens can easily absorb an entire day of your time. Spread out across the neighbourhood, other crowd-pullers include the KunstHausWien, as well as museums homing in on everything from military history to art fakes. Some cracking cafes, delis and restaurants have popped up recently, making breaks between sightseeing all the more pleasurable.

7 Prater & East of the Danube p155

Leopoldstadt, the city's Jewish quarter, is one of Vienna's hippest and most happening districts. The neighbourhood has graffiti art, beach bars by the Danube Canal and a raft of enticing new boutiques, restaurants, galleries and edgy cafes hiding down its still-sleepy backstreets. Its centrepiece is the Prater, and further east is the Danube River and Danube Island recreation area.

8 Schloss Schönbrunn & Around p165

The palace dominates this well-to-do residential neighbourhood and the tight original village streets outside the ancient walls give way to a relatively suburban feel. The ensemble of suburbs adjoining the neighbourhood to the north – Fünfhaus, Rudolfsheim and Ottakring – also make for an interesting taste of everyday Viennese life.

The Hofburg & Around

Neighbourhood Top Five

❶ **Hofburg** (p60) Strolling through the monumental palace complex, exploring courtyards and admiring the elegant gates, impressive squares, statues of the Habsburg rulers and monumental architecture.

❷ **Albertina** (p66) Viewing world-class graphic arts exhibitions and the gallery's collection of original graphics by masters within luxurious palace rooms.

❸ **Kaiserappartements** (p60) Touring the Habsburg imperial apartments, the Sisi Museum and the Silberkammer (Silver Depot).

❹ **Spanish Riding School** (p61) Catching the famous white Lipizzaner stallions during a mesmerising equine ballet performance.

❺ **Neue Burg Museums** (p62) Revelling in the historical musical instruments, arms and armour, and ancient artefacts unearthed during Austrian archaeologists' excavations at Ephesus in Turkey.

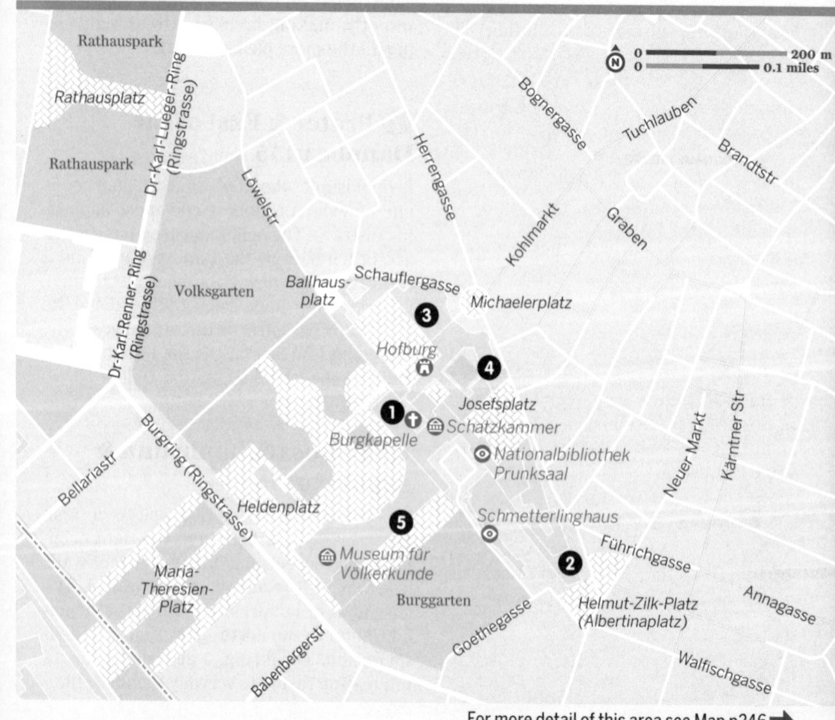

For more detail of this area see Map p246

Explore the Hofburg & Around

One of the most spectacular palace complexes in the Austrian capital, the Hofburg was the seat of the Habsburgs for some six-and-a-half centuries. It can be easily approached from the MuseumsQuartier by crossing Maria-Theresien-Platz, but the the grandest place to start is at the gate on Michaelerplatz, where the Habsburgs used to enter. From here you can stroll from one end to the other in about an hour, with time to stop and admire the architecture. If you plan on visiting several museums, block your calendar for much of the day to see these comfortably. Although visitors are almost always walking through, it rarely feels crowded. Plan to spend at least another four hours taking in the most important sights around the Hofburg – the Albertina graphic-arts gallery, Kaisergruft, where most of the Habsburg royal family are buried, and the Jüdisches Museum (Jewish Museum). The neighbourhood has some good shopping as well as a handful of excellent eating and drinking options, with many more close at hand in the nearby MuseumsQuartier.

Local Life

➡ **Park Life** This epicentral part of town has some of the prettiest parks in Vienna, with the Volksgarten (p64) flanking one side of the Hofburg and the Burggarten (p64) the other. Locals flock here in summer to picnic or simply relax.

➡ **Snack Life** Join opera-going locals dressed in their finery sipping champagne and tucking into sausages at open-air Bitzinger Würstelstand am Albertinaplatz (p69).

➡ **Nightlife** A small but legendary collection of places for drinking or clubbing are here, ranging from coffee houses through Loos American Bar (p70) to Volksgarten ClubDiskothek (p70) and Palffy Club (p71).

Getting There & Away

➡ **U-Bahn** Herrengasse (U3) and Stephansplatz (U1, U3) are closest to the Hofburg, but Museumsquartier (U4) can also be convenient for the Heldenplatz side of the palace complex.

➡ **Tram** Useful for entering from Ringstrasse (D, 1, 2, 71 Dr-Karl-Renner-Ring, Burgring and Kärntner Ring/Oper).

➡ **Bus** Buses 1A and 2A connect Michaelerplatz with Stephansplatz.

Lonely Planet's Top Tip

Although this neighbourhood is full of iconic sights, it's also a part of town that invites aimless strolling to soak up the atmosphere. The Hofburg is most impressive during the quiet hours of early morning or early evening, while the streets between the Hofburg and Stephansplatz, with lots of private art galleries, are best explored in business hours.

Best Places to Eat

➡ Blue Mustard (p69)

➡ Bitzinger Würstelstand am Albertinaplatz (p69)

➡ Meinl's Restaurant (p69)

➡ Trześniewski (p69)

For reviews, see p69. ➡

Best Places to Drink

➡ Loos American Bar (p70)

➡ Café Leopold Hawelka (p70)

➡ Meinl's Weinbar (p70)

➡ Volksgarten ClubDiskothek (p70)

➡ Demel (p71)

➡ Palmenhaus (p71)

For reviews, see p70. ➡

Best Places to Shop

➡ J&L Lobmeyr Vienna (p72)

➡ Meinl am Graben (p72)

➡ Steiff (p72)

➡ Dorotheum (p73)

➡ Bonbons Anzinger (p73)

For reviews, see p72. ➡

GRAPHIA/SHUTTERSTOCK ©

TOP SIGHT
THE HOFBURG

Built as a fortified castle in the 13th century, the home of the Habsburg rulers from Rudolph I in 1279 until the Austrian monarchy collapsed under Karl I in 1918 is the ultimate display of Austria's former imperial power. Today, the impressive palace complex contains the offices of the Austrian president, an ensemble of extraordinary museums and stately public squares.

Kaiserappartements

The **Kaiserappartements** (Imperial Apartments; 01, Michaelerplatz; adult/child €12.90/7.70, incl guided tour €15.90/9.20; ⌚9am-6pm Jul & Aug, to 5.30pm Sep-June) were once the official living quarters of Franz Josef I (1830–1916) and Empress Elisabeth (1837–98; or Sisi, as she was affectionately named). The highlight is the **Sisi Museum**, devoted to Austria's most beloved empress, which has a strong focus on the clothing and jewellery of Austria's monarch and a replica of her personal fitness room complete with rings and bars. Also here is a reconstruction of Sisi's luxurious Pullman coach. Many of the empress' famous portraits are also on show, as is her death mask, made after her assassination in Geneva in 1898.

Multilingual audio guides are included in the admission price. Guided tours take in the Kaiserappartements, the Sisi Museum and the adjoining **Silberkammer**, whose largest silver service caters to 140 dinner guests.

DON'T MISS

- Strolling through the Hofburg
- Kaiserappartements
- Schatzkammer
- Neue Burg Museums
- Spanish Riding School

PRACTICALITIES

- Imperial Palace
- Map p246, D3
- www.hofburg-wien.at
- 01, Michaelerkuppel
- admission free
- 🚌1A, 2A Michaelerplatz, 🚋D, 1, 2, 46, 49, 71 Burgring, Ⓤ Herrengasse

Kaiserliche Schatzkammer

The **Kaiserliche Schatzkammer** (Imperial Treasury; www.kaiserliche-schatzkammer.at; 01, Schweizerhof; adult/child €12/free; ⌚9am-5.30pm Wed-Mon) contains secular and ecclesiastical treasures of priceless value and splendour – the sheer wealth of this collection of crown jewels is staggering. As you walk through the rooms you see a golden rose, diamond-studded Turkish sabres, a 2680-carat Colombian emerald and, the highlight of the treasury, the imperial crown. The wood-panelled **Sacred Treasury** has a collection of rare religious relics: fragments of the True Cross, the Holy Lance that pierced Jesus on the Cross, one of the nails from the Crucifixion, a thorn from Christ's crown and a piece of tablecloth from the Last Supper. Multilingual audio guides cost €4 (the shorter highlight audio tour is free) and are very worthwhile.

Burgkapelle

The **Burgkapelle** (Royal Chapel; ☎01-533 99 27; www.hofmusikkapelle.gv.at; 01, Schweizerhof; ⊙10am-2pm Mon & Tue, 11am-1pm Fri; 🚌2A Heldenplatz, 🚋D, 1, 2, 71 Burgring) originally dates from the 13th century. It received a Gothic makeover from 1447 to 1449, but much of this disappeared during the baroque fad. Its vaulted wooden statuary survived and is testament to those Gothic days. The **Vienna Boys' Choir Mass** (tickets €10-36) takes place here every Sunday at 9.15am between September and June. The chapel is sometimes closed to visitors in July and August, so check ahead in those months.

Spanish Riding School

The world-famous **Spanish Riding School** (Spanische Hofreitschule; ☎01-533 90 31-0; www.srs.at; 01, Michaelerplatz 1; performances €25-217; ⊙hours vary) is a Viennese institution truly reminiscent of the imperial Habsburg era. This unequalled equestrian show is performed by Lipizzaner stallions formerly kept at an imperial stud established at Lipizza (hence the name). These graceful stallions perform an equine ballet to a program of classical music while the audience watches from pillared balconies – or from a cheaper standing-room area – and the chandeliers shimmer above.

There are many different ways to see the Lipizzaner. **Performances** are the top-shelf variant, and for seats at these you will need to book several months in advance. The website lists performance dates and you can order tickets online. As a rule of thumb, performances are at 11am on Sunday from mid-February to June and mid-August to December, with frequent additional performances on Saturday and occasionally other days of the week. For standing-room tickets, book at least one month in advance. During the summer break, it hosts special 'Piber meets Vienna' performances. Visitors to the

VISITING THE IMPERIAL APARTMENTS

Entrance to the Kaiserappartements is via the Kaiserstieg staircase, after which you learn about the Habsburgs and the history of the Hofburg and you can look at a model of the complex. You then enter the Sisi Museum and afterwards the restored apartments of Empress Elisabeth and Kaiser Franz Josef I. The Silberkammer occupies another part of the Reichskanzleitrakt (State Chancery Tract) of the building.

Empress Maria Theresia (1717–80) is immortalised in her robed, operatic glory in the middle of Maria-Theresien-Platz, but Empress Elisabeth, better know as Sisi, is the real darling of the Habsburg show in this part of town. The cult of Sisi knows no bounds in German-speaking countries, due in large part to the trilogy of films from the 1950s starring the Austro-French actress Romy Schneider. She embodied the empress so well that in the popular mind it often seems hard to distinguish Sisi as art and the empress in reality.

Morgenarbeit can drop in for part of a session (morning training sessions; adult/child €15/7.50, 10am to noon Tuesday to Friday January to June and mid-August to December).

One-hour **guided tours** (adult/child €16/8; 2pm, 3pm and 4pm March to late January, 2pm, 3pm and 4pm Tuesday to Sunday late January and February), held in English and German, take you into the performance hall, stables and other facilities. A combined **morning training and tour** (adult/child €31/15) is another option. The visitor centre here sells all tickets.

Neue Burg Museums

The Neue Burg is home to the three **Neue Burg Museums** (01-525 240; www.khm.at; 01, Heldenplatz; adult/child €15/free; 10am-6pm Wed-Sun; D, 1, 2, 71 Burgring, U Herrengasse, Museumsquartier). The **Sammlung alter Musikinstrumente** (Collection of Ancient Musical Instruments) contains a wonderfully diverse array of instruments. The **Ephesos Museum** features artefacts unearthed during Austrian archaeologists' excavations at Ephesus in Turkey between 1895 and 1906. The **Hofjagd- und Rüstkammer** (Arms and Armour) museum contains ancient armour dating mainly from the 15th and 16th centuries. An audio guide costs €4.

THE WHITE HORSE IN HISTORY

The Lipizzaner stallion breed dates back to the 1520s, when Ferdinand I imported the first horses from Spain for the imperial palace. His son Maximilian II imported new stock in the 1560s, and in 1580 Archduke Charles II established the imperial stud in Lipizza (Lipica; today in Slovenia), giving the horse its name. Austria's nobility had good reason for looking to Spain for its horses: the Spanish were considered the last word in equine breeding at the time, thanks to Moors from the 7th century who had brought their elegant horses to the Iberian Peninsula. Italian horses were added to the stock around the mid-1700s (these too had Spanish blood) and by the mid-18th century the Lipizzaner had a reputation for being Europe's finest horses.

Over the centuries, natural catastrophe, but more often war, caused the Lipizzaner to be evacuated from their original stud in Slovenia on numerous occasions. One of their periods of exile from the stud in Lipica was in 1915 due to the outbreak of WWI. Some of the horses went to Laxemburg (just outside Vienna), and others to Bohemia in today's Czech Republic (at the time part of the Austro-Hungarian Empire).

When the Austrian monarchy collapsed in 1918, Lipica passed into Italian hands and the horses were divided between Austria and Italy. The Italians ran the stud in Slovenia, while the Austrians transferred their horses to Piber, near Graz, which had been breeding military horses for the empire since 1798 – at that time stallions were mostly crossed with English breeds.

The fortunes of our pirouetting equine friends rose and fell with the collapse of the Habsburg empire and advent of two world wars. When WWII broke out, Hitler's cohorts goose-stepped in and requisitioned the Piber stud in Austria and started breeding military horses and pack mules there. They also decided to bring the different studs in their occupied regions together under one roof, and Piber's Lipizzaner wound up in Hostau, situated in Bohemia. Fearing the Lipizzaner would fall into the hands of the Russian army as it advanced towards the region in 1945, American forces seized the Lipizzaner and other horses in Hostau and transferred them back to Austria. Today, Piber still supplies the Spanish Riding School with its white stallions.

ationalbibliothek (National Library)

Nationalbibliothek Prunksaal

The **Nationalbibliothek** (National Library) was once the imperial library and is now the largest library in Vienna. The real reason to visit these esteemed halls of knowledge is to gaze on the **Nationalbibliothek Prunksaal** (Grand Hall; ☎01-534 10; www.onb.ac.at; 01, Josefsplatz 1; adult/child €7/free; ⏲10am-6pm Tue, Wed & Fri-Sun, to 9pm Thu; 🚋D, 1, 2, 71 Burgring).

Commissioned by Charles VI, this baroque hall was the brainchild of Johann Bernhard Fischer von Erlach, who died the year the first brick was laid, and finished by his son Joseph in 1735. Leather-bound scholarly tomes line the walls, and the upper storey of shelves is flanked by an elegantly curved wood balcony. Rare ancient volumes (mostly 15th century) are stored within glass cabinets, with pages opened to beautifully illustrated passages of text. A statue of Charles VI stands guard under the central dome, which itself has a magnificent fresco by Daniel Gran depicting the emperor's apotheosis.

Papyrusmuseum

Part of the Nationalbibliothek museum ensemble, along with the Esperantomuseum (p68) and Globenmuseum (p68), the **Papyrusmuseum** (☎01-534 10 420; www.onb.ac.at; 01, Heldenplatz; adult/free €4/free; ⏲10am-6pm Tue, Wed & Fri-Sun, to 9pm Thu; 🚋D, 1, 2, 71 Burgring, UHerrengasse, Museumsquartier)

TIPS FOR THE KAISERLICHE SCHATZKAMMER

Multilingual audio guides cost €4 (the shorter highlight audio tour is free) and are very worthwhile. A combined Schatz der Habsburger (Treasures of the Habsburgs) ticket, which includes the Kunsthistorisches Museum and Neue Burg, costs €20.

The Kaislerliche Schatzkammer dates back to the time of Ferdinand I (1503–64), who commissioned an antiquarian to take care of the collection. In the 18th century under Maria Theresia, the treasures were separated and reorganised, possibly to hide the sale of some treasures to finance the War of the Austrian Succession (1740–48). Under Hitler, all the imperial regalia from the Holy Roman Empire was transferred to Nuremberg, where it had previously been kept for about 400 years from 1424. It was returned to the Hofburg after WWII.

displays an interesting collection of 200 fragments of ancient writing on papyrus from Egypt and also has inscriptions on other media, such as parchment and clay. One of its highlights is a fragment of musical notation on pottery depicting the choral ode from *Orestes*, a tragedy written by the Greek Euripides. An audio guide costs €2.

Burggarten

Tucked behind the Hofburg, the Burggarten (Castle Garden; www.bmlfuw.gv.at/ministerium/bundesgaerten; 01, Burgring; ⏲6am-10pm Apr-Oct, 7.30am-5.30pm Nov-Mar; 🚋D, 1, 2, 46, 49, 71 Burgring, ⓤMuseumsquartier) FREE is a leafy oasis amid the hustle and bustle of the Ringstrasse and Innere Stadt. The marble **statue of Mozart** is the park's most famous tenant, but there's also a **statue of Franz Josef** in military garb. Lining the Innere Stadt side of the Burggarten is the Schmetterlinghaus and the beautiful art nouveau Palmenhaus (p71) bar.

Schmetterlinghaus

Sharing the Habsburg's personal Jugendstil glasshouse (1901) with the Palmenhaus (p71) bar in the Burggarten, the **Schmetterlinghaus** (Butterfly House; ☎01-533 85 70; www.schmetterlinghaus.at; 01, Burggarten; adult/child €6.50/3.50; ⏲10am-4.45pm Mon-Fri, to 6.15pm Sat & Sun Apr-Oct, 10am-3.45pm Nov-Mar; 🚋D, 1, 2, 71 Burgring, ⓤKarlsplatz) has hundreds of fluttering butterflies and a shop stocking a great range of butterfly paraphernalia. Its warm, humid air is especially welcome on chilly days.

Volksgarten

Spreading out between the Burgtheater and Heldenplatz, the **Volksgarten** (People's Garden; www.bmlfuw.gv.at; 01, Dr-Karl-Renner-Ring; ⏲6am-10pm Apr-Oct, 6.30am-7pm Nov-Mar; 🚋D, 1, 2, 46, 49, 71 Dr-Karl-Renner-Ring, ⓤVolkstheater, Herrengasse) FREE is great for relaxing among dignified rose bushes and even more dignified statues. A **monument to Empress Elisabeth** is in the northeast corner, not far from the **Temple of Theseus**, an imitation of the one in Athens (commissioned by Napoleon), and the Volksgarten ClubDiskothek (p70).

HOFBURG PALACE COMPLEX

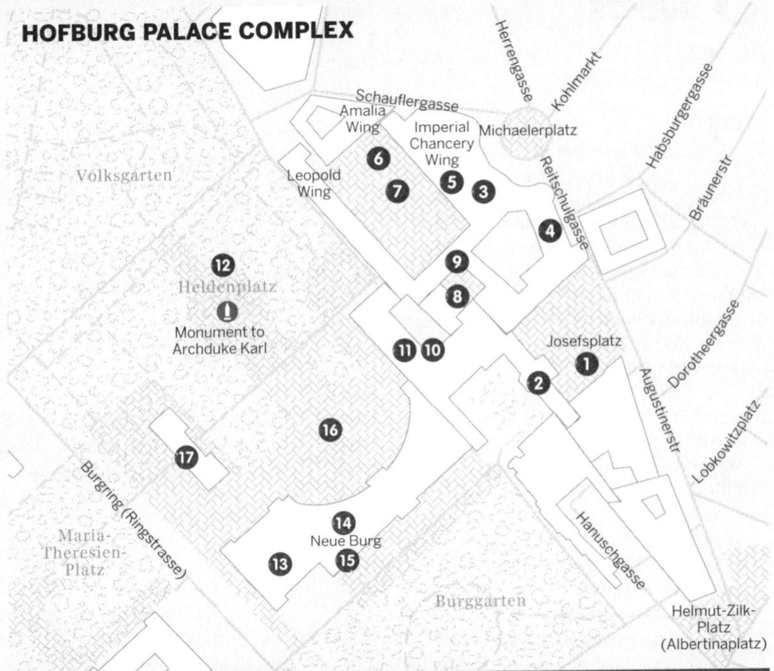

Palace Tour
The Hofburg

LENGTH ONE HOUR TO ONE DAY

The Hofburg is a jigsaw puzzle of monumental buildings. For the full effect, enter from Michaelerplatz, as the monarchs used to. First, though, admire the pretty square just to the south, ❶ **Josefsplatz**, named after Joseph II and adorned with the equestrian monument to Emperor Josef II. Josefsplatz also serves as the entrance to the ❷ **Nationalbibliothek Prunksaal** (p63).

Pass through the ❸ **Michaelertor** and neo-baroque Michaelertrakt. The Michaelerplatz side of the building is lined with statues of Hercules and evocative fountains depicting the Power of the Land and Power of the Sea. On the left of the hall is the ❹ **Spanish Riding School** (p61) and its visitor centre, on the right the ❺ **Kaiserappartements** (p60).

Straight ahead, you reach the large courtyard ❻ **In der Burg**, with a monument to ❼ **Emperor Franz I**, the last in a long line of Holy Roman emperors after Napoleon brought about the collapse of the Reich in 1806.

The oldest part of the Hofburg is the ❽ **Schweizerhof** (Swiss Courtyard), named after the Swiss guards who used to protect its precincts. This is reached via the Renaissance ❾ **Swiss Gate**, which dates from 1553. The 13th-century courtyard gives access to the ❿ **Burgkapelle** (p61) and the ⓫ **Schatzkammer** (p60).

Straight ahead is ⓬ **Heldenplatz** (Hero's Square) and the ⓭ **Neue Burg**, built between the second half of the 19th century and WWI. The Neue Burg houses the three ⓮ **Neue Burg Museums** (p62). The balcony is where Hitler addressed a rally during his triumphant 1938 visit to Vienna after the *Anschluss*. Facing each other on Heldenplatz are monuments to ⓯ **Prince Eugene of Savoy** (closest to the Neue Burg) and ⓰ **Archduke Karl** (Charles of Austria). Pass through the Äusseres Burgtor (Outer Palace Gate) to the Ringstrasse.

SIGHTS

HOFBURG PALACE

See p60.

ALBERTINA GALLERY

Map p246 (www.albertina.at; 01, Albertinaplatz 3; adult/child €12.90/free; ⏲10am-6pm Thu-Tue, to 9pm Wed; 🚋D, 1, 2, 71 Kärntner Ring/Oper, ⓤKarlsplatz, Stephansplatz) Once used as the Habsburgs' imperial apartments for guests, the Albertina is now a repository for what's regularly touted as the greatest collection of graphic art in the world. The permanent Batliner Collection – with over 100 paintings covering the period from Monet to Picasso – and the high quality of changing exhibitions really make the Albertina worthwhile.

Multilingual audio guides (€4) cover all exhibition sections and tell the story behind the apartments and the works on display.

The original focus of the Batliner Collection was French impressionism and post-impressionism, as well as the works of the Swiss Alberto Giacometti, but over time husband and wife benefactors Herbert and Rita Batliner added a substantial number of Russian avant-garde works to create a who's who of 20th-century and contemporary art: Monet, Picasso, Degas, Cézanne, Matisse, Chagall, Nolde, Jawlensky and many more.

Tickets (but not the audio guides) are valid for the whole day, so you can nip out for lunch and return later to finish off a visit.

A branch of the Österreichisches Filmmuseum (p72) is located here.

KAISERGRUFT MAUSOLEUM

Map p246 (Imperial Burial Vault; www.kaisergruft.at; 01, Tegethoffstrasse 2; adult/child €5.50/2.50; ⏲10am-6pm; 🚋D, 1, 2, 71 Kärntner Ring/Oper, ⓤStephansplatz, Karlsplatz) Beneath the **Kapuzinerkirche** (Church of the Capuchin Friars; www.erzdioezese-wien.at; 01, Tegethoffstrasse 2; ⏲8am-6pm), the Kaisergruft is the final resting place of most of the Habsburg royal family, including Empress Elisabeth. Opened in 1633, it was instigated by Empress Anna (1585–1618). Her body and that of her husband, Emperor Matthias (1557–1619), were the first entombed in this impressive vault. A total of 149 Habsburgs are buried here, including 12 emperors and 19 empresses.

English-language, 30-minute guided tours (included in admission) take place at 3.30pm Wednesday to Saturday.

Only three Habsburgs are notable through their absence here. The last emperor, Karl I, was buried in exile in Madeira, and Marie Antoinette (daughter of Maria Theresia) still lies in Paris. The third is Duc de Reichstadt, son of Napoleon's second wife, Marie Louise, who was transferred to Paris as a publicity stunt by the Nazis in 1940. The hearts and organs reside in Augustinerkirche and Stephansdom, respectively.

THEATERMUSEUM MUSEUM

Map p246 (☎01-525 24 3460; www.theatermuseum.at; 01, Lobkowitzplatz 2; adult/child incl all exhibitions €8/free; ⏲10am-6pm Wed-Mon; 🚋D, 1, 2, 62, 71 Kärntner Ring/Oper, ⓤStephansplatz) Housed in the baroque Lobkowitz palace (1694), this museum has a permanent exhibition devoted to Austrian composer Gustav Mahler (1860–1911) and temporary exhibitions on Vienna's theatre history. Since 2014, it has also displayed the collection from the Staatsoper's former museum with portraits of operatic greats, costumes, stage designs and documents spotlighting premieres and highlights like Herbert von Karajan's eight-year reign as director. Opera lovers will enjoy the occasional gem, such as Dame Margot Fonteyn's stub-toed ballet slipper.

A small room hidden towards the back of the 1st floor contains an ensemble of puppets from puppeteer Richard Teschner, vaguely reminiscent of Java's wayang golek wooden puppets. Performances are listed on the website.

JÜDISCHES MUSEUM MUSEUM

Map p246 (Jewish Museum; ☎01-535 04 31; www.jmw.at; 01, Dorotheergasse 11; adult/child incl Museum Judenplatz €10/free; ⏲10am-6pm Sun-Fri; ⓤStephansplatz) Housed inside Palais Eskeles, Vienna's Jüdisches Museum showcases the history of Jews in Vienna, from the first settlements at Judenplatz in the 13th century to the present. Spaces devoted to changing exhibitions are complemented by its permanent exhibition covering 1945 to the present day; the highlight is the startling collection of ceremonial art on the top floor. Combined tickets to the Jüdisches Museum and Museum Judenplatz (p78) are valid for four days.

MICHAELERPLATZ ROMAN RUINS ROMAN SITE

Map p246 (01, Michaelerplatz; 1A, 2A Michaelerplatz, U Herrengasse) FREE Ringed by gorgeous architecture, Michaelerplatz is centred on Roman ruins that are reputed to have been a brothel for soldiers. This cobblestoned circular 'square' is a major pick-up point for tours by *Fiaker* (horse-drawn carriages).

MICHAELERKIRCHE CHURCH

Map p246 (01-533 80 00; www.michaelerkirche.at; 01, Michaelerplatz; church free, crypt tours adult/child €7/3, church tours by donation; 7am-10pm; 1A, 2A Michaelerplatz, U Herrengasse) The Michaelerkirche dates from the 13th century. Its highlight is the burial crypt which you can see on 40-minute bilingual German/English tours at 11am and 1pm Monday to Saturday. Tours take you past coffins, some revealing occupants preserved by the rarefied air of the crypt. One-hour bilingual church tours run at 1pm and 3pm on Wednesday.

AUGUSTINERKIRCHE CHURCH

Map p246 (01-533 09 470; http://augustinerkirche.augustiner.at; 01, Augustinerstrasse 3; 8am-6pm, hours can vary; 1A, 2A Michaelerplatz, U Herrengasse) FREE The real highlight of the 14th-century Gothic Augustinerkirche (Augustinian Church) is not its pale, vaulted interior but a crypt containing silver urns with the hearts of 54 Habsburg rulers. The church hosts regular evening classical music concerts. The website (http://hochamt.augustiner.at) has details. Sometimes on a visit you can catch the choir practising. The crypt is open on Sunday after the 11am Mass (celebrated with a full choir and orchestra) – turn up around 12.30pm. Many Habsburg weddings took place here.

LOOS HAUS HISTORIC BUILDING

Map p246 (www.adolfloos.at; 01, Michaelerplatz; 9am-3pm Mon-Wed & Fri, to 5.30pm Thu; 1A, 2A Michaelerplatz, U Herrengasse) FREE Designed by Adolf Loos, this modernist gem put Franz Josef's nose seriously out of joint when it was completed in 1911. Its intentionally simple facade offended the emperor so deeply that he ordered the curtains to be pulled on all palace windows overlooking the building. Today it houses a bank, with exhibition halls on the upper floors, including displays on this controversial building.

While it was being erected, critics were describing this as a 'house without eyebrows', referring to its lack of window

COMBINATION MUSEUM TICKETS

There are lots of combined options for visiting the Hofburg and nearby museums, including the following:

Sisi Ticket (adult/child €28.80/17) Includes the Imperial Apartments, Sisi Museum and Silberkammer (Imperial Silver Collection) with audio guide, as well as Schloss Schönbrunn and the Hofmobiliendepot (Imperial Furniture Collection).

Neue Burg Museums (adult/child €15/free) Includes all three Neue Burg Museums and the Kunsthistorisches Museum.

Annual ticket Kunsthistorisches Museum (adult/child €34/19) Includes Kunstkammer, Kunsthistorisches Museum, the Neue Burg Museums, Kaiserliche Schatzkammer, Wagenburg, Schloss Ambras Innsbruck and Theatermuseum.

Schatz der Habsburger (Treasures of the Habsburgs; adult/child €20/free) Includes Kunsthistorisches Museum, the Neue Burg Museums and Kaiserliche Schatzkammer.

Masterticket (adult/child €24/free) Includes the Neue Burg Museums, Kunsthistorisches Museum and the Leopold Museum.

Die Kostbarkeiten des Kaisers (Treasures of the Emporers; adult/child €23/free) Includes the Kaiserliche Schatzkammer and Morgenarbeit (morning training sessions) at the Spanish Riding School.

Nationalbibliothek Universal-Wochenticket (€15) Includes entry to the Nationalbibliothek's Esperantomuseum, Globenmuseum and Papyrusmuseum, the Nationalbibliothek Prunksaal and the new Literaturmuseum. Valid for seven days.

LOCAL KNOWLEDGE

ORNATE TOILETS

Built in 1905 by celebrated Czech-born, Vienna-based architect Adolf Loos (1870–1933) and still operating today, the opulent **Adolf Loos' Public Toilets** (Map p246; 01, opposite Graben 22; UStephansplatz) down a flight of steps below Graben were built as a showcase for a toilet manufacturer and retain their mahogany-panelled stalls with opaque-glass doors and exquisite tiling (the original chandeliers have been replaced with electric lighting).

detail, and work had to be stopped until Loos agreed to add the 10 bronze window boxes adorning it today.

GLOBENMUSEUM MUSEUM

Map p246 (01-534 10 710; www.onb.ac.at; 01, Herrengasse 9, 1st fl; adult/child €4/free; 10am-6pm Fri-Wed, to 9pm Thu Jun-Sep, 10am-6pm Tue, Wed & Fri-Sun, to 9pm Thu Oct-May; 1A, 2A Michaelerplatz, UHerrengasse) Part of the Nationalbibliothek collection of museums, along with the Papyrusmuseum (p63) and Esperantomuseum (admission covers all three), this small museum situated inside a former palace (Palais Mollard) is dedicated to cartography. Among the collection of 19th-century globes and maps are some gems dating from the 16th century. Look for the globe made for Emperor Karl V by Mercator in 1541.

A combined ticket that includes the three museums plus the Nationalbibliothek Prunksaal (p63) and the new Literaturmuseum (p81) costs €15/12 per adult/child.

ESPERANTOMUSEUM MUSEUM

Map p246 (01-534 10 730; www.onb.ac.at; 01, Herrengasse 9, ground fl; adult/child €4/free; 10am-6pm Fri-Wed, to 9pm Thu Jun-Sep, 10am-6pm Tue, Wed & Fri-Sun, to 9pm Thu Oct-May; 1A, 2A Michaelerplatz, UHerrengasse) The oft-overlooked Esperantomuseum is mostly devoted to the artificial language created by Dr Ludvik Zamenhof in 1887. The first book in Esperanto, by Dr Zamenhof himself, features among interesting exhibits on artificial languages, such as language used in the *Star Trek* TV series and films. A media terminal explains the language used by the Klingons, reciting lines from Shakespeare's *Hamlet*. Tickets also include entry to the Nationalbibliothek's Globenmuseum and Papyrusmuseum (p63). An audio guide costs €2.

A combined ticket that includes the three museums plus the Nationalbibliothek Prunksaal (p63) and the new Literaturmuseum (p81) costs €15.

PHANTASTENMUSEUM WIEN MUSEUM

Map p246 (International Museum of Fantastic Art; www.palais-palffy.at; 01, Josefsplatz 6; adult/child €9/7; 10am-6pm; 1A, 2A Michaelerplatz, D, 1, 2, 71, 46, 49 Burgring, UHerrengasse) Situated upstairs in Palais Palffy, the Phantastenmuseum Wien exhibits works by 120 artists from the Viennese School of Fantastic Realists, which arose in the 1950s, as well as 30 international artists. Anyone with a passing or deeper interest in the fantastic painting style with surrealistic (sometimes explicit) edges will enjoy the permanent collection and frequently changing temporary exhibitions.

MINORITENKIRCHE CHURCH

Map p246 (01-533 41 62; www.minoritenkirche-wien.info; 01, Minoritenplatz; 8am-6pm; 1A, 2A Michaelerplatz, UHerrengasse) FREE The Minoritenkirche (Minorite Church) is a 13th-century Gothic church that later received a baroque facelift. The stubby edifice was 'shortened' (ie partially destroyed) by the Turks in 1529. The most noteworthy piece inside is a mosaic copy of da Vinci's *Last Supper*, commissioned by Napoleon. Sunday services are held at 8.30am in German and 11am in Italian. The church is used for occasional classical concerts and choir recitals throughout the year – see the website's calendar for details.

HELMUT-ZILK-PLATZ SQUARE

Map p246 (Albertinaplatz; UStephansplatz, Karlsplatz) This attractive square wedged between the Staatsoper and the Albertina stands out for its **Monument Against War & Fascism** by Alfred Hrdlicka (1988). The series of pale block-like sculptures has a dark, squat shape wrapped in barbed wire, representing a Jew scrubbing the floor; poignantly, the greyish block originally came from the Mauthausen concentration camp.

DONNERBRUNNEN FOUNTAIN

Map p246 (Providentiabrunnen; 01, Neuer Markt; UStephansplatz) First installed in 1739 by sculptor Georg Raphael Donner, and replicated in bronze in 1873, this intricate fountain depicts Providentia, the Roman goddess of destiny, at its centre, foreseeing water supplies for Vienna. Surrounding it are the male figures of Traun (with a trident) and Enns (a resting ferryman), representing Upper Austria's rivers, and the female figures of Ybbs (carrying a jug) and March (against a frieze showing a battle, highlighting the river's role as a natural border), representing Lower Austria's rivers.

EATING

★BITZINGER WÜRSTELSTAND AM ALBERTINAPLATZ STREET FOOD €

Map p246 (www.bitzinger-wien.at; 01, Albertinaplatz; sausages €3.40-4.40; 8am-4am; Kärntner Ring/Oper, UKarlsplatz, Stephansplatz) Behind the Staatsoper, Vienna's best sausage stand has cult status. Bitzinger offers the contrasting spectacle of ladies and gents dressed to the nines, sipping beer, wine (from €2.30) or Joseph Perrier Champagne (€19.90 for 0.2L) while tucking into sausages at outdoor tables or the heated counter after performances. Mustard (€0.40) comes in *süss* (sweet, ie mild) or *scharf* (fiercely hot).

LE BOL CAFE €

Map p246 (www.lebol.at; 01, Neuer Markt 14; dishes €4.90-9.10; 8am-11pm Mon-Sat, 10am-11pm Sun; UStephansplatz) French cafe Le Bol specialises in *tartines* (open-faced sandwiches) such as artichoke crème, basil and olive tapenade, brie with chicken and red onion, roast beef, and courgette, tomato and cabbage, along with a wide selection of filled baguettes, *croques madame* and *monsieur* (toasted sandwiches), and wonderful coffee and hot chocolate. It has both individual and communal tables.

TRZEŚNIEWSKI SANDWICHES €

Map p246 (www.trzesniewski.at; 01, Dorotheergasse 1; sandwiches €1.20-3.60; 8.30am-7.30pm Mon-Fri, 9am-6pm Sat, 10am-5pm Sun; UStephansplatz) Trześniewski has been serving exquisite open-faced finger-style sandwiches for over 100 years. Choose from 22 delectable toppings incorporating primarily Austrian-sourced produce – chicken liver, smoked salmon and horseradish cream cheese and wild paprika and red pepper, egg and cucumber – on dark Viennese bread. This branch is the flagship of a now 10-strong chain in Vienna.

★BLUE MUSTARD INTERNATIONAL €€

Map p246 (01-934 67 05; www.bluemustard.at; 01, Dorotheergasse 6-8; 4-course menus €59-63, mains €15-25, street food €4.50-8.50; kitchen 5-10pm Mon-Sat, street-food truck 8am-5pm Mon-Sat, bar 5pm-2am Mon-Thu, 5pm-4am Fri & Sat; UStephansplatz) Backlit wood hand carvings of Stephansdom's Gothic windows, a wall-to-wall neon-lit map of Vienna and a street-food truck parked in the foyer make this one of Vienna's hottest new openings. Alexander Mayer's 'Journey menus' might start in Vienna (*Beuschel* veal ragout) and end in Naples (*Torta Ricotta e Pera* – poached pear and ricotta in an almond-and-hazelnut biscotti) with spectacular cocktail pairings.

Street food from the retro gold truck spans Vietnamese spring rolls to fajitas and falafel. Or drop by the bar for sensational craft cocktail creations, such as El Cipote (tequila, aloe vera liqueur, jalapenos and pineapple juice). Infusions include bacon-infused vodka and sage-infused gin.

CAFÉ MOZART CAFE €€

Map p246 (01-241 00-200; www.cafe-mozart.at; 01, Albertinaplatz 2; mains €15.90-32, cakes & pastries €4.50-8.50; kitchen 11.30am-11.30pm, bar 8am-midnight; ; UKarlsplatz) Opening to a covered terrace, 1794-opened Café Mozart serves classic Viennese cakes – *Apfelstrudel* (apple strudel), *Esterhazy Torte* (layered almond cake), *Sacher Torte* (chocolate cake with apricot jam) and *Rehrücken* (chocolate-almond mousse dipped in dark chocolate) – along with more substantial dishes: *Tafelspitz* (boiled beef) with creamed spinach potato salad, Viennese-style fried chicken with parsley sauce, and beef goulash with bread dumplings.

BIERHOF AUSTRIAN €€

Map p246 (01-533 44 28; http://bierhof.at; 01, Haarhof 3; mains €9.90-23.90; 11.30am-11.30pm; ; UHerrengasse) A narrow passageway opens to a courtyard where the umbrella-shaded tables beneath the trees make a charming spot to dine on homemade classics like *Eiernockerl* (flour-and-egg dumplings), *Tiroler Gröstl* (pork, potatoes and bacon, topped with a fried egg), *Tiroler Leber* (liver dumplings with apple sauce and green beans) and *Wiener Schnitzel* with parsley potatoes. The midweek lunch menu costs just €7.10.

★MEINL'S RESTAURANT INTERNATIONAL €€€

Map p246 (☎01-532 33 34 6000; www.meinlamgraben.at; 01, Graben 19; mains €16-39, 4-/5-course menus €67/85; ⏲noon-midnight Mon-Sat; 📶✍; ⓤStephansplatz) Meinl's combines cuisine of superlative quality with an unrivalled wine list and views of Graben. Creations at its high-end restaurant span calamari and white-truffle risotto, and apple schnapps-marinated pork fillet with green beans and chanterelles. Its on-site providore (p72) has a cafe and sushi bar, and its cellar wine bar (p70) serves great-value lunch menus.

RESTAURANT HERRLICH AUSTRIAN €€€

Map p246 (☎01-53404-920; www.steigenberger.com; 01, Herrengasse 10; 2-/3-course lunch menus €14.90/18.90, mains €15-32; ⏲noon-2.30pm Mon, noon-2.30pm & 6-11pm Tue-Sat, 6-11pm Sun; ⓤHerrengasse) Located inside the Steigenberger Hotel Herrenhof (p193), the upmarket Herrlich focuses on a lighter style of Austrian cooking in a modern setting replete with snow-white tablecloths. It serves classic dishes such as Tyrolean mountain cheese ravioli with brown butter and wild garlic on its changing, seasonal menus.

CAKE WARS: THE SACHER TORTE

Eduard Sacher, the son of the *Sacher Torte* creator Franz Sacher, began working at Demel in 1934, bringing the original recipe and sole distribution rights with him. Between 1938 and 1963 legal battles raged between Demel and Café Sacher over the trademark and title. An out-of-court settlement gave Café Sacher the rights to the phrase 'Original Sacher Torte', and Demel the rights to decorate its torte with a triangular seal reading 'Eduard-Sacher-Torte'. Each cafe still claims to be a cut above the other; try both and decide.

DRINKING & NIGHTLIFE

★MEINL'S WEINBAR WINE BAR

Map p246 (www.meinlamgraben.at; 01, Graben 19; ⏲11am-midnight Mon-Sat; ⓤStephansplatz) In the basement of food emporium Meinl am Graben (p72), this wine cellar stocks a vast selection of Austrian wines along with a smattering of international labels. Over 30 wines are available by the glass; between 11.30am and 2.30pm it also serves superb lunch menus (two-/three-course menus €10.50/13.50). For the full gourmet experience, book into the restaurant (p69).

★CAFÉ LEOPOLD HAWELKA COFFEE

Map p246 (www.hawelka.at; 01, Dorotheergasse 6; ⏲8am-midnight Mon-Wed, to 1am Thu-Sat, 10am-midnight Sun; ⓤStephansplatz) Opened in 1939 by Leopold and Josefine Hawelka, whose son Günter still bakes the house-speciality *Buchteln* (sweet jam-filled, sugar-dusted yeast rolls) to Josefine's secret recipe today, this low-lit, picture-plastered coffee house is a living slice of Viennese history. It was once the hang-out of artists and writers – Friedensreich Hundertwasser, Elias Canetti, Arthur Miller and Andy Warhol included.

★VOLKSGARTEN CLUBDISKOTHEK CLUB

Map p246 (http://volksgarten.at; 01, Burgring 1; ⏲Apr–mid-Sep; 🚋D, 1, 2, 71 Dr-Karl-Renner-Ring, ⓤMuseumsquartier, Volkstheater) Spilling onto the Volksgarten's lawns, these early-19th-century premises are split into three areas: the Wintergarten lounge bar with vintage 1950s furnishings and palms, Cortic Säulenhalle ('column hall'), hosting live music and theme nights, and hugely popular Club-Diskothek (cover charge from €3). Hours vary; check the program online.

★LOOS AMERICAN BAR COCKTAIL BAR

Map p246 (www.loosbar.at; 01, Kärntner Durchgang 10; ⏲noon-5am Thu-Sat, to 4am Sun-Wed; ⓤStephansplatz) Loos is *the* spot in the Innere Stadt for a classic cocktail such as its signature dry martini, expertly whipped up by talented mixologists. Designed by Adolf Loos in 1908, this tiny 27-sq-metre box (seating just 20-or-so patrons) is bedecked from head to toe in onyx and polished brass, with mirrored walls that make it appear far larger.

PALMENHAUS BAR

Map p246 (☎01-533 10 33; www.palmenhaus.at; 01, Burggarten; ⏰10am-midnight Mon-Fri, 9am-midnight Sat, 9am-11pm Sun; 🚋D, 1, 2, 71 Burgring, Ⓤ Karlsplatz, Museumsquartier) Housed in a beautifully restored *Jungendstil* palm house with high arched ceilings, glass walls and steel beams, looking through into the adjacent *Schmetterlinghaus* (butterfly house), the Palmenhouse opens onto a glorious covered summer terrace facing the Burggarten. The relaxed, welcoming ambience makes it ideal for a glass of wine or coffee. DJs occasionally spin on weekend evenings. Classic Austrian dishes (mains €16.80 to €32) such as schnitzel are excellent; reserve ahead if you plan on dining.

CAFÉ SACHER COFFEE

Map p246 (www.sacher.com; 01, Philharmonikerstrasse 4; ⏰8am-midnight; 🚋D, 1, 2, 71 Kärntner Ring/Oper, Ⓤ Karlsplatz) With a battalion of waiters, and air of nobility, this grand cafe is celebrated for its *Sacher Torte*, a wonderfully rich iced-chocolate cake with apricot jam once favoured by Emperor Franz Josef. It has a covered pavement terrace, but for the full-blown experience, head to the opulent chandelier-lit interior.

DEMEL COFFEE

Map p246 (www.demel.at; 01, Kohlmarkt 14; ⏰9am-7pm; 🚌1A, 2A Michaelerplatz, Ⓤ Herrengasse, Stephansplatz) Within sight of the Hofburg, this elegant and regal cafe has a gorgeous rococo period salon. Demel's speciality is the *Ana Demel Torte,* a calorie-bomb of chocolate and nougat, as well as the Eduard-Sacher-Torte. The window displays an ever-changing array of edible art pieces (ballerinas and manicured bonsai, for example).

VILLON WINE BAR

Map p246 (www.villon.at; 01, Habsburgergasse 4; ⏰6pm-midnight Tue-Fri, 7pm-midnight Sat; Ⓤ Herrengasse, Stephansplatz) This 500-year-old wine cellar is sunk 16m deep into the ground, so forget all about your mobile phone working. Spanning four levels, the interior is smart and modern, with light-coloured woods in the main room where you can order wine by the glass or bottle, accompanied by parmesan cheese, bread, olives and Thun ham (a local ham speciality).

PALFFY CLUB CLUB

Map p246 (www.palffyclub.at; 01, Josefsplatz 6; ⏰10pm-late Fri & Sat Aug-May; 🚌1A, 2A Michaelerplatz, 🚋D, 1, 2, 71 Burgring, Ⓤ Herrengasse) This 550-sq-metre club occupies two floors of a 14th-century palace building where a young Mozart performed (and allegedly premiered *The Marriage of Figaro*). Dominated by a glittering 12m chandelier with 80,000 Swarovski crystals, the 1st floor has R&B and '70s & '80s, while the 2nd floor, with house and techno beats, opens at 1am.

PASSAGE CLUB

Map p246 (☎01-961 66 77-0; www.club-passage.at; 01, Burgring 3, Babenberger Passage; ⏰9pm-4am Tue, 10pm-5am Wed & Thu, 11pm-6am Fri & Sat; 🚋D, 1, 2, 71 Burgring, Ⓤ Museumsquartier) Originally a pedestrian underpass, neon-lit Passage is the closest thing in Vienna to a megaclub for a mostly young crowd. The music is loud (noise from the Ringstrasse traffic directly overhead is easily drowned out) and spans anything from early classics to house. Some nights have free admission; others incur a cover charge.

ESTERHÁZYKELLER WINE BAR

Map p246 (☎01-533 34 82; www.esterhazykeller.at; 01, Haarhof 1; ⏰4-11pm Sep-Jun; Ⓤ Stephansplatz, Herrengasse) Tucked in a quiet courtyard just off Kohlmarkt, this *Heurigen* (wine tavern) has an enormous cellar – rustic decor, complete with medieval weaponry and farming tools – where excellent wine is served direct from the Esterházy Palace wine estate in Eisenstadt, as well as beer. The adjoining Esterházy Stüberl (restaurant; mains €9.90 to €24.90) opens from 11am to 10pm September to June.

CAFÉ GRIENSTEIDL COFFEE

Map p246 (☎01-535 26 92-0; www.cafegriensteidl.at; 01, Michaelerplatz 2; ⏰8am-11.30pm; 🚌1A, 2A Michaelerplatz, Ⓤ Herrengasse) Once the *Stammlokal* (local haunt) for Vienna's late-19th-century literary set, Griensteidl holds a prestigious position between the Hofburg and the Loos Haus, and retains its *Jugendstil* lamps and marble-topped tables. Huge windows look out over Michaelerplatz.

CAFÉ TIROLERHOF COFFEE

Map p246 (☎01-512 78 33; 01, Führichgasse 8; ⊙7am-10pm Mon-Sat, 9.30am-8pm Sun; 📶; 🚊D, 1, 2, 71 Kärntner Ring/Oper, UStephansplatz, Karlsplatz) Lovingly renovated *Jugendstil* decor from the 1920s, giant arched windows and homemade *Apfelstrudel* make Tirolerhof an inviting choice in the Innere Stadt.

FLEDERMAUS CLUB

Map p246 (www.fledermaus.at; 01, Spiegelgasse 2; ⊙9pm-late Wed-Mon; UStephansplatz) Fledermaus is among Vienna's most relaxed and down-to-earth clubs in terms of decor and clientele. Its program runs the spectrum of musical styles from the 1950s to '90s, with each night dedicated to a particular movement or epoch. Some nights have free admission; other times there's a cover charge.

CAFÉ BRÄUNERHOF COFFEE

Map p246 (☎01-512 38 93; www.braeunerhof.at; 01, Stallburggasse 2; ⊙8am-9pm Mon-Fri, to 7pm Sat, 10am-7pm Sun; UHerrengasse, Stephansplatz) Little has changed in Bräunerhof from the days when Austria's seminal writer Thomas Bernhard frequented the premises. Classical music features from 3pm to 6pm on weekends.

☆ ENTERTAINMENT

ÖSTERREICHISCHES FILMMUSEUM CINEMA

Map p246 (Austrian Film Museum; ☎01-533 70 54; www.filmmuseum.at; 01, Auginerstrasse 1; adult/child €10.50/6; 🚊D, 1, 2, 71 Kärntner Ring/Oper, UKarlsplatz) Situated inside the Albertina (p66), the Austrian Film Museum shows a range of films with and without subtitles in the original language, featuring a director, group of directors or a certain theme from around the world in programs generally lasting a couple of weeks. Screenings are usually at 6.45pm; check the website for other times.

CONCERTS AT THE HOFBURG

The **Hofburg Concert Halls** (Map p246; ☎01-587 25 52; www.hofburgorchester.at; 01, Heldenplatz; tickets €42-55; 🚊D, 1, 2, 71 Burgring, UHerrengasse), the sumptuous Festsaal and Redoutensaal, are regularly used for Strauss and Mozart concerts, featuring the Hofburg Orchestra and soloists from the Staatsoper and Volksoper. Performances start at 8.30pm and tickets are available online and from travel agents and hotels. Seating is not allocated, so get in early to secure a good seat.

SHOPPING

★STEIFF TOYS

Map p246 (www.steiff-galerie-wien.at; 01, Bräunerstrasse 3; ⊙10am-12.30pm & 1.30-6pm Mon-Fri, 10am-12.30pm & 1.30-5pm Sat; UStephansplatz) Founded in Germany in the late 19th century, Steiff is widely regarded as the original creator of the teddy bear, which it presented at the Leipzig Toy Fair in 1903: an American businessman bought 3000 and sold them under the name 'teddy bear' after US president Theodore ('Teddy') Roosevelt. Today its flagship Austrian shop is filled with adorable bears, along with other premium quality cuddly toys.

★MEINL AM GRABEN FOOD & DRINKS

Map p246 (www.meinlamgraben.at; 01, Graben 19; ⊙8am-7.30pm Mon-Fri, 9am-6pm Sat; UStephansplatz) Vienna's most prestigious providore brims with quality European foodstuffs. Chocolate and confectionery dominate the ground floor, and impressive cheese and cold meats are tantalisingly displayed upstairs. The basement stocks European and Austrian wine and fruit liqueurs and has a classy on-site wine bar (p70); there's also an exceptional on-site restaurant (p69).

★J&L LOBMEYR VIENNA HOMEWARES

Map p246 (www.lobmeyr.at; 01, Kärntner Strasse 26; ⊙10am-7pm Mon-Fri, to 6pm Sat; UStephansplatz) Reached by a beautifully ornate wrought-iron staircase, this is one of Vienna's most lavish retail experiences. The collection of Biedermeier pieces, Loos-designed sets, fine/arty glassware and porcelain on display here glitters from the lights of the chandelier-festooned atrium. Lobmeyr has been in business since 1823, when it exclusively supplied the imperial court.

Today production is more focused towards pieces inspired by the Wiener Werkstätte artists from the early 20th century. This movement sought to bring a philosophy of artistic craftsmanship into functional design, later helping pave the way for art deco.

BONBONS ANZINGER CHOCOLATE

Map p246 (www.bonbons-anzinger.at; 01, Tegetthoffstrasse 7; ⌚8am-6.30pm Mon-Fri, 9am-6pm Sat, noon-4pm Sun; 🚋D, 1, 2, 71 Kärntner Ring/Oper, UKarlsplatz) A jewel box of a chocolate shop, with ceramic-tiled floors, mint-green cabinets, and a dazzling array of handmade truffles and pralines, Bonbons Anzinger has a tiny upstairs tearoom serving coffee, tea and hot chocolate, with a chocolate on the side. Its speciality is the *Mozartkugel*, a dark chocolate-covered ball filled with pistachio marzipan and nougat, along with gingerbread at Christmas.

GMUNDNER CERAMICS

Map p246 (www.gmundner.at; 01, Bräunerstrasse 3; ⌚10am-6pm Mon-Fri, 10am-5pm Sat; UStephansplatz) Gmundner has been manufacturing ceramics by hand since 1492, and it's estimated over 50% of Austrian households hold at least one Gmundner piece. Its plates, casserole dishes, tea and coffee cups and more are all safe to use in microwaves and dishwashers. If you're nervous about transporting these beautiful wares in your luggage, international shipping can be arranged.

OBERLAA FOOD & DRINKS

Map p246 (www.oberlaa-wien.at; 01, Neuer Markt 16; ⌚8am-8pm; UStephansplatz) This much-loved confectioner is famed for its 'Laa-Kronen' – brightly coloured *macarons* in flavours like pistachio, lemon and strawberry, available singly or in gorgeous boxed sets. It also sells beautifully packaged chocolates, loose-leaf teas and homemade ice creams in summer, when you can dine on its pavement terrace. There are nine other branches around town.

ÖSTERREICHISCHE WERKSTÄTTEN GLASS, CERAMICS

Map p246 (www.austrianarts.com; 01, Kärntner Strasse 6; ⌚10am-6.30pm Mon-Fri, to 6pm Sat; UStephansplatz) Established in 1945, Österreichische Werkstätten is dedicated to selling work made by Austrian companies and designed by Austrian designers. Look out for Kisslinger, a family glassware company since 1946, with Klimt- and Hundertwasser-styled designs; Peter Wolfe's more traditional Tirol-style designed glassware; and the world-renowned Riedel wine glasses.

ALTWAREN AUCTIONS

The **Dorotheum** (Map p246; www.dorotheum.com; 01, Dorotheergasse 17; ⌚10am-6pm Mon-Fri, 9am-5pm Sat; UStephansplatz) is among the largest auction houses in Europe and for the casual visitor it's more like a museum, housing everything from antique toys and tableware to autographs, antique guns and, above all, lots of quality paintings. You can bid at the regular auctions held here, otherwise just drop by (it's free) and enjoy browsing.

LODEN-PLANKL CLOTHING

Map p246 (www.loden-plankl.at; 01, Michaelerplatz 6; ⌚10am-6pm Mon-Sat Mar-Jun & Sep-Dec, 10am-5pm Mon-Sat Jan, Feb, Jul & Aug; 🚌1A, 2A Michaelerplatz, UHerrengasse) Kit yourself out Von Trapp family-style at this 180-year-old institution full of handmade embroidered *Dirndls* (women's traditional dress) and blouses, capes, high-collared jackets, and deer-suede and *loden* (a traditional fabric made from boiled and combed wool) coats. Traditional designs share racks with modern variations.

FREYTAG & BERNDT BOOKS, MAPS

Map p246 (www.freytagberndt.com; 01, Wallnerstrasse 3; ⌚9.30am-6.30pm Mon-Fri, to 6pm Sat; 🚌1A, 2A Michaelerplatz, UHerrengasse) The ultimate place to inspire wanderlust, Freytag & Berndt has an extensive collection of guides and maps (many in English) to Vienna, Austria (including some superbly detailed walking maps) and destinations around the globe.

AUGARTEN WIEN CERAMICS

Map p246 (www.augarten.at; 01, Spiegelgasse 3; ⌚10am-6pm Mon-Sat; UStephansplatz) Wiener Porzellanmanufaktur Augarten makes Vienna's finest porcelain – the most delicate of ornaments, vases and dinnerware with traditional hand-painted designs. Tours of the factory (p159) are available.

Stephansdom & the Historic Centre

WEST & NORTH OF STEPHANSPLATZ | SOUTH & EAST OF STEPHANSPLATZ

Neighbourhood Top Five

❶ **Stephansdom** (p76) Marvelling at the intricate details of Vienna's famous landmark and Austria's best-known Gothic cathedral.

❷ **Literaturmuseum** (p81) Learning about Austria's literary luminaries and their seminal works from the 18th century to the present day at this new museum dedicated to Austrian writing.

❸ Historic centre (p84) Exploring the quiet courtyards and lanes of Vienna's historic core at your own pace on a self-guided walking tour.

❹ **Mozarthaus Vienna** (p80) Visiting Wolfgang Amadeus Mozart's only surviving Viennese home, where he composed *The Marriage of Figaro* during his 2½ years here.

❺ **Haus der Musik** (p80) Conducting your own virtual orchestra and engaging with other interactive exhibits at this innovative music museum.

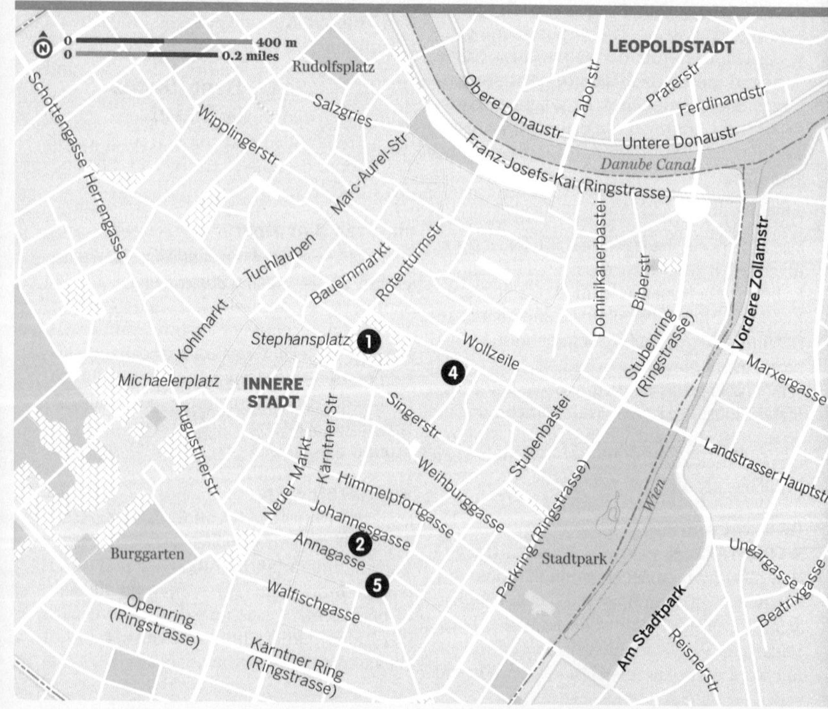

For more detail of this area see Map p244

Explore Stephansdom & the Historic Centre

Vienna's entire Innere Stadt is compact and easily walked – especially its core, the Stephansdom (p76) and historic centre neighbourhood. The city's monumental cathedral makes an ideal starting point; plan to spend half a day exploring it in its entirety, including scaling the south tower's 343 steps for sweeping views over the Innere Stadt's rooftops.

After lunch, head to the Haus der Musik (p80) and Mozarthaus Vienna (p80) to discover the Austrian capital's incredible musical heritage. Other key sights here include the Museum Judenplatz (p78). Keep Vienna's iconic coffee houses on your radar along the way to rest up, rejuvenate and relax into Viennese life.

The historic centre gets very crowded in summer, making early evening one of the best times to stroll around and soak up the atmosphere. After dinner, late on a warm night, is ideal for a romantic stroll through the illuminated streets.

Local Life

➡ **Street Life** Walking the historic centre's main streets in summer can sometimes give you the feeling of being on an ant trail. Take local side lanes like Blutgasse and duck into squares and courtyards along the way. Heiligenkreuzerhof is one of the prettiest. Streets around it, such as Sonnenfelsgasse, Schönlaterngasse and Dr-Ignaz-Seipel-Platz, are also quieter parts of town, as are areas around Ruprechtskirche (p80), Maria am Gestade (p79), and the area between Judenplatz and Am Hof.

➡ **Canal Life** In summer, join locals relaxing along the banks of the Danube Canal, where you'll also find bars, restaurants and the city's oldest jazz club.

➡ **Nightlife** The historic centre is beautiful when lit up at night. Soak it up the way the Viennese do: on a leisurely evening stroll.

Getting There & Away

➡ **U-Bahn** Stephansplatz (U1, U3) and Schwedenplatz (U1, U4) – and to a lesser extent Stubentor (U3), Herrengasse (U3) and Karlsplatz (U1, U2, U4) – are the main stops.

➡ **Tram** Schwedenplatz (1, 2) and Kärntner Ring/Oper (1, 2, D, 71) are the most convenient stops.

➡ **Bus** 1A links Stephansplatz, Schottentor and Michaelerplatz; 3A links Stubentor with Stephansplatz and Börsenplatz.

Lonely Planet's Top Tip

The U-Bahn is handy for connecting to outlying neighbourhoods and crossing the historic centre, and the Ringstrasse trams are good for circumnavigating it, but public transport is limited within the centre itself. Taxis are plentiful but costly due to the plethora of one-way streets and slow-moving traffic, so it's best to explore on foot (nothing is more than a 10- to 20-minute walk).

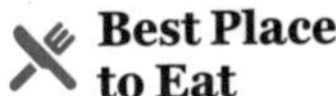

Best Places to Eat

➡ Tian (p87)
➡ Plachutta (p87)
➡ Griechenbeisl (p85)
➡ Wrenkh (p85)
➡ Artner (p87)

For reviews, see p85. ➡

Best Places to Drink

➡ Kruger's American Bar (p87)
➡ Enrico Panigl (p88)
➡ Kleines Café (p89)
➡ Vinogin (p88)
➡ Sky Bar (p88)

For reviews, see p87. ➡

Best Places to Shop

➡ Wiener Rosenmanufaktur (p91)
➡ Wald & Wiese (p87)
➡ Runway (p90)
➡ Schau Schau (p90)

For reviews, see p90. ➡

TOP SIGHT
STEPHANSDOM

Soaring above the surrounding cityscape, Vienna's immense, filagreed Gothic masterpiece Stephansdom (St Stephen's Cathedral) – or Steffl (Little Stephen) as it's locally (and ironically) dubbed – symbolises the city like no other building. Highlights include the cathedral's spectacular main nave with its Gothic stone pulpit and baroque high altar, its *Katakomben* (catacombs), two towers and the cathedral treasures.

History

A church has stood on this site since the 12th century, reminders of which today are the Romanesque Riesentor (Giant Gate) and Heidentürme (Towers of the Heathens) at the entrance and above it. In 1359, at the behest of Habsburg Duke Rudolf IV, Stephansdom began receiving its Gothic makeover and Rudolf earned himself the epithet of 'The Founder' by laying the first stone in the reconstruction.

Stephansdom: Inside & Out

From outside the cathedral, the first thing that will strike you is the glorious tiled roof, with its dazzling row of chevrons on one end and the Austrian eagle on the other.

Inside the cathedral, the magnificent Gothic stone pulpit takes pride of place, fashioned in 1515 by Anton Pilgrim (his likeness appears in the stonework). The pulpit railing is adorned with salamanders and toads, symbolising the battle of good against evil. At the far end of the main nave, the baroque high altar shows the stoning of St Stephen. The chancel to its left has the winged Wiener Neustadt altarpiece, dating from 1447; the right chancel has the

DON'T MISS

- Main nave
- Gothic stone pulpit
- Baroque high altar
- Cathedral south tower
- Cathedral Pummerin (north tower bell)
- *Katakomben* (catacombs)

PRACTICALITIES

- St Stephen's Cathedral
- Map p244, C5
- tours 01-515 323 054
- www.stephanskirche.at
- 01, Stephansplatz
- main nave adult & one child €6, additional child €1.50
- public visits 9-11.30am & 1-4.30pm Mon-Sat, 1-4.30pm Sun
- U Stephansplatz

Renaissance red-marble tomb of Friedrich III. Under his guidance the city became a bishopric (and the church a cathedral) in 1469.

Katakomben

The area around the cathedral was originally a graveyard. But with plague and influenza epidemics striking Europe in the 1730s, Karl VI ordered the graveyard to be closed and henceforth Vienna buried its dead beneath Stephansdom in the **Katakomben** (30min tour adult/child €5.50/2; ⌚tours 10-11.30am & 1.30-4.30pm Mon-Sat, 1.30-4.30pm Sun). Today, they contain the remains of countless victims, which are kept in a mass grave and a bone house. Also on display are rows of urns containing the internal organs of the Habsburgs. One of the many privileges of being a Habsburg was to be dismembered and dispersed after death: their hearts are in the Augustinerkirche in the Hofburg and the rest of their bodies are in the Kaisergruft. Entrance is allowed only on a tour.

Cathedral South Tower

When the foundation stone for the **south tower** (Südturm; adult/child €4.50/2; ⌚9am-5.30pm) was laid in 1359, Rudolf IV is said to have used a trowel and spade made of silver. Two towers were originally envisaged, but the Südturm grew so high that little space remained for the second; in 1433 the tower reached its final height of 136.7m. Today you can ascend the 343 steps to a small platform for one of Vienna's most spectacular views over the Innere Stadt (you don't need a ticket for the main nave).

Cathedral Pummerin

Weighing 21 tonnes, the **Pummerin** (Boomer Bell; adult/child €5.50/2; ⌚9am-5.30pm) is Austria's largest bell and was installed in the 68.3m-high **north tower** in 1957. While the rest of the cathedral was rising up in its new Gothic format, work was interrupted on this tower due to a lack of cash and the fading allure of Gothic architecture. It's accessible only by lift; you don't need a ticket for the main nave.

Dom- & Diözesanmuseum

The **Dom- & Diözesanmuseum** (Cathedral & Diocesan Museum of Vienna; www.dommuseum.at) is a treasure trove of religious art pieces spanning a period of more than 1000 years. Among the collection's extraordinary exhibits are the earliest European portrait – of Duke Rudolph IV (1360) – and two Syrian glass vessels (1280–1310), thought to be among the oldest glass bottles in the world. Check the website for updates on its reopening following extensive renovations.

ANIMAL EL DORADO

Stephansdom is an unlikely El Dorado for animal lovers. The Riesentor (Giant Gate) is packed with basilisks as well as fearsome dragons and lions. Friedrich III's tomb (1513) has some rather hideous creatures (serpents, ugly eagles, lions and a goblin) on top, but you can't get close enough to see these. The zoological highlight, however, is the pulpit, with salamanders and toads, topped off by the pug-faced Fearless Dog, there to ward off evil.

The first church built on the site of the cathedral was a Romanesque church consecrated in 1147. It was remodelled completely and consecrated again in 1263. Entering the cathedral today, you pass though the Riesentor, which dates from the early 13th century. The Heidentürme (Towers of the Heathens) rise above this main portal. The name 'Riesentor' has less to do with the size of the gate than its deep, inward-sloping funnel shape, derived from the old German 'rīsanan' (rising).

STEPHANSDOM CATHEDRAL

See p76.

PETERSKIRCHE CHURCH

Map p244 (Church of St Peter; www.peterskirche.at; 01, Petersplatz; 7am-8pm Mon-Fri, 9am-9pm Sat & Sun; U Stephansplatz) One of the city's prettiest churches, the Peterskirche was built in 1733 according to plans of the celebrated baroque architect Johann Lukas von Hildebrandt. Interior highlights that make a visit highly worthwhile include a fresco on the dome painted by JM Rottmayr and a golden altar depicting the martyrdom of St John of Nepomuk. Regular organ recitals and concerts are also held here; check the program online.

MUSEUM JUDENPLATZ MUSEUM

Map p244 (01-535 04 31; www.jmw.at; 01, Judenplatz 8; adult/child incl Jüdisches Museum €10/free; 10am-6pm Sun-Thu, to 5pm Fri; U Stephansplatz, Herrengasse) The main focus of Museum Judenplatz is on the excavated remains of a medieval synagogue that once stood on Judenplatz, with a film and numerous exhibits to elucidate Vienna's Jewish history. It was built in the Middle Ages, but Duke Albrecht V's 'hatred and misconception' led him to order its destruction in 1421. The basic outline of the synagogue can still be seen here. Combined tickets to the Museum Judenplatz and Jüdisches Museum (p66) are valid for four days.

HOLOCAUST-DENKMAL MEMORIAL

Map p244 (01, Judenplatz; U Stephansplatz) Deliberately reminiscent of a bunker, the steel-and-concrete Holocaust-Denkmal (2000) is a memorial to the 65,000 Austrian Jews who perished in the Holocaust. Designed by British sculptor Rachel Whiteread, this 'nameless library' depicts books with their spines facing inwards, representing the lost knowledge of the Holocaust victims. It's inscribed with the names of Austrian concentration camps where the victims were murdered.

STADTTEMPEL SYNAGOGUE

Map p244 (01-531 041 11; www.ikg-wien.at; 01, Seitenstettengasse 4; tours adult/child €5/free; guided tours 11.30am & 2pm Mon-Thu; U Stephansplatz, Schwedenplatz) Vienna's main synagogue, seating 500 people, was completed in 1826 after *Toleranzpatent* reforms by Joseph II in the 1780s granted rights to Vienna's Jews to practise their religion. This paved the way for improved standing for Jews and brought a rise in fortunes. Built in an exquisite Biedermeier style, the main prayer room is flanked by

GUIDED TOURS & MUSIC IN STEPHANSDOM

Multilingual audio guide tour The most common option to take in the cathedral interior; audio guides costing €8 per adult (including one child under 14; €1.50 per additional child). They're available from 8.30am to 11.30am and 1pm to 5.30pm Monday to Saturday, and from 1pm to 5.30pm Sunday.

All-inclusive tour All-inclusive tours are partly with an audio guide, partly with a tour guide (adult €17.90, including one child under 14; €3 per additional child; seniors and students pay €13.90). Tours take in the cathedral interior, *Katakomben*, south tower and the north tower. Children aren't allowed to do it alone.

Guided tours in English & German English-language tours explain the background of the cathedral and walk you through its main interior features. The 30-minute tours leave at 10.30am Monday to Saturday (adult/child €5.50/2). The same guided tours in German leave at 3pm daily.

Evening roof-walk tours in German These 90-minute south tower tours (adult/child €10/4) depart at 7pm every Saturday from July to September and feature a brisk climb to the top of the south tower.

Special events & Mass The website www.dommusik-wien.at has a program of special concerts and events, but the 10.15am Mass on Sundays (9.30am during the school holidays around July and August) is something special, as it's conducted with full choral accompaniment. Tickets are available online at www.kunstkultur.com.

12 ionic columns and is capped by a cupola. Security is tight; you'll need your passport to gain entry.

When it was built, only Catholic places of worship were allowed to front major streets, so the Stadttempel was built inside an apartment complex, which was the reason it was the sole survivor of 94 synagogues in Vienna following the November Pogroms of 1938.

ANKERUHR MONUMENT

Map p244 (Anker Clock; 01, Hoher Markt 10-11; UStephansplatz, Schwedenplatz) An art nouveau masterpiece created by Franz von Matsch in 1911, this mechanical clock was named after the Anker Insurance Co, which commissioned it. Over a 12-hour period, figures including Roman Emperor Marcus Aurelius (who died in Vienna in AD 180), Joseph Haydn, Eugene of Savoy, Maria Theresia and others pass across the clock face, indicating the time against a static measure showing the minutes. At noon, all the figures trundle past in succession to the tune of organ music.

Once the centre of the Roman outpost, the **Hoher Markt** is Vienna's oldest square.

AM HOF SQUARE

Map p244 (01; UHerrengasse) Before moving to the site of the Hofburg in the late 13th century, the ruling family the Babenbergs resided on this large square. Rising up in the centre is the **Mariensäule** (Mary's Column; 1667), dedicated to the Virgin Mary. Look out too for house **No 11**, where a gold-painted cannonball is a reminder of the 1683 Turkish siege. The former Jesuit monastery **Kirche Am Hof** (01-533 83 94; www.hkm-wien.at; 01, Am Hof; 8am-noon & 4-6pm Mon-Sat, 4-6pm Sun; UHerrengasse, Schottentor) occupies the southeast side. It's now the Croatian Catholic Church.

UHREN MUSEUM MUSEUM

Map p244 (Clock Museum; 01-533 22 65; www.wienmuseum.at; 01, Schulhof 2; adult/child €7/free; 10am-6pm Tue-Sun; 1A, 3A, UHerrengasse) Opened in 1921 in the Hafenhaus, one of Vienna's oldest buildings, the municipal Uhren Museum's three floors are weighed down with an astounding 21,200 clocks and watches, ranging from the 15th century to a 1992 computer clock, with 700 on display at any one time. The collection of Biedermeier and belle époque models will, for most, steal the show. The peace and quiet is shattered at the striking of each hour. Bus to Renngasse.

ARCHIV DES ÖSTERREICHISCHEN WIDERSTANDS MUSEUM

Map p244 (Austrian Resistance Archive; 01-228 94 69-319; www.doew.at; 01, Wipplingerstrasse 8; 9am-5pm Mon-Wed & Fri, to 7pm Thu; UStephansplatz) FREE Housed in the Altes Rathaus (Old City Hall), the Austrian Resistance Archive documents the little-known antifascist resistance force that operated during the Nazi regime; some 2700 resistance fighters were executed by the Nazis and thousands more sent to concentration camps. The exhibition gives in-depth analysis of the Nazi doctrines on homosexuality, 'unworthy' citizens, concentration camps and forced labour, with photos and memorabilia detailing the time before and after the *Anschluss*.

NEIDHART-FRESKEN MUSEUM

Map p244 (01-535 90 65; www.wienmuseum.at; 01, Tuchlauben 19; adult/child €5/free; 10am-1pm & 2-6pm Tue-Sun; UStephansplatz) An unassuming house on Tuchlauben hides a remarkable decoration: the oldest extant secular frescoes in Vienna. The small frescoes, dating from 1407, tell the story of the minstrel Neidhart von Reuental (1180–1240), as well as life in the Middle Ages, in lively scenes. They were discovered when the house was set to be redeveloped into apartments in 1979. The artworks are in superb condition considering their age.

RÖMER MUSEUM MUSEUM

Map p244 (01-535 56 06; www.wienmuseum.at; 01, Hoher Markt 3; adult/child €7/free; 9am-6pm Tue-Sun; 1A, 3A, UStephansplatz) This small expanse of Roman ruins dating from the 1st to the 5th century is thought to be part of the officers' quarters of the Roman legion camp at Vindobona. You can see crumbled walls, tiled floors and a small exhibition of artefacts here, along with a 3D film with English subtitles. Take the bus to Hoher Markt.

MARIA AM GESTADE CHURCH

Map p244 (01-533 95 94-0; www.maria-am-gestade.redemptoristen.at; 01, Passauer Platz; 8am-7pm; 1, 2, UStephansplatz) Originally a wooden church built by Danube boatsmen around 880, Maria am Gestade (Maria on the Riverbank) was built in stone between

1394 and 1414, making it one of Vienna's few surviving Gothic structures. For steep ground the nave was built narrower than the choir (and with a slight bend). In 1805 Napoleon used it to store weapons and horses. The interior has a high vaulted Gothic ceiling and pretty stained glass behind a winged Gothic altar. Tram to Salztorbrücke.

RUPRECHTSKIRCHE CHURCH

Map p244 (St Rupert's Church; 01-535 60 03; www.ruprechtskirche.at; 01, Ruprechtsplatz 1; 10am-noon Mon & Tue, 10am-noon & 3-5pm Wed, 10am-5pm Thu & Fri, 11.30am-3.30pm Sat; 1, 2, USchwedenplatz) Vienna's oldest church is believed to date from 740. The lower levels of the tower date from the 12th century, the roof from the 15th century and the iron Renaissance door on the west side from the 1530s. In summer, its stone walls are clad in ivy. The interior is sleek and worth a quick viewing, with a Romanesque nave from the 12th century. Note that there are no public visiting hours on Sunday due to religious services.

MONUMENT TO THE VICTIMS OF FASCISM MONUMENT

Map p244 (01, Morzinplatz; 1, 2, USchwedenplatz) On the site of the former Gestapo headquarters during the Nazi era at Morzinplatz, this 1985 monument features the Star of David and the pink triangle, representing the Jewish and homosexual victims of the Nazis.

MOZARTHAUS VIENNA MUSEUM

Map p244 (01-512 17 91; www.mozarthausvienna.at; 01, Domgasse 5; adult/child €11/4.50, with Haus der Musik €18/8; 10am-7pm; UStephansplatz) The great composer spent 2½ happy and productive years at this residence between 1784 and 1787. Exhibits include copies of music scores and paintings, while free audio guides recreate the story of his time here. Mozart spent a total of 11 years in Vienna, changing residences frequently and sometimes setting up his home outside the Ringstrasse in the cheaper *Vorstädte* (inner suburbs) when his finances were tight. Of these the Mozarthaus Vienna is the only one that survives.

TOP SIGHT
HAUS DER MUSIK

The Haus der Musik explains the world of sound and music to adults and children alike in an amusing and interactive way (in English and German).

Floor 1 hosts the **Museum of the Vienna Philharmonic**. Find out about the history of the orchestra's famous New Year's concerts and listen to recent concert highlights. You can even compose your own waltz by rolling dice.

Floor 2, called the **Sonosphere**, has plenty of engaging instruments, interactive toys and touch screens. Test the limits of your hearing and play around with sampled sounds to record your own CD (€7). One of the highlights for aficionados of everyday audioscapes is a collection of street and subway sounds from New York, Tokyo and other places.

Floor 3 covers Vienna's classical composers and is polished off with an amusing interactive video in which you conduct the Vienna Philharmonic Orchestra.

Floor 4 has the so-called **Virtostage**, in which your own body language and movements shape the music to create an opera.

DON'T MISS

- Sonosphere
- Virtual conductor
- The Vienna Philharmonic Orchestra concert footage

PRACTICALITIES

- Map p244, C7
- www.hausdermusik.com
- 01, Seilerstätte 30
- adult/child €13/6, with Mozarthaus Vienna €18/8
- 10am-10pm
- D, 1, 2, 71, UKarlsplatz

The exhibition begins on the top floor, overlooking a narrow, closed-in inner courtyard, and covers the society of the late 18th century, providing asides into prominent figures in the court and Mozart's life, such as the Freemasons (to whom he dedicated a number of pieces). Coverage of Mozart's vices – his womanising, gambling and ability to waste excessive amounts of money – gives it an edge.

Retaining its original stucco ceilings, the middle floor concentrates on Mozart's music and his musical influences. It was in this house that he penned *The Marriage of Figaro*. A surreal holographic performance of scenes from *The Magic Flute* is in another room. The final floor has Mozart's bedroom and a few pieces of period furniture in glass cases to give a feel for the era.

FLEISCHMARKT STREET

Map p244 (01, Fleischmarkt; UStephansplatz) Greek merchants settled around Fleischmarkt from about 1700, which gradually became known as the Griechenviertel (Greek quarter). Today it has some attractive art nouveau buildings, such as **No 14**, built by F Dehm and F Olbricht (1899), **No 7** (Max Kropf; 1899) – the childhood home of Hollywood film director Billy Wilder from 1914 to 1924 – and **Nos 1 & 3** (1910). The favourite meeting place of the Greek community was the Griechenbeisl (p85), today one of Vienna's most popular *Beisln* (bistro pubs).

GRIECHENKIRCHE ZUR HEILIGEN DREIFALTIGKEIT CHURCH

Map p244 (Holy Trinity Greek Orthodox Church; 01-533 38 89; www.metropolisvonaustria.at; 01, Fleischmarkt 13; 10am-3pm; 1, 2, USchwedenplatz) Built in 1861 at the behest of the Greek community, the interior of Vienna's main Greek Orthodox church is a glittering blaze of Byzantine designs. A ceiling fresco depicting the prophets surrounded by swirls of gold is augmented by a high altar of 13 panels – each of which features sparkling gilding – and a doorway to the inner sanctum.

LITERATURMUSEUM MUSEUM

Map p244 (Literature Museum; www.onb.ac.at/literaturmuseum; 01, Grillparzerhaus, Johannesgasse 6; adult/child €7/free; 10am-6pm Tue, Wed & Fri-Sun, to 9pm Thu; UStephansplatz) An 1844 Biedermeier building houses Austria's literature museum (opened 2015), containing books, manuscripts, letters, photos, illustrations and personal effects such as desks from the country's most seminal authors, playwrights and poets, from the 18th century to the present day. The celebrated writers represented include Günther Anders, Ingeborg Bachmann, Peter Handke, Robert Menasse, Herta Müller and Hilde Spiel. You can also hear readings and quotes from the museum's 550 hours of audio recordings. Information leaflets are available in English.

FRANZISKANERKIRCHE CHURCH

Map p244 (01-512 45 78 11; http://wien.franziskaner.at; 01, Franziskanerplatz; 7am-8pm; UStephansplatz) This Franciscan church is a glorious architectural deception. Outside it exudes the hallmarks of an early-17th-century Renaissance style, yet inside it is awash with gold and marble decorative features from the baroque era (about 100 years later). The high altar takes the form of a triumphal arch; hidden behind this is Vienna's oldest organ (1642), built by Johann Wöckherl. Concerts (€6) lasting 45 minutes take place at 2pm on Fridays from April to October.

DOMINIKANERKIRCHE CHURCH

Map p244 (Dominican Church; 01-512 91 74; 01, Postgasse 4; 7am-7pm; 2, UStubentor) Vienna's oldest baroque church (consecrated in 1634) is largely the work of Italian architects and artisans, with a spacious interior adorned with white stucco and frescoes. The Dominicans first came to Vienna in 1226, when Leopold VI of Babenberg invited them to settle, but their earliest church burned down less than 50 years later. Its Gothic replacement was dismantled during the first Turkish siege in 1529 and its stone used to fortify the city walls.

POSTSPARKASSE MUSEUM

Map p244 (www.ottowagner.com; 01, Georg-Coch-Platz 2; museum adult/child €8/free; 10am-5pm Mon-Fri; 1, 2, USchwedenplatz) The marble-cased and metal-studded Post Office Savings Bank building is the *Jugendstil* (Art Nouveau) work of Otto Wagner, who oversaw its construction between 1904 and 1906, and again from 1910 to 1912. You can explore the back section of the building, where there's also a small museum with temporary exhibitions on design and a video section on the history of the building.

ANGELINA DIMITROVA/SHUTTERSTOCK ©

1. Holocaust-Denkmal (p78)
A memorial to the 65,000 Austrian Jews who died in the Holocaust.

2. Stephansdom (p76)
Interior of the city's Gothic cathedral, Stephansdom.

3. Stephansplatz
The square is named for its towering cathedral.

4. Peterskirche (p78)
The baroque dome of Peterskirche as seen from the Stephansdom cathedral roof.

4

3

TTSTUDIO/SHUTTERSTOCK ©

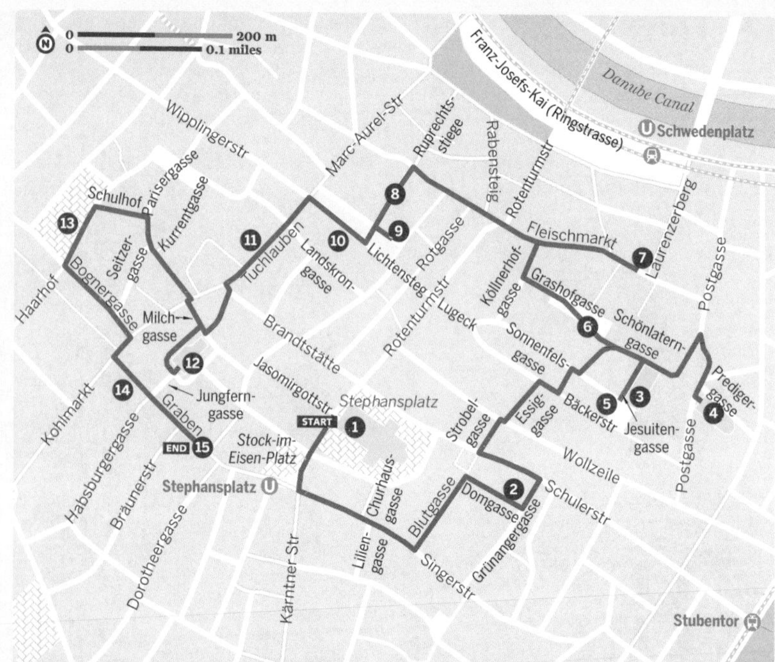

Neighbourhood Walk
The Historic Centre

START STEPHANSDOM
FINISH GRABEN
LENGTH 3KM; 90 MINUTES TO FIVE HOURS

Begin at Vienna's signature cathedral, **1 Stephansdom** (p76). After following a small section of Kärntner Strasse, you'll wind through the atmospheric backstreets to **2 Mozarthaus Vienna** (p80), where the composer lived for almost three years.

A series of narrow lanes leads you down towards two fine baroque churches. The interior of the **3 Jesuitenkirche** (01, Dr-Ignaz-Seipel-Platz 1) is pure deception, with frescoes creating the illusion of a dome, while the 1634 **4 Dominikanerkirche** (p81) is Vienna's finest reminder of the early baroque period of church building. The Jesuitenkirche is opposite the **5 Austrian Academy of the Sciences** (01, Dr-Ignaz-Seipel-Platz 2), housed in a university building dating from 1755.

During daylight hours, you can enter **6 Heiligenkreuzerhof** from the eastern side (at night time, enter from Grasshofgasse). At Christmas, this tranquil courtyard is filled with traditional decorations. Busy **7 Fleischmarkt** (p81) is the heart of the traditional Greek quarter of Vienna, where Greek merchants settled from the 18th century. Climb the stairs and enter lively **8 Judengasse**, the centre of the traditional Jewish quarter. These days, Hoher Markt – Vienna's oldest square – is a busy commercial street; highlights are the art nouveau **9 Ankeruhr** (p79), a mechanical clock with historic figures marking the time as they pass over the clock face and the **10 Römer Museum** (p79), Roman ruins dating from the 1st to the 5th century. You'll then pass the **11 Neidhart-Fresken** (p79) mural and reach the most impressive church this side of Stephansdom, the **12 Peterskirche** (p78), with a golden altar.

Northwest of here, **13 Am Hof** (p79) is spiked by an impressive Mariensäule column. As you walk along Graben back towards Stephansplatz, pop into **14 Adolf Loos' Public Toilets** (p68), replete with mahogany-panelled stalls and exquisite tiling, then admire the gilded baroque **15 Pestsäule memorial** (1693) to Vienna's 75,000 plague victims on Graben.

EATING

For the most authentic Viennese experience, head to a *Beisl* (a small tavern, like a bistro pub). Those on the eastern fringes of the historic centre, and on and around Wollzeile and Himmelpfortgasse, offer the most local experience.

DONUTERIA — SWEETS, BAKERY €

Map p244 (www.donuteria.com; 01, Seilerstätte 30; doughnuts €2.50-5; ⌚9.30am-7pm Mon-Fri, 11am-6pm Sat, noon-5pm Sun; ; 2, 71) Inspired Austrian-flavoured doughnuts at this spiffing new shop include *Apfelstrudel* (apple strudel), the Sacher (chocolate and apricot jam, based on the classic *Sacher Torte*), Styrian (pumpkinseed and hazelnut), Mohn (poppyseed and lemon) and the Mozart (pistachio, marzipan and chocolate), based on the *Mozartkugel,* first created in 1890. Tram to Schwarzenbergplatz.

HIDDEN KITCHEN — DELI €

Map p244 (www.hiddenkitchen.at; 01, Färbergasse 3; light meals €5-8, 3-course lunch €10; ⌚10am-4pm Mon-Fri; ; U Herrengasse, Schottentor) This slick, white-walled deli raises the Viennese salad to a new level. Combinations like couscous with tarragon, cranberries and goat's cheese, fennel-mushroom carpaccio, and bulgur wheat with tomatoes, rocket and feta are fresh and healthy. They also do a fine line in quiches, soups and juices. Get there before the lunch crowds devour all in sight.

CAFÉ KORB — AUSTRIAN €

Map p244 (www.cafekorb.at; 01, Brandstätte 9; mains €5.80-9.80; ⌚8am-midnight Mon-Sat, 10am-midnight Sun; ; U Stephansplatz) Famed for its *Apfelstrudel,* Sigmund Freud's former hang-out is first and foremost a coffee house, but its top-notch Austrian menu places it in the realm of a *Beisl.* The food is classic – including three house-speciality schnitzels, several varieties of *Würstel* (sausages) – and the crowd eclectic and offbeat.

Downstairs, there's a geometric 'art lounge' with a bowling alley, and toilets identified only by abstract anatomical symbols that Freud would have appreciated.

ZANONI & ZANONI — GELATERIA €

Map p244 (01-512 79 79; www.zanoni.co.at; 01, Lugeck 7; ice cream from €1.30; ⌚7.30am-midnight; U Stephansplatz) Opening to a vast summer terrace, this Italian *gelateria* and *pasticceria* has 30 seasonal varieties of gelato, such as vanilla poppyseed, blueberry ricotta, strawberry and lemon, *biscotto,* tiramisu, and chocolate and apricot. It also has vegan ice creams, frozen yoghurts and diabetic-friendly dishes, including crêpes.

★GRIECHENBEISL — BISTRO €€

Map p244 (01-533 19 77; www.griechenbeisl.at; 01, Fleischmarkt 11; mains €15-28; ⌚11.30am-11.30pm; ; 1, 2, U Schwedenplatz) Dating from 1447 and frequented by Beethoven, Brahms, Schubert and Strauss among other luminaries, Vienna's oldest restaurant has vaulted rooms, wood panelling and a figure of Augustin trapped at the bottom of a well inside the front door. Every classic Viennese dish is on the menu, along with three daily vegetarian options. In summer, head to the plant-fringed front garden. Its warren of rooms include the oldest section, the Zither Stüberl, and the Mark Twain Zimmer (named for another former guest), inscribed with the autographs of Twain and others, which has been granted heritage status.

★WRENKH — BISTRO €€

Map p244 (01-533 15 26; www.wrenkh-wien.at; 01, Bauernmarkt 10; mains €8-25; ⌚11am-11pm Mon-Sat; ; U Stephansplatz) Wrenkh specialises in vegetables (lentils in white-wine sauce with bread dumplings; paprika-marinated sweet potato with roasted goat's cheese; creamed spinach-stuffed roast potatoes with apple and celery salad), but also creates some superb fish-based dishes (sautéed mountain-stream trout with cherry-tomato potato salad) and meat options (dry-aged rib-eye with miso and aubergine crème). On weekdays, bargain-priced 2-/3-course lunch menus cost €9.50/10.50.

BREZL GWÖLB — AUSTRIAN €€

Map p244 (01-533 88 11; www.brezl.at; 01, Ledererhof 9; mains €12-20; ⌚11.30am-1am; ; U Schottentor, Herrengasse) Hidden down an alley near Freyung, Brezl Gwölb has won a loyal following for its winningly fresh Austrian home-cooking, served with smiles and a generous dollop of Gothic charm. Atmospherically lit by candles, the crypt-like cellar magics you back in time with its carvings, brick arches, wrought-iron lanterns and alcoves. No wonder the place overflows with regulars.

FRATELLI — ITALIAN €€

Map p244 (01-533 87 45; www.fratelli.at; 01, Rotenturmstrasse 11; pizza €9.20-13.90, pasta

€11.20-17.50, mains €23-38; ⏲11.30am-11.30pm; ⓤStephansplatz) Umbrella-shaded white-clothed tables spread over the square in summer at this elegant Italian restaurant; the frescoed interior has a winding staircase to the cellar. Handmade pastas span meat-filled ravioli with wild mushrooms to linguine with scampi, but the showstoppers are the mains: veal medallions with lemon sauce, grilled sole with caper butter, or whole turbot with Swiss chard and potatoes.

HUTH GASTWIRTSCHAFT AUSTRIAN €€

Map p244 (☎01-513 56 44; www.zum-huth.at; 01, Schellinggasse 5; mains €13.90-18.90; ⏲noon-11pm; 🚋2) One of several local neo-*Beisln* in this under-the-radar part of Innere Stadt, Huth serves superb Viennese classics such as *Wiener Schnitzel* with cranberry sauce and parsley potatoes, *Selchfleisch* (smoked pork with sauerkraut) and desserts including *Topfenstrudel* (quark-filled strudel), in a high-ceilinged main dining room and vaulted brick cellar, as well as a terrace in summer. Tram to Weihburggasse.

MOTTO AM FLUSS INTERNATIONAL €€

Map p244 (☎01-252 55 10; www.mottoamfluss.at; 01, Franz-Josefs-Kai 2; restaurant mains €13-30, cafe dishes €4-10.30; ⏲restaurant 11.30am-2.30pm & 6pm-midnight, cafe 8am-10pm, bar 6pm-4am; 📶🖊; 🚋1, 2, ⓤSchwedenplatz) Located inside the Wien-City ferry terminal, with dazzling views of the Danube Canal, Motto am Fluss' restaurant serves Austro-international cuisine with quality organic meats (vegetarian and vegan options available). Its upstairs cafe does great all-day breakfasts, cakes and pastries, and its bar is a superbly relaxed hang-out for Austrian wines, beers and house-creation cocktails.

HISTORIC GRABEN

Today Vienna's most elegant shopping street, **Graben** (Map p244; 01; ⓤStephansplatz) began life as a ditch dug by the Romans to protect Vindobona. In 1192 Leopold V filled in the ditch and built a defensive city wall that ended at Freyung, using as finance the ransom paid by arch-rival Richard the Lionheart, who at that time was being kept under lock and key in a castle near Dürnstein, on the Danube.

FIGLMÜLLER AUSTRIAN €€

Map p244 (☎01-512 61 77; www.figlmueller.at; 01, Wollzeile 5; mains €9.50-20.50; ⏲11am-9.30pm; 📶; ⓤStephansplatz) Vienna would simply be at a loss without Figlmüller. This famous *Beisl* has a rural decor and some of the biggest (on average 30cm in diameter) and best schnitzels in the business. Wine is from the owner's vineyard, but no beer is served. Its popularity has spawned a second location nearby on **Bäckerstrasse** (Map p244; ☎01-512 17 60; www.figlmueller.at; 01, Bäckerstrasse 6; mains €9.50-22.50; ⏲11.30am-11.30pm; ⓤStephansplatz) with a wider menu (and drinks list).

ZUM SCHWARZEN KAMEEL MODERN EUROPEAN, DELI €€

Map p244 (☎01-533 81 25 11; www.kameel.at; 01, Bognergasse 5; mains €22.50-39.50, 5-course dinner menu €68, with wines €93; ⏲restaurant noon-11pm Mon-Sat, deli 9am-6pm Mon-Sat, patisserie 10am-6pm Mon-Sat; 📶; ⓤStephansplatz, Herrengasse) Zum Schwarzen Kameel is an eclectic deli/patisserie/highbrow-wine-bar hybrid but is above all worth a visit for the inventive cuisine in its wood-panelled restaurant upstairs: grilled lobster with truffled pea ragout, Styrian chicken with saffron risotto, or steak stuffed with blue cheese and grappa-soaked raisins served with roast artichokes. Downstairs, the patisserie serves open-faced sandwiches and steaming soups (€1.30 to €6). Truffle salamis, quail eggs, smoked salmon and cheeses are sold at the deli. Or just drop by for an *Achterl* (0.125L) of wine from among its 800-strong selection.

XPEDIT ITALIAN €€

Map p244 (☎01-512 33 13 23; www.xpedit.at; 01, Wiesingerstrasse 6; pasta €11-13.50, mains €17.50-19.50; ⏲noon-2.30pm & 6-10pm Mon-Fri, 6-10pm Sat; 🚋2) Styled like a Ligurian *osteria*, Xpedit's warehouse decor gives it a contemporary, informal atmosphere. The small menu changes daily in keeping with the seasons but might include a feisty, anchovy-rich penne puttanesca, gnocchi Gorgonzola, or veal steak on polenta with truffle-cream sauce. Reservations are recommended but it's also possible to get dishes to take away. Tram to Julius-Raab-Platz.

BEIM CZAAK BISTRO €€

Map p244 (☎01-513 72 15; www.czaak.com; 01, Postgasse 15; mains €11-18.90; ⏲11am-midnight Mon-Sat; 🚋1, 2, ⓤSchwedenplatz) In business since 1926, Beim Czaak retains a genuine and relatively simple interior, entered via the restaurant's tree-shaded, ivy-clad courtyard garden. Classic Viennese meat dishes dominate the menu, with long-time favourites including schnitzels (gluten-free variations available), *Tafelspitz* (boiled prime beef), beef goulash with bacon and shredded dumplings, and fried Styrian chicken. Midweek lunch menus cost €9.90.

★TIAN VEGETARIAN €€€

Map p244 (☎01-890 46 65-2; www.taste-tian.com; 01, Himmelpfortgasse 23; 2-/3-course lunch menus €29/34, 4-/6-course dinner menus €93/108; ⊙noon-2pm & 5.45-9pm Tue-Sat; ; 2, UStephansplatz) Christian Holper's chandelier-lit, lounge-style restaurant takes vegetarian cuisine to Michelin-starred heights (tomato and white-raspberry soup, *porcini* risotto with spruce shoots, green-almond quinoa with broccoli), with regionally sourced produce – including from Tian's own garden. Wine-paired dinner menus cost €138/173 for four/six courses; on a languid afternoon, try the three-course lunch menu with free-flowing champagne or wine (€99). Tram to Weihburggasse.

★PLACHUTTA AUSTRIAN €€€

Map p244 (☎01-512 15 77; www.plachutta.at; 01, Wollzeile 38; mains €16.50-27.20; ⊙11.30am-11.15pm; UStubentor) If you're keen to taste *Tafelspitz,* you can't beat this specialist wood-panelled, white-tableclothed restaurant. It serves no fewer than 13 varieties from different cuts of Austrian-reared beef, such as *Mageres Meisel* (lean, juicy shoulder meat), *Beinfleisch* (larded rib meat) and *Lueger Topf* (shoulder meat with beef tongue and calf's head). Save room for the Austrian cheese plate.

Its marquee-like outdoor terrace is heated in chilly weather.

ARTNER STEAK €€€

Map p244 (☎01-503 50 34; www.artner.co.at; 01, Franziskanerplatz 5; mains €16-30; ⊙noon-11pm Mon-Sat; ; UStephansplatz) A double-height wall of wine bottles (including vintages from the owners' vineyard) links Artner's ground-floor wood-panelled dining room and romantic vaulted brick cellar. Locally reared, dry-aged Austrian steaks are its signature; there are also two succulent burgers, along with fish dishes. Tables set up on the square opposite in the shadow of the Renaissance-style Franziskanerkirche in summer. Service is outstanding.

LOCAL KNOWLEDGE

VIENNESE HONEY

Some 5000 bee colonies and 600 bee-keepers harvest honey within Vienna's city limits, including on the rooftops of the Rathaus, Staatsoper, Kunsthistorisches Museum, Secession and several hotels. The fruits of their labour are sold at the **Wald & Wiese** (Map p244; www.waldundwiese.at; 01, Wollzeile 19; ⊙9.30am-6.30pm Mon-Fri, 9am-5pm Sat; UStephansplatz) specialist honey boutique, which also sells honey-based beverages including mead, honey-and-whisky liqueur and grappa, along with beeswax candles, hand creams, toothpaste, royal jelly...

During the truffle season, it sells locally harvested truffles and related products (including truffle honey), too.

RESTAURANT BAUER FRENCH €€€

Map p244 (☎01-512 98 71; 01, Sonnenfelsgasse 17; mains €26-35, 5-course menu €85; ⊙6-11pm Mon, noon-3pm & 6-11pm Tue-Fri, closed Sat & Sun; UStephansplatz) Book at least a couple of months in advance and dress the part to dine at white-linen-clothed tables beneath the lavish arched ceilings of this intimate Michelin-starred restaurant, one of Vienna's most exclusive. Chef Walter Bauer's small, seasonal menu is primarily French, with Mediterranean influences; wine pairings are available.

DRINKING & NIGHTLIFE

The historic centre is a hub for everything from cutting-edge cocktail bars and craft-beer bars to relaxed *Vinotheks* (wine bars) and pubs with leafy beer gardens. There are also some lively student haunts, particularly around the *Bermudadreieck* (Bermuda Triangle; p89).

★KRUGER'S AMERICAN BAR BAR

Map p244 (www.krugers.at; 01, Krugerstrasse 5; ⊙6pm-4am Mon-Sat, 7pm-4am Sun; D, 1, 2, 71, UStephansplatz) Retaining some of its original decor from the 1920s and '30s, this dimly lit, wood-panelled American-style bar is a legend in Vienna, furnished with leather

Chesterfield sofas and playing a soundtrack of Frank Sinatra, Dean Martin and the like. The drinks list runs to 71 pages; there's a separate cigar and smoker's lounge. Tram to Kärntner Ring/Oper.

VINOTHEK W-EINKEHR WINE BAR

Map p244 (☎0676 40 82 854; www.w-einkehr.at; 01, Laurenzerberg 1; ⏲3-10pm Tue-Fri, 4-10pm Sat; USchwedenplatz) There are just 15 seats inside this contemporary wine bar and another eight on the summer terrace, so the action often spills onto the pavement (you can also reserve a table). All of the wines here are Austrian, from prestigious viticulture regions including Blaufränkischland and Neusiedler See in Burgenland, and Carnuntum, Wagram and Weinviertel in Lower Austria.

VINOGIN BAR

Map p244 (01, Fleischmarkt 28; ⏲6pm-midnight Mon-Sat; USchwedenplatz) The name says it all: the twin specialities of this new bareboards bar with outsized chalk-scrawled blackboards are wine and gin. Many of the wines are from producers in Vienna's outer districts; there are also Austrian gins as well as boutique international varieties, with over 100 different labels in all. Cash only.

SKY BAR ROOFTOP BAR

Map p244 (www.skybox.at; 01, Kärntner Strasse 19; ⏲10am-2am Mon-Fri, 9.30am-2am Sat, 11am-2am Sun; UStephansplatz) A heart-stopping glass lift/elevator whisks you up to the top floor of the Steffl department store to take in the Innere Stadt's best panoramas from the bar and open-air terrace. One (or more) of its 350 cocktails makes a great accompaniment. Live music plays from 9.30pm Monday to Saturday. During the day it operates as a cafe and restaurant.

FLANAGAN'S IRISH PUB

Map p244 (www.flanagans.at; 01, Schwarzenbergstrasse 1-3; ⏲10am-2am Sun-Thu, to 4am Fri & Sat; 📶; 🚋2, UKarlsplatz) As authentic as it gets: Flanagan's was dismantled brick by brick from its original location in County Cork and rebuilt here in 1996. Soak up hand-pulled pints of Guinness with Irish stew, seafood chowder with soda bread, and fish and chips, as well as traditional Sunday roasts. Its sociable atmosphere peaks when it screens major sporting events. Tram to Schwarzenbergstrasse.

1516 BREWING COMPANY MICROBREWERY, PUB

Map p244 (☎01-961 15 16; www.1516brewingcompany.com; 01, Schwarzenbergstrasse 2; ⏲10am-2am; 🚋2, UKarlsplatz) Copper vats and bare-brick walls create an industrial backdrop at this locally loved venue that brews beers from malted wheat, rye and rice, including unusual varieties, such as Heidi's Blueberry Ale. The awning-shaded terrace gets packed in summer. Arrive early for a good seat when it screens international football (soccer) games. Tram to Schwarzenbergstrasse.

VIS-À-VIS WINE BAR

Map p244 (☎01-512 93 50; www.weibel.at; 01, Wollzeile 5; ⏲4-10.30pm Tue-Fri, 3-10.30pm Sat; UStephansplatz) Tucked down an atmospheric passage, this tiny wine bar only seats 10 people, but it makes up for it with over 350 wines on offer (with a strong emphasis on Austrian drops) and antipasti (including gourmet olives).

KAFFEE ALT WIEN CAFE

Map p244 (☎01-512 52 22; www.kaffeealtwien.at; 01, Bäckerstrasse 9; ⏲10am-2am Sun-Thu, to 3am Fri & Sat; 📶; UStephansplatz) Low-lit and full of character, bohemian Alt Wien is a classic dive attracting students and arty types. It's a one-stop shop for a lowdown on events in the city – every available wall space is plastered with posters advertising shows, concerts and exhibitions. The goulash is legendary and perfectly complemented by dark bread and beer.

VINOTHEKS

The Innere Stadt has some great *Vinotheks* (wine bars) – one of the best is **Enrico Panigl** (Map p244; www.enrico-panigl.at; 01, Schönlaterngasse 11; ⏲6pm-4am Mon-Sat, to 2am Sun; 🚋2, UStephansplatz, Stubentor). Hidden down a narrow passage off Lugeck, this rustic, dark-timber-furnished venue with a vaulted ceiling is one of Vienna's best-kept wine secrets, with 40 rotating Austrian, Italian and Hungarian wines available by the glass and bottle. For a more modern ambience, head for **Wein & Co** (Map p244; www.weinco.at; 01, Jasomirgottstrasse 3-5; ⏲10am-2am Mon-Sat, 3pm-midnight Sun; 📶; UStephansplatz), which is attached to a comprehensive wine shop.

ZWÖLF APOSTELKELLER PUB

Map p244 (Twelve Apostle Cellar; ☎01-512 67 77; www.zwoelf-apostelkeller.at; 01, Sonnenfelsgasse 3; ⏰11am-midnight; Ⓤ Stephansplatz) Occupying a vast, dimly lit tri-level cellar, historic Zwölf Apostelkeller (Twelve Apostle Cellar) has a spirited atmosphere bolstered by traditional *Heuriger* (wine tavern) ballads from 7pm daily. In addition to outstanding local wines there's also a good choice of schnapps and beer.

KLEINES CAFÉ CAFE

Map p244 (01, Franziskanerplatz 3; ⏰10am-2am Mon-Sat, 1pm-2am Sun; 🚊2, Ⓤ Stubentor) Designed by architect Hermann Czech in the 1970s, Kleines Café has a bohemian atmosphere reminiscent of Vienna's heady *Jugendstil* days. It's tiny inside, but the wonderful summer outdoor seating on a cobbled square overlooking the baroque Franziskanerkirche is among the best in the Innere Stadt. Tram to Weihburggasse.

HAAS & HAAS TEAHOUSE

Map p244 (☎01-512 26 66; www.haas-haas.at; 01, Stephansplatz 4; ⏰9am-6.30pm Mon-Fri, to 6pm Sat; Ⓤ Stephansplatz) The fragrance of teas from around the world greets you on entry to Haas & Hass, Vienna's premiere tearoom, with an extensive selection including Assam, Ceylon, Darjeeling, green, herbal and aromatic, as well as coffee. The rear garden is a shaded retreat from inclement weather, while the front parlour has comfy cushioned booths and striking views of Stephansdom.

DIGLAS CAFE

Map p244 (☎01-512 57 65; www.diglas.at; 01, Wollzeile 10; ⏰8am-10.30pm; Ⓤ Stephansplatz) Classic coffee house Diglas has swanky red-velvet booths, an extensive range of coffee and an elegant, venerable clientele. The reputation of Diglas' cakes precedes it, and the *Apfelstrudel* is unrivalled, as are the seasonal apricot or plum dumplings. Live piano music fills the room from 7pm to 10pm Thursday to Saturday.

CAFÉ PRÜCKEL COFFEE

Map p244 (www.prueckel.at; 01, Stubenring 24; ⏰8.30am-10pm; 📶; 🚊2, Ⓤ Stubentor) Unlike other Viennese cafes with sumptuous interiors, Prückel features an intact 1950s design. Intimate booths, strong coffee, diet-destroying cakes and Prückel's speciality – its crispy, flaky apple strudel served with cream – are all big drawcards. Live piano music plays from 7pm to 10pm on Mondays, Wednesdays and Fridays.

BERMUDA TRIANGLE & BEYOND

The hub of the bars in the area Viennese locals call the *Bermudadreieck* (Bermuda Triangle) is between Schwedenplatz, Morzinplatz and the corner of Seitenstettengasse and Judengasse. Most places here draw an early-20s crowd.

WHY NOT? GAY

Map p244 (www.why-not.at; 01, Tiefer Graben 22; cover after midnight €7; ⏰10pm-4am Fri & Sat; 📶; 🚊1, Ⓤ Herrengasse) Why Not? is one of the few Viennese clubs focusing solely on the gay scene. The small club quickly fills up with mainly young guys; there are three bars and a dance floor. Tram to Salztorbrücke.

☆ ENTERTAINMENT

METRO KINOKULTURHAUS CINEMA

Map p244 (☎01-512 18 03; www.filmarchiv.at; 01, Johannesgasse 4; film tickets adult/child €8.50/7; ⏰2-9pm Mon-Fri, 11am-9pm Sat & Sun; Ⓤ Stephansplatz) Part of the Austrian Film Archive, the Metro Kinokulturhaus opened in 2015 and is now a showcase for exhibitions (most are free, though some incur an admission charge). The restored cinema here was first converted for screenings in 1924 and retains its wood panelling and red-velvet interior; it shows historic and art-house Austrian films (in German).

JAZZLAND LIVE MUSIC

Map p244 (☎01-533 25 75; www.jazzland.at; 01, Franz-Josefs-Kai 29; cover €11-20; ⏰7pm-2am Mon-Sat mid-Aug–mid-Jul, live music from 9pm; 🚊1, 2, Ⓤ Schwedenplatz) Buried in a former wine cellar beneath Ruprechtskirche, Jazzland is Vienna's oldest jazz club, dating back nearly 50 years. The music covers the whole jazz spectrum, and features both local and international acts. Past performers have included Ray Brown, Teddy Wilson, Big Joe Williams and Max Kaminsky.

GARTENBAUKINO CINEMA

Map p244 (☎01-512 23 54; www.gartenbaukino.at; 01, Parkring 12; tickets €7.50-13.50; 🚋2, Ⓤ Stubentor, Stadtpark) The interior of the Gartenbaukino has survived since the 1960s. The cinema seats a whopping 736 people, and is packed during Viennale Film Festival (p46) screenings. Its regular screening schedule is filled with art-house films, often in their original language (including English) with German subtitles.

KAMMEROPER THEATRE

Map p244 (☎Wien Ticket 01-588 85; www.theater-wien.at; 01, Fleischmarkt 24; tickets €6-156; 🚋1, 2, Ⓤ Schwedenplatz) The Kammeroper ranks as Vienna's third opera house after the Staatsoper (p103) and Volksoper (p137), and the small venue is perfect for unusual and quirky opera productions. In summer the entire company is transported to the Schlosstheater Schönbrunn to continue performances in more opulent surroundings.

PORGY & BESS JAZZ

Map p244 (☎01-512 88 11; www.porgy.at; 01, Riemergasse 11; ⏰performances from 9pm; 🚋2, Ⓤ Stubentor) The program here features top-range modern jazz acts from around the globe. The dimly lit interior has a capacity of 350, and the vibe is velvety and very grown-up. Book well ahead.

SHOPPING

RUNWAY FASHION & ACCESSORIES

Map p244 (www.runwayvienna.at; 01, Goldschmiedgasse 10; ⏰11am-6.30pm Tue-Fri, to 6pm Sat; Ⓤ Stephansplatz) Runway is a launching pad for up-and-coming Austrian fashion designers, whose creations sit alongside those of their established compatriots. Set over two floors, the chandelier-lit space showcases the direction of womenswear in Vienna and Austria today through its rotating racks of clothes and accessories, as well as through its regular free catwalk shows (check the online calendar for dates).

SCHAU SCHAU FASHION & ACCESSORIES

Map p244 (☎01-533 45 84; www.schau-schau.at; 01, Rotenturmstrasse 11; ⏰10am-6pm Mon-Sat; Ⓤ Stephansplatz) Austrian, German and international celebrities – including Beyoncé – head to this one-off boutique for stunning sunglasses and prescription eyewear. It was founded in the late '70s by optometrist Peter Kozich, who handcrafts frames from natural materials including buffalo horn, gold, platinum and various woods in his 13th-century cottage in Lower Austria. Designs can be made to order.

KISS KISS BANG BANG FASHION & ACCESSORIES

Map p244 (www.kkbb.rocks; 01, Johannesgasse 17; ⏰10am-7pm Mon-Fri, to 6pm Sat; 🚋2, 71, Ⓤ Stadtpark) Trends move at lightning speed at this flagship of plugged-in Austrian boutique KKBB, which sources up-to-the-minute men's, women's and children's fashions from Europe's fashion capitals every three to five weeks. Tram to Schwarzenbergplatz.

DAS NEUE SCHWARZ VINTAGE

Map p244 (www.dasneueschwarz.de; 01, Landskrongasse 1; ⏰10.30am-6.30pm Mon-Sat; Ⓤ Stephansplatz) 'The New Black' stocks a changing array of vintage clothes, shoes and accessories from some of the fashion world's biggest names: Jean Paul Gaultier, Vivienne Westwood, Azzedine Alaïa, Balenciaga, Stella McCartney, Versace, Chloé, Viktor & Rolf, Margiela, Pucci, Miu Miu and Isabel Marant. It has a sister store in Berlin.

SO AUSTRIA HOMEWARES, FASHION & ACCESSORIES

Map p244 (www.so-austria.at; 01, Lugeck 3a; ⏰10am-7pm Mon-Fri, to 6pm Sat; Ⓤ Stephansplatz) Founded by two South Tyroleans with a passion for Austrian home and fashion accessories, this high-quality shop only sells goods handcrafted in Austria: hand towels, tea towels, bags, shoes, jewellery, sculptures, hats, scarves and clothing.

HERZILEIN CHILDREN'S CLOTHING

Map p244 (www.herzilein-wien.at; 01, Wollzeile 17; ⏰10am-7pm Mon-Fri, to 6pm Sat; Ⓤ Stubentor) Viennese-designed and -made clothes for babies and children aged 0 to 12 years here are both functional and playful, such as stripey tops with animal motifs (monkeys, elephants etc). It also makes kids' swimwear, jackets, gloves, scarves and hand-stitched soft toys. Directly across the street is Herzilein's stationery and gift shop; look for the red-and-pink polka dot facades.

ATELIER NASKE JEWELLERY

Map p244 (☎01-316 39 31; www.goldkunst.at; 01, Wipplingerstrasse 7; ⏰3.30-6.30pm Mon &

Tue, 2.30-6.30pm Wed & Thu, by appt Fri & Sat; ⓊStephansplatz) Delicate butterfly pendants, perfectly sculpted rings, cuff links embedded with precious stones and more are all painstakingly hand-tapped by designer Elke Naske. If you commission her for a piece, Naske will make an initial model in silver (as it's less expensive) to make sure it fits correctly.

UNGER UND KLEIN WINE

Map p244 (www.ungerundklein.at; 01, Gölsdorfgasse 2; ⏲3pm-midnight Mon-Fri, 5pm-midnight Sat; 🚊1, ⓊSchwedenplatz) Unger und Klein's small but knowledgeable wine collection spans the globe, but the majority of its labels come from Europe, with the best of Austrian wines – from expensive boutique varieties to bargain-bin bottles. It doubles as a small, laid-back wine bar, with a good selection of wines by the glass; Friday and Saturday evenings get crowded. Tram to Salztorbrücke.

MANNER FOOD

Map p244 (www.manner.com; 01, Stephansplatz 7; ⏲10am-9pm; ⓊStephansplatz) Vienna's favourite sweet since 1898, *Manner* – a glorious concoction of wafers and hazelnut cream – has its own concept store decked out in its signature peachy-pink. Buy the biscuit in every imaginable variety and packaging combination.

ALTMANN & KÜHNE CHOCOLATE

Map p244 (www.altmann-kuehne.at; 01, Graben 30; ⏲9am-6.30pm Mon-Fri, 10am-5pm Sat; ⓊStephansplatz) Behind a modernist facade designed by Josef Hoffmann (a founding member of the visual arts collective Wiener Werkstätte), this small, charming shop is the flagship of century-old chocolatier Altmann & Kühne, which produces handmade chocolates and sweets. Hoffmann also designed the interior as well as the iconic packaging: miniature hat boxes, luggage trunks, glass cabinets, bookshelves and even baroque buildings.

ART UP FASHION & ACCESSORIES

Map p244 (www.artup.at; 01, Bauernmarkt 8; ⏲11am-6.30pm Mon-Fri, to 5pm Sat; ⓊStephansplatz) A key player in Vienna's contemporary art and design scene, Art Up provides space for young designers to get a foothold in the fashion world. The model makes for an eclectic collection – elegant fashion pieces sit alongside quirky accessories (such as Astroturf ties and handbags) as well as ceramics and sculptures.

LOCAL KNOWLEDGE

LOCAL ROSES

At **Wiener Rosenmanufaktur** (Map p244; www.wienerrosenmanufaktur.at; 01, Schönlaterngasse 7; ⏲3-7pm Mon-Fri, 11am-5pm Sat Jul & Aug, 1-6.30pm Mon-Fri, 11am-6.30pm Sat, 2-5pm Sun Sep-Jun; ⓊSchwedenplatz), roses grown by Ingrid Maria Heldstab in her garden in Vienna's 23rd district are used in an incredible array of products, from jams (including spicy versions with ginger), jellies and liqueurs – which you can taste in store – to soaps, aromatic oils and other cosmetics. The tiny shop occupies one of Vienna's oldest buildings, the Basiliskenhaus, which dates from 1212.

WOKA HOMEWARES

Map p244 (www.woka.at; 01, Singerstrasse 16; ⏲10am-6pm Mon-Fri, to 5pm Sat; ⓊStephansplatz) Get a feel for the spectacular Wiener Werkstätte aesthetic and Bauhaus, art deco and Secessionist design, with Woka's reproductions of lamps designed by Adolf Loos, Kolo Moser and Josef Hoffmann, among others.

SPORTS & ACTIVITIES

BADESCHIFF SWIMMING

Map p244 (www.badeschiff.at; 01, Danube Canal; adult/child €5/2.50; ⏲8am-10pm May-Sep, bar 10am-1am year-round, kitchen 10am-10pm year-round; 🚊1, ⓊSchwedenplatz) Swim on (not in!) the Danube. Floating on the bank of the Danube, between Schwedenplatz and Urania, this 28m-long lap pool has multiple decks with umbrella-shaded sun loungers and an open-air football pitch on the platform suspended above. It doubles as a bar at night; in winter the pool closes and the ship is a bar and restaurant only.

The hold of the ship contains a bowling alley and dance floor where DJs spin regularly. Tram to Julius-Raab-Platz.

Karlsplatz & Around Naschmarkt

Neighbourhood Top Five

❶ **Karlskirche** (p94) Riding the lift (elevator) up to this mesmerising church's elliptical copper dome for a close-up view of the incredible frescoes by Johann Michael Rottmayr.

❷ **Secession** (p97) Contemplating the sensuous shapes, gold mosaics and mythological symbolism of Klimt's *Beethoven Frieze* at the 1897-designed exhibition centre of the Vienna Secession movement artists.

❸ **Naschmarkt** (p96) Breathing in the heady aromas of spices, olives, oils and vinegars, cheeses, hams, sausages and much more while snacking your way from stall to delectable stall.

❹ **Akademie der Bildenden Künste** (p96) Viewing Bosch's impressive and gruesome *Triptych of the Last Judgment* altarpiece.

❺ **Staatsoper** (p95) Reliving operatic highs with a guided tour of this resplendent gold-and-crystal-adorned opera house.

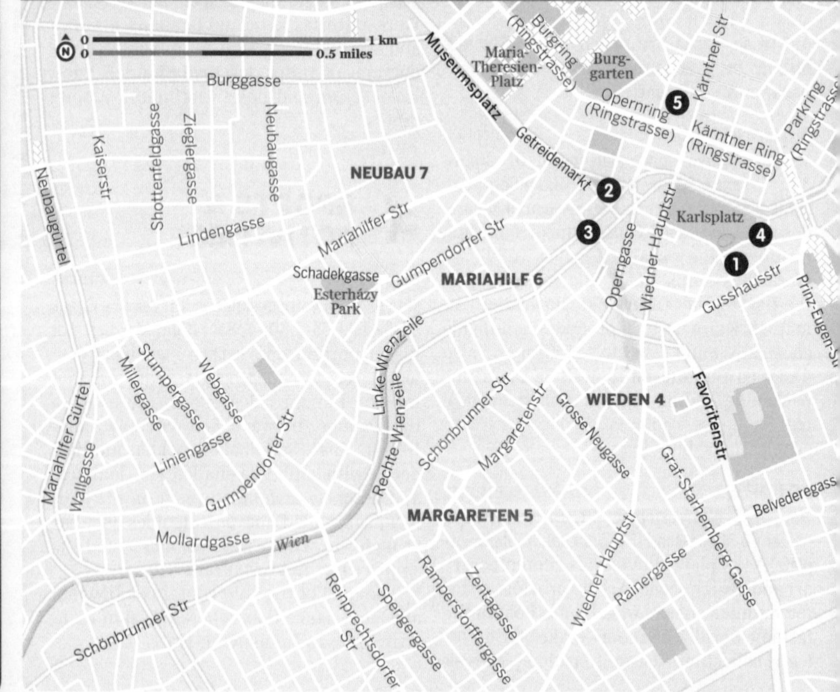

For more detail of this area see Map p248

Explore Karlsplatz & Around Naschmarkt

Spreading south of the Opernring is Vienna's cultured 4th district, Wieden. Here days can be spent gazing upon the baroque frescoes that dance across the Karlskirche, Otto Wagner's art nouveau buildings and Klimt's sensual friezes. Nights lift the curtain on high-calibre opera and classical music in some of the world's finest concert halls. Wander west and within minutes you swing from gilded opulence to the multilingual buzz, street-food sizzle and market-stall banter of the Naschmarkt. Amble south of here to the easygoing Freihausviertel and Vienna suddenly shrinks to village scale, with arty cafes, ateliers and food shops run by folk with genuine passion.

North of Wieden is 6th-district Mariahilf. Give the high-street throngs on Mariahilfer Strasse the slip and you soon find yourself in quintessentially Viennese backstreets, home to speciality shops and old-school *Beisln* (bistro pubs). On the cutting edge of the city's nightlife and design scene is Gumpendorfer Strasse.

Wedged between Wieden and Mariahilf in the 5th district is Margareten, with few heavyweight sights but strong local flavour, particularly around the increasingly fashionable Margaretenplatz.

Local Life

- **Shopping Life** Follow the hungry Viennese to the Naschmarkt (p96) for a world of street food, and scout out delis, design stores and one-of-a-kind boutiques in the artsy **Freihausviertel** and around **Margaretenplatz**.
- **Cafe Life** Great cafes here range from boho Café Jelinek (p101) to starkly contemporary Café Drechsler (p102).
- **Nightlife** Hang out with a young and up-for-it crowd on Gumpendorfer Strasse, crammed with bars, cafes and lounge-style restaurants, or find a more laid-back scene around Schleifmühlgasse.

Getting There & Away

- **U-Bahn** Karlsplatz is well connected to all corners of Vienna, served by the U-Bahn lines U1, U2 and U4. The U4 line to Kettenbrückengasse is handy for Naschmarkt and the Freihausviertel, while the U3 line (Zieglergasse, Neubaugasse etc) is useful for reaching Mariahilfer Strasse. Pilgramgasse (U4) is the most central stop for Margareten, and Taubstummengasse (U1) for Wieden.
- **Tram** Key tram routes include Nos 1 and 62, which stop at Karlsplatz and pass through Wieden.

Lonely Planet's Top Tip

It's a pleasure simply to wander the backstreets of the Freihausviertel, just south of Naschmarkt. One of the neighbourhood's most elegant streets is Mühlgasse, lined with late-19th-century houses with Juliet balconies and ornate doors in the *Jugendstil* (Art Nouveau) style. Numbers 26 and 28 are fine examples.

Best Places to Eat

- Naschmarkt (p96)
- Said the Butcher to the Cow (p98)
- Eis Greissler (p98)
- Vollpension (p98)
- El Burro (p98)

For reviews, see p98.

Best Places to Drink

- Café Sperl (p101)
- Rafael's Vinothek (p99)
- Café Rüdigerhof (p101)
- Juice Deli (p101)

For reviews, see p101.

Best Places to Shop

- Beer Lovers (p105)
- Gegenbauer (p99)
- Flohmarkt (p99)
- Käseland (p99)
- Blühendes Konfekt (p105)

For reviews, see p103.

TOP SIGHT
KARLSKIRCHE

Rising imperiously above Resselpark is Vienna's baroque magnum opus: the Karlskirche. Crowned by a 72m-high copper dome, the church was built between 1716 and 1739 as thanks for deliverance from the 1713 plague. The edifice bears the hallmark of prolific Austrian architect Johann Bernhard Fischer von Erlach, while the interior swirls with the vivid colours of Johann Michael Rottmayr's frescoes.

In the flower-strewn **Resselpark**, a pond centred on a **Henry Moore sculpture** reflects the splendour of the church like a celestial mirror. Your gaze is drawn to the neoclassical portico, the spiralling pillars, which are modelled on Trajan's Column in Rome and embellished with scenes from the life of St Charles Borromeo, as well as cross-bearing angels from the Old and New Testaments intricately carved from white marble. The pediment reliefs depict the suffering of Vienna's plague victims.

Inside, a lift (elevator) soars up into the elliptical cupola for a close-up of Johann Michael Rottmayr's **frescoes** of the glorification of St Charles Borromeo. Look for tongue-in-cheek Counter Reformation details, such as angels setting fire to Martin Luther's German bible. The **high altar** panel, which shows the ascension of St Charles Borromeo, is a riot of golden sunrays and stucco cherubs.

DON'T MISS

- Cupola frescoes
- High altar panel
- Facade from Resselpark

PRACTICALITIES

- St Charles Church
- Map p248, H3
- www.karlskirche.at
- 04, Karlsplatz
- adult/child €8/free
- 9am-6pm Mon-Sat, noon-7pm Sun
- U Karlsplatz

TOP SIGHT
STAATSOPER

Few concert halls can hold a candle to the neo-Renaissance Staatsoper, Vienna's foremost opera and ballet venue. Even if you can't snag performance tickets, you can get a taste of the architectural brilliance and musical genius that have shaped this cultural bastion on a guided tour.

Built between 1861 and 1869 by August Siccardsburg and Eduard van der Nüll, the Staatsoper initially revolted the Viennese public and Habsburg royalty and quickly earned the nickname 'stone turtle'. Despite the frosty reception, it went on to house some of the most iconic directors in history, including Gustav Mahler, Richard Strauss and Herbert von Karajan.

Guided tours take in highlights such as the **foyer**, graced with busts of Beethoven, Schubert and Haydn and frescoes of celebrated operas, and the **main staircase**, watched over by marble allegorical statues embodying the liberal arts. The **Tea Salon** dazzles in 22-carat gold leaf, the **Schwind Foyer** captivates with 16 opera-themed oil paintings by Austrian artist Moritz von Schwind, while the **Gustav Mahler Hall** is hung with tapestries inspired by Mozart's *The Magic Flute*. You'll also get a behind-the-scenes look at the **stage**, which raises the curtain on over 300 performances each year.

DON'T MISS

- Foyer
- Tea Salon
- Gustav Mahler Hall

PRACTICALITIES

- Map p248, G1
- www.wiener-staatsoper.at
- 01, Opernring 2
- D, 1, 2, 71 Kärntner Ring/Oper, U Karlsplatz

SIGHTS

Vienna's history museum, the Wien Museum, is due to reopen in 2019 following a major expansion. Visit www.wienmuseum.at for updates or check with Tourist Info Wien (p224).

KARLSKIRCHE — CHURCH

See p94.

STAATSOPER — NOTABLE BUILDING

See p95.

NASCHMARKT — MARKET

Map p248 (www.wienernaschmarkt.eu; 06, Linke & Rechte Wienzeile; ⏲6am-7.30pm Mon-Fri, to 6pm Sat; ⓤKettenbrückengasse) Vienna's famous market and eating strip (p99) began life as a farmers market in the 18th century, when the fruit market on Freyung was moved here. Interestingly, a law passed in 1793 said that fruit and vegetables arriving in town by cart had to be sold on Naschmarkt, while anything brought in by boat could be sold from the decks.

The fruits of the Orient poured in, the predecessors of the modern-day sausage stand were erected and sections were set aside for coal, wood and farming tools and machines. Officially, it became known as Naschmarkt ('munch market') in 1905, a few years after Otto Wagner bedded the Wien River down in its open-topped stone and concrete sarcophagus. This Otto Wagnerian horror was a blessing for Naschmarkt, because it created space to expand. A close shave came in 1965 when there were plans to tear it down – it was saved, and today the Naschmarkt is not only the place to shop for food but has an antique market (p99) each Saturday.

AKADEMIE DER BILDENDEN KÜNSTE — MUSEUM

Map p248 (Academy of Fine Arts; www.akbild.ac.at; 01, Schillerplatz 3; adult/child €8/free; ⏲10am-6pm Tue-Sun; 🚋D, 1, 2 Kärntner Ring/Oper, ⓤMuseumsquartier, Karlsplatz) Founded in 1692, the Akademie der Bildenden Künste is an often underrated art space. Its gallery concentrates on the classic Flemish, Dutch and German painters, and includes important figures such as Hieronymus Bosch, Rembrandt, Van Dyck, Rubens, Titian, Francesco Guardi and Cranach the Elder, to mention a handful. Hour-long tours (€3, in German only) take place at 10.30am every Sunday. Audio guides cost €2. The supreme highlight is Bosch's impressive and gruesome *Triptych of the Last Judgment* altarpiece (1504–08).

It depicts the banishment of Adam and Eve on the left panel and the horror of Hell in the middle and right panels. The building itself has an attractive facade and was designed by Theophil Hansen (1813–91), of Parlament fame. It still operates as an art school and is famous for turning down Adolf Hitler twice and accepting Egon Schiele (though the latter was happy to leave as quickly as possible). Directly in front of the academy is a **statue of Friedrich Schiller**, the 18th-century German playwright.

HAUS DES MEERES — MUSEUM

Map p248 (House of the Sea; www.haus-des-meeres.at; 06, Fritz-Grünbaum-Platz 1; museum adult/child €16.70/7.60, viewing platform €5; ⏲9am-6pm Fri-Wed, to 9pm Thu; ⓤNeubaugasse) The 'House of the Sea' offers an interesting glimpse into the world of giant fish, reptiles and creepy-crawlies. Aim to visit during feeding time: sharks are fed at 10.30am Monday, 3pm Wednesday and 3.30pm Fridays, while a staff member hops into the shark tank at 6pm Thursday. The piranhas go into a frenzy at 3pm Tuesday, as do reptiles at 7pm Thursday and 10am Sunday. A 192-step exterior staircase leads to the 9th-floor viewing platform.

Its resident freshwater crocodile is fed on 9.30am Saturday. There's a glass tropical house filled with lithe monkeys and a small rain forest with free-flying birds. It occupies the inside of a *Flakturm* (Nazi-built anti-aircraft gun blockhouse tower), giving you a chance to see the interior of one of these monoliths.

HAYDNHAUS — MUSEUM

Map p248 (www.wienmuseum.at; 06, Haydngasse 19; adult/child €5/free; ⏲10am-1pm & 2-6pm Tue-Sun; ⓤZieglergasse) Haydn lived in Vienna during the heady times of Napoleon's occupation, and this exhibition at his last residence focuses on Vienna as well as London during the late 18th and early 19th centuries. An Austrian composer prominent in the classical period, he is most celebrated for his 104 symphonies and 68 string quartets. The small garden here is modelled on the original. Audio guides cost €4.

THIRD MAN PRIVATE COLLECTION — MUSEUM

Map p248 (www.3mpc.net; 04, Pressgasse 25; adult/child €8/4.50, guided tour incl admission €10; ⏲2-6pm Sat, guided tours 2pm Wed;

(U Kettenbrückengasse) Fans of the quintessential film about Vienna from 1948 (voted best British film of the 20th century by the British Film Institute) will enjoy the posters, *The Third Man* paraphernalia and the other 3000-plus objects on show. Stills illustrate the work of Australian-born cinematographer Robert Krasker, who received an Oscar for this film. The museum covers aspects of Vienna before and after 'Harry Lime Time' as well as the film itself. Guided 75-minute tours take place in English. Cash only.

KUNSTHALLE PROJECT SPACE — GALLERY

Map p248 (www.kunsthallewien.at; 04, Treitlstrasse 2; ⏲11am-7pm Fri-Wed, to 9pm Thu; U Karlsplatz) FREE Once the Kunsthalle took up its new residence in the MuseumsQuartier, this glass cube was built on its former site. Its doors were thrown open in 2001 to temporary exhibitions of up-and-coming artists. The website tells you what's on (and any variation in times).

SCHUBERT STERBEWOHNUNG — MUSEUM

Map p248 (www.wienmuseum.at; 04, Kettenbrückengasse 6; adult/child €5/free; ⏲10am-1pm & 2-6pm Wed & Thu; U Kettenbrückengasse) Here, in his brother's apartment, Franz Schubert spent his dying days (40 to be precise) in 1828. While dying of either typhoid fever or syphilis he continued to compose, scribbling out a string of piano sonatas and his last work, *Der Hirt auf dem Felsen* (The Shepherd on the Rock). The apartment (Schubert's Death Apartment) is fairly bereft of personal effects but does document these final days with some interesting Schubi knick-knacks and sounds.

STADTBAHN PAVILLONS — NOTABLE BUILDING

Map p248 (www.wienmuseum.at; 04, Karlsplatz; adult/child €5/free; ⏲10am-6pm Tue-Sun Apr-Oct; U Karlsplatz) Peeking above the Resselpark at Karlsplatz are two of Otto Wagner's finest designs, the Stadtbahn Pavillons. Built in 1898 at a time when Wagner was assembling Vienna's first public transport system (1893–1902), the pavilions are gorgeous examples of *Jugendstil,* with floral motifs and gold trim on a structure of steel and marble. The west pavilion holds an exhibit on Wagner's most famous *Jugendstil* works, the Kirche am Steinhof and Postsparkasse. The eastern pavilion is home to Club U (p102). In 1977, the pavilions were dismantled to make room for the U-Bahn to run beneath them and were rebuilt 1.5m higher.

TOP SIGHT SECESSION

In 1897, 19 progressive artists turned from the mainstream Künstlerhaus artistic establishment to form the Vienna Secession. Among their number were Gustav Klimt, Josef Hoffman, Kolo Moser and Joseph M Olbrich. Olbrich designed their new exhibition centre, combining sparse functionality with stylistic motifs. The building's most striking feature is a delicate golden dome of intertwined laurel leaves that deserves better than the description 'golden cabbage' accorded it by some Viennese.

The 14th exhibition (1902) held here featured the *Beethoven Frieze,* by Klimt, based on Richard Wagner's interpretation of Beethoven's ninth symphony. This 34m-long work was intended as a temporary display, little more than an elaborate poster for the main exhibit, Max Klinger's *Beethoven* monument. Now the star exhibit, it has occupied the basement since 1983.

Inspired by Greek mythology, the frieze is bewitching. The yearning for happiness finds expression in ethereal female figures floating across the walls, a choir of rapturous, flower-bearing angels, and the arts personified as curvaceous, gold-haired nudes who appear to grow like trees. These are juxtaposed by the hostile forces, whose serpent-haired gorgons and beastly portrayals of sickness, madness and death caused outrage in 1902.

DON'T MISS

- *Beethoven Frieze*
- The facade
- Rotating exhibitions of contemporary art

PRACTICALITIES

- Map p248, F2
- www.secession.at
- 01, Friedrichstrasse 12
- adult/child €9/5.50
- ⏲10am-6pm Tue-Sun
- U Karlsplatz

EATING

★VOLLPENSION CAFE €

Map p248 (www.vollpension.wien; 04, Schleifmühlgasse 16; dishes €2.80-7.90; ⏲9am-10pm Tue-Sat, to 8pm Sun; ✍; 🚊1, 62 Wien Paulanergasse) This white-painted brick space with mismatched vintage furniture, tasselled lampshades and portraits on the walls is run by 15 *omas* (grandmas) and *opas* (grandpas) along with their families, with more than 200 cakes in their collective repertoire. Breakfast, such as avocado and feta on pumpernickel bread, is served until 4pm; lunch dishes include a vegan goulash with potato and tofu. Traditional red-wine organic goulash with bread dumplings and frankfurter sausages with fresh horseradish mustard are among the other specialities in store.

★EIS GREISSLER ICE CREAM €

Map p248 (www.eis-greissler.at; 06, Mariahilfer Strasse 33; 1/2/3/4/5 scoops €1.50/2.80/3.80/4.80/5.30; ⏲11am-10pm; UMuseumsquartier) 🍃 The inevitable queue makes Eis Greissler easy to spot. Locals flock here whatever the weather for ice cream made from organic milk, yoghurt and cream from its own farm in Lower Austria, and vegans are well catered for with soy and oat milk varieties. All-natural flavours vary seasonally but might include cinnamon, pear, strawberry, raspberry, chocolate, hazelnut or butter caramel.

EL BURRO STREET FOOD €

Map p248 (www.elburro.at; 04, Margaretenstrasse 9; dishes €7.20-9.60; ⏲11.30am-10pm Mon-Fri, 1-10pm Sat & Sun; 🚊1, 62 Wien Paulanergasse, UTaubstummengasse) At this hip Mexican street-food cantina, first choose your base (burritos, tacos, quesadillas and tostada tortilla bowls), then fillings (beef brisket, pulled pork, sweet potato and beets, octopus ceviche) and toppings (tomato salsa, guacamole, corn, spiced mango, sour cream), plus drinks (craft beers, cocktails, homemade lemonades, Austrian wines). There's a handful of tables inside and more on the summer terrace. Otherwise head to a nearby park.

LE BURGER BURGERS €

Map p248 (www.leburger.at; 07, Mariahilfer Strasse 114; burgers €6.50-9.50; ⏲8am-midnight Mon-Thu, 8am-1am Fri, 9am-10pm Sun; 🚊5 Kaiserstrasse/Mariahilfer Strasse, UWestbahnhof) TV crews descended on this 2016 opening, not least for its rainforest-like vertical garden walls and live DJs (Friday and Saturday nights). But the highlights are the build-your-own burgers themselves. Incorporating 100% Austrian beef (veggie versions are available), they're topped with made-in-house sauces such as spicy ketchup, mango chutney, BBQ and truffle mayo. Sides span fries to onion rings and coleslaw.

AROMAT CREPERIE €

Map p248 (☎01-913 24 53; www.arom.at; 04, Margaretenstrasse 52; crêpes €6.90-10.90; ⏲6-10pm Tue-Sun; UKettenbrückengasse) This funky little crêperie has an open kitchen and often caters for those with an intolerance to wheat and gluten. Daily buckwheat-flour *galettes* depend on the day's market produce but might include chilli con carne, bratwurst with sauerkraut, or aubergine and sour cream. The charming surroundings feature simple Formica tables, 1950s fixtures, a blackboard menu, and one huge glass frontage.

DELICIOUS MONSTER FAST FOOD €

Map p248 (☎01-920 44 54; www.deliciousmonster.at; 04, Gusshausstrasse 12; dishes €6-14; ⏲11am-4pm Mon-Fri; UKarlsplatz) There's always a good buzz at this lunchtime snackeria. Art-adorned walls and gold banquettes create a cool backdrop for satisfying homemade burgers (try the Styrian beef with pumpkin chutney), wraps, baguettes and salads. Find it tucked behind the Karlskirche.

★SAID THE BUTCHER TO THE COW BURGERS, STEAK €€

Map p248 (☎01-535 69 69; http://butcher-cow.at; 01, Opernring 11; mains €10.80-31.90; ⏲kitchen 5-11pm Tue-Sat, bar 5pm-1am Tue & Wed, 5pm-2am Thu-Sat; 🚊D, 1, 2, 71 Kärntner Ring/Oper, UKarlsplatz) Not only does this hip hang-out have a brilliant name, it serves knock-out brioche-bun burgers (chicken teriyaki with wasabi mayo; black tiger prawns with bok choy; red wine vinegar-marinated halloumi with mango chutney; black bean and guacamole with boletus mushrooms), chargrilled steaks, and house-speciality cheesecakes. Better yet, it moonlights as a gin bar with 30 varieties and seven different tonics.

UBL AUSTRIAN €€

Map p248 (☎01-587 64 37; 04, Pressgasse 26; mains €8.50-18; ⏲noon-2pm & 6-10pm Wed-Sun; UKettenbrückengasse) The menu at this much-loved *Beisl* is loaded with Viennese classics, such as *Schinkenfleckerl*

LOCAL KNOWLEDGE

VIENNA'S NASCHMARKT

Vienna's aromatic **Naschmarkt** (www.wienernaschmarkt.eu; ⏲6am-7.30pm Mon-Fri, to 6pm Sat; ⓤKettenbrückengasse) unfurls over 500m along Linke Wienzeile between the U4 stops of Kettenbrückengasse and Karlsplatz. The western (Kettengasse) end has all sorts of meats, fruit and vegetables (including exotic varieties), spices, wines, cheeses, olives, Indian and Middle Eastern specialities and fabulous kebab and falafel stands. In all, there are 123 fixed stalls, including a slew of sit-down restaurants. Another 35 places are allocated for temporary stalls such as farmers stands. The market peters out at the eastern end to stalls selling Indian fabrics, jewellery and trinkets. An adjoining **Flohmarkt** (Flea Market; ⏲6.30am-6pm Sat) sets up on Saturdays.

Naschmarkt Deli (Map p248; www.naschmarkt-deli.at; 04, Naschmarkt stand 421-436; dishes €6.50-16.50; ⏲7am-midnight Mon-Sat; ⓤKettenbrückengasse) Among the enticing stands, Naschmarkt Deli has an edge on the others for its delicious snacks. Breakfast (Turkish, English or prosecco) is served until 4pm. Sandwiches, falafel, big baguettes and chunky lentil soups fill out the menu. DJs play from 5.30pm.

Neni (Map p248; ☎01-585 20 20; http://neni.at; 06, Naschmarkt stand 510; breakfasts €6.50-9.50, mains €12.50-16; ⏲8am-10am & noon-10.30pm Mon-Sat; ✎; ⓤKettenbrückengasse) This industro-cool glass cube combines a cafe, a bar and a restaurant. Dishes such as caramelised aubergine with ginger and chilli are served alongside whole fish with preserved lemon and desserts such as Kanafah (pastry filled with ricotta and mascarpone with chopped pistachios and yoghurt ice cream). Tables fill up fast most nights, so reserve ahead. Cash only.

Umar (Map p248; ☎01-587 04 56; www.umarfisch.at; 04, Naschmarkt stand 76; mains €15-35; ⏲11am-11pm Mon-Sat; ⓤKarlsplatz) Umar is one of the best fish restaurants in Vienna, serving fresh seafood imported from the Mediterranean and beyond at its large Naschmarkt stall. Choose between whole fish, mussels in white-wine sauce and giant shrimps fried in herb butter along with good wines from the Wachau. The midweek lunch menu ($14.90) is a bargain.

Urbanek (Map p248; 04, Naschmarkt stand 46; dishes €5-8; ⏲9am-6.30pm Mon-Thu, 8am-6.30pm Fri, 7.30am-4pm Sat; ⓤKarlsplatz) Stepping inside Urbanek is to enter a world of cured meats in all their different varieties – smoked, salted, cooked or raw. The atmosphere is rarefied but relaxed as you enjoy a glass of wine and perhaps delicately cut slices of Mangalitza pig – a breed prized for its delicious ham. The roast beef is organic, and the selection of cheeses outstanding.

Rafael's Vinothek (Map p248; 06, Naschmarkt stand 121; ⏲10am-7.30pm Mon-Fri, to 6pm Sat; ⓤKettenbrückengasse) Over 450 different wines from all over Austria are stocked at this Naschmarkt *Vinothek*. Many are available to drink at its wine-barrel tables by the glass or bottle, accompanied by cheese and charcuterie platters in a chaotically sociable atmosphere – it's a favourite spot for a tipple for stallholders from the entire market.

Gegenbauer (Map p248; www.gegenbauer.at; 06, Naschmarkt stand 111-112; ⏲9am-6pm Mon-Fri, to 5pm Sat; ⓤKarlsplatz) Some of the world's most fêted chefs use the oils and vinegars from this cornerstone of the Naschmarkt. At his Vienna distillery, Erwin Gegenbauer makes over 70 different vinegars from fruits and vegetables such as asparagus, fig, melon, tomato, as well as beer, along with balsamic varieties from grapes (some aged in oak casks) and 20 flavoured oils.

Käseland (Map p248; www.kaeseland.com; 06, Naschmarkt stand 172; ⏲9am-6.30pm Mon-Fri, 8am-5pm Sat; ⓤKarlsplatz, Kettenbrückengasse) Cheese aficionados find it nearly impossible to tear themselves away from this venerable Naschmarkt stand, which has been in this spot for four decades. Over 100 Austrian cheeses (prized Lüneberg, Montafoner Sauerkäse and Tiroler Graukäse included) are piled high alongside hand-picked varieties from Switzerland, Italy and Hungary. Vacuum packing is available.

(oven-baked ham and noodle casserole), *Schweinsbraten* (roast pork) and four types of schnitzel, and is enhanced with seasonal cuisine throughout the year. You could do worse than finish the hefty meal off with a stomach-settling plum schnapps. The tree-shaded garden is wonderful in summer.

SANTOS
MEXICAN €€

Map p248 (01-942 99 02; www.santos-bar.com; 04, Favoritenstrasse 4-6; mains €9-24.90; 11am-midnight Mon-Fri, to 1am Sat; ; UTaubstummengasse) In a triangular-shaped corner room with floor-to-ceiling glass, this glamorous spot sizzles up classics such as pulled pork tacos, chilli con carne, quinoa and vegetable quesadillas, chicken burritos and marinated steak fajitas. Between 11am and 4pm Monday to Friday, lunch mains drop to €8 to €12.80. Its bar mixes Mexican-styled cocktails including an El Diablo (tequila, crème de cassis and lime).

KOJIRO
SUSHI €€

Map p248 (01-586 62 33; 04, Kühnplatz 4; dishes €8-21; 11am-6.15pm Mon-Fri, 10am-2.30pm Sat; UKettenbrückengasse, Karlsplatz) Locals serious about their sushi flock to this tiny nosh spot near the Naschmarkt, which rolls out brilliantly fresh sushi and sashimi.

HAAS BEISL
AUSTRIAN €€

Map p248 (01-586 25 52; www.haasbeisl.at; 05, Margaretenstrasse 74; mains €10-19; 11.30am-10pm Mon-Sat, to 9pm Sun; UPilgramgasse) Warm and woody, this traditional Margareten *Beisl* is absolutely genuine and a great place to enjoy decent food in a very local atmosphere. Classics such as offal, sweetmeats, goulash and dumplings are prepared the way your grandmother might have done them. Two-course midweek lunch menus cost €7.90.

SILBERWIRT
AUSTRIAN €€

Map p248 (01-544 49 07; www.silberwirt.at; 05, Schlossgasse 21; mains €8-16; noon-midnight; ; UPilgramgasse) This atmospheric neo-*Beisl* offers traditional Viennese cuisine, mostly using organic and/or local produce. A meal might begin with Waldviertel sheep's cheese salad with walnuts and poppy seeds, followed by trout with herby potatoes and almond butter, and *Palatschinken* (pancakes) with homemade apricot jam. A dedicated kids' menu appeals to little appetites. In summer, dine in the tree-shaded garden.

STEMAN
AUSTRIAN €€

Map p248 (01-597 85 09; www.steman.at; 06, Otto-Bauer-Gasse 7; mains €6-16.50; 11am-11pm Mon-Fri; UZieglergasse) Run by the same folk as Café Jelinek (p101), Steman serves good honest Austrian food in a nicely restored, high-ceilinged interior, with tables on the pavement in summer. The mood is laid-back, the service friendly and the menu packed with classics such as goulash and *Käsespätzle* (cheese noodles). The €7.10 two-course lunch (with a daily vegetarian option) is a bargain. Cash only.

ZUM ALTEN FASSL
AUSTRIAN €€

Map p248 (01-544 42 98; www.zum-alten-fassl.at; 05, Ziegelofengasse 37; mains €8.90-15.50; 11.30am-3pm & 5pm-midnight Mon-Fri, 5pm-midnight Sat, noon-3pm & 5pm-midnight Sun; UPilgramgasse) With its private garden amid residential houses and polished wooden interior, this well-kept *Beisl* is a great spot to sample the Viennese favourites and regional specialities, such as *Eierschwammerl* (chanterelles) and *Blunzengröstl* (a potato, bacon, onion and blood sausage fry-up). When it's in season, *Zanderfilet* (fillet of zander) is the chef's favourite. Midweek lunch menus cost €6.30 to €7.80. Between 1974 and 1982 the singer Falco lived upstairs in this building – a plaque marks the spot.

MOTTO
FUSION €€

Map p248 (01-587 06 72; http://motto.wien; 05, Schönbrunner Strasse 30; mains €11-30; kitchen 6pm-midnight, bar to 2am Sun-Thu, to 4am Fri & Sat; UPilgramgasse) The darling of Margareten's dining scene is this theatrical lounge-style restaurant with clever backlighting, high banquettes and DJ beats. Asian, Austrian and Mediterranean flavours are all in the mix, with well-executed dishes from Tandoor catfish and calamari with miso sauce to the signature fillet steak with chocolate-chilli sauce. Reservations are recommended. Enter through the chrome door on Rüdigergasse.

TANCREDI
AUSTRIAN €€

Map p248 (01-941 00 48; www.tancredi.at; 04, Grosse Neugasse 5; mains €13.80-28.80; 11.30am-2.30pm Mon, 11.30am-2.30pm & 6-11pm Tue-Fri, 6-11pm Sat; UTaubstummengasse) An extensive range of Austrian wines complements the expertly prepared regional and fish specialities, seasonal fare and organic dishes at this welcoming spot with warm, pastel-yellow walls, stripped-back wooden floors, fittings from yesteryear and an umbrella-shaded garden. On weekdays, lunch menus cost €9.50 to €16.80. The entrance is on Rubengasse.

DRINKING & NIGHTLIFE

★CAFÉ SPERL COFFEE

Map p248 (www.cafesperl.at; 06, Gumpendorfer Strasse 11; 7am-11pm Mon-Sat, 11am-8pm Sun; ; Museumsquartier, Kettenbrückengasse) With its gorgeous *Jugendstil* fittings, grand dimensions, cosy booths and unhurried air, 1880-opened Sperl is one of the finest coffee houses in Vienna. The must-try is *Sperl Torte,* an almond-and-chocolate-cream dream. Grab a slice and a newspaper (over 10 daily in English, French and German), order a coffee (34 kinds), and join the rest of the people-watching patrons. A live pianist plays from 3.30pm to 5.30pm on Sunday.

JUICE DELI JUICE BAR

Map p248 (www.juicedeli.at; 06, Mariahilfer Strasse 45, shop 20, Raimundhof; 9.30am-7pm Mon-Fri, 11am-6pm Sat; Neubaugasse) Tucked in a courtyard reached via a narrow alleyway leading off Mariahilfer Strasse, this one-off locavore spot uses regionally sourced, seasonal organic fruit, vegetables and herbs in its cold-pressed juices and smoothies such as mango and banana with handmade almond milk. It also has detox water varieties (lemongrass and mint; ginseng...). Plastic packaging is shunned in favour of glass bottles. A handful of tables set up on the tiny terrace out the front in warm weather.

CAFÉ RÜDIGERHOF CAFE

Map p248 (05, Hamburgerstrasse 20; 9am-2am; Kettenbrückengasse, Pilgramgasse) Rüdigerhof's facade is a glorious example of *Jugendstil* architecture, and the '50s furniture and fittings inside could be straight out of an *I Love Lucy* set. The atmosphere is homey and familiar and the wraparound garden huge and shaded. Hearty Austrian fare (huge schnitzels, spinach *Spätzle,* goat's cheese strudel) is way above average. On Saturday mornings it fills with Naschmarkt shoppers.

BIER & BIERLI BAR

Map p248 (http://bierundbierli.at; 01, Operngasse 12; 11am-midnight; D, 1, 2, 71 Kärntner Ring/Oper, Karlsplatz) Over 20,000 beer cans from around the world line the walls of this airy, contemporary bar, which also has a growing collection of beer coasters on the ceiling. Five Austrian beers rotate on the taps, with several more available by the bottle. First-rate Austrian food includes *Tafelspitz* (boiled beef), schnitzels, goulash and fried Styrian chicken. Staff are super-friendly.

KAFFEE FABRIK COFFEE

Map p248 (www.kaffeefabrik.at; 04, Favoritenstrasse 4-6; 8am-6pm Mon-Fri, 11am-5pm Sat; Taubstummengasse) Fabrik's owners travel the world to source beans directly from small organic farms and co-ops in Sumatra, India, Ethiopia, Ecuador and Nicaragua, which they roast in Burgenland and brew to perfection at this pint-sized, whitewashed cafe. Keep an eye out around town, including at festivals, for its cherry-red coffee-cart bike.

FELIXX GAY

Map p248 (www.y-not.at; 06, Gumpendorfer Strasse 5; 6pm-2am; Museumsquartier) Chandeliers, mini disco balls, striped wallpaper and leather lounges make this one of Vienna's classiest gay bars. Themed events include Monday's Long & Strong cocktail night, Friday's DJs and Prosecco and Saturday's Love & Happiness with '70s, '80s and '90s music.

CAFÉ JELINEK COFFEE

Map p248 (www.steman.at; 06, Otto-Bauer-Gasse 5; 9am-9pm; Zieglergasse) With none of the polish or airs and graces of some other coffee houses, this shabbily grand cafe is Viennese through and through. The wood-burning stove, picture-plastered walls and faded velvet armchairs draw people from all walks of life with their cocoon-like warmth. Join locals lingering over freshly roasted coffee, cake and the daily newspapers.

BARFLY'S CLUB COCKTAIL BAR

Map p248 (www.castillo.at; 06, Esterhazygasse 33; 8pm-2am Sun-Thu, to 4am Fri & Sat; Neubaugasse, Zieglergasse) This low-lit, sophisticated bar is famous for its 500-strong cocktail list (the menu is over 1cm thick) and intimate ambience, which attracts a regular crowd of journalists and actors. It's decorated with photos of Ernest Hemingway, Fidel Castro, Che Guevara, the Rat Pack and Marilyn Monroe. At around €14 a pop, drinks aren't cheap, but they're among the city's best.

WIEDEN BRÄU MICROBREWERY

Map p248 (www.wieden-braeu.at; 04, Waaggasse 5; ⌚11.30am-midnight Sep-Jun, 4pm-midnight Sat & Sun Jul & Aug; 📶; Ⓤ Taubstummengasse) *Helles, Märzen* and *Radler* beers are brewed year-round at this upbeat microbrewery, and there are a few seasonal choices, including a ginger beer and hemp beer. All are brewed in keeping with the 1516 German Purity Law and are matched with Austrian classics such as schnitzel and goulash. Retreat to the garden in summer.

EBERT'S COCKTAIL BAR COCKTAIL BAR

Map p248 (www.eberts.at; 06, Gumpendorfer Strasse 51; ⌚6pm-2am Tue-Thu, 7pm-4am Fri & Sat; Ⓤ Neubaugasse, Kettenbrückengasse) Expert bartenders shake things up: all the mixologists here double as instructors at the bartending academy next door. The cocktail list is novel-esque, the vibe stylish, modern minimalism, the tunes jazzy to electronic, and on weekends you'll barely squeeze in.

MON AMI BAR

Map p248 (www.monami.at; 06, Theobaldgasse 9; ⌚6pm-2am Mon-Sat; Ⓤ Museumsquartier) Don't let the sign fool you: this former pet-grooming salon morphed into a lovely '60s-style bar. It mixes excellent cocktails, serves a short but decent beer, wine and snacks list, and attracts a laid-back and unpretentious crowd. DJ Roman Schöny regularly works the decks. Cash only.

LUTZ BAR, CLUB

Map p248 (www.lutz-bar.at; 06, Mariahilfer Strasse 3; ⌚8am-2am Mon-Thu, 8am-3am Fri, 9am-3am Sat, 10am-6pm Sun; 📶; Ⓤ Museumsquartier) A cafe and restaurant by day, at night Lutz morphs into a buzzing bar. Caramel leather armchairs and clean lines create a contemporary backdrop for a frozen mojito or lemongrass fizz – try for a seat by the floor-to-ceiling windows overlooking Mariahilfer Strasse. From 10pm to 6am on Tuesday, Friday and Saturday, a subterranean club plays anything from house to disco.

AUX GAZELLES CLUB

Map p248 (http://auxgazelles.at; 06, Rahlgasse 5; ⌚11pm-5am Fri & Sat; Ⓤ Museumsquartier) Aux Gazelles' club bar has a beautiful Moorish decor. The music is an eclectic mix of smooth ethnic sounds, and there are plenty of dim corners and low, comfy couches. The gigantic venue also incorporates a restaurant serving tajines and sweet Moroccan pastries, a bar and deli, and even a *hammam* (steam bath). Aux Gazelles is one of the few clubs in town where a dress code is enforced.

ROXY CLUB

Map p248 (www.roxyclub.org; 04, Faulmanngasse 2; ⌚11pm-4am Thu-Sat; 🚋D, 1, 2 Kärntner Ring/Oper, Ⓤ Karlsplatz) Hidden behind an inconspicuous blue door, this seminal Viennese venue still manages to run with the clubbing pack, and sometimes leads the way. DJs from Vienna's electronica scene regularly guest on the turntables and most nights it's hard to find a space on the small dance floor. Expect a crowded, but very good, night out. Cash only.

CAFÉ DRECHSLER COFFEE

Map p248 (www.cafedrechsler.at; Linke Wienzeile 22; ⌚8am-midnight Sun-Thu, to 2am Fri & Sat; 📶; Ⓤ Kettenbrückengasse) Sir Terence Conran worked his magic with polished marble bar and table tops, Bauhaus light fixtures and whitewashed timber panels at Drechsler, one of the liveliest coffee houses in town. Food includes its legendary *Gulasch* (goulash). DJs spin in the evening, keeping the vibe upbeat and hip.

CAFÉ SAVOY CAFE

Map p248 (www.savoy.at; 06, Linke Wienzeile 36; ⌚noon-2am Mon-Thu, to 3am Fri & Sat, 9am-2am Sun; 📶; Ⓤ Kettenbrückengasse) Café Savoy is an established gay haunt that has a more traditional cafe feel to it. The clientele is generally very mixed on a Saturday – mainly due to the proximity of the Naschmarkt – but at other times it's filled with men of all ages.

CLUB U BAR, CLUB

Map p248 (www.club-u.at; 04, Künstlerhauspassage; ⌚9pm-4am; Ⓤ Karlsplatz) Club U occupies one of Otto Wagner's Stadtbahn Pavillons (p97) on Karlsplatz. It's a small, student-favourite bar-club with regular DJs and a wonderful outdoor seating area overlooking the pavilions and park.

MANGO BAR GAY, BAR

Map p248 (www.why-not.at; 06, Laimgrubengasse 3; ⌚9pm-6am; Ⓤ Kettenbrückengasse) Mango attracts a young, often men-only, gay crowd with good music, friendly staff and plenty of mirrors to check out yourself and others. It usually serves as a kick-start for a big night out on the town.

ENTERTAINMENT

★STAATSOPER OPERA

Map p248 (☎01-514 44 7880; www.wiener-staatsoper.at; 01, Opernring 2; tickets €10-208, standing room €3-4; 🚋D 1, 2, 71 Kärntner Ring/Oper, UKarlsplatz) The glorious Staatsoper is Vienna's premiere opera and classical-music venue. Productions are lavish, formal affairs, where people dress up accordingly. In the interval, wander the foyer and refreshment rooms to fully appreciate the gold-and-crystal interior. Opera is not performed here in July and August (tours still take place). Tickets can be purchased (p45) up to two months in advance.

Tickets to the annual **Opernball** (www.wiener-staatsoper.at; ⏲Jan/Feb) range from €490 to an eye-watering €21,000 and sell out years in advance.

★MUSIKVEREIN CONCERT VENUE

Map p248 (☎01-505 81 90; www.musikverein.at; 01, Musikvereinsplatz 1; tickets €24-95, standing room €4-6; ⏲box office 9am-8pm Mon-Fri, to 1pm Sat Sep-Jun, 9am-noon Mon-Fri Jul & Aug; UKarlsplatz) The opulent Musikverein holds the proud title of the best acoustics of any concert hall in Austria, which the Vienna Philharmonic Orchestra embraces. The lavish interior can be visited by 45-minute guided tour (in English and German; adult/child €6.50/4) at 10am, 11am and noon Monday to Saturday. Smaller-scale performances are held in the Brahms Saal. There are no student tickets.

Tickets for the famous New Year's Eve concert cost anything from €25 (standing room) to €800; due to high demand, a ballot takes place in January or February – register at www.wienerphilharmoniker.at. Standing-room tickets are available up to seven weeks in advance.

THEATER AN DER WIEN THEATRE

Map p248 (☎01-588 85; www.theater-wien.at; 06, Linke Wienzeile 6; tickets €10-160, standing room €7, student tickets €10-15; ⏲box office 10am-6pm Mon-Sat, 2-6pm Sun; UKarlsplatz) The Theater an der Wien has hosted some monumental premiere performances, including Beethoven's *Fidelio,* Mozart's *Die Zauberflöte* and Strauss Jnr's *Die Fledermaus*. These days, besides staging musicals, dance and concerts, it's re-established its reputation for high-quality opera, with one premiere each month.

Student tickets go on sale 30 minutes before shows; standing-room tickets are available one hour prior to performances.

FILMCASINO CINEMA

Map p248 (☎01-587 90 62; www.filmcasino.at; 05, Margaretenstrasse 78; tickets €7.50-9; UKettenbrückengasse) An art-house cinema of some distinction, Filmcasino screens an excellent mix of Asian and European docos and avant-garde short films, along with independent feature-length films from around the world. Its '50s-style foyer is particularly impressive.

TOP KINO CINEMA

Map p248 (☎01-208 30 00; www.topkino.at; 06, Rahlgasse 1; tickets adult/child €7/6; UMuseumsquartier) Top Kino screens European films and documentaries, generally in their original language with German subtitles, and also holds a variety of themed film festivals throughout the year.

SCHIKANEDER CINEMA

Map p248 (☎01-585 58 88; www.schikaneder.at; 04, Margaretenstrasse 24; tickets adult/child €7/5; ⏲Sep-Jun; UKettenbrückengasse) Located next to the **bar** (⏲7.30pm-4am Mon-Sat, to 2am Sun) of the same name, Schikaneder is the darling of Vienna's alternative cinema scene. The film subject range is quite broad but also highly selective, and art house through and through.

BURG KINO CINEMA

Map p248 (☎01-587 84 06; www.burgkino.at; 01, Opernring 19; tickets €8-9.50; 🚋D, 1, 2 Burgring, UMuseumsquartier) The Burg Kino shows only English-language films. It has regular screenings of *The Third Man,* Orson Welles' timeless classic set in post-WWII Vienna.

SHOPPING

★BEER LOVERS DRINKS

Map p248 (http://beerlovers.at; 06, Gumpendorfer Strasse 35; ⏲11am-8pm Mon-Fri, 10am-5pm Sat; UKettenbrückengasse) A wonderland of craft beers, this emporium stocks over 1000 labels from over 125 different breweries in over 70 styles, with more being sourced every day. Tastings are offered regularly, and cold beers are available in the walk-in glass fridge and in refillable growlers.

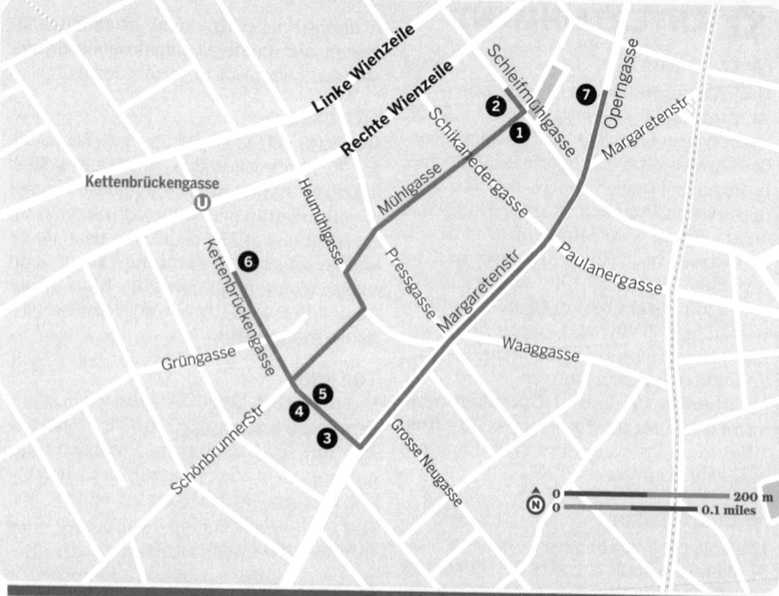

Local Life
Epicure Tour of the Freihausviertel

Once home to impoverished artisans, today the Freihausviertel has been revitalised: its attractive lanes harbour boho cafes, speciality food stores and some of Vienna's most exciting new galleries, ateliers and boutiques. After a morning browsing Vienna's gourmand's fantasyland, the Naschmarkt, continue your spin through the 4th district with this foodie tour.

❶ Literary Lunch

'Spices and books for cooks' is the credo of **Babettes** (Map p248; www.babettes.at; 04, Schleifmühlgasse 17; ⌚10am-7pm Mon-Fri, 10.30am-5pm Sat Sep-Jul, 11am-6pm Mon-Fri, 10am-3pm Aug; Ⓤ Kettenbrückengasse), with a round-the-world tour of cookbooks to browse. On weekdays, a different lunch special (such as curry) sizzles in the open kitchen, prepared with own-brand spices and fresh Naschmarkt produce. Food is served from noon to 2.30pm Monday to Friday. Evening cookery-class themes range from tapas to Tuscan cuisine.

❷ Austrian Bubbly

Toast the start of the afternoon at **Sekt Comptoir** (Map p248; www.sektcomptoir.at; 04, Schleifmühlgasse 19; ⌚5-11pm Mon-Thu, noon-11pm Fri & Sat; Ⓤ Kettenbrückengasse) over a glass of Burgenland *Sekt* (sparkling wine). As it's located just a few blocks from the Naschmarkt, shoppers with bulging grocery bags often spill onto the sidewalk here.

❸ Sugar & Spice

If you're lucky you'll see the Henzl family drying, grinding and blending their home-grown and foraged herbs and spices with sugar and salt at delightfully old-school **Henzls Ernte** (Map p248; www.henzls.at; 05, Kettenbrückengasse 3; ⌚1-6pm Tue-Fri, 9am-5pm Sat; Ⓤ Kettenbrückengasse). Specialities include sloe-berry salt, lavender sugar, wild garlic pesto and green tomato preserve.

❹ Farm Fresh

Nip into farmers' store **Helene** (Map p248; http://bauernladenhelene.at; 05, Kettenbrückengasse 7; ⌚8am-6pm Tue-Fri, to 3pm Sat; Ⓤ Kettenbrückengasse) for a smorgasbord of top-quality regional produce. Besides super-fresh fruit and veg, cheese and meat, you'll find Joseph Brot von Pheinsten organic loaves from the Waldviertel, chestnut, larch and acacia honeys from Lower Austria, and wine and chilli jam from Burgenland.

Naschmarkt (p99)

❺ Apple of a Needle's Eye

At dinky workshop-store **Näherei Apfel** (Map p248; www.naeherei-apfel.at; Kettenbrückengasse 8; ⏲11am-6pm Tue-Fri, 10am-3pm Sat; Ⓤ Kettenbrückengasse), you can buy Burgenland apples dried, preserved, chipped, juiced and by the kilo, browse Ursula's funky sweaters, jersey dresses and bags, and even learn to sew.

❻ Just Desserts

At chocolatier and patisserie **Fruth** (Map p248; www.fruth.at; 04, Kettenbrückengasse 20; ⏲11am-7pm Tue-Fri, 9am-5pm Sat; Ⓤ Kettenbrückengasse), Eduard Fruth creates edible works of art. Deliberate over delicacies including strawberry tartlets, rich truffles and feather-light éclairs.

❼ Afternoon Tea

A boudoir of a French tearoom, **Süssi** (Map p248; ☎01-943 13 24; www.suessi.at; 04, Operngasse 30; desserts €3.50-7, afternoon tea €18; ⏲11am-9pm Tue-Sat, 1-9pm Sun; Ⓤ Karlsplatz) is a real blast from the past with its ruby red chairs, striped wallpaper, lace doilies and candelabras. Brews from Paris-based Mariage Frères are served in proper crockery and go perfectly with the tempting array of *macarons*, quiches, fruit tarts and cream cakes.

It also stocks craft ciders, small-batch liqueurs and boutique nonalcoholic drinks such as ginger beers.

DIE SCHWALBE FASHION & ACCESSORIES

Map p248 (www.die-schwalbe.at; 06, Otto-Bauer-Gasse 24; ⏲11.30am-6.30pm Mon-Sat; Ⓤ Neubaugasse) 'Eco-urban steetwear' here spans hoodies and pullovers to T-shirts, jackets, shorts and pants, plus accessories such as beanies, caps and scarves from small-scale labels including Blueberry Rockster, Habu San, Hemp Hoodlamb and Plasma Lab. Its piercing lounge is open from 1pm to 6.30pm Tuesday to Friday and 1pm to 5pm on Saturdays.

BLÜHENDES KONFEKT FOOD

Map p248 (www.bluehendes-konfekt.com; 06, Schmalzhofgasse 19; ⏲10am-6.30pm Wed-Fri; Ⓤ Zieglergasse, Westbahnhof) 🍃 Violets, forest strawberries and cherry blossom, mint and oregano – Michael Diewald makes the most of what grows wild and in his garden to create confectionery that fizzes with seasonal flavour. Peek through to the workshop to see flowers and herbs being deftly transformed into one-of-a-kind bonbons and mini bouquets that are edible works of art.

WE BANDITS FASHION & ACCESSORIES

Map p248 (http://webandits.tictail.com; 06, Theobaldgasse 14; ⏲noon-7pm Mon-Fri, 11am-6pm Sat; Ⓤ Museumsquartier) No matter how often you visit this boutique, you'll never see the same item twice: owner Sophie Pollak scours the globe (in particular Asia and Scandinavia) for unique men's and women's fashions, and buys one-off pieces (clothing, scarves, shoes, socks, bags, backpacks...) from designers such as Kokoon, Sessun, Delikatessen, UFTD and Royal Republic.

MEIN DESIGN FASHION & ACCESSORIES

Map p248 (www.mein-design.org; 04, Kettenbrückengasse 6; ⏲11am-6pm Tue-Fri, 10am-3pm Sat; Ⓤ Kettenbrückengasse) Boutique owner and designer Ulrike gives young Austrian designers a platform for showcasing their fresh, innovative fashion and accessories at this boutique-workshop, where the accent is on quality and sustainability. Displays change every few months; you might find anything from beautifully made children's clothes to jewellery fashioned from recycled tyres and silk blouses emblazoned with photographs of Vienna icons.

FEINEDINGE CERAMICS

Map p248 (www.feinedinge.at; 05, Margaretenstrasse 35; ⏲10am-6pm Mon-Wed & Sat, to 7.30pm Thu & Fri; ⓤKettenbrückengasse) Sandra Haischberger makes exquisite porcelain that reveals a clean, modern aesthetic at her atelier shop. Her range of home accessories, tableware and lighting is minimalist, but often features sublime details, such as crockery in chalky pastels, filigree lamps that cast exquisite patterns and candle holders embellished with floral and butterfly motifs.

DÖRTHE KAUFMANN CLOTHING

Map p248 (www.doertekaufmann.com; 04, Kettenbrückengasse 17; ⏲1-7pm Tue-Fri, 10am-4pm Sat; ⓤKettenbrückengasse) Dörthe is the designer behind the biannual collections presented at this little boutique, which might include anything from French-style bolero jackets to dresses inspired by bold Nigerian colours and patterns. These feature alongside a snug assortment of chunky hand-knitted hats, gloves, scarves and booties, all beautifully made with merino, mohair or alpaca wool and coloured with natural pigments.

THUM SCHINKENMANUFAKTUR FOOD

Map p248 (www.thum-schinken.at; 05, Margaretenstrasse 126; ⏲7am-noon Mon-Fri; ⓤPilgramgasse) In business since 1860, Thum Schinkenmanufaktur is famed for its traditional Viennese leg hams, bacon, salami from prized Mangalitza pigs, and smoked and truffled meat products.

GABARAGE UPCYCLING DESIGN DESIGN STORE

Map p248 (www.gabarage.at; 06, Schleifmühlgasse 6; ⏲10am-6pm Mon-Thu, 10am-7pm Fri, 11am-5pm Sat; ⓤTaubstummengasse) Recycled design, ecology and social responsibility underpin the quirky designs at Gabarage. Old bowling pins become vases, rubbish bins get a new life as tables and chairs, advertising tarpaulins morph into bags, and traffic lights are transformed into funky lights.

FLO VINTAGE MODE VINTAGE

Map p248 (www.flovintage.com; 04, Schleifmühlgasse 15a; ⏲10am-6.30pm Mon-Fri, to 3.30pm Sat; ⓤKettenbrückengasse) It's surprising a city this enamoured with the glamorous past has few true vintage clothing stores. Spanning 1890 to 1980 pieces, the clothes here are fastidiously and beautifully displayed, from pearl-embroidered art nouveau masterpieces to 1950s and '60s New Look pieces and designer wear of the '70s and '80s (alphabetised from Armani to Zegna). Prices (and quality) are high.

RAVE UP MUSIC

Map p248 (www.rave-up.at; 06, Hofmühlgasse 1; ⏲10am-6.30pm Mon-Fri, to 5pm Sat; ⓤPilgramgasse) Friendly staff, loads of new vinyl and a massive collection make a trip to Rave Up a real pleasure. The store specialises in indie and alternative imports from the UK and US, but you'll find plenty of electronica, hip-hop and retro tunes, and you can listen before you buy, too.

LICHTERLOH HOMEWARES

Map p248 (www.lichterloh.com; 06, Gumpendorfer Strasse 15-17; ⏲11am-6.30pm Tue-Fri, 10am-2pm Sat; ⓤMuseumsquartier) This massive, ultracool space is filled with iconic furniture from the 1900s to 1970s, by names such as Eames, Thonet and Mies van der Rohe. Even if you're not planning to lug home a sleek Danish sideboard, it's worth a look at this veritable gallery of modern furniture design.

SPORTS & ACTIVITIES

KLETTERANLAGE FLAKTURM CLIMBING

Map p248 (☎01-585 47 48; www.alpenverein.wien/flakturm; 06, Esterházypark; climbing incl gear per hr adult/child €45/22; ⏲2pm-dusk Apr-Oct; ⓤNeubaugasse) The stark outside walls of the *Flakturm* (flak tower) in Esterházypark are used for climbing exercises organised by the Österreichischer Alpenverein (Austrian Alpine Club). Twenty routes (gradients four to eight) climb to a maximum height of 34m.

The Museum District & Neubau

Neighbourhood Top Five

❶ **Kunsthistorisches Museum** (p109) Throwing yourself head first into the artistic vortex of the Museum of Art History, a whirl of Habsburg treasures from Egyptian tombs to rare breed Raphael, Dürer and Caravaggio masterworks.

❷ **MuseumsQuartier** (p115) Checking Vienna's cultural pulse during an art-packed day at this vast ensemble of museums, cafes, restaurants and bars inside the Hofburg's former imperial stables.

❸ **Naturhistorisches Museum** (p118) Making a date with the dinosaurs and prehistoric divas at the Museum of Natural History.

❹ **Rathaus** (p120) Revelling in the neo-Gothic riches of the City Hall on a free guided tour.

❺ Neubau's Design Scene (p124) Taking a design-inspired walk through the cobbled backstreets of the Biedermeier Spittelberg neighbourhood.

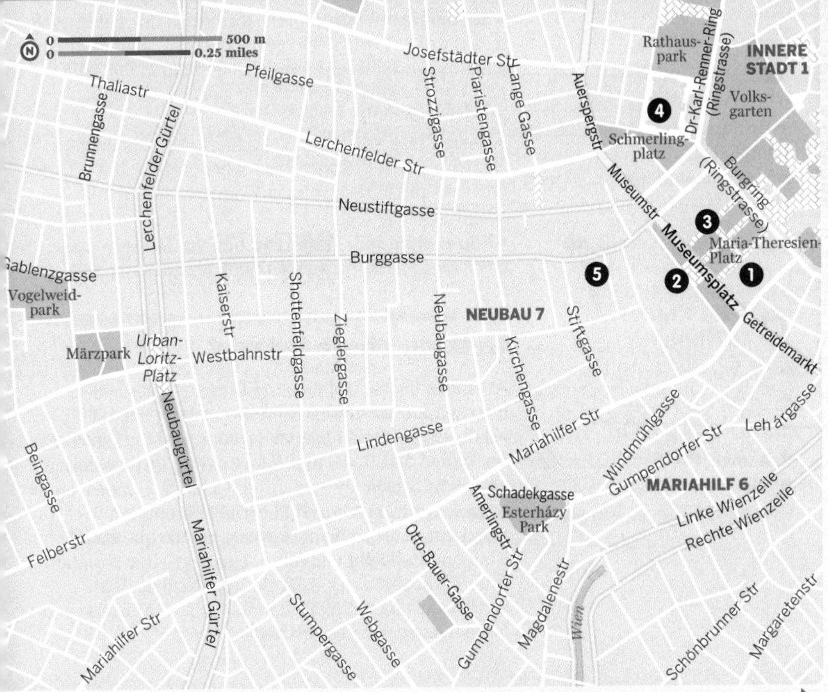

For more detail of this area see Map p252

Lonely Planet's Top Tip

Time your visit to catch one of the neighbourhood sights' free guided tours. Gallery tours that won't cost you a cent include those at the Leopold Museum at 3pm on Sunday, the Kunsthalle Wien at 3pm and 4pm on Saturday and Sunday, and the MUMOK (check schedules online). Best of all are the gratis guided tours of the neo-Gothic Rathaus at 1pm on Monday, Wednesday and Friday.

Best Places to Eat

- Tian Bistro (p121)
- Vestibül (p122)
- Figar (p120)
- Pure Living Bakery (p120)

For reviews, see p120.

Best Places to Drink

- Brickmakers Pub & Kitchen (p122)
- Café Leopold (p123)
- Le Troquet (p123)

For reviews, see p122.

Best Places to Shop

- Die Werkbank (p124)
- Dirndlherz (p126)
- Das Möbel (p124)
- S/GHT (p125)
- Mühlbauer (p126)

For reviews, see p126.

Explore The Museum District & Neubau

The Museum District and Neubau walk a fine line between Habsburg history and modernity. The baroque imperial stables have cantered into the 21st century with their transformation into the MuseumsQuartier (p115), a colossal complex of on-the-pulse bars, cafes, boutiques and museums, including the Leopold (p115), the proud holder of the world's largest Schiele collection. Hang out in the courtyards here in summer and the creativity in the air is palpable.

Just around the corner on Maria-Theresien-Platz is the Kunsthistorisches Museum (p109), an epic and exhilarating journey through art, where Rubens originals star alongside Giza treasures. Its architectural twin is the neoclassical Naturhistorisches Museum (p118) opposite.

When you've had your fill of art and culture, keep tabs on Vienna's evolving fashion and design scene with a mosey around Neubau's backstreet studios and boutiques. After dark, the live-wire clubs and bars tucked under the Gürtel arches, slightly west, are where the young Viennese go to party.

Local Life

- **Schanigärten Life** Join the locals toasting summer at a flurry of *Schanigärten* (pavement cafes and courtyard gardens), including Amerlingbeisl (p122) in Spittelberg, and Kantine (p121) and Café Leopold (p123) in the MuseumsQuartier.
- **Design Life** Mill around Kirchengasse, Lindengasse, Neubaugasse and Zollergasse, where artists and creatives put a fresh spin on Viennese fashion and design.
- **Pop-up Life** Join locals digging into dishes by guest chefs cooking at Brickmakers Pub & Kitchen (p122).

Getting There & Away

- **U-Bahn** Useful U-Bahn stops include Museumsquartier and Volkstheater on the U2 line. The U3 Neubaugasse and Zieglergasse stops, and the U6 stops Burggasse Stadthalle and Thaliastrasse are best for accessing Neubau.
- **Tram** Trams D, 1, 2 and 71 travel around the Ringstrasse, stopping at Rathaus, Dr-Karl-Renner-Ring and Parlament en route. The No 49 line trundles from Dr-Karl-Renner-Ring through Neubau, with handy stops including Stiftgasse/Siebensterngasse and Neubaugasse/Westbahnstrasse.

TOP SIGHT
KUNSTHISTORISCHES MUSEUM

The Habsburgs built many a bombastic palace but, artistically speaking, the Kunsthistorisches Museum is their magnum opus. Occupying a neoclassical building as sumptuous as the art it contains, the museum takes you on a time-travel treasure hunt – from classical Rome to Egypt and the Renaissance. If your time's limited, skip straight to the Old Master paintings in the Picture Gallery.

Picture Gallery

The Kunsthistorisches Museum's vast Picture Gallery is by far and away the most impressive of its collections. Devote at least an hour or two to exploring its feast of Old Masters paintings.

Dutch, Flemish & German Painting

First up is the **German Renaissance**, where Lucas Cranach the Elder stages an appearance with engaging Genesis tableaux like *Paradise* (1530) and *Fall of Man* (aka *Adam and Eve;* 1537). The key focus, though, is the prized Dürer collection. Dürer's powerful compositions, sophisticated use of light and deep feeling for his subjects shine through in masterful pieces like *Portrait of a Venetian Lady* (1505), the spirit-soaring *Adoration of the Trinity* (1511) and the macabre *Martyrdom of the Ten Thousand* (1508).

Rubens throws you in the deep end of **Flemish baroque** painting next, with paintings rich in Counter-Reformation themes and mythological symbolism. The monumental *Miracle of St Francis Xavier* (1617), which

DON'T MISS

- Dutch Golden Age paintings
- Italian, Spanish & French collection
- Kunstkammer
- Offering Chapel of Ka-ni-nisut

PRACTICALITIES

- KHM, Museum of Art History
- Map p252, H4
- www.khm.at
- 01, Maria-Theresien-Platz
- adult/child incl Neue Burg museums €15/free
- ⌚10am-6pm Fri-Wed, to 9pm Thu Jun-Aug, closed Mon Sep-May
- Ⓤ Museumsquartier, Volkstheater

GUIDED TOURS

For more insight, pick up a multilingual audio guide (€4) near the entrance. The KHM runs free guided tours in German, from 30-minute lunchtime tours (12.30pm Tuesday and Thursday) to hour-long tours focusing on a particular artist or period (4pm Wednesday, 10.15am Friday). See www.khm.at for details.

As you climb the ornate main staircase of the Kunsthistorisches Museum, your gaze is drawn to the ever-decreasing circles of the cupola, and marble columns guide the eye to delicately frescoed vaults, roaring lions and Antonio Canova's mighty statue of *Theseus Defeating the Centaur* (1805). Austrian legends Hans Makart and the brothers Klimt have left their hallmark between the columns and above the arcades – the former with lunette paintings, the latter with gold-kissed depictions of women inspired by Greco-Roman and Egyptian art.

used to hang in Antwerp's Jesuit church, the celestial *The Annunciation* (1610), the *Miracles of St Ignatius* (1615) and the *Triptych of St Ildefonso* (1630) all reveal the iridescent quality and linear clarity that underscored Rubens' style. Mythological masterworks move from the gory, snake-riddled *Medusa* (1617) to the ecstatic celebration of love in *Feast of Venus* (1636).

In 16th- and 17th-century **Dutch Golden Age** paintings, the desire to faithfully represent reality through an attentive eye for detail and compositional chiaroscuro is captured effortlessly in works by Rembrandt, Ruisdael and Vermeer. Rembrandt's perspicuous *Self-Portrait* (1652), showing the artist in a humble painter's smock, Van Ruisdael's palpable vision of nature in *The Large Forest* (1655) and Vermeer's seductively allegorical *The Art of Painting* (1665), showing Clio, Greek muse of history, in the diffused light of an artist's studio, are all emblematic of the age.

The final three rooms are an ode to the art of Flemish baroque master **Van Dyck** and Flemish Renaissance painter **Pieter Bruegel the Elder**. Van Dyck's keenly felt devotional works include *The Vision of the Blessed Hermann Joseph* (1630), in which the Virgin and kneeling monk are bathed in radiant light, and *Madonna and Child with St Rosalie, Peter and Paul* (1629). An entire room is given over to Pieter Bruegel the Elder's vivid depictions of Flemish life and landscapes, alongside his biblical star attraction – *The Tower of Babel* (1563).

Italian, Spanish & French Painting

The first three rooms here are given over to key exponents of the **16th-century Venetian** style: Titian, Veronese and Tintoretto. High on your artistic agenda here should be Titian's *Nymph and Shepherd* (1570), elevating the pastoral to the mythological in its portrayal of the futile desire of the flute-playing shepherd for the beautiful maiden out of his reach. Veronese's dramatic depiction of the suicidal Roman heroine *Lucretia* (1583), with a dagger drawn to her chest, and Tintoretto's *Susanna at her Bath* (1556), watched by two lustful elders, are other highlights.

Devotion is central to Raphael's *Madonna of the Meadow* (1506) in room 4, one of the true masterpieces of the **High Renaissance**, just as it is to the *Madonna of the Rosary* (1601), a stirring Counter-Reformation altarpiece by **Italian baroque** artist Caravaggio in the next room. Room 7 is also a delight, with compelling works like Giuseppe Arcimboldo's anthropomorphic paintings inspired by the seasons and elements, such as fruit-filled *Sum-*

mer (1563), *Winter* (1563) and *Fire* (1566). Look out, too, for Venetian landscape painter Canaletto's *Schönbrunn* (1761), meticulously capturing the palace back in its imperial heyday.

Of the artists represented in the final rooms dedicated to **Spanish, French and English** painting, the undoubted star is Spanish court painter Velázquez. Particularly entrancing is his almost 3D portrait of *Infanta Margarita Teresa in a Blue Dress* (1673), a vision of voluminous silk and eight-year-old innocence. Gainsborough's *Suffolk Landscape* (1748), with its feather-light brushwork and suffused colours, and French baroque painter Nicolas Poussin's turbulent *Destruction of the Temple in Jerusalem* (1639) also demand attention.

Kunstkammer

Imagine the treasures you could buy with brimming coffers and the world at your fingertips. The Habsburgs did just that, filling their *Kunstkammer* (cabinet of art and curiosities) with an encyclopaedic collection of the rare and the precious: from narwhal-tusk cups to table holders encrusted with fossilised shark teeth. Its 20 themed rooms containing 2200 artworks open a fascinating window on the obsession with collecting curios in royal circles in Renaissance and baroque times.

The biggest crowd-puller here is Benvenuto Cellini's allegorical **Saliera** (salt cellar), commissioned by Francis I of France in 1540, which is exquisitely handcrafted from rolled gold, ivory and enamel. Among the Kunstkammer's other top-drawer attractions are the wildly expressive, early-17th-century ivory sculpture **Furie** (Master of the Furies), the serenely beautiful **Krumauer Madonna** (1400), a masterpiece of the Bohemian Gothic style, and Gasparo Miseroni's lapis lazuli **Dragon Cup** (1570), a fiery beast glittering with gemstones.

Egyptian & Near Eastern Collection

Decipher the mysteries of Egyptian civilisations with a chronological romp through this miniature Giza of a ground-floor collection, beginning with **pre-dynastic** and **Old Kingdom** treasures. Here the exceptionally well-preserved **Offering Chapel of Ka-ni-nisut** spells out the life of the high-ranking 5th-dynasty official in reliefs and hieroglyphs. The Egyptian fondness for nature and adornment finds expression in artefacts such as a monkey-shaped kohl container and fish-shaped make-up palette.

Stele, sacrificial altar slabs, jewellery boxes, sphinx busts and pharaoh statues bring to life the **Middle Kingdom** and **New Kingdom**. The Egyptian talent for craftsmanship shines in pieces like a turquoise ceramic hippo (2000 BC) and the gold seal ring of Ramses X (1120 BC). The **Late Period** dips into the land of the pharaohs, at a time when rule swung from Egypt to Persia. Scout out the 3000-year-old Book of the Dead of Chonsu-mes, the polychrome mummy board of Nes-pauti-taui and Canopic jars with lids shaped like monkey, falcon and jackal heads.

Stone sarcophagi, gilded mummy masks and busts of priests and princes transport you back to the **Ptolemaic** and **Greco-Roman** period. In the **Near Eastern** collection, the representation of a prowling lion from Babylon's triumphal Ishtar Gate (604–562 BC) is the big attraction.

Greek & Roman Antiquities

This rich Greek and Roman repository reveals the imperial scope for collecting classical antiquities, with 2500 objects traversing three millennia from the Cypriot Bronze Age to early medieval times.

Cypriot and Mycenaean Art catapults you back to the dawn of Western civilisation, 2500 years ago. The big draw here is the precisely carved votive statue

Kunsthistorisches Museum

HALF-DAY TOUR OF THE HIGHLIGHTS

The Kunsthistorisches Museum's scale can seem daunting; this half-day itinerary will help you make the most of your visit.

Ascend the grand marble staircase, marvelling at the impact of Antonio Canova's *Theseus Slaying the Centaur*. Turn right into the Egyptian and Near Eastern Collection, where you can decipher the reliefs of the **Offering Chapel of Ka-ni-nisut** ❶ in room II. Skip through millennia to Ancient Rome, where the intricacy of the **Gemma Augustea Cameo** ❷ in room XVI is captivating. The other wing of this floor is devoted to the Kunstkammer Wien, hiding rarities such as Benvenuto Cellini's golden **Saliera** ❸ in room XXIX.

Head up a level to the Picture Gallery, a veritable orgy of Renaissance and baroque art. Bearing to the East Wing brings you to Dutch, Flemish and German Painting, which starts with Dürer's

LEEMAGE/GETTY IMAGES ©

Gemma Augustea Cameo
Greek & Roman Antiquities, Room XVI
Possibly the handiwork of imperial gem-cutter Dioscurides, this sardonyx cameo from the 1st century AD shows in exquisite bas-relief the deification of Augustus, in the guise of Jupiter, who sits next to Roma. The defeated barbarians occupy the lower tier.

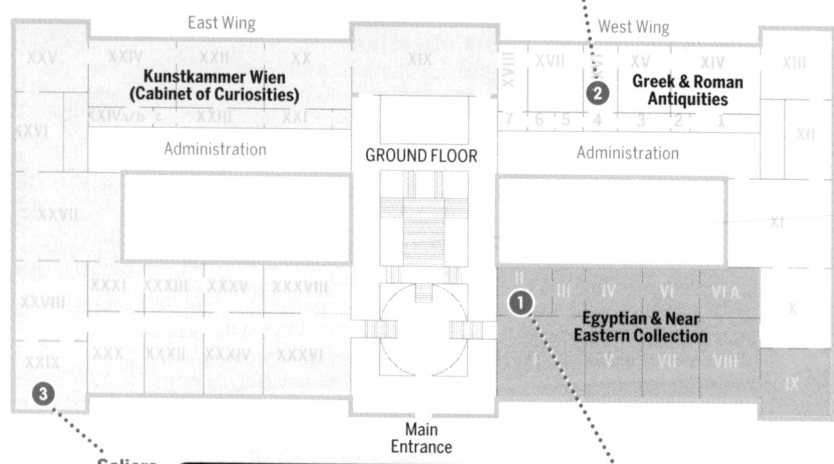

Saliera
Kunstkammer Wien, Room XXIX
Benvenuto Cellini's hand-wrought gold salt cellar (1543) is a dazzling allegorical portrayal of Sea and Earth, personified by Tellus and trident-bearing Neptune. They recline on a base showing the four winds, times of day and human activities.

DIETER NAGL/AFP/GETTY IMAGES ©

Offering Chapel of Ka-ni-nisut
Egyptian & Near Eastern Collection, Room II
Reliefs and hieroglyphs depict the life of high-ranking 5th-dynasty official Ka-ni-nisut, together with his wife, children and entourage of mortuary priests and servants. This 4500-year-old tomb chamber is a spectacular leap into the afterlife.

spirit-lifting **Adoration of the Trinity** ❹ in room XV, takes in meaty Rubens and Rembrandt works en route, and climaxes with Pieter Bruegel the Elder's absorbingly detailed **The Tower of Babel** ❺ in room X. Allocate equal time to the Italian, Spanish and French masters in the halls opposite. Masterpieces including Raphael's **Madonna of the Meadow** ❻ in room 4, Caravaggio's merciful **Madonna of the Rosary** ❼ in room V and Giuseppe **Arcimboldo's Summer** ❽ in room 7 steal the show.

TOP TIPS

» Pick up an audio guide and a floor plan in the entrance hall to orientate yourself.

» Skip to the front of the queue by booking your ticket online.

» Visit between 6pm and 9pm on Thursday for fewer crowds.

» Flash photography is not permitted.

The Tower of Babel

Dutch, Flemish & German Painting, Room X

The futile attempts of industrial souls to reach godly heights are magnified in the painstaking detail of Bruegel's *The Tower of Babel* (1563). Rome's Colosseum provided inspiration.

ART MEDIA/PRINT COLLECTOR/GETTY IMAGES ©

Madonna of the Meadow

Italian, Spanish & French Painting, Room 4

The Virgin Mary, pictured with infants Christ and St John the Baptist, has an almost iridescent quality in Raphael's seminal High Renaissance 1506 masterpiece, set against the backdrop of a Tuscan meadow.

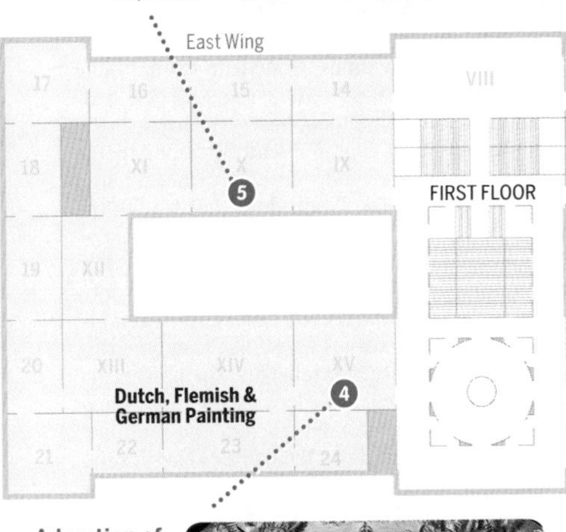

Adoration of the Trinity

Dutch, Flemish & German Painting, Room XV

Dürer's magnum opus altarpiece was commissioned by Nuremberg merchant Matthäus Landauer in 1511. Angels, saints and earthly believers surround the Holy Trinity, while Dürer hides in the bottom right-hand corner.

DEA PICTURE LIBRARY/GETTY IMAGES ©

Madonna of the Rosary

Italian, Spanish & French Painting, Room V

Caravaggio's trademark chiaroscuro style brings depth, richness and feeling to this 1607 masterpiece. Holding infant Jesus, the Madonna asks St Dominic to distribute rosaries to the barefooted poor who kneel before her.

Summer

Italian, Spanish & French Painting, Room 7

Italian court painter Giuseppe Arcimboldo's *Summer* (1563) was a hit with the Habsburgs. The most striking of his four seasons cycle, this masterwork celebrates seasonal abundance in the form of a portrait composed of fruit and vegetables.

COIN COLLECTION

A piggy bank of gigantic Habsburg proportions, this coin collection is one of the world's best. Covering three halls and three millennia on the 3rd floor, the 2000 notes, coins and medallions on display are just a tiny fraction of the Kunsthistorisches Museum's 700,000-piece collection.

The coin collection's first hall presents medals of honour, first used in Renaissance Italy around 1400, and showcases gold and silver House of Habsburg wonders. The second hall travels through monetary time, from the birth of the coin in Lydia in the 7th century BC to the 20th century. Look out for classical coins, like the stater embellished with a lion head, in circulation under Alyattes, King of Lydia (619–560 BC), and Athenian coins featuring the goddess Athena and her pet owl. The third hall stages one-off exhibitions.

Dining in the Kunsthistorisches Museum

of a man wearing a finely pleated tunic. Among the muses, torsos and mythological statuettes in **Greek Art** is a fragment from the Parthenon's northern frieze showing two bearded men. The arts flourished in **Hellenistic** times, evident in exhibits like the *Amazonian Sarcophagus*, engraved with warriors so vivid you can almost hear their battle cries. In **pre-Roman Italy**, look for sculptures of Athena, funerary crowns intricately wrought from gold, and a repoussé showing the Titans doing battle with the Gods.

The sizeable **Roman** stash includes the 4th-century AD *Theseus Mosaic* from Salzburg, a polychrome, geometric marvel recounting the legend of Theseus. You'll also want to take in the captivating 3rd-century AD *Lion Hunt* relief and the 1st-century AD *Gemma Augustea,* a sardonyx bas-relief cameo. Early medieval show-stoppers include the shimmering golden vessels from the **Treasure of Nagyszentmiklós**, unearthed in 1799 in what is now Romania.

Kunsthistorisches Museum Dining

A meal under the dome is unforgettable. The Kunsthistorisches Museum runs gourmet evenings (6.30pm to 10pm Thursday; adult/child €44/25 excluding museum admission and drinks), and also serves breakfast (10am to 12.30pm; per person €19.90 excluding admission). You're free to wander through the museum to admire the artworks between courses.

TOP SIGHT
MUSEUMSQUARTIER

Baroque heritage and the avant-garde collide at the MuseumsQuartier, one of the world's most ambitious cultural spaces. Spanning 90,000 sq metres, this ensemble of museums, cafes, restaurants, shops, bars and performing arts venues occupies the former imperial stables designed by Fischer von Erlach in 1725. You can't see it all in a day, so selectively is the way to go.

Leopold Museum

The **Leopold Museum** (www.leopoldmuseum.org; 07, Museumsplatz 1; adult/child €13/8; ⏲10am-6pm Fri-Wed, to 9pm Thu Jun-Aug, 10am-6pm Wed & Fri-Mon, to 9pm Thu Sep-May) is named after Rudolf Leopold, a Viennese ophthalmologist who, on buying his first Egon Schiele (1890–1918) for a song as a young student in 1950, started to amass a huge private collection of mainly 19th-century and modernist Austrian artworks. In 1994 he sold the lot – 5266 paintings – to the Austrian government for €160 million (sold individually, the paintings would have made him €574 million), and the Leopold Museum was born. Café Leopold (p123) is located on the top floor.

The Leopold has a white limestone exterior, open space (the 21m-high glass-covered atrium is lovely) and natural light flooding most rooms. Considering Rudolf Leopold's love of Schiele, it's no surprise the museum contains the world's largest collection of the painter's work: 41 paintings and 188 drawings and graphics. Among the standouts are the ghostly *Self Seer II Death and Man* (1911), the mournful *Mother with Two Children* (1915) and the caught-in-the-act *Cardinal and Nun* (1912).

Other artists well represented include Albin Egger-Lienz, with his unforgiving depictions of pastoral life, Richard Gerstl and Austria's third-greatest expressionist, Oskar Kokoschka. Of the handful of works on display by Klimt, the unmissable is the allegorical *Death and Life*

DON'T MISS

- Schiele collection at the Leopold Museum
- Viennese Actionism at the MUMOK
- Cafe life in the courtyard in summer

PRACTICALITIES

- Museum Quarter; MQ
- Map p252, G4
- www.mqw.at
- 07, Museumsplatz
- ⏲information & ticket centre 10am-7pm
- ⓤMuseumsquartier, Volkstheater

CHILDREN'S THEATRE

Dschungel Wien (☎01-522 07 20; www.dschungelwien.at; 07, Museumsplatz 1; adult/child tickets from €6/4.50; ⊙box office 2.30-6.30pm Mon-Fri, 4.30-6.30pm Sat & Sun) covers the spectrum, from drama and puppetry to music, dance and narrative theatre. There are generally several performances daily in German and occasionally in English; see the website for details.

The MuseumsQuartier's courtyards host a winter and summer program of events, from film festivals to Christmas markets, literary readings to DJ nights; see www.mqw.at for details. They are also a popular hang-out in the summer months when the cafe terraces hum with life.

DANCE

Tanzquartier Wien (☎01-581 35 91; www.tqw.at; 07, Museumsplatz 1; tickets €10-57; ⊙box office 10am-4.30pm mid-Jul–Aug, 9am-7.30pm Mon-Fri, 10am-7.30pm Sat Sep–mid-Jul) is Vienna's first dance institution. It hosts local and international performances with a strong experimental nature. Unsold tickets (€8) go on sale 15 minutes before showtime.

(1910), a swirling amalgam of people juxtaposed by a skeletal grim reaper. Works by Loos, Hoffmann, Otto Wagner, Waldmüller and Romako are also on display.

MUMOK

The dark basalt edifice and sharp corners of **MUMOK** (Museum Moderner Kunst; Museum of Modern Art; www.mumok.at; 07, Museumsplatz 1; adult/child €11/free; ⊙2-7pm Mon, 10am-7pm Tue, Wed & Fri-Sun, 10am-9pm Thu) are a complete contrast to the MQ's historical sleeve. Inside, MUMOK is crawling with Vienna's finest collection of 20th- and 21st-century art, centred on fluxus, nouveau realism, pop art and photo-realism. The best of expressionism, cubism, minimal art and Viennese Actionism is represented in a collection of 9000 works that are rotated and exhibited by theme – but take note that sometimes all the Actionism is packed away to make room for temporary exhibitions. Viennese Actionism evolved in the 1960s as a radical leap away from mainstream art in what some artists considered to be a restrictive cultural and political climate. Artists like Günter Brus, Otto Mühl, Hermann Nitsch and Rudolf Schwarzkogler aimed to shock with their violent, stomach-churning performance and action art, which often involved using the human body as a canvas. They were successful: not only did their work shock, some artists were even imprisoned for outraging public decency. Other well-known artists represented throughout the museum – Pablo Picasso, Paul Klee, René Magritte, Max Ernst and Alberto Giacometti – are positively tame in comparison. Check the program before visiting with children to ensure exhibits are suitable.

Kunsthalle Wien

The **Kunsthalle** (Arts Hall; ☎01-521 890; www.kunsthallewien.at; 07, Museumsplatz 1; both halls adult/child €12/free; ⊙11am-7pm Fri-Wed, to 9pm Thu) is a collection of exhibition halls used to showcase local and international contemporary art. Its high ceilings, open planning and functionality have helped the venue leapfrog into the ranks of the top exhibition spaces in Europe. Programs, which run for three to six months, rely heavily on photography, video, film, installations and new media. Weekend visits include one-hour guided tours in English and German. The Saturday tours (Halle 1 at 3pm, Halle 2 at 4pm) focus on a theme, while Sunday tours (same times) give an overview.

Architekturzentrum Wien

The **Architekturzentrum Wien** (Vienna Architecture Centre; ☎01-522 31 15; www.azw.at; 07, Museumsplatz 1; exhibition prices vary, library admission free; ⊙architecture centre 10am-7pm, library 10am-5.30pm Mon, Wed & Fri, to 7pm Sat & Sun, closed Thu) collectively encompasses

MUSEUMQUARTIER COMPLEX

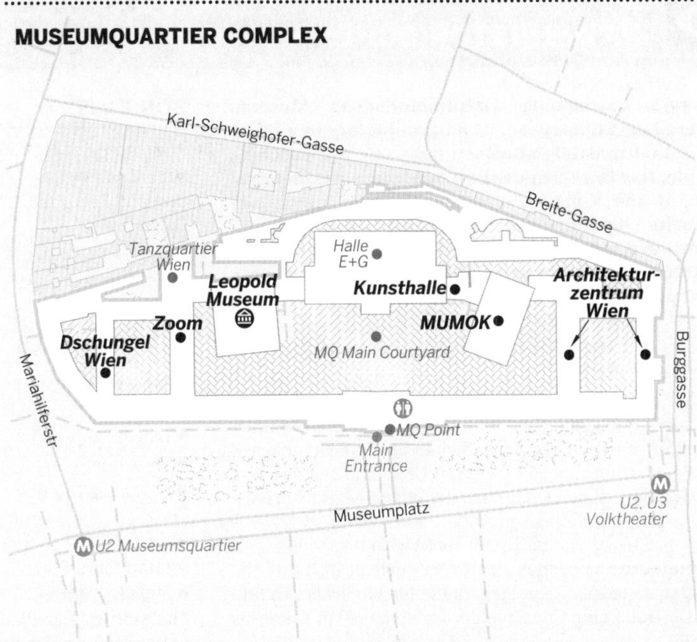

three halls used for temporary exhibitions, a library and a cafe. Exhibitions focus on international architectural developments, and change on a regular basis. The extensive library is open to the public. The centre also organises regular walking tours through Vienna on Sunday (in German), covering various architectural themes. You need to book ahead; see the website for dates and prices.

Zoom

Kids love this hands-on **children's museum** (01-524 79 08; www.kindermuseum.at; 07, Museumsplatz 1; exhibition adult/child €4/free, activities child €4-6, accompanying adult free; 12.45-5pm Tue-Sun Jul & Aug, 8.30am-4pm Tue-Fri, 9.45am-4pm Sat & Sun Sep-Jun, activity times vary; U Museumsquartier, Volkstheater), an arts-and-crafts session with lots of play thrown in. Budding Picassos have the chance to make, break, draw, explore and be creative in the 'Atelier'. 'Exhibition' stages a new exhibition every six months, while 'Ocean' appeals to tots with its mirrored tunnels, grottoes and ship deck for adventure play that stimulates coordination. For children aged eight to 14, there is an animated film studio and the future-focused Lab Club. Activities last about 1½ hours and spots can be reserved from the ticket office or by booking online.

MQ TICKETS & INFORMATION

Combined MuseumsQuartier tickets are available from the **MQ Point** (01-523 58 81-17 31; www.mqpoint.at; 07, Museumsplatz 1; 10am-7pm) . The **MQ Kombi Ticket** (€32) includes entry into every museum (Zoom only has a reduction) and a 30% discount on performances in the Tanzquartier Wien; the **MQ Art Ticket** (€26) gives admission into the Leopold Museum, MUMOK, Kunsthalle and reduced entry into Zoom, plus a 30% discount on the Tanzquartier Wien.

TOP SIGHT
NATURHISTORISCHES MUSEUM

Vienna's astounding Naturhistorisches Museum covers four billion years of natural history in a blink. With its exquisitely stuccoed halls and eye-catching cupola, this late-19th-century building is the identical twin of the Kunsthistorisches Museum which sits opposite. Among its minerals, fossils and dinosaur bones are one-of-a-kind finds like the miniscule 25,000-year-old Venus of Willendorf and a peerless 1100-piece meteorite collection.

Ground Floor: Meteorites, Dinosaurs & Prehistoric Finds

The ground floor leads in with a treasure chest of minerals, fossils and gemstones, with star exhibits like the 115kg chunk of smoky quartz from Switzerland's Tiefen glacier, a 6.2kg platinum nugget from the Urals and the dazzling 'Blumenstrauss' gemstone bouquet which Maria Theresia gave to Emperor Franz I in 1760.

Room 5 blasts you into outer space with the world's largest **meteorite** collection, featuring such beauties as the Martian meteorite Chassigny that landed in France in 1815 and the iron Cabin Creek meteorite, which fell in Arkansas in 1886.

For kids and **dinosaur** fans, the big-hitters hang out in room 10 on the ground floor. On a raised platform loom the skeletons of a diplodocus, iguanodon and a 6m-tall animatronic replica of an allosaurus. Keep an eye out, too, for the skeleton of an archelonischyros, the largest turtle ever.

Rooms 11 to 13 spell out **prehistory** in artefacts, with curiosities such as the coat of a woolly mammoth and Neanderthal tools. Two of the museum's tiniest stunners vie for attention here: the buxom Stone Age starlet the Venus of Willendorf, just 11cm tall, and her curvy, 32,000-year-old rival Fanny of Galgenberg, one of the world's oldest female statuettes, named after famous Viennese dancer Fanny Elster (1810–84).

Occupying rooms 14 to 15, the **anthropological collection**, which reopened in January 2013, brings to life hominid evolution and themes such as bipedalism and brain development at hands-on stations. You can determine the gender, age and cause of death of a virtual skeleton at the CSI table, take and email a prehistoric photo of yourself and spot the difference between Neanderthals and *Homo sapiens* by touching skulls.

First Floor: Zoology

The 1st floor is a taxidermist's dream. Spotlighting zoology and entomology, the collection slithers, rattles, crawls, swims and swings with common, endangered and extinct species, from single-cell organisms to large mammals. Show-stoppers include a 1.4m-long giant clam in room 23, a 5.5m Amazonian anaconda in room 27, a Galapagos giant tortoise in room 28 and two-toed sloths, found in 1831 in Brazil, in room 33.

Rooftop Tours

Panoramic rooftop tours take you onto the building's roof to view the ornate architecture up-close; children under 12 aren't allowed.

DON'T MISS

- Meteorite collection
- Venus of Willendorf and Fanny of Galgenberg
- Dinosaurs in room 10
- Rooftop tours

PRACTICALITIES

- Museum of Natural History
- Map p252, G4
- www.nhm-wien.ac.at
- 01, Maria-Theresien-Platz
- adult/child €10/free, rooftop tours €8
- 9am-6.30pm Thu-Mon, to 9pm Wed, rooftop tours in English 3pm Fri, Sat & Sun
- U Museumsquartier, Volkstheater

SIGHTS

KUNSTHISTORISCHES MUSEUM — MUSEUM

See p109.

MUSEUMSQUARTIER — MUSEUM

See p115.

NATURHISTORISCHES MUSEUM — MUSEUM

See p118.

HOFMOBILIENDEPOT — MUSEUM

Map p252 (www.hofmobiliendepot.at; 07, Andreasgasse 7; adult/child €9.50/6, incl 1hr tour €11.50/7; ⌚10am-6pm; Ⓤ Neubaugasse) The Habsburgs stashed away the furniture not displayed in the Hofburg, Schönbrunn, Schloss Belvedere and their other palaces at the Hofmobiliendepot. A romp through this regal attic of a museum, covering four floors and 165,000 objects, provides fascinating insight into furniture design, with highlights such as a display of imperial travelling thrones, Emperor Maximilian's coffin and Empress Elisabeth's neo-Renaissance bed from Gödöllő Castle. One of the more underrated museums in the city, it's included in the Sisi Ticket (p67).

Biedermeier aficionados will gravitate to the 2nd floor, where over a dozen rooms are beautifully laid out in the early-19th-century style, and a few dozen chairs from the era can be tested by visitors. In all, it's the most comprehensive collection of Biedermeier furniture in the world. The 4th floor displays *Jugendstil* furniture from the likes of Otto Wagner, Loos and Hoffmann.

BURGTHEATER — THEATRE

Map p252 (☎01-514 44 4140; www.burgtheater.at; 01, Universitätsring; tours adult/child €7/3.50; ⌚tours 3pm Sep-Jun; 🚋D, 1, 2 Rathaus, Ⓤ Rathaus) This stately Renaissance-style theatre (p125) sits with aplomb on the Ringstrasse. Designed by Gottfried Semper and Karl Hasenauer in 1888, it was restored to its pre-WWII glory in 1955. The company dates to 1741, making it Europe's second oldest. If the walls could talk, they'd tell of musical milestones like the premiere of Mozart's *The Marriage of Figaro* (1786) and Beethoven's *First Symphony* (1800). For a behind-the-scenes look at this magnificent theatre, join one of the regular guided tours.

Tours zip through its history, architecture and technological wizardry: besides taking in portraits of famous Austrian actors and busts of well-known playwrights, you'll get to appreciate the full-on effect of the foyer ceiling frescoes painted by the Klimt brothers. English tours run Friday to Sunday only; otherwise they are in German with English summary.

PALAIS EPSTEIN — LANDMARK

Map p252 (☎01-401 10 2400; www.palaisepstein.at; 01, Dr-Karl-Renner-Ring 1; tours adult/child €5/3; ⌚tours 11am & 2pm Sat mid-Sep–mid-Jul; 🚋D, 1, 2 Dr-Karl-Renner-Ring, Ⓤ Volkstheater) Designed by Theophil von Hansen, the same architect who created the plans for the Österreichisches Parlament (Austrian parliament) next door, Palais Epstein houses Austrian national parliament administrative offices. You can take tours in German through its hallowed halls (the glass atrium rises an impressive four floors) and visit its *bel étage* rooms. The only way to see inside is by taking a tour.

With a filigree ceiling of gold lacework and circular frescoes (Hansen based it on detail in the Santa Maria dei Miracoli in Venice), the *Spielzimmer* (play room) is a highlight.

JUSTIZPALAST — NOTABLE BUILDING

Map p252 (☎01-521 52-0; www.ogh.gv.at; 01, Schmerlingplatz 11; ⌚7.30am-4.30pm Mon-Fri; 🚋D, 1, 2 Burgring, Ⓤ Volkstheater) Completed in 1881, the Justizpalast is home to the supreme court. It's an impressive neo-Renaissance building that – as long as

NIGHT AT THE NATURHISTORISCHES MUSEUM

If you're keen to re-create the Ben Stiller *Night at the Museum* experience, book a **Nacht im Museum**. Adults (€200) receive a gala dinner, torch/flashlight tour of the permanent collections and champagne on the roof terrace before bedding down next to the dinosaurs and breakfast the following morning at the cafe. Children (€75) must be accompanied by an adult, and also get a torch/flashlight tour. Both adults and children need to bring their own sleeping bag. Check dates and make reservations on the museum's website or at its shop.

you're not being dragged in wearing handcuffs – is also interesting inside. The 23m-high central hall is a majestic ensemble of staircase, arcades, glass roofing and an oversized statue of Justitia poised with her sword and law book. To enter, you pass through airport-style security; bring photo ID.

The cafe on the top floor is open to the general public and has great views across the Hofburg.

HAUPTBÜCHEREI WIEN LIBRARY

Map p252 (www.buechereien.wien.at; 07, Urban-Loritz-Platz; ⌚11am-7pm Mon-Fri, to 5pm Sat; Ⓤ Burggasse-Stadthalle) Vienna's central city library straddles the U6 line, its pyramid-like steps leading up to the enormous main doors, which are two storeys tall. At the top of the library is the Café Oben (p123), which has far-reaching views to the south.

EATING

FIGAR CAFE €

Map p252 (www.figar.net; 07, Kirchengasse 18; breakfast €5.50-9, mains €10-15; ⌚kitchen 8am-10.30pm Mon-Fri, 9am-4pm Sat & Sun, bar to midnight Sun-Wed, to 2am Thu-Sat; Ⓤ Neubaugasse) Splashed with a street-art-style mural, Neubau's hottest brunch spot serves spectacular breakfasts until 2pm including Working Class Hero (sausage, mushrooms, homemade baked beans, spinach and skewered roast cherry tomatoes) and Chosen (Viennese Thum ham, chorizo, Emmental and scrambled eggs), plus yoghurt, muesli, porridge and pastries. At night it morphs into a craft cocktail bar with a soundtrack of house music.

Lunch mains range from organic salads to lamb fillet with thyme and cucumber yoghurt, grilled salmon with spinach potato salad and cheese burgers with chilli tomato confit and rosemary potato fries.

PURE LIVING BAKERY CAFE €

Map p252 (www.purelivingbakery.com; 07, Burggasse 68; dishes €3.20-8.40; ⌚9am-9pm; 🚋46 Strozzigasse/Lerchenfelder Strasse) Opening to a wraparound terrace, Vienna's second, larger Pure Living Bakery (p172) has the same beach-house vibe, with retro furniture, organic coffee and superfood shakes. Vitamin-packed light bites span bagels such as Health is Wealth (avocado, tomato, cucumber and iceberg lettuce) and California Cool Classic (Atlantic smoked salmon,

TOP SIGHT RATHAUS

The crowning glory of the Ringstrasse boulevard's 19th-century architectural ensemble, Vienna's neo-Gothic City Hall was completed in 1883 by Friedrich von Schmidt of Cologne Cathedral fame and modelled on Flemish city halls. From the fountain-filled **Rathauspark**, where Josef Lanner and Johann Strauss I, fathers of the Viennese waltz, are immortalised in bronze, you get the full effect of its facade of lacy stonework, pointed-arch windows and spindly turrets.

For an insight into the Rathaus' history, take the free guided tour that leads through the **Arkadenhof**, one of Europe's biggest arcaded inner courtyards, and the barrel-vaulted **Festsaal** (Festival Hall), which hosts the Concordia Ball in June. Look for the reliefs of composers Mozart, Haydn, Gluck and Schubert in the orchestra niches. In the **Stadtsitzungsaal** (Council Chamber), a 3200kg-heavy, flower-shaped chandelier dangles from a coffered ceiling encrusted with gold-leaf rosettes and frescoes depicting historic events such as the foundation of the university in 1365. Other tour highlights include the **Stadtsenatssitzungssaal** (Senate Chamber), the **Wappensäle** (Coat of Arms Halls) and the **Steinsäle** (Stone Halls).

DON'T MISS

- Rathauspark
- Arkadenhof
- Festsaal
- Stadtsitzungsaal

PRACTICALITIES

- City Hall
- Map p252, G1
- www.wien.gv.at
- 01, Rathausplatz 1
- admission free
- ⌚tours 1pm Mon, Wed & Fri Sep-Jun, 1pm Mon-Fri Jul & Aug
- 🚋D, 1, 2 Rathaus, Ⓤ Rathaus

brie and cream cheese) to pastas, salads, cakes, cookies and artisan ice cream.

LIEBLING CAFE €

Map p252 (☎01-990 58 77; 07, Zollergasse 6; dishes €3-8.50; ⏲9am-midnight Mon-Sat, to 10pm Sun; 📶🖉; Ⓤ Neubaugasse) There's no sign hanging above the door at Liebling, where distressed walls and a mishmash of flea market furniture create a funkily shabby backdrop. Sip fresh-squeezed juices and lunch on wholesome day specials such as spinach-feta strudel, goat's cheese panna cotta or rich tomato soup, polished off with a slice of chocolate-lavender cake. Cash only.

PIZZERIA-OSTERIA DA GIOVANNI ITALIAN €

Map p252 (☎01-523 77 78; http://giovanniwien.com; 07, Sigmundsgasse 14; pizza €4.90-13.90, mains €12.80-18.90; ⏲6-11.30pm Mon-Thu, noon-3pm & 6-11.30pm Fri & Sat; 👪; 🚋49 Stiftgasse, Ⓤ Volkstheater) A slice of the south in the cobbled heart of Spittelberg, this homey Italian restaurant specialises in thin, crispy pizzas and homemade pastas, such as spinach ravioli with truffle-cream sauce. The handful of tables fills quickly, so it's worth booking. In warm weather, more tables open up in the rear covered courtyard.

TART'A TATA CAFE €

Map p252 (07, Lindengasse 35; dishes €4-6.50; ⏲8am-7pm Mon-Sat; Ⓤ Neubaugasse) This retro-cool French cafe wouldn't look out of place in Paris' Le Marais. It does a delectable line in quiches, crêpes, pure-butter croissants and patisserie, including a superb *tarte aux fraises* (strawberry tart).

DIE BURGERMACHER BURGERS €

Map p252 (www.dieburgermacher.at; 07, Burggasse 12; burgers €8.50-10.50; ⏲5-10.30pm Tue-Fri, noon-10.30pm Sat, noon-9.30pm Sun; 🖉; Ⓤ Volkstheater) 🌿 The burgers at this small, alternative joint are made using organic ingredients and include meat and vegetarian options, from halloumi cheese to Mexican varieties. If you can't get a table, grab a spot at the side bench or order takeaway.

KANTINE CAFE €

Map p252 (☎01-523 82 39; www.mq-kantine.at; 07, Museumsplatz 1; mains €8.50-13.50; ⏲kitchen 11am-midnight, bar 9am-2am; 📶🖉; Ⓤ Museumsquartier) This upbeat cafe/bar in the former stables of the emperor's personal steeds is the most laid-back spot to eat in the MuseumsQuartier. Lit by a disco ball, the vaulted interior has comfy chairs for lounging, surfing and refuelling over a salad, pita wrap or one of 40 cocktails. In summer, tables spill out onto the patio on MuseumsQuartier's main square.

Glühwein (mulled wine) keeps things warm in winter.

ST JOSEF VEGETARIAN €

Map p252 (☎01-526 68 18; 07, Mondscheingasse 10; plate small/large €8.30/9.20; ⏲8am-5pm Mon-Fri, to 4pm Sat; 🖉; 🚋49 Siebensterngasse, Ⓤ Neubaugasse) 🌿 St Josef is a canteen-like all-organic vegetarian place that cooks to a theme each day (Indian, for instance) and gives you the choice of a small or large plate filled with the various offerings. It has a sparse, industrial character, which is part of its charm, a young and arty vibe, plus super-friendly staff.

GRADWOHL BAKERY €

Map p252 (www.gradwohl.info; 07, Zieglergasse 1; dishes €1.50-3.50; ⏲7am-6pm Mon-Fri, to noon Sat; Ⓤ Zieglergasse) 🌿 Part of a chain known for its organic wholegrain bread, this handy branch just off Mariahilfer Strasse makes a quick, healthy stop for a freshly prepared sandwich or baguette.

MASCHU MASCHU II MIDDLE EASTERN €

Map p252 (☎01-990 47 13; www.maschu-maschu.at; 07, Neubaugasse 20; falafel €5.40-7.90, mains €7.20-19.80; ⏲10.30am-midnight; 🖉; Ⓤ Neubaugasse) This Neubau outpost of the Maschu Maschu minichain is a fully fledged restaurant with sunny streetside seating – when the weather's playing along – and a menu loaded with lamb dishes. Its **Innere Stadt branch** (Map p244; ☎01-533 29 04; www.maschu-maschu.at; 01, Rabensteig 8; dishes €5.40-8.90; ⏲10.30am-midnight; 🖉; 🚋1, 2, Ⓤ Schwedenplatz) primarily does takeaway.

★TIAN BISTRO VEGETARIAN €€

Map p252 (☎01-890 466 532; www.tian-bistro.com; 07, Schrankgasse 4; mains €10-18; ⏲11.30am-10pm Mon-Fri, 9am-10pm Sat & Sun; 🖉; 🚋49 Siebensterngasse/Stiftgasse, Ⓤ Volkstheater) Colourful tables set up on the cobbled laneway outside Tian Bistro in summer, while indoors, a glass roof floods the atrium-style, greenery-filled dining room in light. It's the cheaper, more relaxed offspring of Michelin-starred vegetarian restaurant Tian (p87), and serves sublime vegetarian and vegan dishes such as black truffle risotto with Piedmont hazelnuts, as well as serving breakfast until 2pm on weekends.

GLACIS BEISL BISTRO €€

Map p252 (☎01-526 56 60; http://glacisbeisl.at; 07, Breite Gasse 4; mains €7.60-17.80; ⏲kitchen noon-11pm, bar 11am-2am; ; UVolkstheater) Hidden downstairs along Breite Strasse in the MuseumsQuartier (follow the signs from MUMOK), Glacis Beisl does an authentic goulash, an accomplished *Wiener Schnitzel* and some other very decent Austrian classics, which you can wash down with local Viennese reds and whites. In summer, dine beneath the walnut trees among flowering geraniums in the sprawling courtyard.

AMERLINGBEISL AUSTRIAN €€

Map p252 (☎01-526 16 60; www.amerlingbeisl.at; 07, Stiftgasse 8; mains €7-16; ⏲kitchen noon-midnight, bar 9am-2am; 49 Stiftgasse, UVolkstheater) This tucked-away Spittelberg *Beisl* is an enchanting summer choice for its cobbled, lantern-lit courtyard swathed in ivy and vines. The seasonally inspired food hits the mark, too, whether you opt for pasta like fettuccine with wild garlic or mains such as crispy schnitzel with cranberry sauce, local *Würstel* (sausage) with potato salad or light dishes like smoked trout salad. Look out for the weekly cocktail special (€5).

HALLE INTERNATIONAL €€

Map p252 (☎01-523 70 01; www.diehalle.at; 07, Museumsplatz 1; mains €8.50-18.90, 2-course lunch menus €8.90-9.90; ⏲kitchen 10am-midnight, bar to 2am; ; UMuseumsquartier) Halle is the versatile resident eatery of the Kunsthalle, with a good buzz and optical tricks like cylindrical lamps and low tables. The chefs whip up antipasti, risottos, pastas, salads, plus several Austrian all-rounders like goulash and pan-Asian dishes. On steamy summer days it's usually a fight for a shaded outside table between the Kunsthalle and MUMOK.

KONOBA DALMATIAN €€

Map p252 (☎01-929 41 11; www.konoba.at; 08, Lerchenfelder Strasse 66-68; mains €12-19; ⏲5pm-midnight; UThaliastrasse) Few restaurants in the city come close to Konoba's expertise with fish. The Dalmatian chefs know their product inside out and serve some of the freshest catch in town. Zander and *Goldbrasse* (sea bream) are often on the menu, but expect to find a healthy array of seasonal dishes too. The open-plan interior creates a convivial atmosphere.

GAUMENSPIEL BISTRO €€

Map p252 (☎01-526 11 08; www.gaumenspiel.at; 07, Zieglergasse 54; mains €18-28, 4-/5-course menus €36/48; ⏲6-10.30pm Mon-Sat; ; 49 Westbahnstrasse/Zieglergasse, UBurggasse Stadthalle) There's a real neighbourly feel to this *Beisl,* where a red-walled, wood-floored interior and tiny courtyard garden create a pleasantly low-key backdrop for fine dining. Mediterranean-Austrian specialities reveal an attentive eye for quality, detail and presentation – be it goat's cheese soufflé with dates or wild duck with rose hip–red cabbage and mandarin polenta.

VESTIBÜL AUSTRIAN €€€

Map p252 (☎01-532 49 99; www.vestibuel.at; 01, Universitätsring 2; 3-course lunch menu €31, 3-/4-course dinner menus €53/67, mains €16-42; ⏲noon-2.30pm & 6-10.30pm Mon-Fri, 6-10.30pm Sat; D, 1, 2 Rathaus, Stadiongasse, URathaus) In the southern wing of the Burgtheater, Vestibül is a showpiece of marble columns and stucco topped off with a glorious sparkling mirrored bar. The menu is a contemporary take on traditional cuisine with a strong regional and seasonal focus; expect such dishes as lobster meat with sauerkraut and saffron-poached catfish with root vegetables and meadow herbs. Reservations recommended.

DRINKING & NIGHTLIFE

★BRICKMAKERS PUB & KITCHEN CRAFT BEER

Map p252 (☎01-997 44 14; www.brickmakers.at; 07, Zieglergasse 42; ⏲4pm-2am Mon-Fri, 10am-2am Sat, 10am-1am Sun; UZieglergasse) British racing-green metro tiles, a mosaic floor and a soundtrack of disco, hip-hop, funk and soul set the scene for brilliant craft beers and ciders: there are 30 on tap at any one time and over 150 by the bottle. Pop-ups take over the kitchen, and at lunch and dinner guest chefs cook anything from gourmet fish and chips to BBQ-smoked beef brisket.

LE TROQUET — BAR

Map p252 (www.letroquet.at; 07, Kirchengasse 18; ⏲11am-2am Mon-Sat, 5pm-2am Sun; ⓤNeubaugasse) French is lingua franca at Le Troquet, which is styled like a Parisian cafe with a zinc bar. Wines and craft beers are sourced from all over France, and cocktails are retro (Harvey Wallbanger, Cuba Libre). Classic French cafe dishes include *croques monsieur* and *madame* (toasted ham and cheese sandwiches, the latter with a fried egg on top).

DONAU — CLUB

Map p252 (www.donautechno.com; 07, Karl-Schweighofer-Gasse 10; ⏲8pm-4am Mon-Thu, to 6am Fri & Sat, to 2am Sun; ⓤMuseumsquartier) DJs spin techno to a pumped crowd at this columned, strikingly illuminated club. It's easily missed – look for the grey metal door. It has its own on-site *Würstelstand* (sausage stand).

DACHBODEN — BAR

Map p252 (www.25hours-hotels.com; 07, Lerchenfelder Strasse 1-3; ⏲3pm-1am; 📶; ⓤVolkstheater) Housed in the 25hours Hotel (p195), Dachboden has stunning views of Vienna's skyline from its beach bar–style decked terrace. DJs spins jazz, soul and funk on Wednesday and Friday nights. Inside, wooden crates and mismatched vintage furniture are scattered across the raw-concrete floor beneath chandeliers. Besides Fritz cola and an array of wines, beers and speciality teas, there are tapas-style snacks.

SIEBENSTERNBRÄU — MICROBREWERY

Map p252 (www.7stern.at; 07, Siebensterngasse 19; ⏲11am-midnight; ⓤNeubaugasse) Swig some of Vienna's finest microbrews at this lively, no-nonsense brewpub. Besides hoppy lagers and malty ales, there are unusual varieties like hemp, chilli and wood-smoked beer. Try them with pretzels or pub grub like schnitzel, goulash and pork knuckles (lunch mains €6.90, dinner mains €7.50 to €18.90). The courtyard garden fills up quickly in the warmer months. Takeaway refillable growlers are available.

ROTE BAR — BAR

Map p252 (www.rotebar.at; 07, Neustiftgasse 1; ⏲10pm-2am Mon-Fri, to 4am Sat, to 1am Sun; ⓤVolkstheater) Look for the small door to the left of the Volkstheater's main entrance to find the stairs up to this marble-, chandelier- and thick-red-velvet-curtain–bedecked bar. It's a gorgeous space for cocktails or by-the-glass wines with antipasti. It hosts regular events, from Wednesday-night performance art sessions to DJ-fuelled Saturday dance nights, plus occasional tango nights, poetry readings and more.

CAFÉ LEOPOLD — BAR

Map p252 (www.cafe-leopold.at; 07, Museumsplatz 1; ⏲10am-midnight Sun-Wed, to 4am Thu, to 6am Fri & Sat; 📶; ⓤMuseumsquartier, Volkstheater) The pick of the MuseumsQuartier bars, Café Leopold sits on top of the Leopold Museum. Its design is sleek, with spacey lighting and a conservatory overlooking the action on MuseumsQuartier's square, and the atmosphere is more club than bar. DJs feature Thursday to Saturday; hip-hop figures prominently. In chilly months, the outdoor terrace becomes a winter garden.

EUROPA — BAR

Map p252 (www.europa-lager.at; 07, Zollergasse 8; ⏲9am-5am; 📶; ⓤNeubaugasse) A long-standing fixture of the 7th district, Europa is a chilled spot any time of the day or night. During daylight hours, grab a window table for coffee and food. In the evening, perch at the bar and listen to the DJs spin tunes. Breakfast (9am and 3pm daily) caters to a hungover clientele; Sunday features a sumptuous breakfast buffet.

CAFÉ OBEN — CAFE

Map p252 (www.oben.at; 07, Urban-Loritz-Platz 2a; ⏲10am-11pm Mon-Thu, 9am-11pm Fri & Sat, 10am-3pm Sun; ⓤBurggasse-Stadthalle) *Oben* ('up') on top of the Hauptbücherei Wien (p120), the rooftop terrace here provides a sweeping vista of Vienna to the south. Come for a coffee, Upper Austria–sourced organic juice, Viennese wine, Austrian beer, schnapps or cocktails with a view, or a good-value, two-course lunch (€7.50 to €9.80). Sunday brunch (€18.80) is extremely popular.

WIRR — BAR

Map p252 (http://wirr.at; 07, Burggasse 70; ⏲8am-2am Sun-Fri, to 4am Sat; ⓤVolkstheater, Burggasse-Stadthalle) On weekends it's often hard to find a seat on the time-worn sofas at this colourful, alternative bar whose walls are covered in local artists' work. Eclectic club nights – which range from '60s pop to Balkan rhythms – are held downstairs.

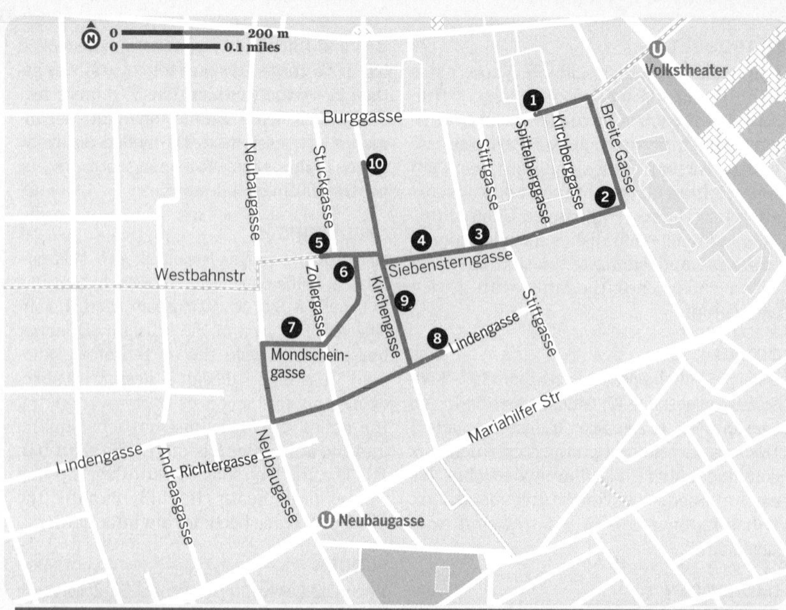

Local Life
Neubau's Design Scene

The ultimate place to tap into Vienna's burgeoning fashion and design scene is the happening 7th district, Neubau, a hotbed of creativity where you'll often see artisans at work. This half-day stroll takes you to boutiques showcasing creations by the city's most exciting designers, ateliers and fashion-focused cafes. For the inside scoop, visit www.7tm.at.

❶ Coffee & Shopping

Das Möbel (Map p252; http://dasmoebel.at; 07, Burggasse 10; ⏲2pm-midnight Mon-Fri, 10am-midnight Sat & Sun; ⓤVolkstheater) is as much of a hip cafe as a shop, but it showcases some of the funkiest and most original furniture in Vienna by local artists and designers, which is all for sale.

❷ The Workbench

Furniture, lamps, rugs, vases, jewellery, watches, graphic art, bags, even bicycles are among the creations you might find on display at **Die Werkbank** (Map p252; www.werkbank.cc; 07, Breite Gasse 1; ⏲noon-6.30pm Tue-Fri, 11am-5pm Sat; ⓤVolkstheater) – 'The Workbench' – an all-white space that operates as a design collective, where some of Vienna's most innovative designers showcase their works.

❸ Experimental Fashion

All of the women's casual wear pieces at **Wiener Konfektion** (Map p252; www.wienerkonfektion.at; 07, Siebensterngasse 20; ⏲12.30-6.30pm Wed-Fri, noon-5pm Sat; 🚋49 Siebensterngasse) are designed and made in Vienna by experimental owner/designer Maria Fürnkranz-Fielhauer, who uses contemporary fabrics, denim and wool blends but especially vintage '60s and '70s fabrics to create T-shirts, skirts, dresses, sweat pants and more.

❹ Art Deco & Bauhaus Designs

Holzer Galerie (Map p252; www.galerieholzer.at; 07, Siebensterngasse 32; ⏲10am-noon & 2-6pm Mon-Fri, to 5pm Sat; 🚋49 Siebensterngasse, ⓤNeubaugasse) is the place for high-quality, highly polished furniture, ornaments, lighting and art mainly from the art deco and Bauhaus periods, plus easier-to-transport art deco–inspired jewellery.

❺ Handcrafted Bags

Understated clutch, shoulder and tote bags, crafted from vegetable-tanned leather by **Ina Kent** (Map p252; www.inakent.com; 07, Siebensterngasse 50; ⏰11am-7pm Mon-Fri, to 6pm Sat; 🚊49 Siebensterngasse, Ⓤ Volkstheater), are coveted by locals. Attached to the boutique is Ina's workshop where you may spot her crafting the pieces for sale.

❻ Applied Arts

Schauraum (Map p252; ☎01-676 757 67 00; www.schauraum.at; 07, Siebensterngasse 33; ⏰by appointment; 🚊49 Siebensterngasse, Ⓤ Neubaugasse) zooms in on unusual applied arts. Besides cutting-edge tableware and accessories, you'll find Karin Merkl's clever, versatile jumpers, scarves and jackets made from merino wool or silk.

❼ Fashion Forward

A serious designer store in a stark all-white 480-sq-metre space, **Park** (Map p252; www.park.co.at; 07, Mondscheingasse 20; ⏰10am-7pm Mon-Fri, to 6pm Sat; Ⓤ Neubaugasse) stocks fashion books, magazines, accessories and furnishings as well as cutting-edge fashion.

❽ Catwalk Trends

Silky, curve-enhancing dresses, separates and swimwear by design maven **Elke Freytag** (Map p252; http://elkefreytag.com; 07, Lindengasse 14; ⏰noon-6pm Wed-Fri, 10am-3pm Sat; 🚊49 Siebensterngasse, Ⓤ Neubaugasse) regularly grace catwalks in Vienna and beyond.

❾ Emerging Talent

Forward-looking boutique **S/GHT** (Map p252; www.sight.at; 07, Kirchengasse 24; ⏰11am-6pm Mon-Sat; Ⓤ Neubaugasse) promotes emerging Austrian labels such as Katharina Schmid, Meshit and Sightline along with breakthrough international designers.

❿ Unique Jewellery

At the **Schmuckladen** (Map p252; http://baustelle.schmuckladen.org/wordpress; 07, Kirchengasse 40; ⏰1-6.30pm Wed, 11am-6.30pm Thu & Fri, 11am-5pm Sat; 🚊49 Siebensterngasse, Ⓤ Volkstheater) workshop, goldsmith Ilga puts her own imaginative spin on jewellery, from fragile silver leaf necklaces to quirky button rings.

FRAUENCAFÉ LESBIAN, CAFE

Map p252 (http://frauencafe.com; 08, Lange Gasse 11; ⏰6pm-midnight Thu & Fri, plus special events; Ⓤ Rathaus, Volkstheater) A strictly women-, lesbian- and transgendered-only cafe-bar, Frauencafé has long been a favourite of Vienna's lesbian scene. It has a homely, relaxed feel and is located away from the hub of gay and lesbian bars around Die Villa (p225).

☆ ENTERTAINMENT

★BURGTHEATER THEATRE

Map p252 (National Theatre; ☎01-514 44 4440; www.burgtheater.at; 01, Universitätsring 2; seats €7.50-61, standing room €3.50, students €9; ⏰box office 9am-5pm Mon-Fri; 🚊D, 1, 2 Rathaus, Ⓤ Rathaus) The Burgtheater hasn't lost its touch over the years – this is one of the foremost theatres in the German-speaking world, staging some 800 performances a year, which reach from Shakespeare to Woody Allen plays. The theatre also runs the 500-seater Akademietheater, which was built between 1911 and 1913.

Tickets at the Burgtheater and Akademietheater sell for 75% of their face value an hour before performances. Advance bookings are recommended, although, depending on the performance, some last-minute tickets may be available.

VOLKSTHEATER THEATRE

Map p252 (☎01-521 11-400; www.volkstheater.at; 07, Neustiftgasse 1; tickets €11-53; ⏰box office 10am-7.30pm Mon-Sat; Ⓤ Volkstheater) With a seating capacity close to 1000, the Volkstheater is one of Vienna's largest theatres. Built in 1889, the interior is suitably grand. While most performances are translations (anything from Woody Allen to Ingmar Bergman to Molière), only German-language shows are staged. Students can buy unsold tickets for €5 one hour before performances start. Advance bookings are necessary.

VIENNA'S ENGLISH THEATRE THEATRE

Map p252 (☎01-402 12 60; www.englishtheatre.at; 08, Josefsgasse 12; tickets €24-47; ⏰box office 10am-7.30pm Mon-Fri, 5-7.30pm Sat performance days mid-Aug–Jun, closed Jul–mid-Aug; 🚊2 Rathaus, Josefstädter Strasse, Ⓤ Rathaus) Founded in 1963, Vienna's English Theatre is the oldest foreign-language theatre in

Vienna (with the occasional show in French or Italian). Productions range from timeless pieces, such as Shakespeare, to contemporary works and comedies. Students receive a 20% discount. Standby tickets for €10 go on sale 15 minutes before showtime.

SHOPPING

★DIRNDLHERZ — CLOTHING

Map p252 (http://dirndlherz.at; 07, Lerchenfelder Strasse 50; 11am-6pm Thu & Fri, to 4pm Sat; U Volkstheater) Putting her own spin on alpine fashion, Austrian designer Gabriela Urabl creates one-of-a-kind, high-fashion *Dirndls* (women's traditional dress), from sassy purple-velvet bosom-lifters to 1950s-style gingham numbers and *Dirndls* emblazoned with quirky motifs like pop-art and punk-like conical metal studs. T-shirts with tag-lines like *'Mei Dirndl is in da Wäsch'* ('My *Dirndl* is in the wash') are also available.

MÜHLBAUER — HATS

Map p252 (www.muehlbauer.at; 07, Neubaugasse 34; 10am-6.30pm Mon-Fri, to 6pm Sat; U Neubaugasse) This large boutique of Austrian milliner **Mühlbauer** (Map p246; 01, Seilergasse 10; 10am-6.30pm Mon-Fri, to 6pm Sat; U Stephansplatz) uses materials such as felt, alpaca wool, mohair, rabbit, suede, cashmere, straw, seaweed, fur, merino wool and moleskin. Every style imaginable is available, including new collections each season. Or you can have one custom made in four weeks – shipping is available worldwide.

SCHOKOV — CHOCOLATE

Map p252 (www.schokov.com; 07, Siebensterngasse 20; noon-6.30pm Mon-Fri, 10am-6pm Sat; 49 Stiftgasse, U Volkstheater) Thomas Kovazh turned his chocolate-making dream into reality when he opened this sleek gallery-style shop. Today, Schokov sells some of Vienna's best pralines and truffles (over 200 varieties). Chilli, lavender, sea-salt, potato and pepper chocolate – you'll find them all in bar form here, alongside top Austrian brands like Zotter and Berger. A 1½-hour, 20-chocolate tasting workshop costs €29.

ART POINT — FASHION & ACCESSORIES

Map p252 (http://artpoint.eu; 07, Neubaugasse 35; 11am-7pm Mon-Fri, to 5pm Sat; 49 Neubaugasse, Westbahnstrasse, U Neubaugasse) This boutique-design platform presents Lena Kvadrat's latest Austrian-Russian collection. Versatility is the hallmark, with pieces often layering fabrics so that they can be worn in different ways to create unique looks.

MOTMOT — FASHION & ACCESSORIES

Map p252 (www.motmotshop.com; 07, Kirchengasse 36; noon-7pm Tue-Fri, to 5pm Sat; U Volkstheater, Neubaugasse) This husband-and-wife team (both former graphic designers) creates custom clothes with fun flair – each piece is screenprinted by hand on American Apparel T-shirts and sweatshirts; choose from the 20-plus designs (imagine a comic book come to life) and colours. They also sell mugs, buttons, posters and art books.

GÖTTIN DES GLÜCKS — FASHION & ACCESSORIES

Map p252 (www.goettindesgluecks.com; 07, Kirchengasse 17; 11am-2pm & 2.30-6.30pm Mon-Fri, 11am-5pm Sat; U Neubaugasse) Austria's first fair-fashion label conforms to the fair-trade model throughout the production process through relationships with sustainable producers in India, Mauritius and beyond. The result is supple, delicious cotton jerseys, skirts, and shorts for men and women, with the comfort of sleepwear in stylish, casual daywear.

SPORTS & ACTIVITIES

WIENER EISTRAUM — ICE SKATING

Map p252 (www.wienereistraum.at; 01, Rathausplatz; adult/child from €4, pre-heated skate hire €7.50/5.50; 9am-10pm late Jan-early Mar; D, 1, 2 Rathaus, U Rathaus) In the heart of winter, Rathausplatz transforms into two connected ice rinks covering a total of 8000 sq metres. It's a magnet for the city's ice skaters, and the rinks are complemented by DJs, food stands, special events and *Glühwein* bars. The skating path zigzags through the nearby park and around the entire square.

There's a free skating area and free equipment for beginners and children, open 9am to 4pm Monday to Friday, 8am to 10pm Saturday and Sunday. At 5pm Monday to Friday, eight curling lanes set up here.

Alsergrund & the University District

Neighbourhood Top Five

❶ **Sigmund Freud Museum** (p130) Getting in touch with your inner Freudian as you explore his former home, with exhibits providing a tantalising insight into the life of the father of psychoanalysis.

❷ **Palais Liechtenstein** (p129) Tiptoeing through the palace's baroque apartments and landscaped gardens on a guided tour.

❸ **University Main Building** (p129) Going for an wander through the arcades and courtyards of Vienna's 650-year-old university.

❹ **Beethoven Pasqualatihaus** (p129) Conjuring Beethoven's Foutth, Fifth and Seventh Symphonies in the airy apartment in which they were written.

❺ **Schubert Geburtshaus** (p129) Catching a concert in the composer's childhood home.

❻ **Café Central** (p135) Listening to a pianist play in the vaulted, marble-columned grandeur of this touristy cafe.

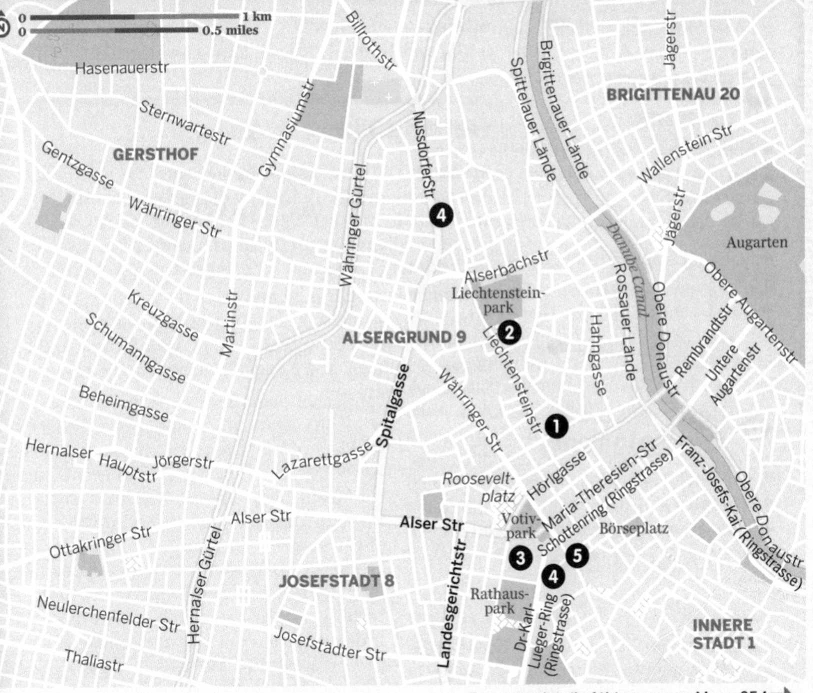

For more detail of this area see Map p254

Lonely Planet's Top Tip

This neighbourhood throws itself into a festive summer vortex when it plays host to the Summer Stage (p26), with food pavilions and stages strung along Rossauer Lände, on the banks of the Danube Canal. The mood is incredibly upbeat, and there are regular concerts – some free – reaching from jazz to tango, rock to pop. It's on evenings between 5pm and 1am from May to September (take the U4 to Rossauer Lände). The website has the inside scoop.

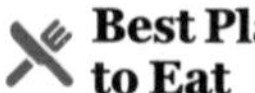

Best Places to Eat

- Punks (p134)
- Flein (p132)
- Wetter (p134)
- Mamamon (p131)

For reviews, see p131.

Best Places to Drink

- Achtundzwanzig (p135)
- Botanical Gardens (p135)
- Lane & Merriman's (p135)
- Weinstube Josefstadt (p136)
- POC Cafe (p135)

For reviews, see p135.

Best Entertainment

- Volksoper (p137)
- B72 (p137)
- Miles Smiles (p138)

For reviews, see p137.

Explore Alsergrund & the University District

The cool but far from contrived neighbourhoods of the 8th, 9th and 16th are decidedly local and best experienced at a laid-back Viennese pace. These are streets made for wandering and stopping for well-made coffees, a sneaky Gruner Veltiner or quietly smart lunches, rather than ticking off iconic museums or wow-factor vistas. Once you leave the corporate types behind around the Innere Stadt, campus life and its cafes, bars and little shops begin in Alsergrund Vorstadt. In Josefstädterstrasse and the little streets running north you'll find a similar mix, or else wander west towards Ottakring for bass-thumping bars and upbeat music haunts hidden under the Gürtel's railway arches.

Local Life

- **Street Markets** Feel Vienna's multiethnic pulse while snacking and strolling around Brunnenmarkt (p132), and find farm-fresh produce at the Bauernmarkt (p132) and Freyung market (p138).
- **Backstreets** This is a terrific neighbourhood for getting off the beaten track. Slip down quiet, tree-lined backstreets to find little-known sights like the Museum für Volkskunde (p131).
- **Cafes** Coffee kings POC (p135), studenty Café Stein (p135) and Tunnel (p136) all have a loyal local following.

Getting There & Away

- **U-Bahn** The closest stops to the centre for reaching Alsergrund and the university district are Schottentor and Rathaus on the U2 line. The U6 line follows the Gürtel further west; useful stops include Alser Strasse, Josefstädter Strasse and Währingerstrasse-Volksoper.
- **Tram** Schottentor is a handy stop on the Ring. Other tram lines serving this neighbourhood include 44, which runs from Schottentor along Alser Strasse to the Hernalser Gürtel, and 5 and 33, which trundle along Josefstädterstrasse.

SIGHTS

PALAIS LIECHTENSTEIN PALACE

Map p254 (☎01-319 57 67; www.liechtensteinmuseum.at; 09, Fürstengasse 1; tours €20; ⊙guided tours 3pm 1st & 3rd Fri of the month; 🚋D, Ⓤ Rossauer Lände) Once the architectural muse of Italian landscape painter Canaletto, Palais Liechtenstein is a sublime baroque palace that sits in beautifully landscaped and sculpture-dotted grounds. It also houses the private art collection of Prince Hans-Adam II of Liechtenstein (whose family resided in Vienna until the Nazi *Anschluss* in 1938), with around 200 paintings and 50 sculptures dating from 1500 to 1700. The palace can be visited twice monthly on hour-long guided tours (in German; English-language audio guide available). Book ahead.

On the ground floor, the unmissable **Gentlemen's Apartment Library** is a magnificent neoclassical hall containing about 100,000 books and frescoes by Johann Michael Rottmayr. Upstairs is the **Herkulessaal** (Hercules Hall) – so named for the Hercules motifs within its ceiling frescoes by renowned Roman painter Andrea Pozzo (1642–1709). Surrounding the hall are seven **art galleries** providing a trip through 200 years of art history, including such stunners as Raphael's *Portrait of a Man* (1503) and Rubens' intensely perceptive *Portrait of Clara Serena Rubens* (1616), alongside masterpieces of the Van Dyck and Frans Hals ilk. Keep an eye out for one of the world's most valuable pieces of furniture, the **Florentine Badminton Cabinet**, made for the British nobleman Henry Somerset, the 3rd Duke of Beaufort, in the 1720s.

To get here take tram D to Seegasse.

UNIVERSITY MAIN BUILDING UNIVERSITY

Map p254 (☎01-427 70, tours 01-427 71 7525; www.univie.ac.at; 01, Dr-Karl-Lueger-Ring 1; guided tours adult/child €5/3; ⊙7am-10pm Mon-Fri, to 7pm Sat, guided tours in English 11.30am Sat; 🚋D, 1, 2, Ⓤ Schottentor) FREE Founded in 1365, Vienna's venerable university was the first in the German-speaking countries. Today it enrols up to 95,000 students. Grand Duke Rudolph IV (1339–65) used Paris' Sorbonne as his inspiration, and it was just as well he wasn't around in 1520 during the Reformation, because in that year his 'Sorbonne' was shoe-horned into the Church.

In fact, occasional head-clinching between religious and secular institutions over the centuries is a feature of Vienna's university history. When Maria Theresia squeezed the Church out of Austrian universities during the Enlightenment in the mid-18th century, she almost made the uni trim and fit for the modern age. (We say 'almost' because the first woman wasn't admitted until 1897.) During the Nazi era, about half the professors and tutors had to pack their bags due to either their politics or their 'race'.

One-hour **guided tours** take you through the late-19th-century neo-Renaissance and neo-baroque arcades, reading room and, when possible, the decorative main ceremonial chamber. They leave from the porter's office in the entrance hall.

Directly opposite the university is the **Votivkirche** (Votive Church; www.votivkirche.at; 09, Rooseveltplatz; ⊙2-6pm Mon-Fri, 9am-1pm & 4-6pm Sat, to 1pm Sun) FREE, and also the **Mölker Bastei**, one of the couple of remaining sections of the old city walls.

BEETHOVEN PASQUALATIHAUS MUSEUM, HOUSE

Map p254 (www.wienmuseum.at; 01, Mölker Bastei 8; adult/child €5/free; ⊙10am-1pm & 2-6pm Tue-Sun; 🚋D, 1, 2, Ⓤ Schottentor) Beethoven resided on the 4th floor of this house from 1804 to 1814 (he apparently lived in around 80 places in his 35 years in Vienna, but thankfully not all of them are museums). During that time he composed Symphonies 4, 5 and 7 and the opera *Fidelio,* among other works. His two rooms (plus another two from a neighbouring apartment) have been converted into this airy museum, which has a not-too-overwhelming collection of portraits, articles and personal belongings. The house is named after its long-time owner, Josef Benedikt Freiherr von Pasqualati.

SCHUBERT GEBURTSHAUS MUSEUM, HOUSE

Map p254 (www.wienmuseum.at; 09, Nussdorfer Strasse 54; adult/child €5/free; ⊙10am-1pm & 2-6pm Tue-Sun; 🚋37, 38, Ⓤ Währinger Strasse) The house where Schubert was born in 1797 (in the kitchen) was known at that time as *Zum roten Krebsen* (The Red Crab), but Schubert probably didn't remember much about that – he and his family toddled off to greater things when he was five. Apart from his trademark glasses, the house is rather short on objects. But devoted 'Schubertologists' might like to trek here, especially to catch the occasional concert. Tram to Canisiusgasse.

PALAIS DAUN-KINSKY NOTABLE BUILDING

Map p254 (www.palaisevents.at; 01, Freyung 4; ⌚10am-6pm Mon-Fri; UHerrengasse, Schottentor) Built by Hildebrandt in 1716, Palais Kinsky has a classic baroque facade; its highlight is an elaborate, three-storey stairway off to the left of the first inner courtyard, with elegant banisters graced with statues at every turn. The ceiling fresco is a fanciful creation filled with podgy cherubs, bare-breasted beauties and the occasional strongman. The palace now contains gift shops and upmarket restaurants.

SCHOTTENKIRCHE CHURCH

Map p254 (www.schotten.wien; 01, Freyung; ⌚museum 11am-5pm Tue-Sat, church shop 10am-6pm Mon-Fri, to 5pm Sat, closed Mon in high season; UHerrengasse, Schottentor) FREE The Schottenkirche (Church of the Scots), at the northern end of Herrengasse, was founded by Benedictine monks probably originating from Scotia Maior (Ireland); the present facade dates from the 19th century. The interior has a beautifully frescoed ceiling and terracotta-red touches. Although the main nave can only be entered during services at noon and 6pm daily, it's possible to peek through the gates. A small art and artefacts **museum** (adult/child €8/2) in the adjoining monastery displays religious pieces, but of more interest is the church **shop**, which has homemade schnapps, honey and jams.

KUNSTFORUM GALLERY

Map p254 (www.bankaustria-kunstforum.at; 01, Freyungasse 8; adult/child €11/4; ⌚10am-7pm Sat-Thu, to 9pm Fri; UHerrengasse) This private museum gets about 300,000 visitors each year, and for good reason – it stages an exciting program of changing exhibitions, usually highlighting crowd-pleasing modernist or big-name contemporary artists. The work of Miquel Barceló, Fernando Botero, Frida Kahlo, Balthus and Martin Kippenberger have all had their turn in recent years.

PIARISTENKIRCHE CHURCH

Map p254 (www.mariatreu.at; 08, Jodok-Fink-Platz; ⌚8am-6pm; URathaus) FREE The Piaristenkirche (Church of the Piarist Order), or Maria Treu Church, is notable for two interior features. The stunning **ceiling frescoes**, completed by Franz Anton Maulbertsch in 1753, depict various stories from the Bible, while the **organ** holds the distinction of being used by Anton Bruckner for his entry examination into the music academy.

TOP SIGHT
SIGMUND FREUD MUSEUM

The father of modern psychoanalysis spent his most prolific years in this house, and developed his most groundbreaking theories here. He and his family moved there in 1891 and stayed until forced into exile by the Nazis in 1938. Freud's youngest daughter, Anna, helped to transform the apartment into this museum in 1971.

Explore the rooms and picture Freud puffing on a cigar as he pondered the unconscious. These include the exquisitely furnished, if a tad claustrophobic, **waiting room**, where the Wednesday Psychological Society first met in 1902; the **consulting room** that once contained Freud's famous couch (now in London); and **Freud's study**. An **audio guide** gives background on exhibits and interview excerpts, including one where Freud talks about psychoanalytic theory.

There are also original editions of books, typescripts and cabinets devoted to Freud's obsessions (travelling, collecting antiquities, and, yes, smoking), as well as screenings of black-and-white Edison movies like *An Artist's Dream*. Another room is devoted to Anna Freud, born here in 1895, who became a leading light in the field of child psychoanalysis.

DON'T MISS

- The waiting room
- The consulting room
- Anna Freud's mirror in her father's study

PRACTICALITIES

- Map p254, F4
- www.freud-museum.at
- 09, Berggasse 19
- adult/child €10/4
- ⌚10am-6pm
- D, USchottentor, Schottenring

BETHAUS JEWISH SITE

Map p254 (Alten AKH University; 09, Spitalgasse 2, Courtyard 6, Alten AKH; USchottentor) FREE This tiny Jewish prayer house, replete with an atrium roof, is part of the Alten AKH university campus; it was originally built in 1903 for Jewish patients of the hospital. Destroyed by the Nazis in 1938, it was completely reimagined in postmodernist style in the 1970s, and functions today both as a memorial and as a contemporary art installation. Mostly it's locked, but you can see inside. The transparent floor chronicles the prayer house's fate: one level depicts Max Fleischer's original design from 1903; above that is a text from the Gestapo about the pogroms of 1938 against Vienna's Jews; the third layer is a plan of the transformer station. The atrium roof is a glass version of Fleischer's original roof. Bulgarian-born artist Minna Antova was responsible for these conceptual features, which successfully capture a mood of vulnerability.

JOSEPHINUM MUSEUM

Map p254 (www.josephinum.meduniwien.ac.at; 09, Währinger Strasse 25; adult/child €8/free, guided tours €4; 4-8pm Wed, 10am-6pm Fri-Sat, guided tour 11am Fri; ; UWähringer Strasse/Volksoper) Architecture fans sometimes visit this Enlightenment-era complex for its superb 1785 neo-classical structures alone, although Joseph II's medical academy for army surgeons does, in fact, house the city's most unusual museum. The highlight is its collection of 200-year-old anatomical and obstetric models made of wax: while designed as visual aids for teaching, they were also intended for public viewing and to this day are exhibited in their original display cases, made of rosewood and Venetian glass.

Three rooms of this earnest gore can occasionally make you feel like you've wandered onto the set of a horror movie or some hitherto unexplored part of your psyche. If you are confident you can hold down your breakfast, don't forget to save enough time to also see the large collection of medical instruments – 'everything from tourniquets to cystoscopes', the website promises – death masks and an oddly compelling collection of oil paintings, watercolours and photographs depicting operations and medical conditions.

MUSEUM FÜR VOLKSKUNDE MUSEUM

Map p254 (www.volkskundemuseum.at; 08, Laudongasse 15-19; adult/child €8/free; 10am-5pm Tue-Sun; 5, 33, URathaus) Housed in turn-of-the-18th-century Palais Schönborn, this folklore museum gives a taste of 18th- and 19th-century rural dwellings, and is stocked with handcrafted sculptures, paintings and furniture from throughout Austria and its neighbouring countries. Many of the pieces have a religious or rural theme, and telltale floral motifs are everywhere. Temporary exhibitions are regularly featured. Tram to Laudongasse.

EATING

★MAMAMON THAI €

Map p254 (01-942 31 55; www.mamamonthaikitchen.com; 08, Albertgasse 15; mains €7-9.50; 11.30am-9.30pm Mon-Fri, noon-9.30pm Sat; UJosefstädter Strasse, Rathaus) Owner Piano, who named her restaurant for her mum Mon, has spiced up Vienna's burgeoning Southeast Asian food scene with a menu of southern Thai flavours, street-style decor and an indie soundtrack. On mild nights, a young, happy crowd spills out into the courtyard, while single diners pull up a stool at the large communal table or window seats within.

LEONES GELATO GELATERIA €

Map p254 (www.leones.at; 08, Langegasse 78; 1/2/3 scoops €1.80/3.30/4.50; noon-10pm; UAlser Strasse) This smart eat-in gelateria does everything right. Flavours keep it simple and veer towards the traditional, so there are no gaudy colours or chocolate-bar varieties. These are all kept fresh under the oh-so-Italian domed metal lids. Coffee is also the business here: as an added bonus, have it frappé style or as an *affogato* (coffee-based dessert).

SUPPENWIRTSCHAFT SOUP €

Map p254 (www.suppenwirtschaft.at; 09, Servitengasse 6; dishes €4.80-6.60; 11.30am-6pm Mon-Fri; ; URossauer Lände) This chic little eat-in and takeaway kitchen focuses mainly on soups and a few curries and salads from a weekly menu; it fits in well with the genteel style of Servitengasse. All dishes are made fresh each day using ingredients foraged at the Naschmarkt. Everything is half-price from 5pm to 6pm.

SOUPKULTUR SOUP €

Map p254 (www.soupkultur.at; 01, Wipplingerstrasse 32; soups €2.40-4.90, salads €5-9;

⌚11.30am-3.30pm Mon-Thu, to 3pm Fri, closed Sat & Sun; ✎; 🚊D, 1, ⓊSchottentor) Organic produce and aromatic spices are blended, sliced and chopped into an assortment of different soups and salads each week, ranging from red-lentil soup to traditional Hungarian goulash, Caesar salad to Thai papaya salad. There's token seating, but count on taking it away via cup or container – a leafy park is just around the corner. Tram to Wipplingerstrasse.

CAFÉ HUMMEL CAFE €

Map p254 (www.cafehummel.at; 08, Josefstädterstrasse 66; mains €8-17; ⌚7am-midnight Mon-Sat, 8am-midnight Sun; 📶; 🚊2, ⓊJosefstädter Strasse) Unpretentious Hummel welcomes all comers with a classic *Kaffeehaus* vibe. Cakes are baked on the premises, and mains like goulash and schnitzel satisfy. In summer, it's easy to spend a few hours sitting outside, mulling over the international papers and watching the world go by. Breakfast runs to 11am during the week, and a very civilised 2pm on weekends. Tram to Albertgasse.

KENT TURKISH €

Map p254 (☎01-405 91 73; www.kent-restaurant.at; 16, Brunnengasse 67; mains €8-15; ⌚6am-2am; ✎; ⓊJosefstädter Strasse) Kent means 'small town' in Turkish, an appropriate name considering the restaurant's seemingly perpetual expansion. In summer the tree-shaded garden is one of the prettiest in the city, and the food is consistently top-notch. Menu highlights include shish kebab and *ispanakli pide* (long Turkish pizza with sheep cheese, egg and spinach). Everything is available for takeaway or delivery.

★FLEIN AUSTRIAN €€

Map p254 (☎01-319 76 89; 09, Boltzmanngasse 2; mains €9.20-19.50; ⌚11.30am-3pm & 5.30-11.30pm Mon-Fri; 🚊38, 41, ⓊSchottentor) Deep in the University district, rustic Flein is hidden behind high walls and an unassuming green door. Up the garden path is an exquisitely simple, ridiculously atmospheric room; for balmy nights, there are tables spaced here and there under the trees. Food combines traditional dishes with some lovely, Italian-influenced cooking, and surprises with the occasional international twist (hello, kimchi!).

★PUNKS MODERN EUROPEAN €€

Map p254 (☎0664 275 70 72; www.punks.wien; 08, Florianigasse 50; small plates €4.50) The

Local Life
Stroll from Brunnenmarkt to Yppenplatz

This Saturday morning stroll dipping into Vienna's 16th district, Ottakring, takes you for a ramble around the city's liveliest and longest street market, Brunnenmarkt. Once an overlooked backwater, this edgy, ethnically diverse neighbourhood is now firmly on the city's hipster radar. Discover its independent boutiques, delis and cafes and get to know the new Vienna.

1 Street Market

Begin Saturday Viennese-style with a mooch around **Brunnenmarkt** (Map p254; 16, Brunnengasse; ⌚6am-6.30pm Mon-Fri, to 2pm Sat; 🚊2, ⓊJosefstädter Strasse). Haphazard mountains of fabrics, clothing, fruit and veg, spices and coffee, cheese and meat – this market has the lot. Most stall owners are Turkish or Balkan, and Brunnengasse itself is lined with grocery stores, cafes and bakeries, where you can find authentic pide (Turkish pizza), flat bread, halva and baklava.

2 Farm Fresh

The delis and boutiques on tree-dotted Yppenplatz are open most days, but the square is at its bustling best at the **Bauernmarkt** (Map p254; 16, Yppenplatz; ⌚9am-1pm Sat; 🚊2, ⓊJosefstädter Strasse), when farmers from Vienna's rural fringes sell their fruit, vegetables, meat, honey, preserves, wine and dairy goods. In summer, the cafe crowds spill out onto pavement terraces and the square fills with chatter and street entertainers.

3 Brunch Break

You could live in Vienna for a year and happily have a new lunchtime favourite in Yppenplatz each Saturday. The current darling is new kid on the block **Yppenplatz 4** (Map p254; www.yppenplatz4.at; 16, Yppenplatz 4; mains €9-12.80; ⌚10am-11pm Mon-Sat; 🚊2, ⓊJosefstädter Strasse), right in the very centre of the market.

Brunnenmarkt

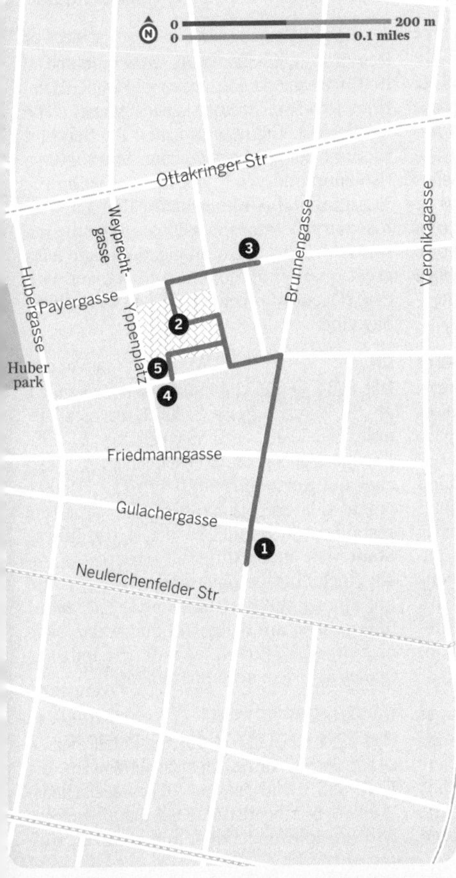

❹ Design District

Young designers and makers have set up shop on Yppenplatz, with a growing crop of cool boutiques and seasonal pop-ups adding to the market mix. A relative old-timer, **Y5** (Map p254; http://y5vienna.wordpress.com; 16, Yppenplatz 5; ⏲10am-3pm Sat; 🚊2, Ⓤ Josefstädter Strasse) 🍃 showcases young design talent via its program of designers-in-residence, all of whom have a commitment to sustainable practices.

❺ Deli Delight

Just across the way, deli **La Salvia** (Map p254; www.lasalvia.at; 16, Yppenplatz; antipasta plates €7-10, pasta €9-12; ⏲4-10pm Tue-Thu, 10am-10pm Fri, 9am-4pm Sat; 🚊2, Ⓤ Josefstädter Strasse) attracts gourmands with its picnic antipasti and stock of brilliant Italian wines, Prosecco, oils and *dolci* (sweets), as well as specialities like wild-boar salami. Taste its wares and revive over a perfectly made cappuccino or Aperol spritz in the bistro-cafe, or stay for lunch.

name might be a giveaway, but this guerilla-style restaurant *is* indeed shaking up an otherwise genteel neighbourhood. Patrick Müller, Anna Schwab and René Steindachner have 'occupied' a former wine bar and eschewed the usual refit or any form of interior decoration; the focus is, quite literally, on the kitchen, with a menu of inventive small dishes prepared behind the bar.

WETTER

ITALIAN €€

Map p254 (01-406 07 75; www.wettercucina.at; 16, Payergasse 13/4; mains €9-20; 5pm-midnight Tue-Fri, 10am-10pm Sat; 4) Italian food is commonplace in Vienna, but it can get a bit same-same. With its pretty *platz*-side outlook, Wetter would be appealing whatever the menu, and it's great for a market pit-stop espresso. But its well-cooked regional specialities – from roast wild boar and Genovese-style tripe to flash-fried sardines and fat, housemade ravioli – that bring in the locals. Tram to Yppengasse.

CAFÉ FRANÇAIS

FRENCH €€

Map p254 (01-319 09 03; www.cafe-francais.at; 09, Währingerstrasse 6-8; mains €8-19.50; 9am-midnight Mon-Sat) The Viennese flock to this big, bold and sexy French all-rounder. Big windows and park views make it a lovely morning spot and small dishes like Provençal-style sardines, fish soup or Moroccan *harira* soup make for a great lunch. Night-time brings the after-work, well-to-do *apero* crowd and dinner service with hearty (if not always entirely authentic) mains.

LA TAVOLOZZA

ITALIAN €€

Map p254 (01-406 37 57; www.latavolozza.at; 08, Florianigasse 37; pizza €7-14.50, mains €14.50-22; 5pm-midnight Mon-Fri, from noon Sat & Sun; 2, URathaus) You'll feel part of the *famiglia* at this friendly neighbourhood Italian place, where tightly packed tables are lit by candlelight. The food is superb: crisp bread fresh from a wood oven is followed by generous, well-seasoned portions of grilled fish and meat, washed down with beefy Chianti reds. Seasonal specialities like truffles often star on the menu. Tram to Lederergasse.

STOMACH

AUSTRIAN €€

Map p254 (01-310 20 99; 09, Seegasse 26; mains €12-20; 4pm-midnight Wed-Sat, 10am-10pm Sun; URossauer Lände) Stomach has been serving seriously good food for years. The menu brims with carefully plated meat, fish and vegetable dishes, including Styrian roast beef, cream-of-pumpkin soup, and, when in season, wild boar and venison. The interior is authentically rural, and the overgrown garden pretty. 'Stomach', interestingly, comes from rearranging the word Tomaschek, the butcher's shop originally located here.

RASOULI

INTERNATIONAL €€

Map p254 (01-403 13 47; www.rasouli.at; 16, Payergasse 12; mains €9-14.50, breakfast €4.50-12, lunch specials €6-12; 9.30am-midnight Tue-Fri, 9am-midnight Sat, 9.30am-6pm Sun; 2, UJosefstädter Strasse) With an open kitchen and a creative menu playing up seasonal organic produce, herbs and spices, Rasouli is understandably one of the most popular hang-outs on Yppenplatz. When the sun's out, snag a spot on the pavement terrace for homemade ice tea, lunch specials and themed breakfasts ranging from American to Greek. Tram to Neulerchenfelder Strasse.

AN-DO FISCH

SEAFOOD €€

Map p254 (01-308 75 76; www.andofisch.at; 16, Brunnenmarkt 161; mains €14-24; 11am-11pm Mon-Sat; UJosefstädter Strasse) The landlocked Viennese are mad for fish and this is a long-time favourite. Start with a fish soup and you'll feel like you're by the Atlantic. Mains like grilled calamari with rosemary potatoes, scallops with olive risotto or sea bass are simple, but made with great-quality ingredients and cooked with care. Friendly, relaxed staff add to the holiday vibe.

EN

JAPANESE €€

Map p254 (01-532 44 90; www.restaurant-en.at; 01, Werdertorgasse 8; lunch menus €9-15, mains €8.50-28; 11.30am-2.30pm & 5.30-10.30pm Mon-Sat; ; USchottenring) A Tokyo chef and Hokkaido staff banded together to create this exceptionally relaxed Japanese restaurant in a quiet corner of the Innere Stadt. The many different varieties of sushi (including octopus and sweet shrimp) are among the best in Vienna. The *gyoza* (dumplings) are delightful and warm sake or *genmaicha* (green tea with roasted rice) makes a perfect accompaniment.

GASTHAUS WICKERL

AUSTRIAN €€

Map p254 (01-317 74 89; 09, Porzellangasse 24a; mains €10-19; 9am-midnight Mon-Fri, from 10am Sat, 11am-11pm Sun; URossauer Lände) Wickerl is a beautiful *Beisl* (small tavern) with an all-wood finish and a warm, welcoming mood. Seasonal fare, such as *Kürbisgulasch* (pumpkin goulash) in autumn, *Marillenknödel* (apricot dumplings) in summer and *Spargel* (asparagus) in spring, are mixed in with the usual Viennese offerings of *Tafelspitz* (prime boiled beef), *Zwiebelrostbraten* (steak with onions) and veal or pork schnitzel.

SCHNATTL — INTERNATIONAL €€€

Map p254 (01-405 34 00; www.schnattl.com; 08, Lange Gasse 40; mains €23-28, 3-course menus from €35; 11.30am-5pm Mon-Thu, to midnight Fri, closed Sat & Sun; ; 2, URathaus) Despite weekday-only opening hours, Schnattl is a culinary institution in Josefstadt, particularly beloved by thespians and other arty types. The inner courtyard is perfect for summer dining, while bottle-green wood panelling creates a cosy mood inside. The chef plays up seasonal specialities like creamy chestnut soup and meltingly tender organic beef, matured on the bone and served with green-pepper gnocchi.

Tram to Rathaus or Josefstädter Strasse.

DRINKING & NIGHTLIFE

★ACHTUNDZWANZIG — WINE BAR

Map p254 (www.achtundzwanzig.at; 08, Schlösslegasse 28; 4pm-1am Mon-Thu, to 2am Fri, 7pm-2am Sat; 5, 43, 44, USchottentor) Austrian wine fans with a rock-and-roll sensibility will feel like they've found heaven at this black-daubed *vinothek* (wine bar) that vibes casual but takes its wines super seriously. Wines by the glass are all sourced from small producers – many of them are organic or minimal-intervention and friends of the owners – and are well priced at under €4 a glass. Nicely done cold plates mean you can kick on and make a night of it. Tram to Lange Gasse.

★POC CAFE — COFFEE

Map p254 (www.poccafe.com; 08, Schlösselgasse 21; 8am-5pm Mon-Fri; 5, 43, 44, USchottentor) Friendly Robert Gruber is one of Vienna's coffee legends and his infectious passion ripples through this beautifully rambling, lab-like space. POC stands for 'People on Caffeine'; while filter, espresso-style or a summertime iced cold-brew are definitely this place's raison d'etre, it's also known for moreish sweets like the killer poppy-seed cake, cheesecake or seasonal fruit tarts. Tram to Lange Gasse.

CAFÉ STEIN — CAFE

Map p254 (www.cafestein.at; 09, Währinger Strasse 6-8; 8am-1am Mon-Sat, 9am-1am Sun; ; D, 1, 2, USchottentor) During the day this multi-level cafe is a popular haunt of students from the nearby university; come evening the clientele metamorphoses into spritz-swilling city workers and DJs bring out their decks. The all-day menu is extensive. During the summer there's outside seating, which enjoys pretty views of the Votivkirche. Sister cocktail bar **Botanical Gardens** (www.botanicalgarden.at; 09, Währinger Strasse 6-8; 5pm-3am Tue-Sat) is hidden below.

CAFÉ CENTRAL — CAFE

Map p254 (www.palaisevents.at; 01, Herrengasse 14; 7.30am-10pm Mon-Sat, 10am-10pm Sun; ; UHerrengasse) Coffee-house legend alert: Trotsky came here to play chess, and turn-of-the-century literary greats like Karl Kraus and Hermann Bahr regularly met here for coffee. Its marble pillars, arched ceilings and chandeliers now mostly play host to tourists, and the queues can be tedious, but once in it's a deliciously storied setting for a *melange* and slices of chocolate-truffle *Altenbergtorte*.

LANE & MERRIMAN'S — IRISH PUB

Map p254 (01-402 47 64; www.laneandmerrimans.net; 09, Spitalgasse 3; 4pm-midnight Mon, Tue & Thu, 11am-midnight Wed, Fri & Sat; UAlser Strasse) Yes, it's an Irish pub – there's that iconic Jane Bown portrait of Samuel Beckett in the window. But forget your preconceptions: David Gannon's contemporary take on the much-maligned institution is a delight. David will probably steer you towards an Austrian bio beer over Guinness; you're equally welcome in for a pot of tea and a slice of chocolate cake.

KAFFEEMODUL — COFFEE

Map p254 (www.kaffeemodul.at; 08, Josefstädterstrasse 35; 7.30am-5.30pm Mon-Fri, 10am-2pm Sat) Can't take another milky *melange*? Head here for espressos, flat whites and cold brew. Billed as 'Vienna's smallest coffee shop', happy conversation bats from one side to the other of the tiny, bench-lined space, and from the stools streetside. There's nothing but coffee, apart from cookies, but what's on offer is direct-trade, small-batch roasted and expertly made.

CAFÉ CI — CAFE

Map p254 (www.ci.or.at; 16, Payergasse 14; mains €7-11, snacks €4.50-7.50; ⏲8am-2am Mon-Sat, from 10am Sun; 🚊2, ⓊJosefstädter Strasse) Something's always happening at this cafe founded to support new immigrants 30 years ago, be it a reading, an exhibition or language or dance classes. Come summer, its terrace throngs with Ottakringer locals sipping organic beers; in winter they retreat inside to browse the daily papers and dig into heart-warming goulash or *ćevapčići* (spicy Serbian sausages). Tram to Neulerchenfelder Strasse/Brunnengasse.

TUNNEL — BAR, CAFE

Map p254 (www.tunnel-vienna-live.at; 08, Florianigasse 39; ⏲9am-2am Mon-Sat, to midnight Sun; 📶; 🚊2, ⓊRathaus) This laid-back, endearingly boho cafe attracts students and all comers. By day it's a relaxed spot to grab an ancient wooden table and flick through a communal book or magazine with coffee or opt for lunchtime beers and Latin American snacks. The mood cranks up a notch with (mostly free) gigs at 9pm, from folk to indie, Latin to jazz.

The full line-up is posted online and includes pub quizzes in German, occasional English-speaking stand-up comedy and a big screen for big football matches. Tram to Lederergasse.

CAFÉ LANDTMANN — CAFE

Map p254 (www.landtmann.at; 10, Universitätsring 4; ⏲7.30am-midnight; 📶; 🚊D, 1, 2, ⓊRathaus) Freud, Mahler and Marlene Dietrich all had a soft spot for this coffee house, which opened its doors in 1873. Today, it attracts politicians and theatre-goers with its elegant interior and close proximity to the Burgtheater, Rathaus and Parliament. The list of traditional coffee specialities is formidable and the dessert menu features *Sacher Torte* (chocolate cake) and *Apfelstrudel* (apple strudel).

There's free live piano music from 8pm to 11pm, Sunday to Tuesday. Tram to Rathausplatz.

HALBESTADT BAR — COCKTAIL BAR

Map p254 (www.halbestadt.at; 09, Stadtbogen 155; ⏲7pm-2am Mon-Thu, to 3am Fri & Sat; ⓊNussdorferstrasse) The impeccable hospitality starts when you can't open the glass door. The host swings it forth, escorts you in and offers to advise you on your order. More than 500 bottles grace the walls of the tiny, atmospheric space under the *Bogen* (railway arch) and mixologists hold court creating enticing cocktails. Note there's no bookings; it fills up fast.

FLEX — CLUB

Map p254 (www.flex.at; 01, Augartenbrücke; ⏲9pm-6am Tue-Sat, club from 11pm; 🚊1, 2, ⓊSchottenring) Down by a graffiti-strewn stretch of the Danube, Flex might attract a very young and mainstream crowd these days but still manages a semblance of its one-time edginess. The sound system is rumoured to be one of Europe's best, entry prices are usually reasonable and dress code unheard of. Local and international DJs are joined by occasional live acts.

CAFÉ BERG — CAFE

Map p254 (www.cafe-berg.at; 09, Berggasse 8; ⏲10am-midnight Mon-Sat, to 11pm Sun; 📶; 🚊D, 1, ⓊSchottentor) Café Berg is Vienna's leading gay bar, although it's welcoming to all walks of life. Its staff are some of the nicest in town, the layout sleek and smart, and the vibe chilled. It's a brilliant all-rounder too, with breakfast and lunch served during the day and events and wine in the evening.

WEINSTUBE JOSEFSTADT — WINE BAR

Map p254 (08, Piaristengasse 27; ⏲4pm-midnight Apr-Dec, closed Jan-Mar; ⓊRathaus) Weinstube Josefstadt is one of the loveliest *Stadtheurigen* (city wine taverns) in Vienna. A leafy green oasis spliced between towering residential blocks, its tables of friendly, well-liquored locals are squeezed in between the trees and shrubs looking onto a pretty, painted *Salettl,* or wooden summerhouse. Wine is local and cheap, food is typical, with a buffet-style meat and fritter selection.

Note that the location is not well signposted – the only indication of its existence is a metal *Busch'n* (green wreath) hanging from a doorway.

LOFT — BAR, CLUB

Map p254 (www.theloft.at; 07, Lerchenfelder Gürtel 37; ⏲7pm-2am Wed & Thu, 8pm-4am Fri & Sat late Aug–mid-Jun, closed mid-Jun–late Aug; ⓊThaliastrasse) 'Working hard for better parties in Vienna' is the catchphrase of this young Gürtel live wire and you can believe the hype. Nearly all events are free and there's something happening most nights: Wednesday art-house film screenings, Thursday table football tournaments,

Friday and Saturday clubbing to DJs with a playlist jumping from electro to old school.

RHIZ BAR, CLUB

Map p254 (www.rhiz.org; 08, U-Bahnbogen (Lerchenfelder Gürtel) 37; 6pm-4am Mon-Thu, 8pm-5am Fri & Sat; ; 2 Josefstädter Strasse, U Josefstädter Strasse) Rhiz' brick arches and glass walls are reminiscent of many bars beneath the U6 line, but its status as a stalwart of the city's electronica scene gives it the edge over the competition. Black-clad boozers and an alternative set cram the interior to hear DJs and live acts year-round, while in summer the large outdoor seating area fills to overflowing.

MAS! BAR

Map p254 (www.restaurante-mas.at; 08, Laudongasse 36; 6pm-midnight Mon-Thu, 5pm-2am Fri & Sat, 10.30am-midnight Sun; 5, 33, U Alser Strasse) A designer bar specialising in cocktails with the bonus of a Mexican food menu, Mas! attracts a well-groomed, local set. Choose from a high, wobbly stool at the long, shimmering bar backed by an enormous light installation, or, for a more intimate evening, a low, dimly lit table. The boozy Mexican brunch (€18) on Sunday is legendary. Tram to Laudongasse.

ENTERTAINMENT

VOTIVKINO CINEMA

Map p254 (01-317 35 71; www.votivkino.at; 09, Währinger Strasse 12; ; U Schottentor) Built in 1912, the Votiv is one of the oldest cinemas in Vienna. It's been extensively updated since then and is now among the best cinemas in the city. Its three screens feature a mix of Hollywood's more quirky ventures and art-house films in their original language.

The 11am Tuesday screening is reserved for parents with babies, and weekend afternoons feature special matinées for kids.

VOLKSOPER OPERA, DANCE

Map p254 (People's Opera; 01-514 44 3670; www.volksoper.at; 09, Währinger Strasse 78; Sep-Jun; U Währinger Strasse) Offering a more intimate experience than the Staatsoper, the Volksoper specialises in operettas, dance performances, musicals and a handful of standard, heavier operas. Standing and impaired-view tickets go for between €3 to €10 and, like many venues, there is a plethora of discounts and reduced tickets for sale 30 minutes before performances. The Volksoper closes for July and August.

B72 LIVE MUSIC

Map p254 (www.b72.at; 08, Hernalser Gürtel 72; 8pm-4am Sun-Thu, to 6am Fri & Sat; 44, U Alser Strasse) Fringe live acts, alternative beats and album launches are the mainstay of B72's entertainment line-up, which all attract a predictably youthful crowd. Its tall glass walls and arched brick interior are typical of most bars along the Gürtel, as is the happy grunginess. Its name comes from its location, *Bogen* 72. Tram to Hernalser Gürtel.

WUK ARTS CENTRE

Map p254 (Workshop & Culture House; 01-40 12 10; www.wuk.at; 09, Währinger Strasse 59; information 9am-8pm Mon-Fri, 3-8pm Sat & Sun; U Währinger Strasse) WUK is many things to many people. It hosts a number of events in its concert hall: mid-size international and local rock acts vie with clubbing nights, classical concerts, film evenings, theatre and children's shows. Women's groups, temporary exhibitions and practical skills workshops are also on-site, along with a cafe with a fabulous cobbled courtyard.

DE FRANCE CINEMA

Map p254 (01-317 52 36; www.defrance.at; 01, Schottenring 5; D, 1, 2, U Schottentor) De France screens films in their original language, with subtitles, in its two small cinemas. The schedule includes a healthy dose of English-language films.

CAFÉ CONCERTO LIVE MUSIC

Map p254 (www.cafeconcerto.at; 16, Lerchenfelder Gürtel 53; 7pm-2am Tue-Sat; ; U Josefstädter Strasse) Concerto is another of the bars on the Gürtel that hosts local live acts. Jazz and singer-songwriters feature heavily on the program, which is also peppered with DJs, and both the cellar and ground-level bar are used for concerts. Entry is often free.

MILES SMILES LIVE MUSIC

Map p254 (www.miles-smiles.at; 08, Lange Gasse 51; 8pm-2am Sun-Thu, to 4am Fri & Sat; U Rathaus) One of two bars in town named after legend Miles Davis, Miles Smiles is for the discerning jazz fan who knows when to clap for the solo. Live acts are irregular but always enthralling, and the atmosphere enthusiastic and energetic.

CAFÉ CARINA LIVE MUSIC

Map p254 (www.cafe-carina.at; 08, Josefstädterstrasse 84; ⏲6pm-2am Mon-Thu, to 6am Fri & Sat; ⓤJosefstädter Strasse) Small, alternative and pleasantly dingy, Carina is a musicians' (and a drinker's) bar. Local bands perform most nights – only a few feet from a normally enthusiastic audience – and the music is invariably folk, jazz or country.

THEATER IN DER JOSEFSTADT THEATRE

Map p254 (☎01-427 003 00; www.josefstadt.org; 08, Josefstädterstrasse 26; ⏲box office 10am-performance time Mon-Fri, 1pm-performance time Sat & Sun; 2, ⓤRathaus) Theater in der Josefstadt is another theatre in the Volkstheater mould, with an ornate interior and traditional German productions. One hour before performances, tickets are available to students and school children for €6; same-day standing-room tickets are also available for €6 at 1pm for afternoon productions, and at 3pm for evening productions. Tram to Stadiongasse.

SHOPPING

STAUD'S FOOD

Map p254 (www.stauds.com; 16, Yppenplatz; ⏲8am-12.30pm Tue-Sat, 3.30-6pm Fri; 2, ⓤJosefstädter Strasse) Ask the Viennese who makes Austria's best jam and you'll invariably hear 'Staud's'. Hans Staud is rigorous about sourcing the finest ingredients for his sweet and savoury preserves. This pavilion shop stocks vegetables with pickled oomph, chutneys, wine jellies, horseradishes, jams and compotes like tangy greengage, apricot and wild lingonberry, all of which make unique gifts. Tram to Neulerchenfelder Strasse.

FESCH'MARKT MARKET

(www.feschmarkt.info; 16, Ottakringer Brauerei, Ottakringer Platz; 44) Austria's young creative makers emerge from their studios with over 200 stalls selling design, fashion, food, drinks and produce. It's held over three days in the lovely Ottakringer brewery and is a great way to experience Austria's newly youthful design scene. Check the website for dates; there are also markets held in Graz, Linz and Feldkirch. Tram to J.N.Berger-Platz.

IMPERIAL ARCADE

With its hexagonal skylight, allegorical sculptures and beautifully lit arcades in Italian Renaissance style, **Palais Ferstel** (Map p254; 01, Strauchgasse 4; ⏲10am-6.30pm Mon-Fri, to 6pm Sat; ⓤHerrengasse) hearkens back to a more glamorous age of consumption. Opened in 1860, it sidles up to the ever-grand Café Central (p135) and likewise bears the hallmark of architect Heinrich von Ferstel, the Habsburgs' blue-eyed boy in the mid-19th century.

Today, it shelters upmarket delis, jewellers and chocolatiers; pop in for a mosey through even if you have no intention of buying.

DIE HÖLLEREI FOOD & DRINKS

Map p254 (www.diehoellerei.at; 08, Florianigasse 13; ⏲11am-6.30pm Tue-Fri, 10am-1pm Sat; ⓤRathaus) Alexandra Höller is passionate about Austrian produce and stocks a beautiful range of the best. Take home unusual bounty such as apricot-seed or saffron gin, moist almond cake in a jar, or wonderful pasta and jams from over the border in Südtirol. You can also pick up a bottle of bubbly or wine here.

XOCOLAT CHOCOLATE

Map p254 (www.xocolat.at; 09, Servitengasse 5; ⏲10am-6pm Mon-Fri, 9am-1pm Sat; ⓤRossauer Lände) This upmarket *Konditorei* (cake shop) offers 40-odd varieties of beautifully decorated handmade chocolates, pralines and truffles – some of which qualify as tiny edible works of art. You can also visit the factory where the chocolates are made.

BIO-MARKT FREYUNG MARKET

Map p254 (01, Freyungasse; ⏲9am-6pm Fri & Sat; ⓤHerrengasse, Schottentor) Great for picking up some picnic fixings, this low-key market exclusively sells organic produce from farmers. Find everything from wood-fired oven bread, fruit, fish and meat to honey, cheese, wine and even pumpkin-seed oil here.

Schloss Belvedere to the Canal

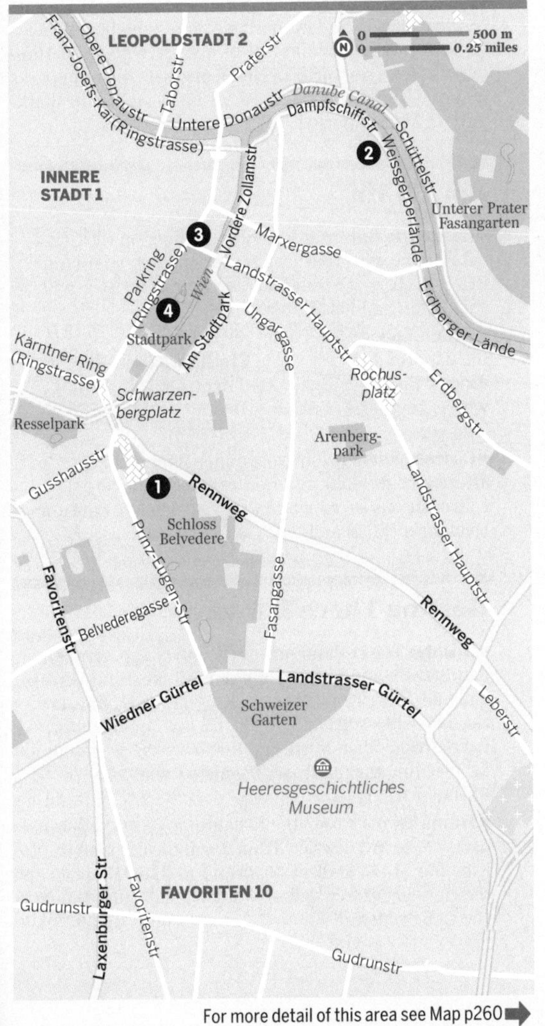

For more detail of this area see Map p260

Neighbourhood Top Five

❶ **Schloss Belvedere** (p141) Drawing breath as you ramble through lavishly frescoed apartments, sculpture-strewn gardens and a gallery home to the ultimate embrace: Klimt's *The Kiss*.

❷ **KunstHausWien** (p150) Being dazzled by Hundertwasser's wonky floors, madcap mosaics and hallucinatory colours.

❸ **Museum für Angewandte Kunst** (p149) Rewinding a century to the dawn of a modernist age at the MAK.

❹ **Stadtpark** (p140) Humming 'The Blue Danube' as you waltz across this garden to Strauss' golden statue.

❺ **21er Haus** (p145) Zooming in on contemporary art with an Austrian slant at this modernist gallery.

Lonely Planet's Top Tip

Time your visit right and you can save on sight admissions. The Museum für Angewandte Kunst is free from 6pm to 10pm on Tuesday, tickets for KunstHausWien are half-price on Monday, while the Heeresgeschichtliches Museum won't cost you a cent on the first Sunday of the month.

Best Places to Eat

- Steirereck im Stadtpark (p152)
- Meierei im Stadtpark (p151)
- Lingenhel (p150)
- Joseph Brot (p151)
- Café Goldegg (p150)

For reviews, see p150.

Best Places to Drink

- Strandbar Herrmann (p152)
- Café am Heumarkt (p152)
- Café Zartl (p152)
- Urania (p152)
- Salm Bräu (p152)

For reviews, see p152.

Best Entertainment

- Radiokulturhaus (p152)
- Konzerthaus (p154)
- Kursalon (p154)
- Arnold Schönberg Center (p154)

For reviews, see p152.

Explore Schloss Belvedere to the Canal

If you only see one palace in Vienna, make it Schloss Belvedere. What giddy romance is evoked in its sumptuously frescoed baroque halls, replete with Klimt, Schiele and Kokoschka artworks; what stories are conjured wandering its landscaped gardens, which drop like the sudden fall of a theatre curtain to reveal Vienna's skyline. Belvedere is overwhelming in both scale and substance: a day-long marathon of a sight that engrosses from start to finish.

As compelling as Belvedere is, it can be rewarding to explore lesser-known corners of Vienna's third district, Landstrasse, too. Here elegant backstreets lead to art nouveau cafes, low-key market squares and houses bearing the psychedelic imprint of artistic wild child Hundertwasser. The spirits of classical greats linger in parks and cemeteries: from Strauss on a pedestal in the Stadtpark to Mozart buried at St Marxer Friedhof.

Local Life

- **Canalside Summer** Embrace summer on the Costa del Danube with your feet in the sand and your bum in a deckchair at Strandbar Herrmann (p152) or with a cocktail in hand at Urania (p152).
- **Green Spaces** Seek quiet respite with a wander in the dappled leafiness of the **Stadtpark** (Map p260; City Park) or the headstone-dotted Zentralfriedhof (p151), where the ghosts of Strauss, Beethoven and Brahms hold court.
- **Coffee Houses** Hone your inner *Wiener* with afternoons devoted to coffee, cake and drawn-out conversations at old-world Café Zartl (p152), Café am Heumarkt (p152) and Café Goldegg (p150).

Getting There & Away

- **U-Bahn** The U-Bahn makes the quick hop between Landstrasse and the rest of Vienna. Taubstummengasse and Südtiroler Platz stations, both on the U1 line, are close to Schloss Belvedere. The U3 line to Stubentor, Landstrasse-Wien Mitte and Rochusgasse are handy for reaching the Stadtpark, Danube Canal and Rochusplatz.
- **Trams** Trams trump the U-Bahn for access to some parts of the 3rd district. Tram 2 trundles around the Ring (for MAK, Stadtpark), tram 1 to Radetzkyplatz (for the Hundertwasser sights), while trams 71 and D take you to Belvedere.

TOP SIGHT
SCHLOSS BELVEDERE & GARDENS

A masterpiece of total art, Belvedere is one of the world's finest baroque palaces. Designed by Johann Lukas von Hildebrandt (1668–1745), it was built as a summer residence for the brilliant military strategist Prince Eugene of Savoy, conqueror of the Turks in 1718. Eugene had grown up around the court of Louis XIV and it shows – this is a chateau to rival Versailles.

Oberes Belvedere

Rising splendidly above the gardens and commanding sweeping views of Vienna's skyline, the **Oberes Belvedere** (Upper Belvedere; Map p260; 03, Prinz-Eugen-Strasse 27; adult/child €14/free; ⏲10am-6pm) is one of Vienna's unmissable sights. Built between 1717 and 1723, its peerless art collection, showcased in rooms replete with marble, frescoes and stucco, attests to the unfathomable wealth and cultured tastes of the Habsburg Empire.

Ground Floor: Medieval & Modern Art

The **Sala Terrena** is a grand prelude to the ground floor, with four colossal Atlas pillars supporting the weight of its delicately stuccoed vault. Spread across four beautifully frescoed rooms, **Medieval Art** leads you through the artistic development of the age, with an exceptional portfolio of Gothic sculpture and altarpieces, many from Austrian abbeys and monasteries. Top billing goes to the Master of Grosslobming's sculptural group, whose fluid, expressive works embodied the figurative ideal; among them is the faceless *St George with Dragon* (1395), with a rather tame-looking dragon at his feet. Other heavenly treasures include Joachim's polyptych *Albrechtsaltar* (1435), one of the foremost examples of Gothic realism, and the *Znaim*

DON'T MISS

- The Klimt collection
- Sala Terrena
- The gardens
- The Impressionist collection
- Marmorsaal

PRACTICALITIES

- Map p260, B4
- www.belvedere.at
- adult/child Oberes Belvedere €14/free, Unteres Belvedere €12/free, combined ticket €20/free
- ⏲10am-6pm
- 🚊D, 71 Schwarzenbergplatz, UTaubstummengasse, Südtiroler Platz

COMBINED TICKETS

Ordering printable tickets online saves time, but they can't be exchanged or refunded. Several money-saving combined ticket options are available, including one covering the Upper Belvedere, Lower Belvedere and 21er Haus (adult/under 19 years €23/free) and another covering the Upper and Lower Belvedere (adult/under 19 years €20/free). Combined tickets are valid for two weeks after the first visit.

The Nazis seized the property of the wealthy Jewish Bloch-Bauer family following the 1938 Anschluss. Among their substantial collection were five Klimt originals, including the *Portrait of Adele Bloch-Bauer I (1907)*. The stolen paintings hung in the Oberes Belvedere until 2006, when a US Supreme Court ruled the Austrian government must return the paintings to their rightful owner, Adele Bloch-Bauer's niece and heir Maria Altmann. The portrait alone fetched US$135 million at auction, at the time the highest price ever paid for a painting, and today hangs in the New York Neue Galerie.

Altar (1445), a gilded glorification of faith showing the Passion of Christ.

Modern Art & Interwar Period is strong on Austrian expressionism. Attention-grabbers here include Oskar Kokoschka's richly animated portrait of art nouveau painter *Carl Moll* (1913). Egon Schiele is represented by works both haunting and beguiling, such as *Death and the Maiden* (1915) and his portrait of six-year-old *Herbert Rainer* (1910). Other standouts include Oskar Laske's staggeringly detailed *Ship of Fools* (1923) and Max Oppenheimer's musical masterpiece *The Philharmonic* (1935), with a baton-swinging Gustav Mahler.

First Floor: From Klimt to Baroque

The 1st-floor **Vienna 1880–1914** collection is a holy grail for Klimt fans, with an entire room devoted to erotic golden wonders such as *Judith* (1901), *Salome* (1909), *Adam and Eve* (1917) and *The Kiss* (1908). Works by German symbolist painter Max Klinger (1857–1920), as well as portraits by Secessionist Koloman Moser and Norwegian expressionist Edvard Munch, also feature. The centrepiece is the **Marmorsaal**, a chandelier-lit marble, stucco and trompe l'oeil confection, crowned by Carlo Innocenzo Carlone's ceiling fresco (1721–23) celebrating the glorification of Prince Eugène. **Baroque & Early-19th-Century Art** pays tribute to Austrian masters of the age, endowed with highlights such as Johann Michael Rottmayr's lucid *Susanna and the Elders* (1692) and Paul Troger's chiaroscuro *Christ on the Mount of Olives* (1750).

Second Floor: Impressionists & Romantics

In **Neoclassicism, Romanticism & Biedermeier Art**, you'll find outstanding works such as Georg Waldmüller's *Corpus Christi Morning* (1857), a joyous snapshot of impish lads and flower girls bathed in honeyed light. Representative of the neoclassical period are clearer, more emotionally restrained pieces such as Jacques-Louis David's gallant *Napoleon on Great St Bernard Pass* (1801) and François Gérard's portrait *Count Moritz Christian Fries and Family* (1804). The romantic period is headlined by the wistful, brooding landscapes and seascapes of 19th-century German painter Caspar David Friedrich.

French masters share the limelight with their Austrian and German contemporaries in **Realism & Impressionism**, where you'll feel the artistic pull of Renoir's softly evocative *Woman after the Bath* (1876), Monet's sun-dappled *Garden at Giverny* (1902) and Van Gogh's *Plain at Auvers* (1890), where wheat fields ripple under a billowing sky. Lovis Corinth's tranquil *Woman Reading Near a Goldfish*

Tank (1911) and Max Liebermann's *Hunter in the Dunes* (1913) epitomise the German Impressionist style.

Gardens

Belvedere: 'beautiful view'. The reason for this name becomes apparent in the baroque **garden** (03, Rennweg/Prinz-Eugen-Strasse; ⏲6.30am-8pm, shorter hours in winter; 🚋D) linking the upper and lower palaces, which was laid out around 1700 in classical French style by Dominique Girard, a pupil of André le Nôtre of Versailles fame. Set along a **central axis**, the gently sloping garden commands a broad view of Vienna's skyline, with the Stephansdom and the Hofburg punctuating the horizon.

The three-tiered garden is lined by clipped box hedges and flanked by ornamental parterres. As you stroll to the **Lower Cascade**, with its frolicking water nymphs, look out for Greco-Roman statues of the eight muses and cherubic putti embodying the 12 months of the year. Mythical beasts squirt water across the **Upper Cascade**, which spills down five steps into the basin below. Guarding the approach to the Oberes Belvedere are winged sphinxes, symbols of power and wisdom, which look as though they are about to take flight any minute.

South of the Oberes Belvedere is the **Alpengarten** (www.bundesgaerten.at; 03, Prinz-Eugen-Strasse 27; adult/child €3.50/2.50; ⏲10am-6pm late Mar-early Aug; 🚋D, O, 18, Ⓤ Südtiroler Platz), a Japanese-style garden nurturing alpine species, at its fragrant best from spring to summer, when clematis, rhododendrons, roses and peonies are in bloom. North from here is the larger **Botanischer Garten** (www.botanik.univie.ac.at; 03, Rennweg 14; ⏲10am-1hr before dusk; 🚋71, O) FREE, belonging to the Vienna University, with tropical glasshouses and 11,500 botanical species, including Chinese dwarf bamboo and Japanese plum yews.

SCHLOSS BELVEDERE AND GARDENS

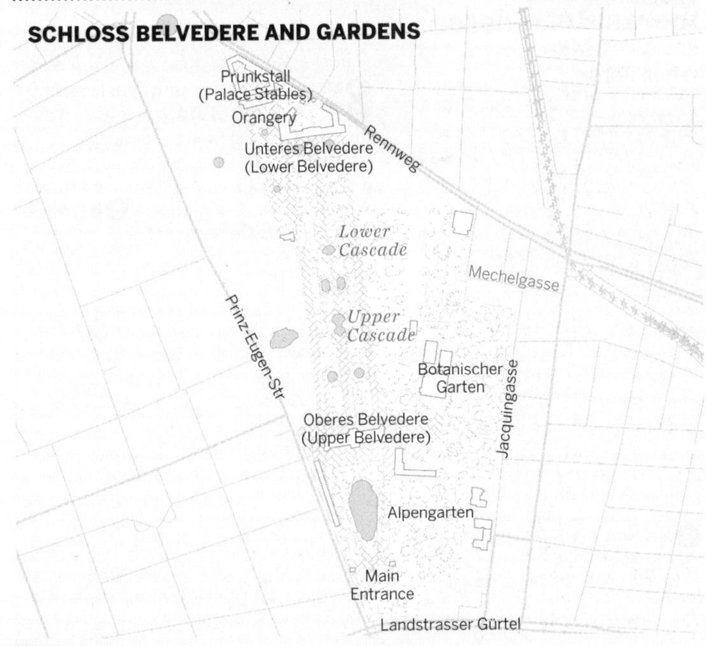

OBERES BELVEDERE

Second Floor

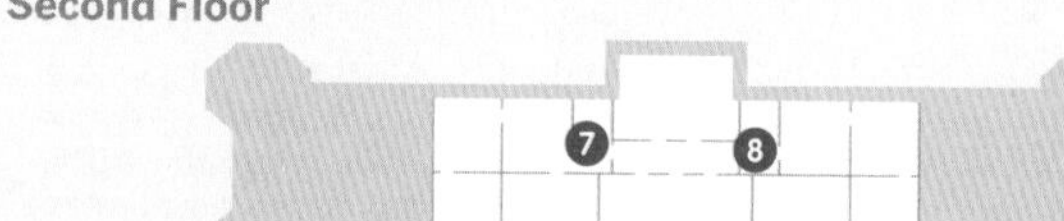

First Floor

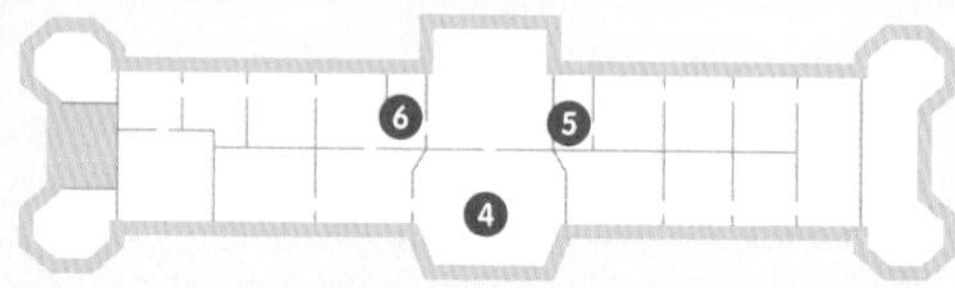

Ground Floor

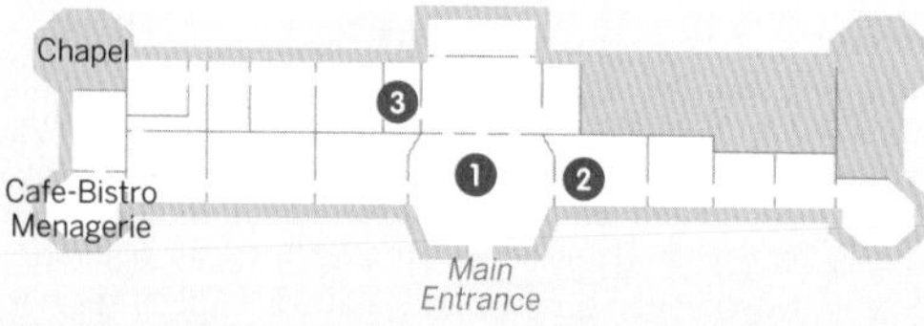

Museum Tour
Oberes Belvedere

LENGTH FOUR HOURS

The Upper Belvedere's scale can be overwhelming. This half-day itinerary will help you pin down the highlights, though bear in mind that paintings are frequently shifted around for exhibitions.

Gaze up to the Atlas pillars supporting the 1 **Sala Terrena** and turn right into 2 **Medieval Art**, displayed in frescoed halls. You'll be drawn to the Gothic brilliance of the Master of Grosslobming's sculptures, such as *St George with Dragon* and *Kneeling Mary*. Note the soul-stirring *Albrechtsaltar* and the *Znaim Altar* depicting the Passion of Christ. Andreas Lackner created the *Abtenauer Altar* (1518), a gilded trio of bishops that presided over the high altar of the parish church of Abtenau in Salzburg. Exit and turn left into 3 **Modern Art & Interwar Period**, with evocative pieces such as Egon Schiele's portrait of *Herbert Rainer* and Max Oppenheimer's *The Philharmonic*.

Saunter up the ornately stuccoed Prunkstiege staircase, pausing to marvel at the fresco-and-marble opulence of the 4 **Marmorsaal**. Now turn right to reach 5 **Vienna 1880–1914**, a peerless repository of fin de siècle and Secessionist art. The Klimt collection is second to none, shimmering with golden-period stunners such as *Judith* and *The Kiss*. Across in 6 **Baroque & Early-19th-Century Art**, look out for light-fantastic works such as Johann Michael Rottmayr's *Susanna and the Elders* and Paul Troger's *Christ on the Mount of Olives*.

On the 2nd floor, turn left into 7 **Neoclassicism, Romanticism & Biedermeier Art**. Notice neoclassical wonders such as François Gérard's *Count Moritz Christian Fries and Family*, then move past landscapes and still-lifes to the Romantic era. Look out for Caspar David Friedrich's *Rocky Landscape of the Elbe Sandstone Heights*. Georg Waldmüller's mirthful *Corpus Christi Morning* takes pride of place in the Biedermeier collection. Round out with Impressionist masterworks in 8 **Realism & Impressionism**, where exceptional works include Max Liebermann's *Hunter in the Dunes*, Monet's *Woman after the Bath* and Van Gogh's *Plain at Auvers*.

Unteres Belvedere

Built between 1712 and 1716, **Unteres Belvedere** (Lower Belvedere; 03, Rennweg 6; adult/child €12/free; ⏲10am-6pm Thu-Tue, to 9pm Wed; 🚋D) is a baroque feast of state apartments and ceremonial rooms. Most lavish of all is the red marble **Marmorsaal**, an ode to Prince Eugène's military victories, with stucco trophies, medallions and Martino Altomonte's ceiling fresco showing the glorification of the prince and Apollo surrounded by muses. At eye level are sculptures taken from Georg Raphael Donner's mid-18th-century **fountain** on Neuer Markt. Snake-bearing Providentia (Prudence) rises above four putti grappling with fish, each of which symbolises a tributary of the Danube.

In the **Groteskensaal**, foliage intertwines with fruit, birds and mythological beasts in the fanciful grotesque style that was all the rage in baroque times. This leads through to the **Marmorgalerie**, a vision of frilly white stucco and marble, encrusted with cherubs and war trophies. The niches originally displayed three classical statues from Herculaneum (now in Dresden), which inspired baroque sculptor Domenico Parodito to create the neoclassical statues you see today. Maria Theresia put her stamp on the palace in the adjacent **Goldkabinett**, a mirrored cabinet dripping in gold.

Temporary exhibitions are held in the **Orangery**, with a walkway gazing grandly over Prince Eugène's private garden. Attached to the Orangery is the **Prunkstall**, the former royal stables, where you can now trot through a 150-piece collection of Austrian medieval art, including religious scenes, altarpieces, sculpture and Gothic triptychs.

21er Haus

The modernist, glass-and-steel **Austria Pavilion**, designed by Karl Schwanzer for Expo 58 in Brussels, was reborn as the **21er Haus** (www.21erhaus.at; 03, Arsenalstrasse 1; adult/under 18yr €7/free; ⏲11am-6pm Tue & Thu-Sun, to 9pm Wed; 🚋D, O, 18, Ⓤ Südtiroler Platz) in 2011, with exhibitions devoted to 20th- and 21st-century art, predominantly with an Austrian focus. Adolf Krischanitz left his clean aesthetic imprint on the open-plan gallery, which sits just south of the Oberes Belvedere in the **Schweizergarten**.

The gallery's dynamic approach embraces an artist-in-residence scheme and a changing rota of contemporary exhibitions. On permanent display is a peerless collection of sculptures by Viennese artist Fritz Wotruba (1907–75), many of which deconstruct the human form into a series of abstract, geometric shapes that have more than an element of cubism about them.

Klimt in Vienna

The works of Gustav Klimt (1862–1918) – the shining star of Austria's Jugendstil (Art Nouveau) age – are as resonant and alluring today as they were when he sent ripples of scandal through the rigid artistic establishment in fin de siècle Vienna with his exotic, erotic style. For total immersion, your first port of call should be the Belvedere (p141), which is home to the world's largest Klimt collection.

The Kiss (1908; Upper Belvedere)

Klimt believed that all art is erotic, and gazing upon this most sensual of artworks, who can disagree? A couple draped in elaborate robes are shown entwined in an embrace in a flowered meadow. Rumours suggest this was Klimt and his lifelong lover, Emilie Flöge, a porcelain-skinned, red-headed beauty. With a sinuous waterfall of gold-leaf and elaborate patterning set against a stardust backdrop, the couple appear to transgress the canvas with their dreamlike, rapturous state.

Adam & Eve (1918; Upper Belvedere)

Klimt was working on this biblical wonder when he suddenly died of a stroke on 6 February 1918. The painting is an ode to the female form Klimt so adored. Adam is less prominent in the background, while in the foreground stands Eve, a celestial vision of radiant skin, voluptuous curves and a cascade of golden hair, with anemones scattered at her feet.

Judith (1901; Upper Belvedere)

One of Klimt's seminal art works, this is an entrancing evocation of the Old Testament heroine Judith, a rich widow

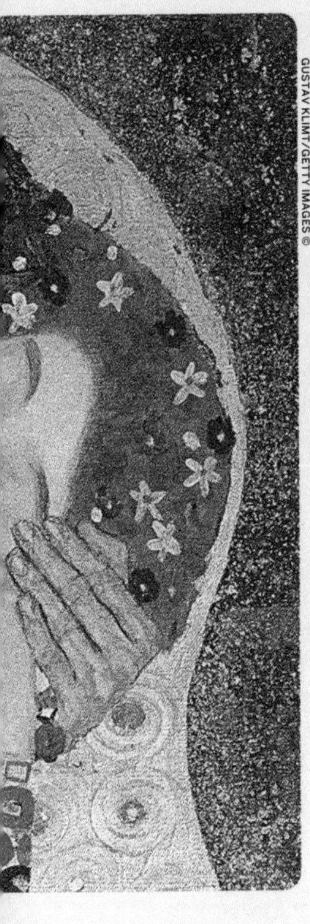

GUSTAV KLIMT/GETTY IMAGES ©

SUPERSTOCK/GETTY IMAGES ©

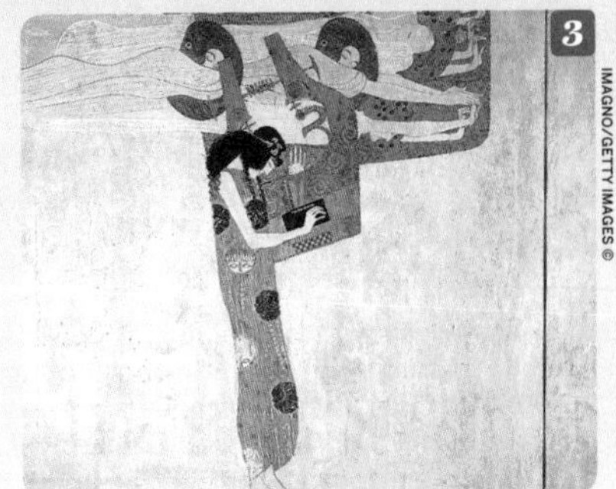

IMAGNO/GETTY IMAGES ©

1. *The Kiss* (detail)
2. *Here's a Kiss to the Whole Word* (detail of *Beethoven Frieze*)
3. *Beethoven Frieze* (detail)

who charms and decapitates Holofernes (look for his severed head in the right-hand corner of the canvas). Here Judith is presented as a femme fatale: a pouting, bare-breasted Assyrian goddess with a halo of dark hair and a glimmer of ecstatic desire in her eye. The use of gold-leaf and mosaic-like detail is typical of Klimt's golden period, which was inspired by Byzantine imagery he saw in Venice.

The Beethoven Frieze (1902; Secession)

Painted for the 14th Vienna Secessionist exhibition, this monumental frieze is a phantasmagorical depiction of Beethoven's Ninth Symphony, anchored in mythological symbolism and the conflict of good and evil. Nymph-like creatures drift across the walls in flowing white robes with choirs of flower-bearing angels. The trio of gorgons (symbolising sickness, madness and death) and the three women (embodying lasciviousness, wantonness and intemperance) caused widespread outrage – the latter were considered pornographic.

Klimt & the Female Form

Klimt's fascination with women is a common thread in many of his paintings. He was most at ease in women's company and lived with his mother and two sisters even at the height of his career. Despite his long-term relationship with the fashion designer Emilie Flöge, Klimt had countless affairs with his models – in his studio, he apparently wore nothing under his artist's smock – and he fathered around 14 illegitimate children. Though of humble origins, Klimt rapidly climbed the social ladder and was sought out by high-society ladies wishing to have their portrait done.

TOP SIGHT

HEERESGESCHICHTLICHES MUSEUM

More riveting than it sounds, the Heeresgeschichtliches Museum presents a fascinating romp through 400 years of Austro-European military history. In the wake of the 1848 rebellion, Franz Josef I strengthened his defences by ordering the building of the fortress-like Arsenal. This sprawling barracks and munitions depot, completed in 1856, harbours Vienna's oldest public museum.

The museum's whimsical red-brick **arsenal**, with its dome, crenellations, vaulted ceilings, frescoes and columns, is a potpourri of Byzantine, Hispano-Moorish and neo-Gothic styles. Spread over two floors, the permanent collection takes a deep breath and plunges headfirst into military history, from the Thirty Years' War (1618–48) to WWII.

On the **ground floor**, the room dedicated to the assassination of Archduke Franz Ferdinand in Sarajevo in 1914 – which triggered a chain of events culminating in the start of WWI – steals the show. Further displays home in on WWI and WWII, with excellent displays including Nazi propaganda and Wehrmacht uniforms.

Moving up a level, the **1st floor** races you back to the Thirty Years' War, the Ottoman Wars in the 16th and 17th centuries and the Napoleonic Wars (1789 to 1815). In the former, the biggest crowd-puller is a monumental painting showing the 1683 Battle of Vienna.

DON'T MISS

- Archduke Franz Ferdinand's car
- WWI and WWII halls
- Peeter Snayers' Thirty Years' War paintings

PRACTICALITIES

- Museum of Military History
- Map p260, C7
- www.hgm.or.at
- 03, Arsenal
- adult/under 19yr €6/free, 1st Sun of month free
- 9am-5pm
- Südtiroler Platz

VVOE/SHUTTERSTOCK ©

TOP SIGHT

MUSEUM FÜR ANGEWANDTE KUNST

Housed in a stately neo-Renaissance pile on the Ring, Vienna's Museum für Angewandte Kunst (MAK) is a stunning tribute to applied arts and crafts, gathered around an arcaded, sky-lit courtyard.

On the **ground floor**, exhibition halls are devoted to different styles. One, for instance, is hung with elaborately patterned 16th- and 17th-century Persian, Indian, Turkish and Egyptian carpets, while another spotlights mid-19th century bentwood Thonet chairs – now a Viennese coffeehouse fixture.

In the baroque, rococo and classical collection, the star attraction is the 1740 porcelain room from the **Palais Dubský** in Brno. Italian Renaissance needlepoint lace, jewel-coloured Biedermeier *Steingläser* glasses and Styrian medieval liturgical vestments are other treasures.

The **1st floor** whisks you into Vienna's artistic golden age, from 1890 to 1938. The prized **Wiener Werkstätte** collection, the world's most comprehensive, collates postcards, furniture, fabric patterns, ceramics and distinctive metalwork by modernism pioneers Josef Hoffmann and Koloman Moser and their contemporaries.

The **basement** Study Collection zooms in on materials: glass and ceramics, metal, wood and textiles, with everything from exquisite Japanese lacquerware to unusual furniture (note the red-lips sofa).

DON'T MISS

- Palais Dubský porcelain room
- Thonet chairs
- Wiener Werkstätte collection
- Klimt's sketch for the Palais Stoclet frieze

PRACTICALITIES

- MAK, Museum of Applied Arts
- Map p260, B2
- www.mak.at
- 01, Stubenring 5
- adult/under 19yr €9.90/free, 6-10pm Tue free, tours €2
- 10am-6pm Wed-Sun, to 10pm Tue, English tours noon Sun
- Stubentor, U Stubentor

SIGHTS

SCHLOSS BELVEDERE PALACE

See p141.

HEERESGESCHICHTLICHES MUSEUM MUSEUM

See p148.

MUSEUM FÜR ANGEWANDTE KUNST MUSEUM

See p149.

KUNSTHAUSWIEN MUSEUM

Map p260 (Art House Vienna; www.kunsthauswien.com; 03, Untere Weissgerberstrasse 13; adult/child €11/5; ⌚10am-6pm; 🚊1, O Radetzkyplatz) The KunstHausWien, with its bulging ceramics, wonky surfaces, checkerboard facade, Technicolour mosaic tilework and rooftop sprouting plants and trees, bears the inimitable hallmark of eccentric Viennese artist and ecowarrior Friedensreich Hundertwasser (1928–2000), who famously called the straight line 'godless'. It is an ode to his playful, boldly creative work, as well as to his green politics.

FÄLSCHERMUSEUM MUSEUM

Map p260 (Museum of Art Fakes; www.faelschermuseum.com; 03, Löwengasse 28; adult/child €5.50/3; ⌚10am-5pm Tue-Sun; 🚊1 Hetzgasse) Wow, a museum with Schiele, Raphael, Rembrandt and Marc Chagall paintings that nobody knows about? Well, that's because they are all fakes, though spotting the difference is a near impossibility for the untrained eye. The tiny, privately run Fälschermuseum opens a fascinating window on the world of art forgeries. Besides giving background on the who, how, when and what, the museum recounts some incredible stories about master forgers who briefly managed to pull the wool over the experts' eyes.

HUNDERTWASSERHAUS LANDMARK

Map p260 (03, cnr Löwengasse & Kegelgasse; 🚊1 Hetzgasse) This residential block of flats bears all the wackily creative hallmarks of Hundertwasser, Vienna's radical architect and lover of uneven surfaces, with its curvy lines, crayon-bright colours and mosaic detail.

It's not possible to see inside, but you can cross the road to visit the **Kalke Village** (Map p260; www.kalke-village.at; 03, Kegelgasse 37-39; ⌚9am-6pm; 🚊1 Hetzgasse) FREE, also the handiwork of Hundertwasser.

EATING

CAFÉ GOLDEGG CAFE €

Map p260 (www.cafegoldegg.at; 04, Argentinierstrasse 49; snacks €3.50-6, mains €10-13; ⌚8am-8pm Mon-Fri, 9am-8pm Sat, 9am-7pm Sun; 📶🖉; Ⓤ Südtiroler Platz) Goldegg is a coffee house in the classic Viennese mould, with its green velvet booths, wood panelling, billiard tables and art nouveau sheen – but with a twist. Staff are refreshingly attentive, and alongside menu stalwarts such as goulash, you'll find lighter dishes like toasted paninis with homemade basil pesto and Ayurvedic vegetable curries.

HIDDEN KITCHEN PARK DELI €

Map p260 (www.hiddenkitchen.at; 03, Invalidenstrasse 19; main, salad & soup €10; ⌚8am-5pm Mon-Fri, 10am-4pm Sat; Ⓤ Wien Mitte) Fresh, healthy food takes centre stage at the modern, buzzy Hidden Kitchen Park. The emphasis is on top-quality produce in creative salads such as lemon-herb couscous and rocket with antipasti and polenta crumble, wholesome stews and soups.

THAT'S AMORE PIZZA €

Map p260 (☎01-343 95 18; www.thatsamore.at; 03, Messenhausergasse 13; pizza €6-14, 2-course lunch €8.50; ⌚11.30am-3pm & 5.30-11pm Mon-Sat, 5.30-11pm Sun; Ⓤ Kardinal-Nagl-Platz, Rochusgasse) The authentically Neopolitan pizzas are love at first bite for many at That's Amore – soft, chewy and with tangy-sweet tomato toppings. A relaxed atmosphere, chipper staff and wallet-friendly prices make this a winner.

CAFE MENTA CAFE €

Map p260 (☎01-966 84 23; www.cafementa.at; 03, Radetzkyplatz 4; lunch €7.50, tasting platter €13, mains €7.50-15.50; ⌚8.30am-midnight) Cafe Menta cuts a nouveau-retro look, with its mint-green walls, bright, wood-floored interior and contemporary bistro seating. Mezze-style sharing plates are the way to go for a taste of mini dishes such as sea-bass kebabs and aubergine halloumi rolls. It also rustles up tasty salads, soups, pasta and ciabattas (including some vegan options) and a cooling homemade mint ice tea.

★LINGENHEL MODERN EUROPEAN €€

Map p260 (☎01-710 15 66; www.lingenhel.com; 03, Landstrasser Hauptstrasse 74; mains €19-24; ⌚shop 8am-8pm, restaurant 8am-10pm Mon-Sat; Ⓤ Rochusgasse) One of Vienna's most exciting gastro newcomers, Lingenhel is an

WORTH A DETOUR

ZENTRALFRIEDHOF

When a Wiener says, *'Er hat den 71er genommen'* ('He took the No 71'), they are, metaphorically speaking, referring to the end of the line: **Zentralfriedhof** (www.friedhoefewien.at; 11, Simmeringer Hauptstrasse 232-244; ⌚7am-8pm, shorter hours in winter; 🚋6, 71 Zentralfriedhof). The cemetery's mammoth scale (2.4 sq km, more than three million resting residents) has made its tram line a euphemism for death. One of Europe's biggest cemeteries, this is where rich and poor, Buddhists and Jews, Catholics and Protestants lie side by side in eternal slumber under ash and maple trees. With leafy avenues and overgrown monuments, it is a remarkably calming place to wander.

The cemetery has three gates: the first leads to the old Jewish graves; the second, the main gate, directs you to the tombs of honour and the **Dr Karl Lueger Kirche**, the cemetery's perkily domed art nouveau church, which bears the hallmark of Austrian architect Max Hegele. The third is closer to the Protestant and new Jewish graves. The **information centre** and map of the cemetery are at Gate Two.

Just beyond Gate Two are the all-star **Ehrengräber** (Tombs of Honour). Besides the clump of big-name composers such as Beethoven, Brahms, Johann Strauss Father and Son, and Schubert, lie Austrian luminaries including artist Hans Makart, sculptor Fritz Wotruba, architect Adolf Loos, and 1980s pop icon Falco. Mozart may have a monument here, but he is buried in an unmarked grave in the **St Marxer Friedhof** (Cemetery of St Marx; Map p260; www.friedhoefewien.at; 03, Leberstrasse 6-8; ⌚7am-7pm, shorter hours in winter; ⓤZippererstrasse).

ultra-slick deli-shop-bar-restaurant, lodged in a 200-year-old house. Salamis, wines and own-dairy cheeses tempt in the shop, while much-lauded chef Daniel Hoffmeister helms the kitchen in the pared-back, white-washed restaurant. The season-inflected food – simple as char with kohlrabi and pork belly with aubergines – tastes profoundly of what it ought to.

MEIEREI IM STADTPARK
AUSTRIAN €€

Map p260 (☎01-713 31 68; http://steirereck.at; 03, Am Heumarkt 2a; set breakfasts €20-24, mains €11.50-22; ⌚8am-11pm Mon-Fri, 9am-7pm Sat & Sun; 🖉; ⓤStadtpark) In the green surrounds of Stadtpark, the Meierei is most famous for its goulash served with lemon, capers and creamy dumplings (€18) and its selection of 120 types of cheese. Served until noon, the bountiful breakfast features gastronomic show-stoppers such as poached duck egg with sweet potato, cress and wild mushrooms, and warm curd-cheese strudel with elderberry compote.

JOSEPH BROT
BISTRO €€

Map p260 (03, Landstrasser Hauptstrasse 4; breakfast €6.70-14.60, lunch mains €12.50-17.50; ⌚bakery 7.30am-9pm Mon-Fri, 8am-6pm Sat & Sun, bistro 8am-9pm Mon-Fri, 8am-6pm Sat & Sun; ⓤWien Mitte) Purveyors of some of Vienna's finest bread, Joseph Brot's newest bakery, bistro and patisserie is a winner. Besides wonderfully fresh loaves – organic olive-tomato ciabatta and rye-honey-lavender, for instance – it does wholesome breakfasts, speciality teas, healthy smoothies and utterly divine pastries. Season-driven specials such as sea bream with tomatoes, artichokes and olives star on the lunch menu in the stripped-back bistro.

RESTAURANT INDUS
INDIAN €€

Map p260 (☎01-713 43 44; www.restaurantindus.at; 03, Radetzkystrasse 20; mains €11-16.50; ⌚11.30am-2.30pm & 6-11pm Sun-Fri, 6-11pm Sat; 🖉; 🚋1, O Radetzkyplatz) Subtle back-lighting, clean lines and scatter cushions in zingy colours create a warm yet minimalist aesthetic at Indus. The mood is laid-back and the biryanis, tandooris, curries and dhals are spot on. The house special is chicken curry with mango, and there are options for vegetarians.

GASTHAUS WILD
AUSTRIAN €€

Map p260 (☎01-920 94 77; http://gasthaus-wild.at; 03, Radetzkyplatz 1; 2-course lunch menus €8.30-10.30, mains €11-27.50; ⌚9am-1am Mon-Fri, to midnight Sun; 🖉; 🚋1, O Radetzkyplatz) Gasthaus Wild, formerly a dive of a *Beisl* (bistro pub), has in recent years morphed into a great *neo-Beisl*. Its dark, wood-panelled interior retains a traditional look, and the menu includes flavoursome favourites such as goulash, schnitzel with potato salad, and paprika chicken with *Spätzle* (egg noodles). The menu changes regularly, the vibe is relaxed, the staff welcoming and the wine selection good.

GMOAKELLER AUSTRIAN €€

Map p260 (☎01-712 53 10; www.gmoakeller.at; 03, Am Heumarkt 25; mains €9-18; ⏰11am-midnight Mon-Sat; UStadtpark) Sizzling and stirring since 1858, this atmospheric cellar is as traditional as it gets, with parquet floors, brick vaults and warm wood panelling. The classic grub – *Zwiebelrostbraten* (onion-topped roast beef) or Carinthian *Kas'nudeln* (cheese noodles) – goes nicely with tangy Austrian wines. Tables spill out onto the pavement in summer.

★STEIRERECK IM STADTPARK GASTRONOMY €€€

Map p260 (☎01-713 31 68; http://steirereck.at; 03, Am Heumarkt 2a; mains €48-52, 6-/7-course menus €142/152; ⏰11.30am-2.30pm & 6.30pm-midnight Mon-Fri; UStadtpark) Heinz Reitbauer is at the culinary helm of this two-starred Michelin restaurant, beautifully lodged in a 20th-century former dairy building in the leafy Stadtpark. His tasting menus are an exuberant feast, fizzing with natural, integral flavours that speak of a chef with exacting standards. Wine pairing is an additional €79/89 (six/seven courses).

DRINKING & NIGHTLIFE

★STRANDBAR HERRMANN BAR

Map p260 (www.strandbarherrmann.at; 03, Herrmannpark; ⏰10am-2am Apr-early Oct; 📶; 🚊0 Hintere Zollamstrasse, USchwedenplatz) You'd swear you're by the sea at this hopping canalside beach bar, with beach chairs, sand, DJ beats and hordes of Viennese livin' it up on summer evenings. Cocktails are two for the price of one during happy hour (6pm to 7pm). Cool trivia: it's located on Herrmannpark, named after picture-postcard inventor Emanuel Herrmann (1839–1902).

SALM BRÄU MICROBREWERY

Map p260 (www.salmbraeu.com; 03, Rennweg 8; ⏰11am-midnight; 🚊71 Unteres Belvedere, UKarlsplatz) Salm Bräu brews its own *Helles, Pils* (pilsner), *Märzen* (red-coloured beer with a strong malt taste), *G'mischt* (half *Helles* and half *Dunkel* – dark) and *Weizen* (full-bodied wheat beer, slightly sweet in taste). It is smack next to Schloss Belvedere and hugely popular, with a happy hour from 3pm to 5pm Monday to Friday and noon to 4pm Saturday.

CAFÉ AM HEUMARKT COFFEE

Map p260 (03, Am Heumarkt 15; ⏰9am-11pm Mon-Fri; UStadtpark) Look for the house number, not the name, as there's no sign at this old-school charmer of a coffee house. Inside it's a 1950s time warp – all shiny parquet, leather banquettes and marble tables. Do as the locals do: grab a newspaper, play billiards and unwind over coffee and no-nonsense Viennese grub.

CAFÉ ZARTL COFFEE

Map p260 (03, Rasumofskygasse 7; ⏰7am-11pm; 📶; 🚊1 Rasumofskygasse, URochusgasse) A withered beauty of a coffee house, Zartl pings you back to when it opened in 1883, with its striped banquettes, cocoon-like warmth and, at times, somnambulant staff. Come for lazy breakfasts, people-watching and coffee with delightfully flaky strudel. You'll be mostly among regulars.

URANIA BAR

Map p260 (www.barurania.com; 01, Uraniastrasse 1; ⏰9am-midnight Mon-Fri, 2pm-midnight Sat, 9am-6pm Sun; 🚊2 Julius-Raab-Platz, USchwedenplatz) Another addition to the canal's ever-increasing stock of bars, Urania occupies the 1st floor of a rejuvenated cinema and observatory complex. Its slick, clean decor, elevated position overlooking the canal and extensive cocktail selection are all big pluses.

ENTERTAINMENT

RADIOKULTURHAUS CONCERT VENUE

Map p260 (☎01-501 70 377; http://radiokulturhaus.orf.at; 04, Argentinierstrasse 30a; tickets €7-27; ⏰box office 4-7pm Mon-Fri; 🚊D Plösslgasse, UTaubstummengasse) Expect anything from odes to Sinatra and R.E.M. or an evening dedicated to Beethoven and Mozart at the Radiokulturhaus. Housed in several performance venues including the Grosser Sendesaal – home to the Vienna Radio Symphony Orchestra and the Klangtheater (used primarily for radio plays) – this is one of Vienna's cultural hot spots.

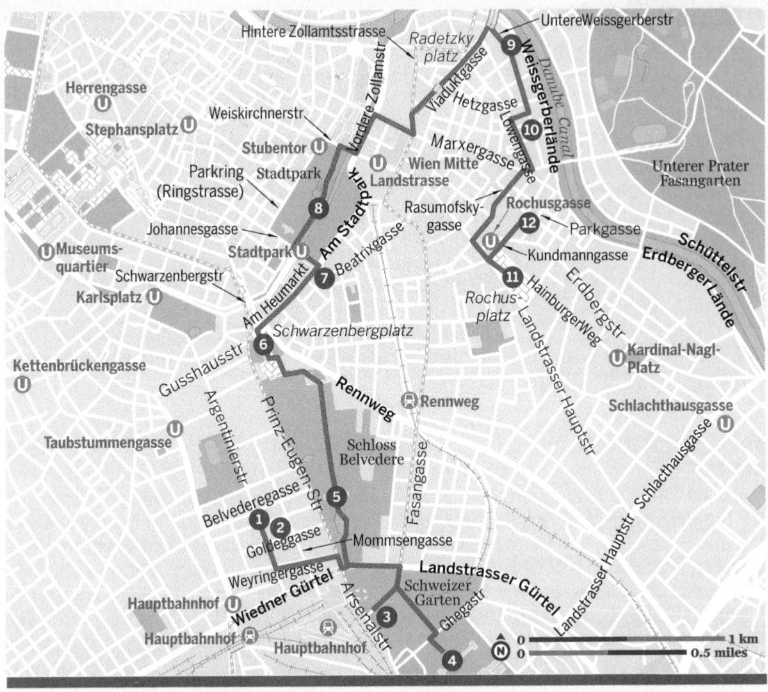

Neighbourhood Walk
Grand Designs in Landstrasse

START SANKT-ELISABETH-PLATZ
END WITTGENSTEINHAUS
LENGTH 8KM; TWO TO FOUR HOURS

Begin by soaking up the vibe of ❶ **Sankt-Elisabeth-Platz**, dwarfed by neo-Gothic Sankt-Elisabeth-Kirche, then nip around the corner to ❷ **Café Goldegg** (p150) for coffee with a dash of art nouveau flair. This old-school coffee house is off the tourist radar so you'll be mingling with Viennese over coffee, strudel or a day special. Wandering south through the sculpture-dotted Schweizergarten, you'll see the cubical ❸ **21er Haus** (p145), Belvedere's repository for contemporary art. Nearby sits the imposing Arsenal, built in the wake of the 1848 rebellion, which harbours the ❹ **Heeresgeschichtliches Museum** (p148) – a vast repository spelling out Austrian history in artefacts.

Backtrack to the ❺ **Belvedere Gardens** (p143), a swooping ribbon of greenery that threads together the two wings of the baroque palace. A brisk 30-minute walk takes in their cascading waterfalls, topiary, sculptures of muses, sphinxes and mythical beasties and ornamental parterres. Emerge at ❻ **Schwarzenbergplatz**, a grand square flanked to the north by a statue of Karl von Schwarzenberg, who led Austrian and Bohemian troops in the Battle of Leipzig (1813).

Rest over a drink in nearby ❼ **Café am Heumarkt** (p152) before tracing the Wien River north through the ❽ **Stadtpark**. Pause for golden snapshots of the memorial commemorating Johann Strauss, king of the waltz. Walk 10 minutes north to spy the chessboard-like facade of ❾ **KunstHausWien** (p150). A five-minute mosey south reveals another of Hundertwasser's creations: the trippy, rainbow-bright ❿ **Hundertwasserhaus** (p150).

Head south to the ⓫ **Rochusmarkt**, where market stalls sell flowers, fruit, meat, cheese, wine and more, then east to the ⓬ **Wittgensteinhaus** at Parkgasse 18. Designed by Paul Engelmann, a student of modernist legend Adolf Loos, and the philosopher Ludwig Wittgenstein, this building has strict lines and a stepped design reminiscent of the Bauhaus style. It's now occupied by the Bulgarian embassy.

WORTH A DETOUR

OBERLAA THERME WIEN

Rest museum-weary feet or escape the city for a day at **Oberlaa Therme Wien** (01-680 09; www.thermewien.at; 11, Kurbadstrasse 14; adult/child 3hr €18.50/12.50, full day €25.90/16; 9am-10pm Mon-Sat, 8am-10pm Sun; ; 67 Oberlaa-Therme Wien), Austria's largest thermal baths. The water here bubbles at a pleasant 27°C to 36°C and jets, whirlpools, waterfalls and grotto-like pools pummel and swirl you into relaxation. Besides a jigsaw of indoor and outdoor pools, there is an area where kids can splash, dive and rocket down flumes, a sauna complex where grown-ups can detox in herb-scented steam rooms with names like 'morning sun' and 'rainbow', as well as gardens with sun loungers, outdoor massage and games such as volleyball and boules for warm-weather days.

The best way to reach the thermal baths is by taking U1 to Reumannplatz, then catching tram 67 to Oberlaa Therme Wien. It's around a 10-minute tram ride from Reumannplatz.

ARNOLD SCHÖNBERG CENTER CLASSICAL MUSIC

Map p260 (01-712 18 88; www.schoenberg.at; 03, Schwarzenbergplatz 6, entrance at Zaunergasse 1; 10am-5pm Mon-Fri; D Schwarzenbergplatz, U Stadtpark) A brilliant repository of Arnold Schönberg's archival legacy and a cultural centre and celebration of the Viennese school of the early 20th century honouring the Viennese-born composer, painter, teacher, theoretician and innovator known for his 12-tone technique. The exhibition hall hosts intimate classical concerts, which in-the-know Wiener flock to.

AKADEMIETHEATER THEATRE

Map p260 (01-514 44 41 40; www.burgtheater.at; 03, Lisztstrasse 1; tickets €7-61; 4A, U Stadtpark) Opened in 1922, the 500-seat Akademietheater is the second venue of Vienna's highly esteemed Burgtheater. It stages predominantly contemporary productions.

KONZERTHAUS CONCERT VENUE

Map p260 (01-242 002; www.konzerthaus.at; 03, Lothringerstrasse 20; box office 9am-7.45pm Mon-Fri, to 1pm Sat, plus 45min before performance; D Gusshausstrasse, U Stadtpark) The Konzerthaus is a major venue in classical-music circles, but throughout the year ethnic music, rock, pop or jazz can also be heard in its hallowed halls. Up to three simultaneous performances, in the Grosser Saal, the Mozart Saal and the Schubert Saal, can be staged; this massive complex also features another four concert halls.

Students can pick up €16 tickets 30 minutes before performances; children receive 50% discount.

KURSALON CLASSICAL MUSIC

Map p260 (01-512 57 90; www.kursalonwien.at; 01, Johannesgasse 33; tickets €42-95, concert with 3-course dinner €74-127, with 4-course dinner €79-132; 2 Weihburggasse, U Stadtpark) Fans of Strauss and Mozart will love the performances at Kursalon, which holds daily evening concerts at 8.15pm devoted to the two masters of music in a splendid, refurbished Renaissance building. Also popular is the concert and dinner package (three- or four-course meal (not including drinks) at 6pm, followed by the concert) in the equally palatial on-site restaurant.

SPORTS & ACTIVITIES

3 CITY WAVE WATER SPORTS

Map p260 (www.3citywave.at; 03, Schwarzenbergplatz; 10am-10pm Sun-Thu, to 11pm Fri & Sat mid-Jun–Sep; U Stadtpark, Karlsplatz) Surfing? In the heart of Vienna? Yep. This artificial wave in front of the Hochstrahlbrunnen fountain on Schwarzenbergplatz draws novices and pros alike. A 50-minute free-surfer session costs €39. Kids' surf camps are also available.

WIENER EISLAUFVEREIN ICE SKATING

Map p260 (www.wev.or.at; 03, Lothringerstrasse 22; adult/child €7/6, boot hire €6.50; 9am-8pm Sat-Mon, to 9pm Tue-Fri; D Schwarzenbergplatz, U Stadtpark) Fancy a twirl? At 6000 sq metres, the Wiener Eislaufverein is the world's largest open-air ice-skating rink. It's close to the Ringstrasse and Stadtpark. Remember to bring mittens and a hat.

Prater & East of the Danube

Neighbourhood Top Five

❶ **Prater** (p157) Enjoying a slice of Viennese park life, with boulevards for strolling, woods for roaming and a funfair. Take a nostalgic twirl above the capital in the Riesenrad, at its twinkling best after dark.

❷ **Johann Strauss Residence** (p159) Waltzing over to where ball chart-topper 'The Blue Danube' was composed.

❸ **Porzellanmuseum im Augarten** (p159) Eyeing banquet-worthy porcelain in the making behind the scenes at the museum.

❹ **Madame Tussauds Vienna** (p159) Meeting Freud, Klimt, Falco and a host of other Austrian waxwork wonders.

❺ **Donauinsel** (p163) Relaxing Viennese-style at a riverside beach or bar in summer.

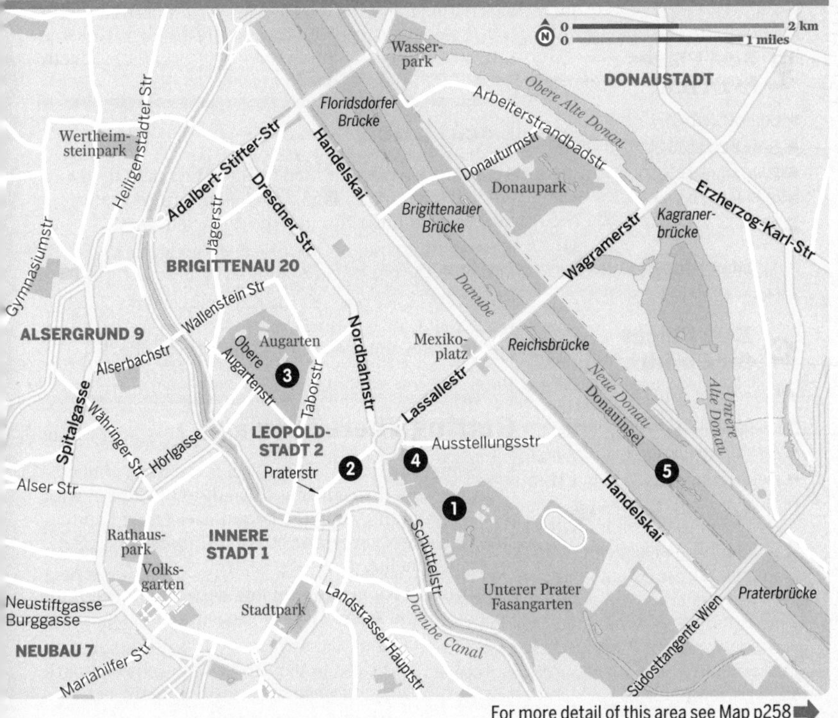

For more detail of this area see Map p258

Lonely Planet's Top Tip

For a truly Viennese experience, visit the 2nd district on a Saturday. Begin with a morning's mooch around the farmers market at Karmelitermarkt, stopping for brunch at one of the deli-cafes, then head southeast for a lazy stroll around the Prater or northwest to the baroque gardens of the Augarten.

Best Places to Eat

- Skopik & Lohn (p161)
- Harvest (p160)
- Schank zum Reichsapfel (p160)
- Spezerei (p161)
- Restaurant Mraz & Sohn (p161)

For reviews, see p160.

Best Places to Drink

- Le Loft (p161)
- Sperlhof (p162)
- Balthasar (p162)
- Fluc (p162)
- Tachles (p162)

For reviews, see p161.

Best Places for Children

- Riesenrad (p157)
- Planetarium (p158)
- Alte Donau (p164)
- Donauinsel (p163)

For reviews, see p159.

Explore Prater & East of the Danube

Between the bends of the Danube Canal and the Danube, Leopoldstadt in Vienna's 2nd district is just a couple of U-Bahn stops from the Innere Stadt, but feels light years away in spirit at times. Here, you can easily tiptoe off the beaten track; not least in the 4.5km ribbon of greenery that is the Prater. The Riesenrad rises above it all, rotating slowly to maximise the skyline views. To the west unfurl the manicured baroque gardens of the Augarten, home to a world-famous porcelain maker.

Leopoldstadt itself is worth more than a cursory glance, with boutiques, delis and cafes continuing to pop up on and around Karmelitermarkt, bringing a dash of gentrification to a once decidedly working-class area. The market, at its vibrant best on a Saturday morning, was once the centre of a flourishing Jewish quarter, which was all but extinguished during WWII. Yet a glimmer of that legacy is still visible in the district's sprinkling of kosher shops and men wearing wide-brimmed fedoras.

Strung along the banks of the Danube further north is Donaustadt, the 22nd district, whose personality swings between the forests of glass-and-steel skyscrapers in the UNO-City and the serene, deer-dotted woodlands of the Nationalpark Donau-Auen. The long slither of an island called Donauinsel is a much-loved summertime hangout of the Wiener for its bars, water-based action and urban beaches.

Local Life

- **Outdoors** Ah, what could be more Viennese than a languid bike ride through the chestnut-filled Prater (p157) or a saunter through the Augarten (p159).
- **Views** Riesenrad not your scene? Join locals to play 'I Spy' with the city's iconic landmarks at Le Loft (p161).
- **Markets** Scoot through the Karmelitermarkt (p162) Wiener-style on a Saturday morn for farm-fresh, organic grub, followed by brunch at a curbside deli.

Getting There & Away

- **U-Bahn** Praterstern (U1 and U2) is the main public transport link through Leopoldstadt to the Prater, with the U1 continuing on to the Donauinsel. Other handy stops include Nestroyplatz (U1) and Taborstrasse (U2) for the Karmelitermarkt.
- **Tram** Tram No 1 is a useful link between the southern portions of the Prater and the Ringstrasse.

MAYLAT/SHUTTERSTOCK ©

TOP SIGHT
PRATER

The Prater describes two distinct areas of parkland, which together comprise the city's favourite outdoor playground. First up, as you enter, is the Würstelprater, with all the roller-coaster-looping, dodgem-bashing fun of the fair, where the iconic Riesenrad turns. The Unterer Prater is a vast swath of woodland park, where Habsburgs once went hunting. Today, it is perfect for gentle bike rides, walks and warm-day picnics.

DON'T MISS

- Riesenrad
- Hauptallee
- Lusthaus
- Planetarium
- Pratermuseum

PRACTICALITIES

- Map p258, D6
- www.wiener-prater.at
- [family-friendly icon]
- UPraterstern

Würstelprater

No matter how old you are, you're forever 10 years old with money burning a hole in your pocket at the **Würstelprater** (rides €1.50-5). Come summer, this funfair throngs with excitable tots and big kids, gorging on doughnuts and lugging around hoopla-won teddies. The fairground's 250 attractions reach from old-school ghost trains and merry-go-rounds to g-force, human cannon-like rides.

Several recent white-knuckle additions to the funfair have cranked up the fear factor, including the **Turbo Boost** that spins at 100km/h, the **Ejection Seat**, a ball that dangles daredevils 90m above the ground, and the **Space Shot**, which shoots thrill-seekers like bullets at up to 80km/h. The 4km **Liliputbahn** (mini railway; www.liliputbahn.com; complete circuit adult/child €4/2.50; mid-Mar–late Oct) trundles between the Würstelprater and the Ernst-Happel-Stadion.

Riesenrad

Top of every Volksprater wish-list is the **Riesenrad** (www.wienerriesenrad.com; 02, Prater 90; adult/child €9.50/4; 9am-11.45pm, shorter hours in winter; [family-friendly icon]; UPraterstern); at least for anyone of an age to recall Orson Welles' cuckoo clock speech in British film noir *The Third Man* (1949), set in a shadowy postwar Vienna. This icon also achieved celluloid fame in the

UNTERER PRATER IN SUMMER

While the Unterer Prater can be virtually empty save for the odd horse-drawn carriage and jogger on a monochrome winter's day, warmer weather brings out the Viennese in droves. Hand-holding couples, families, cyclists, inline skaters, BMX bikers, horse riders and dog walkers all gravitate towards this patch of greenery to stretch their legs and find cool respite under thickets of trees. In mid-April, crowds and runners descend on the park for the Vienna Marathon.

Kids can swing, slide and climb to their hearts' content at the Jesuitenwiese playground, Vienna's biggest, in the Unterer Prater. This meadow is also where friends and families convene to picnic, play beach volleyball or toss a frisbee.

James Bond flick *The Living Daylights,* and *Before Sunrise,* directed by Richard Linklater.

Built in 1897 by Englishman Walter B Basset to celebrate the Golden Jubilee of Emperor Franz Josef I, the Ferris wheel rises to 65m and takes about 20 minutes to rotate its 430-tonne weight one complete circle – giving you ample time to snap some fantastic shots of the city spread out at your feet. It survived bombing in 1945 and has had dramatic lighting and a cafe at its base.

Planetarium

The **Planetarium** (www.planetarium-wien.at; 02, Oswald-Thomas-Platz 1; adult/child €9/6.50; ⏲show times vary; UPraterstern), Vienna's extraterrestrial and interstellar viewfinder, is located on the edge of the Würstelprater behind the Riesenrad. Shows change on a regular basis, but usually focus on how the Earth fits into the cosmological scheme of things. Shows are in German.

Pratermuseum

Sharing the same building as the Planetarium, this **municipal museum** (www.wienmuseum.at; 02, Oswald-Thomas-Platz 1; adult/under 19yr €5/free; ⏲10am-1pm & 2-6pm Tue-Sun Mar-Oct, 10am-1pm & 2-6pm Fri-Sun Nov-Feb; UPraterstern) traces the history of the Würstelprater and its woodland neighbour. For all the life and splendour the Prater has seen, unfortunately its museum has only a rather dull mix of photos and stories, mainly from the 19th century. The antique slot machines, some of which are still functioning, are the museum's saving grace.

Unterer Prater

Few places in Vienna can match the Unterer Prater for fresh air, exercise and a burst of seasonal colour. Spread across 60 sq km, central Vienna's biggest park comprises woodlands of poplar and chestnut, meadows and tree-lined boulevards, as well as children's playgrounds, a swimming pool, golf course and race track.

Fringed by statuesque chestnut trees that are ablaze with russet and gold in autumn and billowing with delicate white blossom in late spring, the **Hauptallee** avenue is the Unterer Prater's central 4.5km vein, running as straight as a die from the Praterstern to the Lusthaus (p161). Originally erected as a 16th-century hunting lodge, the Lusthaus pavilion was rebuilt in 1783 to host imperial festivities and the like. Today, it shelters a chandelier-lit cafe and restaurant.

SIGHTS

PRATER PARK

See p157.

PORZELLANMUSEUM IM AUGARTEN MUSEUM

Map p258 (Augarten Porcelain Museum; www.augarten.at; 02, Obere Augartenstrasse 1; adult/child €7/5, incl guided tour €11/9; ⌚10am-6pm Mon-Sat; UTaborstrasse) Restored to its former glory and reopened in 2011, this imperial pleasure palace harbours a new museum dedicated to exquisite Augarten porcelain. Founded in 1718, Augarten is the second-oldest porcelain manufacturer in Europe. A chronological spin of the museum takes in lavish rococo creations, boldly coloured Biedermeier pieces, Spanish Riding School equestrian figures and the simpler porcelain fashionable in the 1950s. One-hour tours of the premises are available at 2pm and 3pm on Saturdays, when you can learn about the process of turning white kaolin, feldspar and quartz into delicate creations through the process of moulding, casting, luting, glazing and painting. It's free to get a glimpse of some of Augarten's fabulously detailed creations in the shop, open during the regular opening hours.

AUGARTEN PARK

Map p258 (www.kultur.park.augarten.org; 03, Obere Augartenstrasse; ⌚6am-dusk; UTaborstrasse) This landscaped park from 1775 is dotted with open meadows and criss-crossed by tree-lined paths. You can kick a ball in one section, let the kids stage a riot in a playground in another, or visit the **porcelain museum**. Among the park's most eye-catching features are the austere *Flaktürme* (flak towers) in its northern and western corners.

WIENER KRIMINALMUSEUM MUSEUM

Map p258 (www.kriminalmuseum.at; 02, Grosse Sperlgasse 24; adult/child €6/3; ⌚10am-5pm Tue-Sun; UTaborstrasse) The Vienna Crime Museum is another gruesome chapter in the Viennese obsession with death. It takes a tabloid-style look at crimes and criminals in Austria and dwells on murders in the last 100 years or so with particularly grisly relish; there are skulls of earlier criminals, and even an 18th-century head pickled in a jar.

MADAME TUSSAUDS VIENNA MUSEUM

Map p258 (www.madametussauds.com/wien; 02, Riesenradplatz 1; adult/child €20.50/16.50; ⌚10am-8pm, shorter hours in winter; UPraterstern) This waxwork wonderland in the Würstelprater is a stage for a host of sculpted celebrities – Nicole Kidman, Michael Jackson and Johnny Depp star among them. Other figures such as Emperor Franz Josef and his beloved Sisi, Klimt, Freud and Falco give the experience a distinctly Austrian edge. There are hands-on exhibits that let you interact with the wax, from taking an IQ test with Albert Einstein to composing with Mozart and Beethoven.

JOHANN STRAUSS RESIDENCE MUSEUM

Map p258 (www.wienmuseum.at; 02, Praterstrasse 54; adult/under 19yr €5/free; ⌚10am-1pm & 2-6pm Tue-Sun; UNestroyplatz) Strauss the Younger called Praterstrasse 54 home from 1863 to 1878 and composed *the* waltz, 'The Blue Danube', under its high ceilings. Inside you'll find an above-average collection of Strauss and ballroom memorabilia, including an Amati violin said to have belonged to him and oil paintings from his last apartment, which was destroyed during WWII. The rooms are bedecked in period furniture from Strauss' era. The residence is a municipal museum.

DONAUTURM TOWER

Map p258 (www.donauturm.at; 22, Donauturmstrasse 4; adult/child €7.90/5.70, combined ticket incl Riesenrad €13.50/7.40; ⌚10am-midnight; UKaisermühlen Vienna International Centre) At 252m, the Danube Tower in Donaupark is Vienna's tallest structure. Its revolving restaurant at 170m allows fantastic panoramic views of the city and beyond – the food tends to be tried and trusted Viennese favourites. The adventurous can bungee jump off the side of the tower; see the website for details.

UNO-CITY NOTABLE BUILDING

Map p258 (☎01-260 60 3328; www.unvienna.org; 22, Wagramer Strasse 5; adult/child €10/4; ⌚11am, 2pm & 3.30pm Mon-Fri; UKaisermühlen Vienna International Centre) UNO-City, or Vienna International Centre as it is officially known, is home to a variety of international organisations, but mainly houses the UN's third-largest office in the world. Multilingual guided tours lasting about one hour take you through conference rooms and exhibitions on UN activities and give you an insight into what goes on behind usually closed doors. The complex was the picture of modernism way back in 1979 when it was built; today it looks less than fab. It

WORTH A DETOUR

INTO THE WOODS: THE WIENERWALD

If you really want to get into the great outdoors, scamper across to the Wienerwald. The Austrian capital's rural escape vault, this 45km swath of forested hills, fringing the capital from the northwest to the southeast, was immortalised in 'Tales from the Vienna Woods,' the concert waltz by Johann Strauss Junior in 1868.

These woods are made for walking and the city council website (www.wien.gv.at/umwelt/wald/freizeit/wandern/wege) details nine walks, a couple of which take you into the forest. You'll need about three hours to complete the 7.2km trail No 4, which threads up to the **Jubiläumswarte**. Rising above the Wienerwald's green canopy, this lookout tower offers sweeping views from the uppermost platform that take in most of Vienna and reach as far as the 2076m hump of Schneeberg. The climb to the top is exhilarating. Grab some picnic supplies, jump on tram 49 to Bahnhofstrasse, and walk in the direction of the tram to Rosentalgasse, then follow the signs. From the Jubiläumswarte, the trail is mainly through suburbs, so it's nicer to return the way you came.

A slightly longer alternative is trail No 1, an 11km loop, which starts in Nussdorf (take tram D from the Ring) and climbs **Kahlenberg** (484m), a vine-streaked hill commanding fine city views. On your return to Nussdorf you can undo all that exercise by imbibing at a *Heuriger* (wine tavern). You can spare yourself the leg work by taking the Nussdorf-Kahlenberg 38A bus in one or both directions.

Another way of exploring the Wienerwald on your own is on one of the 46 marked mountain-bike trails. These are signposted and graded according to difficulty. The website www.wienerwald.info lists and maps the routes.

does have a rather glamorous extraterritorial status, though, so bring your passport when visiting.

EATING

ZUR REZEPTION CAFE €

Map p258 (02, Grosse Sperlgasse 6; breakfast €6.80-8.90; ⏲9am-6pm Sat-Tue, 9am-11pm Wed-Fri) Blown-up family photos, vintage cabinets and the skeletal frames of old lampshades adorn this wonderfully retro cafe. It does a proper espresso, satisfying breakfasts prepared with produce from the nearby Karmelitermarkt, tasty sandwiches and home-cooked classics like Carinthian pasta with sweet and savoury fillings. The vibe is nicely chilled out.

HARVEST VEGAN €

Map p258 (☎0676 492 77 90; http://harvest-bistrot.at; 02, Karmeliterplatz 1; mains €10-12, brunch €15.50, lunch €8.80; ⏲11am-11pm Mon, Tue, Thu & Fri, 10am-6pm Sat & Sun; 🌱; 🚋Karmeliterplatz (Taborstrasse), UNestroyplatz) A bubble of bohemian warmth, Harvest swears by seasonality in its super-healthy vegetarian and vegan dishes, swinging from lentil, pear, walnut and smoked tofu salad to coconutty vegetable curries. Candles, soft lamp light and mismatched vintage furniture set the scene, and there's a terrace for summer dining. Alt Wien roasted coffee, homemade cakes and weekend brunches round out the picture.

SCHANK ZUM REICHSAPFEL AUSTRIAN €

Map p258 (☎01-212 25 79; http://zumreichsapfel.at; 02, Karmeliterplatz 3; mains €7.50-14.20; ⏲4pm-midnight Mon-Sat; 🚋Karmeliterplatz (Taborstrasse), UNestroyplatz) This is a delightfully warm, wooden *Heuriger* (wine tavern) in the traditional mould, with dark wood panelling, a tiled oven and a jovial crowd of locals digging into platters of rustic bread, speck, ham, sausage and salami, and sipping Austrian wines. More substantial mains hailing from Carinthia are of the *Schopfbratl* (pork roast) with dumplings, goulash and *Kasnudeln* (cheese noodles) ilk.

BITZINGER WÜRSTELSTAND FAST FOOD €

Map p258 (☎01-729 17 44; www.bitzinger-wien.at; 02, Beim Riesenrad; sausage €1.80-4.40; ⏲10am-1am Mon & Wed-Sun, 10am-4am Thu, Fri & Sat; UPraterstern) An outpost of Vienna's most famous sausage stand, this one sits below the Riesenrad in the Prater. Grab your *Bratwurst* or cheesy *Käsekrainer* here before or after hitting the rides.

STEWART CAFE €

Map p258 (www.stew-art.at; 02, Praterstrasse 11; soups €4.50, lunch mains €6.70-7.50; ⏲11am-3pm Mon-Fri; 🌱; 🚋2 Gredlerstrasse, USchwedenplatz) Come lunchtime this small, modern cafe buzzes with hungry locals, who come to slurp comforting soups and fill up on good-value day specials such as Panang curry, couscous stew and pumpkin quiche with alpine cheese. Everything is homemade and brilliantly fresh. There's plenty of choice for vegetarians, and many dishes are lactose and gluten free.

SCHÖNE PERLE — BISTRO €

Map p258 (01-890 32 04; www.schoene-perle.at; 02, Grosse Pfarrgasse 2; midday menu €7.20, mains €6.50-19; 11am-midnight Mon-Fri, 10am-midnight Sat & Sun; ; Taborstrasse) UFO-shaped lights cast a contemporary glow over minimalist Schöne Perle (beautiful pearl), which serves everything from lentil soups through *Tafelspitz* (prime boiled beef) to vegetarian and fish mains, all of which are created with organic produce. Wines are from Austria, as are the large array of juices.

★SKOPIK & LOHN — MODERN EUROPEAN €€

Map p258 (01-219 89 77; www.skopikundlohn.at; 02, Leopoldsgasse 17; mains €13-27; 6pm-1am Tue-Sat; Taborstrasse) The spidery web of scrawl that creeps across the ceiling at Skopik & Lohn gives an avant-garde edge to an otherwise French-style brasserie – all wainscoting, globe lights, cheek-by-jowl tables and white-jacketed waiters. The menu is modern European, with a distinct Mediterranean slant, with spot-on dishes like slow-braised lamb with mint-pea puree, almonds and polenta, and pasta with summer truffle and monkfish.

SPEZEREI — ITALIAN €€

Map p258 (0699 1720 0071; www.spezerei.at; 02, Karmeliterplatz 2; antipasti €7.50-14, lunch special €9; 11.30am-11pm Mon-Sat; ; 2 Karmeliterplatz, Taborstrasse) Wine bottles line the walls of this intimate, friendly *Vinothek* (wine bar). Top-quality wines are matched with a tempting array of antipasti and freshly made pasta, such as homemade *fusilli* (spiral-shaped pasta) filled with vanilla mozzarella or tomato-chilli sauce. The pavement terrace bubbles with life in summer.

TEMPEL — INTERNATIONAL €€

Map p258 (01-214 01 79; www.restaurant-tempel.at; 02, Praterstrasse 56; mains €15.50-26, 2-/3-course lunch €14.50/18; noon-3pm & 6pm-midnight Tue-Fri, 6pm-midnight Sat; Nestroyplatz) Rudi runs a tight ship at this intimate bistro, hidden in a courtyard off Praterstrasse. Presented with an eye for detail, dishes such as duo of quail with beetroot marmalade and chanterelle goulash reveal true depth of flavour and a passion for seasonality. The selection of Austrian wines is excellent, as is the outdoor seating on warm summer evenings.

LUSTHAUS — AUSTRIAN €€

(01-728 95 65; 02, Freudenau 254; mains €11-19; noon-10pm Mon-Fri, to 6pm Sat & Sun, shorter hours winter; ; 77A) A stroll along the Prater's chestnut-shaded avenues works up an appetite for all-Austrian grub at this former 16th-century Habsburg hunting lodge. The pavilion was rebuilt in 1783 to host imperial festivities and the like. Today, it shelters a chandelier-lit cafe and restaurant serving classics like beef broth with sliced pancakes, *Wiener Schnitzel* and *Marillenknödel* (apricot dumplings).

RESTAURANT MRAZ & SOHN — INTERNATIONAL €€€

Map p258 (01-330 45 94; www.mraz-sohn.at; 20, Wallenstein Strasse 59; 4-/6-/9-course menu €65/86/112; 7pm-midnight Mon-Fri; 5 Rauscherstrasse, Jägerstrasse) Mraz & Sohn is not only a snappy name, it really is a family-owned-and-run restaurant. The highly esteemed *chef de cuisine,* Markus Mraz, is the creative force behind the two Michelin stars and other accolades awarded for dishes that shine with creative flair and taste profoundly of their main ingredients – be it succulent Wagyu beef or octopus.

DRINKING & NIGHTLIFE

★LE LOFT — BAR

Map p258 (02, Praterstrasse 1; 10am-2am; 2 Gredlerstrasse, Schwedenplatz) Wow, what a view! Take the lift to Le Loft on the Sofitel's 18th floor to reduce Vienna to toy-town scale in an instant. From this slinky, glass-walled lounge, you can pick out landmarks such as the Stephansdom and the Hofburg over a pomegranate martini or mojito. By night, the backlit ceiling swirls with an impressionist painter's palette of colours.

★SUPERSENSE — CAFE

Map p258 (02, Praterstrasse 70; lunch special €5.50-6.50, breakfast €3.80-8; 9am-7pm Mon-Fri, 10am-5pm Sat) Housed in an ornate Italianate mansion dating to 1898, this retro-grand cafe brings a breath of cool new air to the Prater area. The cafe at the front, which rolls out locally roasted coffee, great breakfasts and day specials, gives way to a store that trades in everything from vinyl to cult Polaroid cameras, calligraphy sets and hand-bound notebooks.

BALTHASAR CAFE

Map p258 (☎0664 381 68 55; http://balthasar.at; 02, Praterstrasse 38; ⏰7.30am-7pm Mon-Fri, 9am-5pm Sat; Ⓤ Nestroyplatz) With pops of bold colour and lampshades that look like deflated golden helium balloons, this quirky cafe brews some of Vienna's best coffee – including a feisty espresso. The pastries, baguettes and brownies are good, too.

SPERLHOF COFFEE

Map p258 (02, Grosse Sperlgasse 41; ⏰4pm-1.30am; @; Ⓤ Taborstrasse) Every Viennese coffee house ought to be just like the wood-panelled, poster-plastered, eccentric Sperlhof, which opened in 1923. It still attracts a motley crowd of coffee sippers, daydreamers, billiard and ping-pong players and chess whizzes today. If you're looking for a novel, check out the table of secondhand books.

FLUC CLUB

Map p258 (www.fluc.at; 02, Praterstern 5; ⏰6pm-4am; Ⓤ Praterstern) Located on the wrong side of the tracks (Praterstern can be rough around the edges at times) and housed in a converted pedestrian passage, Fluc is the closest that Vienna's nightlife scene comes to anarchy – without the fear of physical violence.

CAFE ANSARI CAFE

Map p258 (☎01-276 51 02; www.cafeansari.at; 02, Praterstrasse 15; 2-course lunch €10.80, mains €11-28.50; ⏰8am-11.30pm Mon-Sat, 9am-3pm Sun) Wood floors, turquoise tiles and cosy niches create a stylishly contemporary look at this cafe, with pavement seating on Praterstrasse. The menu has a pinch of the orient and Georgia, taking you through from creative breakfasts to antipasti and mains like sweet potato-papaya cakes with chilli dip, and braised lamb with pumpkin, plums and creamy polenta.

ADRIA BAR

Map p258 (☎0660 12 71 784; www.adriawien.at; 02, Obere Donaustrasse 77; ⏰10am-1am; 🚊Salztorbrücke, Ⓤ Schottenring) Summer days on the Danube Canal are best spent lolling in a deckchair at this urban beach, where you can chill over a craft beer, ice cream or Aperol spritz.

TACHLES BAR

Map p258 (www.cafe-tachles.at; 02, Karmeliterplatz 1; ⏰4pm-1am Mon-Thu, to 2am Fri & Sat, to midnight Sun; 📶; 🚊2 Karmeliterplatz, Ⓤ Taborstrasse) Smack on the main square in up-and-coming Leopoldstadt, this bohemian cafe-bar attracts an intellectual and laid-back crowd of locals in its relaxed, wood-panelled surrounds. Small bites with a Slavic slant – *pierogi* (Polish dumplings), for instance – are on offer and it hosts occasional live music and readings.

KARMELITERMARKT FOR FOODIES

Set in an architecturally picturesque square, the **Karmelitermarkt** (Map p258; 02, Karmelitermarkt; ⏰6am-7.30pm Mon-Fri, to 5pm Sat; 🚊2 Karmeliterplatz, Ⓤ Taborstrasse) reflects the ethnic diversity of its neighbourhood; you're sure to see Hasidic Jews on bikes shopping for kosher goods here. On Saturday the square features a **Bauernmarkt**, where farmers set up stalls brimming with seasonal goods from fruit and veg to cheese, freshly baked bread, specialty salamis and organic herbs. The Viennese fill their bags here in the morning before doing brunch or lunch in one of the deli-cafes, many with outdoor seating. Take their lead and rest at one of these favourites:

Kaas am Markt (www.kaasammarkt.at; 02, Karmelitermarkt 33-36; light meals & mains €5-9; ⏰9am-6pm Tue-Fri, 8am-2pm Sat; ✎) 🍃 Deli-restaurant making the most of farm-fresh and organic produce. Sells picnic goodies like cheeses, salamis, preserves and apricot liqueur.

Zimmer 37 (02, Karmelitermarkt 37-39; lunch mains €6.90-7.90; ⏰10.30am-7.30pm Tue-Fri, 8am-3pm Sat; ✎) 🍃 Cosy, oft-candlelit cafe rustling up wholesome lunches like white bean chilli and homemade pasta.

Tewa (☎0676 84 77 41 211; http://tewa-karmelitermarkt.at; 02, Karmelitermarkt 26-32; breakfast €5.50-9.80, lunch €6.90-7.90; ⏰7am-11pm Mon-Sat) Great bagels, wraps, salads and breakfasts. The terrace is packed when the sun's out.

ENTERTAINMENT

★MUTH CONCERT VENUE

Map p258 (☎01-347 80 80; www.muth.at; 02, Obere Augartenstrasse 1e; Vienna Boys' Choir Fri performance €39-89; ⏲4-6pm Mon-Fri & 1 hour before performances; ⓤTaborstrasse) This striking baroque meets contemporary concert hall is the new home of the Wiener Sängerknaben, or Vienna Boys' Choir, who previously only performed at the Hofburg. Besides Friday-afternoon choral sessions with the angelic-voiced lads, the venue also stages a top-drawer roster of dance, drama, opera, classical, rock and jazz performances. The acoustics are second to none in the 400-seat auditorium and there's a cafe where you can grab a drink before or after a show.

ODEON CONCERT VENUE

Map p258 (☎01-216 51 27; www.odeon-theater.at; 02, Taborstrasse 10; tickets €25-32; ⏲6pm–performance time; 🚊2 Gredlerstrasse, ⓤSchwedenplatz) This oft-forgotten performance venue looks grand from the outside but the interior doesn't impress as much – come for the performance versus a palatial theatre experience. Anything from classical concerts to flamenco are held within its walls.

SHOPPING

TIEMPO BOOKS

Map p258 (http://tiempo.at; 02, Taborstrasse 17a; ⏲10am-6pm Mon-Fri, 10am-3pm Sat; 🚊Karmeliterplatz (Taborstrasse), ⓤTaborstrasse) Travel journals, art books, Vienna-related books, calendars and postcards line the shelves at this bookstore. You can sip a coffee while you browse.

SONG FASHION & ACCESSORIES

Map p258 (www.song.at; 02, Praterstrasse 11-13; ⏲1-7pm Tue-Fri, 10am-6pm Sat; 🚊2 Marienbrücke, ⓤSchwedenplatz) A holy grail for style seekers, this industrial-minimalist gallery and boutique hosts rotating exhibitions of modern art and is a showcase for designer furnishings, jewellery, accessories and fashion from the revered likes of Dries van Noten, Comme des Garçons and Paul Harnden.

STILWERK WIEN DESIGN

Map p258 (www.stilwerk.de/wien; 02, Praterstrasse 1; ⏲10am-7pm Mon-Fri, to 6pm Sat; 🚊2 Marienbrücke, ⓤSchwedenplatz) Plug into Vienna's contemporary design scene at this cluster of concept and interior stores in the glass-clad Design Tower.

NAGY STRICKDESIGN FASHION & ACCESSORIES

Map p258 (02, Krummbaumgasse 2-4; ⏲2-6pm Tue-Fri, 11am-1pm Sat; ⓤTaborstrasse) The stripy cotton and viscose knitwear here is both classic and up-to-the-minute, with flattering shapes and vivid colours, and designs for hot and cold weather. There are also linen pants and skirts in a refreshing range of bright colours and casual styles.

VORGARTENMARKT MARKET

Map p258 (www.vorgartenmarkt.at; 02, Ennsgasse; ⏲8am-6pm Tue-Fri, 8am-1pm Sat; ⓤVorgartenstrasse) Sandwiched between the Danube Canal and the Danube River, this organic market trades in everything from fruit and veg to meat, fish, bread and flowers.

HANNOVERMARKT MARKET

Map p258 (20, Hannovergasse; ⏲6am-7.30pm Mon-Fri, 6am-6pm Sat; ⓤJägerstrasse) The stalls are heaped with fresh regional produce and Asian foods at this local market.

SPORTS & ACTIVITIES

★DONAUINSEL ISLAND

Map p258 (ⓤDonauinsel) The svelte Danube Island stretches some 21.5km from opposite Klosterneuburg in the north to the Nationalpark Donau-Auen in the south and splits the Danube in two, creating a separate arm known as the Neue Donau (New Danube). Created in 1970, it has sections of beach (don't expect much sand) for swimming, boating and a little waterskiing.

The tips of the island are designated FKK (*Freikörperkultur;* free body culture) zones reserved for nudist bathers, who also enjoy dining, drinking, walking, biking and inline skating *au naturel* – it's quite a sight. Concrete paths run the entire length of the island, and there are bicycle and inline-skate rental stores. Restaurants and snack bars are dotted along the paths, but the highest concentration of bars – collectively known as Sunken City and Copa Cagrana – is near Reichsbrücke and the U1 Donauinsel stop. In late June the island hosts the **Donauinselfest** (https://donauinselfest.at; ⏲late Jun) FREE.

PEDAL POWER CYCLING

Map p258 (☎01-729 72 34; www.pedalpower.at; 02, Ausstellungsstrasse 3; bike rental per hr/half-/full day €6/19/30, guided bike tours €29-64, Segway tours €79; ⏲8.30am-7pm Apr-Oct; ⓤPrat-

WORTH A DETOUR

DONAU-AUEN NATIONAL PARK

A vast ribbon of greenery looping along the Danube from the fringes of Vienna to the Slovakian border, the 9300-hectare **Nationalpark Donau-Auen** (01-400 04 9495; www.donauauen.at; 22, Dechantweg 8; national park house 10am-6pm Wed-Sun Mar-Oct; 91A, 92A, 93A, S80) is one of the last remaining major wetlands in Europe. Established in 1996, the park comprises around 65% forest, 20% lakes and waterways and 15% meadows, which nurture some 700 species of fern and flowering plants.

The park's quieter reaches attract abundant birdlife and wildlife, such as red deer, beavers, fire-bellied toads, eagles, kites and a high density of kingfishers. The wienlobAU National Park House, located at the northern entrance to the park, offers a series of themed guided tours, ranging from winter walks to birdwatching rambles, most of which cost around €10/5 for adults/children. Boat tours into the national park leave from Salztorbrücke and last 4½ hours; booking is necessary. See the website for further details.

erstern) Pick up city and mountain bikes here, or hook onto one of the Segway tours, covering the main city highlights including the Ringstrasse, the Rathaus, Hofburg and more, or guided bike tours ranging from a three-hour spin of the city's standout sights to an all-day pedal through the Wachau Valley vineyards. Visit the website for further details. For an extra €6, you can arrange for bikes to be dropped off and picked up at your hotel. Child seats/helmets are an extra €5/3.

ALTE DONAU WATER SPORTS

Map p258 (22, Untere Alte Donau; U Alte Donau) The Alte Donau, a landlocked arm of the Danube, is separated from the Neue Donau by a sliver of land. It carried the main flow of the river until 1875. Now the 160-hectare water expanse is a favourite of Viennese sailing and boating enthusiasts, and also attracts swimmers, walkers, fisherfolk and, in winter (if it's cold enough), ice skaters.

STRANDBAD ALTE DONAU SWIMMING

Map p258 (22, Arbeiterstrandbadstrasse 91; adult/child €5.50/3; 9am-8pm Mon-Fri, 8am-8pm Sat & Sun May–mid-Sep; U Alte Donau) This bathing area makes great use of the Alte Donau during the summer months. It's a favourite of Viennese locals and gets extremely crowded at weekends during summer. Facilities include a restaurant, beach-volleyball court, playing field, slides and plenty of tree shade.

SAILING SCHOOL HOFBAUER BOATING

Map p258 (01-204 34 35; www.hofbauer.at; 22, An der Obere Alte Donau 191; Apr-Oct; U Alte Donau) Hofbauer rents sailing boats (€16.50 per hour) and row boats (€11 per hour) on the eastern bank of the Alte Donau and can provide lessons (in English) for those wishing to learn or brush up on their skills. Pedal boats (€14 per hour) and surf boards (€15.50) are also available for hire.

LOBAU OUTDOORS

(91A, 92A, 93A, S80) This is for those who want to go off-piste in summer. The Lobau, at the southern extremes of Donaustadt, is an area of dense scrub and woodland home to the western extension of the Nationalpark Donau-Auen, with an abundance of small lakes, and walking and cycling trails. In summer, Vienna's alternative crowd flock to the Lobau for skinny-dipping.

COPA CAGRANA RAD UND SKATERVERLEIH CYCLING

Map p258 (01-263 52 42; www.fahrradverleih.at; 22, Am Damm 1; per hr/half-/full day from €5/15/25; 9am-6pm Mar-Oct, to 9pm May-Aug; U Kaisermühlen Vienna International Centre) All manner of bikes are on offer here – city, mountain, trekking, kids' and more. Also has tandems (€12/60 per hour/day), rickshaws (€15/75 per hour/day) and rollerblades (€6/30 per hour/day).

STRANDBAD GÄNSEHÄUFEL SWIMMING

Map p258 (www.gaensehaeufel.at; 22, Moissigasse 21; adult/child €5.50/3; 9am-8pm Mon-Fri & 8am-8pm Sat & Sun May–mid-Sep; U Kaisermühlen Vienna International Centre) Gänsehäufel occupies half an island in the Alte Donau. It does get crowded in summer, but there's normally enough space to escape the mob. There's a swimming pool and FKK (read: nudist) area. The playground, slides, splash areas and mini golf keep kids amused for hours. Besides swimming, Gänsehäufel offers activities like tennis, volleyball and a climbing zone.

Schloss Schönbrunn & Around

Neighbourhood Top Five

❶ **Schloss Schönbrunn** (p167) Wandering the gloriously over-the-top baroque state apartments and lazing in the fountain-dotted gardens of Vienna's paean to the giddy, gilded late Habsburg era.

❷ **Klimt Villa** (p171) Diving into the sensual, colour-charged imagination of Klimt at his last studio.

❸ **Hermesvilla** (p172) Wandering in Empress Elisabeth's footsteps at this 19th-century mansion romantically nestled in woodland.

❹ **Kirche am Steinhof** (p173) Being amazed by the art nouveau grace of this gold-topped church, Otto Wagner's magnum opus.

❺ **Orangery** (p174) Enjoying the rousing melodies of Strauss and Mozart in Schönbrunn's former imperial greenhouse.

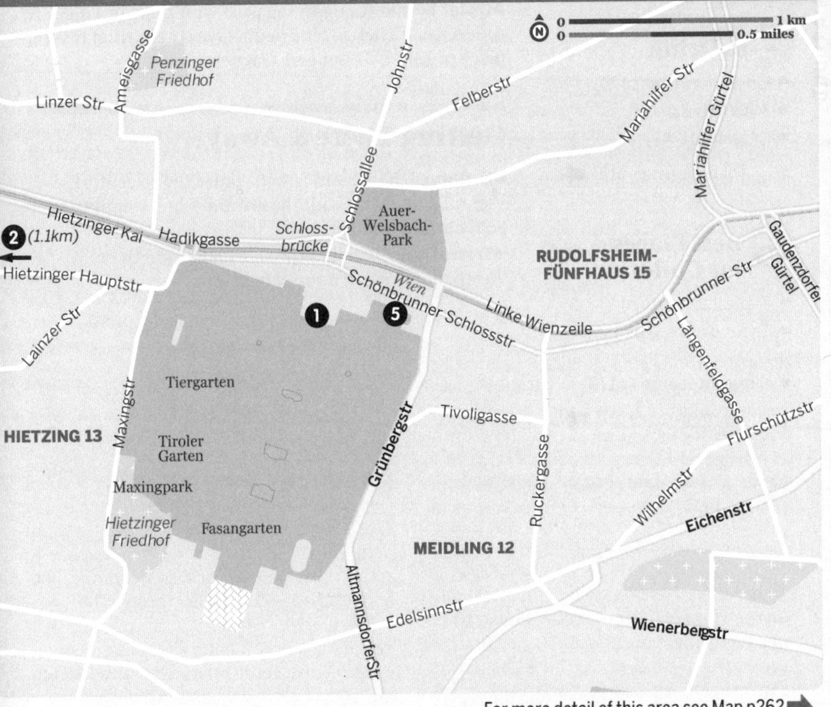

For more detail of this area see Map p262

Lonely Planet's Top Tip

Because of the popularity of the palace, tickets are stamped with a departure time, and there may be a time lag before you're allowed to set off in summer, so buy your ticket straight away and explore the gardens while you wait. Or skip to the front of the queue by buying your ticket in advance online (www.schoenbrunn.at). Simply print the ticket yourself and present it when you enter.

Best Places to Eat

- Pure Living Bakery (p172)
- Quell (p173)
- Waldemar (p172)

For reviews, see p172.

Best Places to Drink

- Café Gloriette (p174)
- Aida (p173)
- Reigen (p174)

For reviews, see p173.

Best Places for Children

- Tiergarten (p168)
- Technisches Museum (p171)
- Kindermuseum (p170)

For reviews, see p171.

Explore Schloss Schönbrunn & Around

Few sights in Vienna enthral like Schloss Schönbrunn. The vision of its imposing baroque facade, glowing like warm butter on a sunny afternoon, is not one you are likely to forget in a hurry. You can almost picture the Habsburgs swanning around the fragrant rose beds and mythological fountains in the French-style formal gardens, which provide a harmonious backdrop for the baroque palace, a Unesco World Heritage site.

The palace and gardens' size means it's best tackled in either a morning or afternoon, or better still over a day, with stops for refreshment within the grounds itself or in one of Hietzing's gently upmarket eating and drinking options. Klimt's Villa and the Hofpavallon can also be visited with an additional hour or so.

Local Life

- **Hang-outs** Kick back with coffee and cake in the garden of the cute-as-a-button Pure Living Bakery (p172). Or quaff microbrews in the tree-shaded courtyard of Brandauers Schlossbräu (p173).
- **Shop** Give the crowds the slip and window shop in Altgasse and Hietzinger Hauptstrasse.
- **Quiet Moments** Calm the pace with time for quiet reflection at Hietzinger Friedhof (p171), the final resting place of Klimt, Moser and Wagner.

Getting There & Away

- **U-Bahn** Schönbrunn is well connected to central Vienna by subway, with the green U4 line stopping at Schönbrunn and Hietzing.
- **Tram** Tram 58 makes the short hop from the Westbahnhof station to Schönbrunn.

TOP SIGHT
SCHLOSS SCHÖNBRUNN

The Habsburg Empire is revealed in all its frescoed, gilded, chandelier-lit glory in the wondrously ornate apartments of Schloss Schönbrunn, which are among Europe's best-preserved baroque interiors. Stories about the first public performance of wunderkind Mozart or Empress Elisabeth's extreme beauty and fitness regimes bring Austrian history to life as you wander the 40 rooms open to the public.

DON'T MISS

- Great Gallery
- Neptunbrunnen
- Gloriette
- Wagenburg

PRACTICALITIES

- Map p262, C3
- www.schoenbrunn.at
- 13, Schönbrunner Schlossstrasse 47
- adult/child Imperial Tour €13.30/9.80, Grand Tour €16.40/10.80, Grand Tour with guide €19.40/12.30
- 8.30am-6.30pm Jul & Aug, to 5.30pm Sep, Oct & Apr-Jun, to 5pm Nov-Mar
- U Hietzing

State Apartments

The frescoed **Blue Staircase** makes a regal ascent to the palace's upper level. First up are the 19th-century apartments of Emperor Franz Josef I and his beloved wife Elisabeth, a beauty praised for her tiny waist and cascading tresses. The tour whisks you through lavishly stuccoed, chandelier-lit apartments such as the **Billiard Room**, where army officials would pot a few balls while waiting to attend an audience, and Franz Josef's **study**, where the emperor worked tirelessly from 5am. The iron bedstead and washstand for morning ablutions in his bedroom reveal his devout, highly disciplined nature.

Empress Elisabeth, or 'Sisi' as she is fondly nicknamed, whiled away many an hour penning poetry in the ruby-red **Stairs Cabinet**, and brushing up on various European languages while her ankle-length locks were tended in the privacy of her **dressing room**. Blue-and-white silk wall hangings adorn the **imperial bedroom** that Franz and Sisi sometimes shared. The neo-rococo **Empress' Salon** features portraits of some of Maria Theresia's 16 children, including Marie Antoinette in hunting garb, poignantly oblivious to her fate at the French guillotine in 1793. Laid with leaded crystal and fragile porcelain, the table in the **Marie**

SCHÖNBRUNN ZOO

Founded in 1752 as a menagerie by Franz Stephan, the **Schönbrunn Tiergarten** (www.zoovienna.at; adult/child €18.50/9; ⏲9am-6.30pm high season, to 4.30pm low season; 👪) is the world's oldest zoo. It houses some 750 animals, including giant pandas, emus, armadillos and Siberian tigers. Feeding times are staggered throughout the day – maps on display tell you who's dining when. The zoo's layout is reminiscent of a bicycle wheel, with pathways as spokes and an octagonal pavilion at its centre. The pavilion dates from 1759 and was used as the imperial breakfast room.

The small **Wüstenhaus** (Desert House; ☎01-877 92 94 390; 13, Maxingstrasse 13b; adult/child €6/4.50; ⏲9am-6pm May-Sep, to 5pm Oct-Apr) near the Palmenhaus makes good use of the once disused Sonnenuhrhaus (Sundial House) to re-create arid desert scenes. There are four sections – Northern Africa and the Middle East, Africa, the Americas and Madagascar – with rare cacti and live desert animals, such as the naked mole rat from East Africa. A combined ticket for the Palmenhaus and Wüstenhaus costs €6.

Antoinette Room is where Franz Josef used to dig into hearty meals of goulash and schnitzel (health-conscious Sisi preferred beef broth and strawberries out of view).

More portraits of Maria Theresia's brood fill the **Children's Room** and the **Balcony Room**, graced with works by court painter Martin van Meytens. Keep an eye out for the one of ill-fated daughter **Maria Elisabeth**, considered a rare beauty before she contracted smallpox. The disease left her so disfigured that all hope of finding a husband vanished, and she entered convent life.

In the exquisite white-and-gold **Mirror Room**, a six-year-old Mozart performed for a rapturous Maria Theresia in 1762. According to his father Leopold, 'Wolferl leapt onto Her Majesty's lap, threw his arms around her neck and planted kisses on her face.' Fairest of all, however, is the 40m-long **Great Gallery** (pictured p167) where the Habsburgs threw balls and banquets, a frothy vision of stucco, mirrors and gilt chandeliers, topped with a fresco by Italian artist Gregorio Guglielmi showing the glorification of Maria Theresia's reign. Decor aside, this was where the historic meeting between John F Kennedy and Soviet leader Nikita Khrushchev took place in 1961.

Wandering through the porcelain-crammed **Chinese Cabinets** brings you to the equestrian fanfare of the **Carousel Room** and the **Hall of Ceremonies**, with five monumental paintings showing the marriage of Joseph, heir to the throne, to Isabella of Parma in 1760. Mozart, only four at the time of the wedding, was added as an afterthought by the artist, who took several years to complete the picture, by which time the virtuoso was a rising star.

If you have a Grand Tour ticket, you can continue through to the palace's **east wing**. Franz Stephan's apartments begin in the sublime **Blue Chinese Salon**, where the intricate floral wall paintings are done on Chinese rice paper. The jewel-box *pietra dura* tables, inlaid with semi-precious stones, are stellar examples of Florentine craftsmanship. The negotiations that led to the collapse of the Austro-Hungarian Empire in 1918 were held here. A century before, Napoleon chose Schönbrunn as his HQ when he occupied Vienna in 1805 and 1809 and the **Napoleon Room** was where he may have dreamed about which country to conquer next. Look for the portrait of his only legitimate son, the Duke of Reichstadt, shown as a cherubic lad in the park at Laxenburg Palace.

Passing through the exquisite rosewood **Millions Room**, the **Gobelin Salon**, filled with Flemish tapestries, and the **Red Salon** brimming with Habsburg portraits, you reach Maria Theresia's **bedroom**, with a throne-like red velvet and gold embroidered four-poster bed. This is where Franz Josef was born in 1830. Gilt-framed portraits of the Habsburgs hang on the red-damask walls of Archduke Franz Karl's **study**, and the tour concludes in the **Hunting Room**, with paintings noting Schönbrunn's origins as a hunting lodge.

Gardens

The beautifully tended formal **gardens** (www.schoenbrunn.at; 13, Schloss Schönbrunn; ⏲6.30am-dusk) FREE of the palace, arranged in the French style, are appealing whatever the season: a symphony of colour in the summer and a wash of greys and browns in winter. The grounds, which were opened to the public by Joseph II in 1779, hide a number of attractions in the tree-lined avenues that were arranged according to a grid and star-shaped system between 1750 and 1755. From 1772 to 1780 Ferdinand Hetzendorf added some of the final touches to the park under the instructions of Joseph II: fake **Roman ruins** (www.schoenbrunn.at; 13, Schloss Schönbrunn; adult/child €3.60/2.80; ⏲8.30am-6.30pm Jul & Aug, to 5.30pm Apr-Jun, Sep & Oct, to 5pm Nov-Mar) in 1778; the **Neptunbrunnen** (Neptune Fountain; www.schoenbrunn.at; adult/child €3.60/2.80; ⏲8.30am-6.30pm Jul & Aug, to 5.30pm Apr-Jun, Sep & Oct, to 5pm Nov-Mar), an equally empire-boosting Greek-mythology-themed folly in 1781; and the crowning glory, the **Gloriette** (adult/child €3.60/2.80; ⏲9am-6pm, closed early Nov–mid-Mar), in 1775. The view from here is, as the names suggests, glorious.

The original **Schöner Brunnen** (Fountain), from which the palace gained its name, now pours through the stone pitcher of a nymph near the Roman ruins. The garden's 630m-long **Irrgarten** (Maze; adult/child €5.30/3; ⏲8.30am-5.30pm) is a classic hedge design based on the original maze that occupied its place from 1720 to 1892; adjoining this is the **Labyrinth**, a playground with games, climbing equipment and a giant mirror kaleidoscope.

SCHLOSS SCHÖNBRUNN AND GARDENS

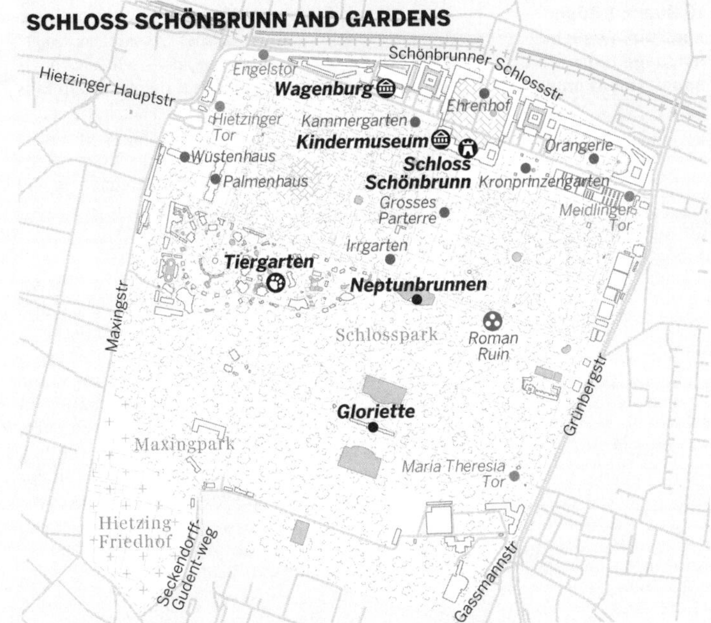

PALMENHAUS

Londoners may think they're experiencing déjà vu on sighting the **Palm House** (Palm House; Map p262; www.schoenbrunn.at; 13, Maxingstrasse 13b; adult/child €6/4.50; ⌚9.30am-6.30pm May-Sep, to 5pm Oct-Apr; 🚊10, 58, 60, Ⓤ Hietzing). This was built in 1882 by Franz Segenschmid as a replica of the one in London's Kew Gardens. Inside is a veritable jungle of tropical plants from around the world. A combined ticket for the Palmenhaus and Wüstenhaus costs €6.

Guided tours of the Kindermuseum (in German) depart at 10.30am, 1.30pm and 3pm. English-language tours are by appointment only.

Gloriette (p169)

To the east of the palace is the Kronprinzengarten (p172), a replica of the baroque garden that occupied the space around 1750.

Kindermuseum

Schönbrunn's **Children's Museum** (www.kaiserkinder.at/kindermuseum.html; 13, Schloss Schönbrunn; adult/child €8.80/6.70; ⌚10am-5pm; 👪) does what it knows best: imperialism. Activities and displays help kids discover the day-to-day life of the Habsburg court, and then don princely or princessly outfits and start ordering the serfs (parents) around. Other rooms devoted to toys, natural science and archaeology all help to keep them entertained.

Wagenburg

The **Wagenburg** (Imperial Coach Collection; www.kaiserliche-wagenburg.at; 13, Schloss Schönbrunn; adult/child €8/free; ⌚9am-5pm mid-Mar–Nov, 10am-4pm Dec–mid-Mar) is *Pimp My Ride* imperial style. On display is a vast array of carriages, including Emperor Franz Stephan's coronation carriage, with its ornate gold plating, Venetian glass panes and painted cherubs. The whole thing weighs an astonishing 4000kg. Also look for the dainty child's carriage built for Napoleon's son, with eagle-wing-shaped mudguards and bee motifs.

SIGHTS

SCHLOSS SCHÖNBRUNN PALACE

See p167.

KLIMT VILLA MUSEUM

(www.klimtvilla.at; 13, Feldmühlgasse 11; adult/child €10/5; ⏰10am-6pm Thu-Sat Apr-Dec; 🚊58) The Klimt Villa, which opened to the public in September 2012 following a complete makeover, immerses you in the sensual world of Vienna's most famous Secessionist. Set in landscaped grounds in a leafy corner of Hietzing, the 1920s neo-baroque villa was built on and around the site of the original rustic studio, the artist's last, where he worked from 1911 to 1918.

Standouts include carefully reproduced furnishings and carpets, as well as Gustav Klimt's headily erotic sketches of his models. Just as special is the intimate atmosphere of strolling through the painter's one-time gardens, where two of his rose bushes still produce blowsy, fragrant flowers. While it can take a little imagination to sense the studio, Moritz Nähr's original photos give a sense of life here, with Klimt and his entourage draped in flowing haute-bohemian robes, as depicted in portraits such as *Adele Bloch-Bauer II* and *Frederike Beer* (both of which Klimt painted here).

TECHNISCHES MUSEUM MUSEUM

Map p262 (www.technischesmuseum.at; 14, Mariahilfer Strasse 212; adult/under 19yr €12/free; ⏰9am-6pm Mon-Fri, 10am-6pm Sat & Sun; 👪; 🚊52, 58 Winckelmannstrasse, Ⓤ Schönbrunn) Opened in 1918, the Technical Museum is dedicated to science, technology and engineering. There are loads of hands-on gadgets allowing you to conduct experiments, but the most interesting aspect of the museum is its historical collection. There's a Mercedes Silver Arrow from 1950, a model-T Ford from 1923 and penny-farthing bicycles to name a few.

Its small musical instrument collection focuses mainly on keyboard instruments, so if this is your main interest, head for the Neue Burg museums instead. The permanent exhibition is complemented by temporary ones; anyone with an engineering bent will absolutely love it here, as will two- to six-year-olds, for the well-thought-out Das Mini section.

HOFPAVILLON HIETZING LANDMARK

Map p262 (www.wienmuseum.at; 13, Schönbrunner Strasse; adult/child €5/free; ⏰10am-1pm & 2-6pm Sat & Sun; Ⓤ Hietzing) Built between 1898 and 1899 by Otto Wagner as part of Vienna's new *Stadtbahn* (metro) system, and recently restored to its former glory, the Hofpavillon Hietzing was a private station for the imperial court. Its white facade, decorated with wrought ironwork, is easily spotted just east of the U4 Hietzing stop.

The wood-panelled interior was designed by Wagner in conjunction with Josef Olbrich; its opulent art nouveau style was signature Wagner and greatly influenced much subsequent architectural design.

HIETZINGER FRIEDHOF CEMETERY

Map p262 (www.friedhoefewien.at; 13, Maxingstrasse 15; audio guide €7; ⏰7am-dusk;

TICKETS FOR SCHLOSS SCHÖNBRUNN

If you plan to see several sights at Schönbrunn, it's worth purchasing one of the combined tickets. Prices vary according to whether it's summer season (April to October) or winter. The best way to get a ticket is to buy it in advance online. Print the ticket yourself and present it when you enter.

The summer season **Classic Pass** (adult/under 19 years €21.60/13.40) is valid for a Grand Tour of Schloss Schönbrunn (including all 40 rooms open to the public) and visits to the Kronprinzengarten (Crown Prince Garden), Irrgarten (Maze) and Labyrinth, Gloriette with viewing terrace, and Hofbackstube Schönbrunn (p173), with the chance to watch apple strudel being made and enjoy the result with a cup of coffee. A **Classic Pass 'light'** (adult/under 19 years €13.90/9.50) excludes the apple strudel show. The Court Bakery Schönbrunn can be viewed separately (it's inside Café Residenz).

The summer **Gold Pass** (adult/under 19 years €55.50/30.50) includes the Grand Tour, Crown Prince Garden, Tiergarten, Palmenhaus, Wüstenhaus, Wagenburg, Gloriette, Maze and Labyrinth, and Court Bakery Schönbrunn.

WORTH A DETOUR

LAINZER TIERGARTEN

At 25 sq km, the **Lainzer Tiergarten** (www.lainzer-tiergarten.at; 13, Hermesstrasse; 8am-dusk; 60B Hermesstrasse, 60 Hermesstrasse) is the largest (and wildest) of Vienna's city parks. The 'zoo' refers to the abundant wild boar, deer, woodpeckers and squirrels that freely inhabit the densely forested park, and the famous Lipizzaner horses that summer here. Opened by Emperor Ferdinand I in 1561, the park was once the hunting ground of Habsburg royalty. Today it offers extensive walking possibilities through lush woodlands of beech and oak, as well as attractions such as the **Hubertus-Warte** (508m), a viewing platform on top of Kaltbründlberg.

On the eastern edge of the park sits the stately **Hermesvilla** (www.wienmuseum.at; 13, Lainzer Tiergarten; adult/child €6/free; 10am-6pm Tue-Sun mid-Mar–early Nov; 60B Hermesstrasse, 60 Hermesstrasse), commissioned by Franz Josef I and presented to his wife as a gift. It is named after the white marble statue of Hermes, which guards the garden in front of the palace. Built by Karl von Hasenauer between 1882 and 1886, with Klimt and Hans Makart on board as interior decorators, the villa is plush – it's more a mansion than simply a 'villa'. Empress Elisabeth's bedroom is totally over the top, with the walls and ceiling covered in motifs from Shakespeare's *A Midsummer Night's Dream*. A visit also takes in the room where Elisabeth, or 'Sisi', used to exercise rigorously in order to keep her famous 16in waist.

UHietzing) FREE Aficionados of Vienna's Secessionist movement will want to make the pilgrimage to the Hietzinger cemetery to pay homage to some of its greatest members. Klimt, Moser and Wagner are all buried here. Others buried in the cemetery include Engelbert Dollfuss, leader of the Austro-Fascists, assassinated in 1934, and composer Alban Berg.

KRONPRINZENGARTEN GARDENS

Map p262 (Privy Garden; www.schoenbrunn.at; adult/student & child €3.60/2.80; 8.30am-6.30pm Jul & Aug, to 5.30pm Apr-Jun, Sep & Oct, to 5pm Nov-Mar) With its ornate parterres, octagonal pools and pergolas, the Kronprinzengarten is a replica of the original baroque garden created in the 1750s.

EATING

WALDEMAR CAFE €

Map p262 (0664 361 61 27; www.waldemar-tagesbar.at; 13, Altgasse 6; sandwiches €4.90-6, lunch mains €4.30-6.90; 7.30am-8pm Mon-Fri, 9am-8pm Sat & Sun; UHietzing) This stylish and airy breakfast-to-aperitif spot is unashamedly internationalist in both its menu and look. Join the casual-chic locals for baguettes and jam or a choice from the dedicated 'müsli & co' menu, or pop in for a groaning toasted sandwich or steaming bowl of Thai green curry or dhal at lunchtime. Sweet staff also turn out good coffee.

PURE LIVING BAKERY CAFE €

Map p262 (www.purelivingbakery.com; 13, Altgasse 12; cakes & snacks €4-10.50; 9am-9pm; ; UHietzing) Inspired by her time in the USA, sweet-toothed traveller Kirsten has brought the laid-back mood and food of a US deli to Vienna. Decked out with surf boards and coffee sacks, wicker chairs and holiday snapshots, this living room of a cafe is the place to unwind over an organic quinoa salad, freshly toasted bagel with smoked salmon and avocado, or superfood smoothie.

Pot plants and pink and blue deckchairs lend a personal touch to the pretty garden, where you can easily while away a sunny afternoon reading a magazine, sipping a shake and nibbling on locally baked goodies such as deep-filled apple pie, warm cinnamon rolls and giant cookies. Gluten-free options are available.

MAFIOSI PIZZA €

Map p262 (01-892 72 28; www.pizzeria-mafiosi.at; 15, Reindorfgasse 15; pizza €3.20-5.60; 11am-midnight; UGumpendorfer Strasse) The woody Naples-meets-alpine-chalet interior is an inviting setting for authentic pizzas, which start at a wallet-friendly €3.20. Add that to cheap booze (€2 for a beer) and you can see why students love the place.

HOFBACKSTUBE SCHÖNBRUNN BAKERY €

Map p262 (Court Bakery Schönbrunn; ☎01-24 100-300; per person incl strudel/coffee & strudel €5/10; ⊙10am-5pm Apr-Oct, to 4pm Nov-Mar, shows on the hour) Sure, it's a little touristy, but if you fancy snagging some tips on how to knock up a perfectly crisp apple strudel, you could do worse than stop by this basement bakery, with live shows on the hour. Enjoy the result with a cup of coffee.

MAXING STÜBERL AUSTRIAN €€

Map p262 (www.maxingstueberl.at; mains €9-18.50; ⊙11am-2pm Mon-Sat; UHietzing) Once the favourite of Johann Strauss, this traditional wood-clad dining room serves up fabulously traditional dishes made with only the best produce from owner Christine Schenk's home region of Pielachtal in lower Austria. Music and candles only add to the atmosphere.

BRANDAUERS SCHLOSSBRÄU AUSTRIAN €€

Map p262 (☎01-879 59 70; www.bierig.at; 13, Am Platz 5; mains €10-16; ⊙10am-1am; ; UHietzing) This microbrewery in the Viennese mould rolls out hoppy house brews, speciality beers (including an organic one) and decent pub grub. Famous spare ribs served with lashings of potatoes feature alongside vegetarian options and the usual hearty suspects such as goulash, cheese-laden dumplings and schnitzel. The €9.90 lunch buffet represents great value. Sit in the leafy courtyard when the sun's out.

HOLLEREI VEGETARIAN €€

Map p262 (☎01-892 33 56; www.hollerei.at; 15, Hollergasse 9; lunch menus €7.90-12.30, mains €14-15.50; ⊙11.30am-3pm & 6-11pm Mon-Sat, 11.30am-3pm Sun; ; UMeidling Hauptstrasse, Schönbrunn) This wood-panelled, all-vegetarian bistro is known for its seasonal salads, soups and pasta dishes. Whether you go for quinoa with sweet potato and date and nut pesto, homemade spinach gnocchi with sun-dried tomatoes or red Thai curry with almond rice, the wholesome food has a welcome freshness. See the website for details on the monthly cookery course (€50).

QUELL AUSTRIAN €€

Map p262 (☎01-893 24 07; www.gasthausquell.at; 15, Reindorfgasse 19; mains €7-14; ⊙11am-midnight Mon-Fri; ; UGumpendorfer Strasse) Time stands still at Quell, a traditional *Beisl* in suburban Rudolfsheim-Fünfhaus. The wood-panelled interior looks as if it's been untouched for years, the archaic wooden chandeliers and ceramic stoves wouldn't be out of place in a folklore museum, and some guests look as though they've been frequenting the place for decades. The menu is thoroughly Viennese, with goulash, pork cutlets and schnitzel featuring heavily.

That said, there is also a surprising number of fish and vegetarian options. Genial staff and quiet streetside seating add to the attractions.

DRINKING & NIGHTLIFE

AIDA CAFE

Map p262 (13, Maxingstrasse 1; ⊙8am-7pm Mon-Fri, 9am-7pm Sat; UHietzing) Just a short amble from the Hietzing Gate to Schloss Schönbrunn, this cafe is a fine spot to escape the crowds, sip a *melange* and dig into delectable pastries, tortes and cakes (€2 to €4) after a visit to the palace.

WORTH A DETOUR

KIRCHE AM STEINHOF

Perched on the crest of the Baumgartner Höhe in Vienna's 14th district, **Kirche am Steinhof** (☎910 60-11 204; 14, Baumgartner Höhe 1; tour €8, art nouveau tour, incl church €12; ⊙4-5pm Sat, noon-4pm Sun, tours 3-4pm Sat, 4-5pm Sun; 47A, 48A Baumgartner Höhe), built from 1904 to 1907, is the crowning glory of Otto Wagner. It's a steepish walk up to the church, nestled in the grounds of the Psychiatric Hospital of the City of Vienna and commanding fine views of the city.

Kolo Moser chipped in with the mosaic windows, and the roof is topped by a copper-covered dome that earned the nickname *Limoniberg* (Lemon Mountain) from its original golden colour. It's a bold statement in an asylum that has other art nouveau buildings, and it could only be pushed through by Wagner because the grounds were far from the public gaze. The church interior can only be visited by guided tour.

U4 CLUB

Map p262 (www.u-4.at; 12, Schönbrunner Strasse 222; ⌚10pm-5.30am Tue-Sat; Ⓤ Meidling Hauptstrasse) U4 was the birthplace of techno clubbing in Vienna way back when, and its longevity is a testament to its ability to roll with the times. A fairly young, studenty crowd are its current regulars, and while the music isn't as cutting edge as it used to be, it still manages to please this crowd.

CAFÉ GLORIETTE COFFEE

Map p262 (www.gloriette-cafe.at; 13, Gloriette; ⌚9am-dusk; Ⓤ Schönbrunn, Hietzing) Café Gloriette occupies the neoclassical Gloriette, high on a hill behind Schloss Schönbrunn, built for the pleasure of Maria Theresia in 1775. With sweeping views of the Schloss, its magnificent gardens and the districts to the north, Gloriette has arguably one of the best vistas in all of Vienna. It's a welcome pit stop after the short climb up the hill.

ENTERTAINMENT

REIGEN LIVE MUSIC

Map p262 (☎01-894 00 94; www.reigen.at; 14, Hadikgasse 62; ⌚6pm-2am Sun-Thu, to 4am Fri & Sat; Ⓤ Hietzing) Reigen's tiny stage is the setting for jazz, blues, Latin and world music in a simple space housing rotating art and photography exhibits, so you can groove while perusing art.

ORANGERY CONCERT VENUE

Map p262 (☎01-812 50 04; www.imagevienna.com; 13, Schloss Schönbrunn; tickets €42-126; Ⓤ Schönbrunn) Schönbrunn's lovely former imperial greenhouse is the location for year-round Mozart and Strauss concerts. Performances last around two hours and begin at 8.30pm daily.

MARIONETTEN THEATER PUPPET THEATRE

Map p262 (☎01-817 32 47; www.marionettentheater.at; 13, Schloss Schönbrunn; tickets full performances adult €11-39, child €9-25; ⌚box office on performance days from 11am; Ⓤ Schönbrunn) This small theatre in Schloss Schönbrunn puts on marionette performances of the much-loved productions *The Magic Flute* (2½ hours) and *Aladdin* (1¼ hours). They're a delight for kids young, old and in between. The puppet costumes are exceptionally ornate and eye-catching.

SHOPPING

1130WEIN FOOD & DRINKS

Map p262 (www.1130wein.at; Lainzerstrasse 1; ⌚10am-7pm Mon-Fri, to 3pm Sat; Ⓤ Hietzing) Pop into this neighbourhood *Vinothek* (wine shop) for tastings with the delightful Robert Sponer-Triulzi, who stocks a huge range of interesting, top-quality (though not always expensive) wines from all over Austria. He'll challenge you with a new varietal or two and make sure you come away with a drop you'll love. There's chilled whites if you're picnicking.

GOLD N' GUITARS MUSIC

Map p262 (13, Maxingstrasse 2; ⌚10am-12.30pm & 2-6pm Mon-Fri, 9am-12.30pm Sat; Ⓤ Hietzing) This is one of a kind in Vienna: owner and guitar craftsman Michael Eipeldauer restores and sells contraguitars, also known as a *Schrammelguitar,* used for folk music, jazz and other styles – they have a standard neck and a second fretless one for bass notes. A prize piece is a Biedermeier model from the 1840s.

Expect to pay between €1600 (used) and €3500 (new). Stylish secondhand East German guitars such as models from Musima, as well as Arthur Lang jazz guitar classics, glisten on stands around the store.

Day Trips from Vienna

Salzburg p176

Crowned by its hilltop fortress, Mozart's birthplace and the backdrop for the evergreen musical *The Sound of Music* has a fairy-tale charm.

Krems an der Danau p185

Gateway to the Wachau, quaint Krems centres on its historic core by the Danube and makes an ideal starting point for a loop through the beautiful Danube Valley.

Melk & Around p188

Easily reached from the Austrian capital, Stift Melk and nearby Shallaburg castle are an unmissable architectural duo.

Salzburg

Explore

Visiting Salzburg from Vienna is doable in two days, but consider tagging on a third day to explore at a more leisurely pace. High on your itinerary for day one should be the Unesco-listed baroque *Altstadt* (old town), which is burrowed below steep hills, with the main trophy sights clustering on the left bank of the Salzach River. You can walk everywhere in this compact, largely pedestrianised city.

On your second day, whizz up to the medieval clifftop fortress, Festung Hohensalzburg, for sublime city and mountain views, or take a spin around the galleries and Mozart museums. With an extra day, you could take a tour of locations featured in *The Sound of Music*.

Base yourself centrally to see Salzburg beautifully illuminated at night. Classical music performances and beer gardens are the big draws after dark.

The Best...

➡**Sight** *Altstadt* (old town)

➡**Place to Eat** Magazin (p182)

➡**Place to Drink** Augustiner Bräustübl (p182)

Top Tip

The **Salzburg Card** (1-/2-/3-day card €27/36/42). The card gets you entry to all of the major sights and attractions and unlimited use of public transport (including cable cars).

Getting There & Away

Car & Motorcycle The A1 motorway links Vienna to Salzburg; it's approximately a three-hour drive.

Train Frequent trains link Vienna with Salzburg (€51.90, 2½ to three hours). Österreiche Bundesbahn (ÖBB; www.oebb.at) is the main operator. Trains depart from the Wien Hauptbahnhof, with some services also stopping at Wien Meidling. Vienna's Westbahnhof is the terminus for the Westbahn (https://westbahn.at) intercity service to/from Salzburg.

Need to Know

➡**Area Code** ☎0662

➡**Location** 296km west of Vienna

➡**Main Tourist Office** (☎0662-88 98 70; www.salzburg.info; Mozartplatz 5; ⏲9am-7pm Mon-Sat, 10am-6pm Sun)

SIGHTS

RESIDENZPLATZ — SQUARE

With its horse-drawn carriages, palace and street entertainers, this baroque square is the Salzburg of a thousand postcards. Its centrepiece is the **Residenzbrunnen**, an enormous marble fountain. The plaza is the late-16th-century vision of Prince-Archbishop Wolf Dietrich von Raitenau who, inspired by Rome, enlisted Italian architect Vincenzo Scamozzi to design it.

★RESIDENZ — PALACE

(www.domquartier.at; Residenzplatz 1; DomQuartier ticket adult/child €12/5; ⏲10am-5pm Wed-Mon) The crowning glory of Salzburg's new DomQuartier, the Residenz is where the prince-archbishops held court until Salzburg became part of the Habsburg Empire in the 19th century. An audio-guide tour takes in the exuberant **state rooms**, lavishly adorned with tapestries, stucco and frescoes by Johann Michael Rottmayr. The 3rd floor is given over to the **Residenzgalerie**, where the focus is on Flemish and Dutch masters. Must-sees include Rubens' *Allegory on Emperor Charles V* and Rembrandt's chiaroscuro *Old Woman Praying*.

Nowhere is the pomp and circumstance of Salzburg more tangible than at this regal palace. A man of grand designs, Wolf Dietrich von Raitenau, the prince-archbishop of Salzburg from 1587 to 1612, gave the go-ahead to build this baroque palace on the site of an 11th-century bishop's residence.

DOM — CATHEDRAL

(Cathedral; www.salzburger-dom.at; Domplatz; ⏲8am-7pm Mon-Sat, 1-7pm Sun May-Sep, shorter hours rest of year) FREE Gracefully crowned by a bulbous copper dome and twin spires, the Dom stands out as a masterpiece of baroque art. Bronze portals symbolising faith, hope and charity lead into the cathedral. In the nave, both the intricate stucco and Arsenio Mascagni's ceiling frescoes recounting the Passion of Christ guide the eye to the polychrome dome.

Italian architect Santino Solari redesigned the cathedral during the Thirty Years' War and it was consecrated in 1628. Its origins, though, date to an earlier cathedral founded by Bishop Virgil in 767.

For more on the history, hook onto one of the free **guided tours**, offered 2pm Monday to Friday in July and August.

ERZABTEI ST PETER MONASTERY

(St Peter's Abbey; www.stift-stpeter.at; St Peter Bezirk 1-2; catacombs adult/child €2/1.50; ⏲church 8am-noon & 2.30-6.30pm, cemetery 6.30am-7pm, catacombs 10am-6pm) A Frankish missionary named Rupert founded this abbey church and monastery in around 700, making it the oldest in the German-speaking world. Though a vaulted Romanesque portal remains, today's church is overwhelmingly baroque, with rococo stucco, statues – including one of archangel Michael shoving a crucifix through the throat of a goaty demon – and striking altar paintings by Martin Johann Schmidt.

Take a stroll around the **cemetery**, where the graves are miniature works of art with intricate stonework and filigree wrought-iron crosses. Composer Michael Haydn (1737–1806), opera singer Richard Mayr (1877–1935) and renowned Salzburg confectioner Paul Fürst (1856–1941) lie buried here; the last is watched over by skull-bearing cherubs. The cemetery is home to the **catacombs** – cave-like chapels and crypts hewn out of the Mönchsberg cliff face.

★FESTUNG HOHENSALZBURG FORT

(www.salzburg-burgen.at; Mönchsberg 34; adult/child/family €12/6.80/26.20, incl funicular €15.20/8.70/33.70; ⏲9am-7pm) Salzburg's most visible icon is this mighty, 900-year-old cliff-top fortress, one of the biggest and best preserved in Europe. It's easy to spend half a day up here, roaming the ramparts for far-reaching views over the city's spires, the Salzach River and the mountains. The fortress is a steep 15-minute jaunt from the centre or a speedy ride up in the glass **Festungsbahn funicular** (Festungsgasse 4; one way/return adult €6.80/8.40, child €3.70/4.60; ⏲9am-8pm, shorter hours in winter).

The fortress began life as a humble bailey, built in 1077 by Gebhard von Helffenstein at a time when the Holy Roman Empire was at loggerheads with the papacy. The present structure, however, owes its grandeur to spendthrift Leonard von Keutschach, prince-archbishop of Salzburg from 1495 to 1519 and the city's last feudal ruler.

Highlights of a visit include the **Golden Hall** (where lavish banquets were once held) with a gold-studded ceiling imitating a starry night sky. Your ticket also gets you into the **Marionette Museum**, where skeleton-in-a-box Archbishop Wolf Dietrich steals the (puppet) show, as well as the **Fortress Museum**, which showcases a 1612 model of Salzburg, medieval instruments, armour and some pretty gruesome torture devices. The Golden Hall is the backdrop for year-round **Festungskonzerte** (fortress concerts), which often focus on Mozart's works. See www.mozartfestival.at for times and prices.

MOZARTS GEBURTSHAUS MUSEUM

(Mozart's Birthplace; www.mozarteum.at; Getreidegasse 9; adult/child €10/3.50; ⏲8.30am-7pm Jul & Aug, 9am-5.30pm Sep-Jun) Wolfgang Amadeus Mozart, Salzburg's most famous son, was born in this bright yellow townhouse in 1756 and spent the first 17 years of his life here. Today's museum harbours a collection of instruments, documents and portraits. Highlights include the mini-violin he played as a toddler, plus a lock of his hair and buttons from his jacket. In one room, Mozart is shown as a holy babe beneath a neon-blue halo – we'll leave you to draw your own analogies.

MOZART-WOHNHAUS MUSEUM

(Mozart's Residence; www.mozarteum.at; Makartplatz 8; adult/child €10/3.50; ⏲8.30am-7pm Jul & Aug, 9am-5.30pm Sep-Jun) Tired of the cramped living conditions on Getreidegasse, the Mozart family moved to this more spacious abode in 1773, where a prolific Wolfgang composed works such as the *Shepherd King* (K208) and *Idomeneo* (K366). Emanuel Schikaneder, a close friend of Mozart and the librettist of *The Magic Flute,* was a regular guest here. An audio guide accompanies your visit, serenading you with opera excerpts. Alongside family portraits and documents, you'll find Mozart's original fortepiano.

★SALZBURG MUSEUM MUSEUM

(www.salzburgmuseum.at; Mozartplatz 1; adult/child €8.50/3; ⏲9am-5pm Tue-Sun, to 8pm Thu; 👪) Housed in the baroque Neue Residenz palace, this flagship museum takes you on a fascinating romp through Salzburg past and present. Ornate rooms showcase everything from Roman excavations to royal portraits. There are free **guided tours** at 6pm every Thursday.

Salzburg

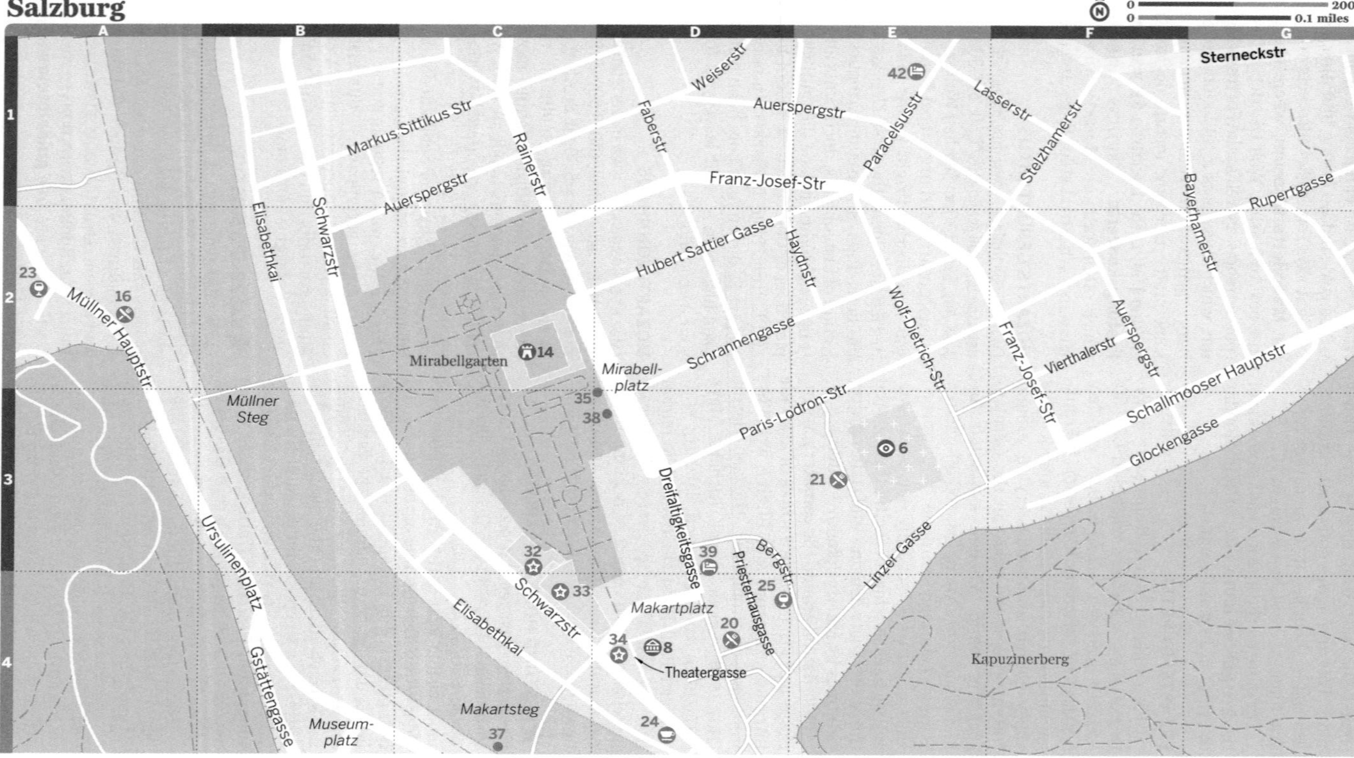
0 200 m
0 0.1 miles
A
B
C
D
E
F
G
1
2
3
4
Sterneckstr
Weiserstr
Markus Sittikus Str
Rainerstr
Faberstr
Auerspergstr
Paracelsusstr
Lasserstr
Stelzhamerstr
Bayerhamerstr
Rupertgasse
Franz-Josef-Str
Elisabethkai
Schwarzstr
Hubert Sattler Gasse
Haydnstr
Wolf-Dietrich-Str
Vierthalerstr
Schallmooser Hauptstr
Glockengasse
Schrannengasse
Mirabell-
platz
Mirabellgarten
Paris-Lodron-Str
Müllner Hauptstr
Müllner
Steg
Dreifaltigkeitsgasse
Priesterhausgasse
Bergstr
Linzer Gasse
Makartplatz
Theatergasse
Ursulinenplatz
Gstättengasse
Museum-
platz
Makartsteg
Kapuzinerberg
6
8
14
16
20
21
23
24
25
32
33
34
35
37
38
39
42

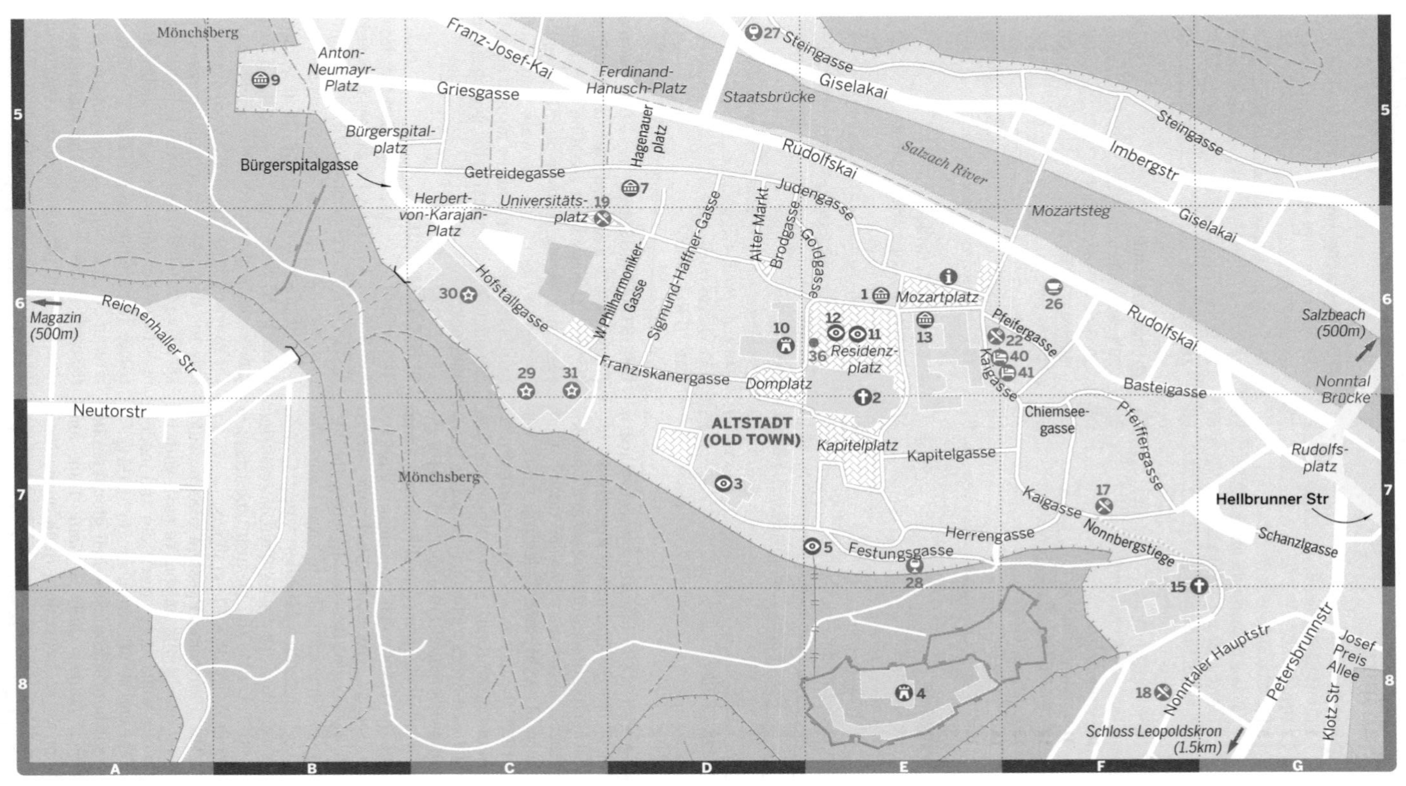

Mönchsberg
Anton-Neumayr-Platz
Franz-Josef-Kai
Ferdinand-Hanusch-Platz
27 Steingasse
Giselakai
Staatsbrücke
Griesgasse
Steingasse
Imbergstr
Bürgerspitalplatz
Bürgerspitalgasse
Hagenauerplatz
Rudolfskai
Salzach River
Getreidegasse
Herbert-von-Karajan-Platz
Universitätsplatz
Judengasse
Mozartsteg
Giselakai
Alter Markt
Brodgasse
Goldgasse
W Philharmoniker-Gasse
Sigmund-Haffner-Gasse
Hofstallgasse
Mozartplatz
Reichenhaller Str
Magazin (500m)
Pfeifergasse
Residenzplatz
Rudolfskai
Salzbeach (500m)
Franziskanergasse
Domplatz
Kaigasse
Basteigasse
Nonntal Brücke
Neutorstr
ALTSTADT (OLD TOWN)
Chiemseegasse
Kapitelplatz
Kapitelgasse
Pfeiffergasse
Rudolfsplatz
Mönchsberg
Kaigasse
Hellbrunner Str
Herrengasse
Nonnbergstiege
Schanzlgasse
Festungsgasse
Nonntaler Hauptstr
Petersbrunnstr
Josef Preis Allee
Klotz Str
Schloss Leopoldskron (1.5km)

Salzburg

Sights

1 Christmas Museum ... E6
2 Dom ... E7
3 Erzabtei St Peter ... D7
4 Festung Hohensalzburg ... E8
5 Festungsbahn Funicular ... E7
6 Friedhof St Sebastian ... E3
7 Mozarts Geburtshaus ... D5
8 Mozart-Wohnhaus ... D4
9 Museum der Moderne ... B5
10 Residenz ... D6
11 Residenzbrunnen ... E6
12 Residenzplatz ... E6
13 Salzburg Museum ... E6
14 Schloss Mirabell ... C2
15 Stift Nonnberg ... G7

Eating

16 Bärenwirt ... A2
17 Cook & Wine ... F7
18 Green Garden ... F8
19 Grünmarkt ... C6
20 Johanneskeller im Priesterhaus ... D4
21 Ludwig ... E3
M32 ... (see 9)
22 Zwettler's ... E6

Drinking & Nightlife

23 Augustiner Bräustübl ... A2
24 Café Bazar ... D4
25 Enoteca Settemila ... D4
26 Kaffee Alchemie ... F6
27 Steinterrasse ... D5
28 StieglKeller ... E7

Entertainment

29 Felsenreitschule ... C6
30 Grosses Festpielhaus ... C6
31 Haus für Mozart ... C6
32 Mozarteum ... C3
33 Salzburger Marionettentheater ... C4
Schlosskonzerte ... (see 14)
34 Schlosskonzerte Box Office ... D4

Sports & Activities

35 Fräulein Maria's Bicycle Tours ... D3
36 Rikscha Tours ... E6
37 Salzburg Schifffahrt ... C4
38 Salzburg Sightseeing Tours ... D3

Sleeping

39 Gästehaus im Priesterseminar ... D3
40 Hotel Wolf ... F6
41 Weisse Taube ... F6
42 YOHO Salzburg ... E1

A visit starts beneath the courtyard in the strikingly illuminated **Kunsthalle**, presenting rotating exhibitions of art. Upstairs, prince-archbishops glower down from the walls at **Mythos Salzburg**, which celebrates the city as a source of artistic and poetic inspiration. Showstoppers include Carl Spitzweg's renowned painting *Sonntagsspaziergang* (Sunday Stroll; 1841), the portrait-lined **prince-archbishop's room** and the **Ständesaal** (Sovereign Chamber), an opulent vision of polychrome stucco curling around frescoes depicting the history of Rome according to Titus Livius. The early-16th-century Milleflori tapestry, Archbishop Wolf Dietrich's gold-embroidered pontifical shoe, and Flemish tapestries are among other attention-grabbers.

The **Panorama Passage** also provides some insight into Salzburg's past, with its Roman walls and potter's kiln and models of the city at different points in history.

Salzburg's famous 35-bell **glockenspiel**, which chimes daily at 7am, 11am and 6pm, is on the western flank of the Neue Residenz.

CHRISTMAS MUSEUM MUSEUM

(Mozartplatz 2; adult/child €6/3; ⏲10am-6pm Wed-Sun) If you wish it could be Christmas every day, swing on over to this recently opened museum. The private collection brings festive sparkle in the form of advent calendars, hand-carved cribs, baubles and nutcrackers.

SCHLOSS MIRABELL PALACE

(Mirabellplatz 4; ⏲Marble Hall 8am-4pm Mon, Wed & Thu, 1-4pm Tue & Fri, gardens 6am-dusk) FREE Prince-Archbishop Wolf Dietrich built this splendid palace in 1606 to impress his beloved mistress Salome Alt. It must have done the trick because she went on to bear him some 15 children (sources disagree on the exact number – poor Wolf was presumably too distracted by spiritual matters to keep count). Johann Lukas von Hildebrandt, of Schloss Belvedere fame, remodelled the palace in baroque style in 1721. The lavish interior, replete with stucco, marble and frescoes, is free to visit. The **Marmorsaal** (Marble Hall) provides a sublime backdrop for evening chamber concerts (p183).

The flowery parterres, rose gardens and leafy arbours are less crowded first thing in the morning and early evening. The lithe *Tänzerin* (dancer) sculpture is a great spot to photograph the gardens with the fortress as a backdrop. *Sound of Music* fans will of course recognise the Pegasus statue, the steps and the gnomes of the Zwerglgarten (Dwarf Garden), where the mini von Trapps practised their 'Do-Re-Mi'.

★MUSEUM DER MODERNE GALLERY

(www.museumdermoderne.at; Mönchsberg 32; adult/child €8/6; ⏲10am-6pm Tue-Sun, to 8pm Wed) Straddling Mönchsberg's cliffs, this contemporary glass-and-marble oblong of a gallery stands in stark contrast to the fortress, and shows first-rate temporary exhibitions of 20th- and 21st-century art. The works of Alberto Giacometti, Dieter Roth, Emil Nolde and John Cage have previously been featured. There's a free **guided tour** of the gallery at 6.30pm every Wednesday. The **Mönchsberg Lift** (Gstättengasse 13; one-way/return €2.30/3.60, incl gallery entry €9.10/6.50; ⏲8am-7pm Mon, to 9pm Tue-Sun) whizzes up to the gallery year-round.

While you're up here, take in the far-reaching views across Salzburg over coffee or lunch at **M32** (☎0662-84 10 00; www.m32.at; Mönchsberg 32; 2-course lunch €16, mains €23-40; ⏲9am-1am Tue-Sun;).

FRIEDHOF ST SEBASTIAN CEMETERY

(Linzer Gasse 41; ⏲9am-6.30pm) Tucked behind the baroque Sebastianskirche (St Sebastian's Church), this peaceful cemetery and its cloisters were designed by Andrea Berteleto in Italianate style in 1600. Mozart family members and well-known 16th-century physician Paracelsus are buried here, but out-pomping them all is Prince-Archbishop Wolf Dietrich von Raitenau's mosaic-tiled mausoleum, an elaborate memorial to himself.

STIFT NONNBERG CONVENT

(Nonnberg Convent; Nonnberggasse 2; ⏲7am-dusk) FREE A short climb up the Nonnbergstiege staircase from Kaigasse or along Festungsgasse brings you to this Benedictine convent, founded 1300 years ago and made famous as the nunnery in *The Sound of Music*. You can visit the beautiful rib-vaulted **church**, but the rest of the convent is off-limits. Take €0.50 to switch on the light that illuminates the beautiful **Romanesque frescoes**.

UNTERSBERG MOUNTAIN, VIEWPOINT

(www.untersbergbahn.at; cable car up/down/return €15/13.50/23.50, free with Salzburg Card; ⏲8.30am-5.30pm Jul-Sep, shorter hours rest of year, closed Nov–mid-Dec) Rising above Salzburg and straddling the German border is the rugged 1853m peak of Untersberg. Spectacular views of the city, the Rositten Valley and the Tyrolean, Salzburg and Bavarian alpine ranges unfold from the summit. The mountain is a magnet to local skiers in winter, and hikers, climbers and paragliders in summer. From the cable car top station, short, easy trails lead to nearby viewpoints at **Geiereck** (1805m) and **Salzburg Hochthron**, while others take you much deeper into the Alps.

Temperatures can feel significantly cooler up here than down in the valley and trails are loose underfoot, so bring a fleece or jacket and sturdy footwear if you plan on doing some walking.

A cable car runs every half-hour to the peak. To reach the cable car valley station, take bus 25 from Salzburg's *Hauptbahnhof* or Mirabellplatz to St Leonhard and the valley station.

EATING

GRÜNMARKT MARKET €

(Green Market; Universitätsplatz; ⏲7am-7pm Mon-Fri, to 3pm Sat) A one-stop picnic shop on one of Salzburg's grandest squares, for regional cheese, ham, fruit, bread and gigantic pretzels.

LUDWIG BURGERS €

(☎0662-87 25 00; www.ludwig-burger.at; Linzer Gasse 39; burgers €6.90-10.80; ⏲11am-10pm;) Gourmet burger joints are all the rage in Austria at the moment and this hip newcomer fits the bill nicely, with its burgers made from organic, regional ingredients, which go well with hand-cut fries and homemade lemonade and shakes. It also rustles up superfood salads and vegan nut-mushroom-herb burgers. An open kitchen is the centrepiece of the slick, monochrome interior.

BÄRENWIRT AUSTRIAN €€

(☎0662-42 24 04; www.baerenwirt-salzburg.at; Müllner Hauptstrasse 8; mains €9-19; ⏲11am-11pm) Sizzling and stirring since 1663, Bärenwirt is Austrian through and through. Go for hearty *Bierbraten* (beer roast) with dumplings, locally caught trout or organic wild-boar *Bratwurst*. A tiled oven warms the woody, hunting-lodge-style interior in winter, while the river-facing terrace is a summer crowd-puller. The restaurant is 500m north of Museumplatz.

JOHANNESKELLER IM PRIESTERHAUS
AUSTRIAN €€

(☎0662-265536; www.johanneskeller.at; Richard-Mayr-Gasse 1; mains €10-20; ⏲5pm-midnight Tue-Sat) Full of cosy nooks and crannies, this brick-vaulted cellar is reached via a steep flight of stairs. The menu is succinct but well thought-out, with mains swinging from classic Austrian – Styrian pork roast with dumplings and sauerkraut, say – to Mediterranean numbers like gyros (rotisserie meat) with tzatziki. It's all bang on the money.

ZWETTLER'S
AUSTRIAN €€

(☎0662-84 41 99; www.zwettlers.com; Kaigasse 3; mains €9.50-21; ⏲11.30am-1am Tue-Sat, to midnight Sun) This gastro-pub has a lively buzz on its pavement terrace. Local grub such as schnitzel with parsley potatoes and venison ragout goes well with a cold, foamy Kaiser Karl wheat beer. The two-course lunch is a snip at €7.90.

COOK & WINE
ITALIAN €€

(☎0662-23 16 06; www.cookandwine.at; Kaigasse 43; mains €15-26.50; ⏲11.30am-11pm Tue-Sat) Highly regarded chef and food and wine connoisseur Günther Grahammer is the brains behind this slick new operation. It combines a wine bar, a cookery school and a smart, bistro-style restaurant serving Italian-inflected dishes along the lines of antipasti, meltingly tender veal cheeks, or trilogy of regional fish cooked on a hot stone.

GREEN GARDEN
VEGETARIAN €€

(☎0662-84 12 01; www.thegreengarden.at; Nonntaler Hauptstrasse 16; mains €9.50-15; ⏲noon-2pm & 5.30-9pm Tue-Sat; 🔌) 🌿 The Green Garden is a breath of fresh air for vegetarians and vegans. Locavore is the word at this bright, modern cottage-style restaurant, pairing dishes like wild herb salad, lemon-goat's-cheese tortellini with asparagus and vegan burgers with organic wines in a totally relaxed setting.

★MAGAZIN
MODERN EUROPEAN €€€

(☎0662-841 584 20; www.magazin.co.at; Augustinergasse 13a; 2-course lunch €16, mains €27-41, tasting menus €71-85; ⏲11.30am-2pm & 6-10pm Tue-Sat) In a courtyard below Mönchsberg's sheer rock wall, Magazin shelters a deli, wine store, cookery school and restaurant. Chef Richard Brunnauer's menus fizz with seasonal flavours: dishes like marinated alpine char with avocado and herb salad and saddle of venison with boletus mushrooms are matched with wines from the 850-bottle cellar, and served alfresco or in the industrial-chic, cave-like interior.

DRINKING & NIGHTLIFE

★AUGUSTINER BRÄUSTÜBL
BREWERY

(www.augustinerbier.at; Augustinergasse 4-6; ⏲3-11pm Mon-Fri, from 2.30pm Sat & Sun) Who says monks can't enjoy themselves? Since 1621, this cheery, monastery-run brewery has been serving potent homebrews in beer steins in the vaulted hall and beneath the chestnut trees in the 1000-seat beer garden. Get your tankard filled at the foyer pump and visit the snack stands for hearty, beer-swigging grub like *Stelzen* (ham hock), pork belly and giant pretzels.

★ENOTECA SETTEMILA
WINE BAR

(Bergstrasse 9; ⏲5-11pm Tue-Sat) This bijou wine shop and bar brims with the enthusiasm and passion of Rafael Peil and Nina Corti. Go to sample their well-curated selection of wines, including Austrian, organic and biodynamic ones, with *taglieri* – sharing plates of cheese and *salumi* – salami, ham, prosciutto and the like – from small Italian producers.

★KAFFEE ALCHEMIE
CAFE

(www.kaffee-alchemie.at; Rudolfskai 38; ⏲7.30am-6pm Mon-Fri, 10am-6pm Sat & Sun) Making coffee really is rocket science at this vintage-cool cafe by the river, which plays up high-quality, fair-trade, single-origin beans. Talented baristas knock up spot-on espressos (on a Marzocco GB5, in case you wondered), cappuccinos and speciality coffees, which go nicely with the selection of cakes and brownies. Not a coffee fan? Try the super-smooth coffee-leaf tea.

CAFÉ BAZAR
CAFE

(www.cafe-bazar.at; Schwarzstrasse 3; ⏲7.30am-7.30pm Mon-Sat, 9am-6pm Sun) At this cafe, all chandeliers and polished wood, locals enjoy the same river views today over breakfast, cake and intelligent conversation as Marlene Dietrich did in 1936.

STIEGLKELLER BEER HALL

(Festungsgasse 10; ⌚11am-11pm) For a 365-day taste of Oktoberfest, try this cavernous, Munich-style beer hall, which shares the same architect as Munich's Hofbräuhaus. It has an enormous garden above the city's rooftops and a menu of meaty mains (€11 to €18) such as fat pork knuckles and schnitzel. Beer is cheapest from the self-service taps outside.

STEINTERRASSE COCKTAIL BAR

(Giselakai 3; ⌚7am-midnight Sun-Thu, to 1am Fri & Sat) Hotel Stein's chichi 7th-floor terrace attracts Salzburg's Moët-sipping socialites and anyone who loves a good view. It isn't cheap, but it's the best spot to see the *Altstadt* light up against the theatrical backdrop of the fortress.

ENTERTAINMENT

SCHLOSSKONZERTE CLASSICAL MUSIC

(www.schlosskonzerte-salzburg.at; ⌚concerts 8pm) A fantasy of coloured marble, stucco and frescoes, Schloss Mirabell's baroque Marmorsaal is the exquisite setting for chamber-music concerts. Internationally renowned soloists and ensembles perform works by Mozart and other well-known composers such as Haydn and Chopin. Tickets costing between €31 and €37 are available online or at the **box office** (☎0662-84 85 86; Theatergasse 2; ⌚10am-3pm Mon-Fri, to 1pm Sat).

MOZARTEUM CLASSICAL MUSIC, OPERA

(☎0662-87 31 54; www.mozarteum.at; Schwarzstrasse 26) Opened in 1880 and revered for its supreme acoustics, the Mozarteum highlights the life and works of Mozart through chamber music (October to June), concerts and opera. The annual highlight is **Mozart Week** in January.

★SALZBURGER MARIONETTENTHEATER PUPPET THEATRE

(☎0662-87 24 06; www.marionetten.at; Schwarzstrasse 24; tickets €20-37; 👪) The red curtain goes up on a miniature stage at this marionette theatre, a lavish stucco, cherub and chandelier-lit affair founded in 1913. The repertoire star is *The Sound of Music,* with a life-sized Mother Superior and a marionette-packed finale. Other enchanting productions include Mozart's *The Magic Flute* and Tchaikovsky's *The Nutcracker*. All have multilingual surtitles.

SALZBURG FESTIVAL ART

(Salzburger Festspiele; www.salzburgerfestspiele.at; ⌚Jul & Aug) The absolute highlight of the city's events calendar is the Salzburg Festival. It's a grand affair, with some 200 productions – including theatre, classical music and opera – staged in the impressive surrounds of the **Grosses Festpielhaus** (☎0662-804 50; Hofstallgasse 1), **Haus für Mozart** (House for Mozart; ☎0662-804 55 00; www.salzburgerfestspiele.at; Hofstallgasse 1) and the baroque **Felsenreitschule** (Summer Riding School; Hofstallgasse 1). Tickets vary in price between €11 and €430; book well ahead.

SPORTS & ACTIVITIES

FRÄULEIN MARIA'S BICYCLE TOURS CYCLING

(www.mariasbicycletours.com; Mirabellplatz 4; adult/child €30/18; ⌚9.30am Apr-Oct, plus 4.30pm Jun-Aug) Belt out *The Sound of Music* faves as you pedal on one of these jolly 3½-hour bike tours, taking in locations from the film including the Mirabellgarten, Stift Nonnberg, Schloss Leopoldskron and Hellbrunn. No advance booking is necessary; just turn up at the meeting point on Mirabellplatz.

RIKSCHA TOURS TOURS

(☎0662-634 02 40; www.rikschatours.at; Residenzplatz; ⌚May-Sep) Whizzing around Salzburg by rickshaw is the latest thing – the clued-up guides fill you in on anecdotes as they pedal. Tours range from a 40-minute spin of the historic centre (€36) to a 75-minute 'Round of Music' tour taking in the film locations of...you guessed it.

SALZBURG SIGHTSEEING TOURS BUS

(☎0662-88 16 16; www.salzburg-sightseeing-tours.at; Mirabellplatz 2; ⌚office 8am-6pm) Sells a 24-hour ticket (adult/child €18/9) for a multilingual hop-on/hop-off bus tour of the city's key sights and *Sound of Music* locations.

SALZBURG SCHIFFFAHRT CRUISE

(Makartsteg; adult/child €15/7.50; ⌚mid-Mar–Oct) A boat ride along the Salzach is a leisurely way to pick out Salzburg's sights. Hour-long cruises depart from Makartsteg bridge, with some of them chugging on to

DIY SOUND OF MUSIC TOUR

Do a Julie and sing as you stroll on a self-guided tour of *The Sound of Music* film locations. Let's start at the very beginning:

The Hills Are Alive Cut! Make that *proper* mountains. The opening scenes were filmed around the jewel-coloured Salzkammergut lakes. Maria makes her twirling entrance on alpine pastures just across the border in Bavaria.

A Problem Like Maria Nuns waltzing on their way to mass at Benedictine Stift Nonnberg (p181) is fiction, but it's fact that the real Maria von Trapp intended to become a nun here before romance struck.

Have Confidence Residenzplatz (p176) is where Maria belts out 'I Have Confidence' and playfully splashes the spouting horses of the Residenzbrunnen fountain.

So Long, Farewell The grand rococo palace of **Schloss Leopoldskron** (www.schloss-leopoldskron.com; Leopoldskronstrasse 56-58), a 15-minute walk from Festung Hohensalzburg, is where the lake scene was filmed. Its Venetian Room was the blueprint for the Trapps' lavish ballroom, where the children bid their farewells.

Do-Re-Mi The Pegasus fountain, the steps with fortress views, the gnomes...the Mirabellgarten at Schloss Mirabell (p180) might inspire a rendition of 'Do-Re-Mi' – especially if there's a drop of golden sun.

Sixteen Going on Seventeen The loved-up pavilion of the century hides out in **Hellbrunn Park** (www.hellbrunn.at; Fürstenweg 37; adult/child/family €12.50/5.50/26.50, gardens free; ⏲9am-5.30pm Apr-Oct, to 9pm Jul & Aug; 👪), where you can act out those 'Oh, Liesl'/'Oh, Rolf' fantasies.

Edelweiss & Adieu The Felsenreitschule (p183) is the dramatic backdrop for the Salzburg Festival in the movie, where the Trapp Family Singers win the audience over with 'Edelweiss' and give the Nazis the slip with 'So Long, Farewell'.

Climb Every Mountain To Switzerland, that is. Or content yourself with alpine views from Untersberg (p181), which appears briefly at the end of the movie when the family flees the country.

Schloss Hellbrunn (adult/child €18/10, not including entry to the palace).

SALZBEACH BEACH

(Volksgarten; ⏲9am-10pm May-Sep) FREE Salzburg's urban beach – complete with sand, potted palms and *Strandkörbe* (wicker-basket chairs) – sprouts up in the Volksgarten each summer. Besides lounging, there's a volleyball court and open-air events over the course of the summer, from free musical gigs to cinema nights.

SLEEPING

YOHO SALZBURG HOSTEL €

(☎0662-87 96 49; www.yoho.at; Paracelsusstrasse 9; dm €19-23, d €72-93; @📶) Free wi-fi, secure lockers, comfy bunks, plenty of cheap beer and good-value schnitzels – what more could a backpacker ask for? Except, perhaps, a merry sing-along with *The Sound of Music* screened daily (yes, *every* day) at 7pm. The friendly crew can arrange tours, adventure sports such as rafting and canyoning, and bike hire.

★GÄSTEHAUS IM PRIESTERSEMINAR GUESTHOUSE €€

(☎0662-877 495 10; www.gaestehaus-priesterseminar-salzburg.at; Dreifaltigkeitsgasse 14; s €65-85, d €116-130) Ah, the peace is heavenly at this one-time seminary tucked behind the Dreifältigkeitskirche. Its bright, parquet-floored rooms were recently given a total makeover, but the place still brims with old-world charm thanks to its marble staircase, antique furnishings and fountain-dotted courtyard. It's still something of a secret, though, so whisper about it quietly...

WEISSE TAUBE HISTORIC HOTEL €€

(☎0662-84 24 04; www.weissetaube.at; Kaigasse 9; s/d/tr/q €143/155/281/324; 📶) Housed in a listed 14th-century building in a quiet corner of the *Altstadt*, the 'white dove' is a solid choice. Staff go out of their way to help and the warm-coloured rooms are well kept (some have fortress views). Breakfast is a generous spread.

★VILLA TRAPP HOTEL €€€

(☎0662-63 08 60; www.villa-trapp.com; Traunstrasse 34; s €65-130, d €114-280, ste €290-580; P 📶 👪) Marianne and Christopher have transformed the original von Trapp family home into a beautiful guesthouse (for guests only, we might add). The 19th-century villa is elegant, if not *quite* as palatial as in the movie, with tasteful wood-floored rooms and a balustrade for sweeping down à la Baroness Schräder.

HOTEL WOLF HISTORIC HOTEL €€€

(☎0662-843 45 30; www.hotelwolf.com; Kaigasse 7; s €108-138, d €198-238, ste €218-258; 📶) Tucked in a quiet corner of the *Altstadt*, Hotel Wolf occupies a lovingly converted 15th-century building. Uneven stone staircases and antique furnishings are a nod to its past, while the light, parquet-floored rooms range from modern to rustic.

Krems an der Danau

Explore

Krems, as it's more commonly known, is the prettiest of the larger towns on the Danube and marks the beginning of the Wachau. Enjoyable eating and drinking, an atmospheric historical centre, rivers of top-quality wine from local vineyards and a couple of excellent museums attract visitors in summer but the rest of the year it's considerably quieter. Aimless wandering is the best plan of attack, stopping by churches and museums, strolling the banks of the Danube and sampling the local tipples as you go.

Krems comprises three parts: Krems to the east, the small settlement of Stein (formerly a separate town) to the west, and the connecting suburb of Und. Hence the local witticism: *Krems und Stein sind drei Städte* (Krems and Stein are three towns). A day is ample time to explore the trio.

The Best...

- **Sight** Kunsthalle Krems
- **Place to Eat** Zum Kaiser von Österreich (p188)
- **Place to Drink** Weinstein (p188)

Top Tip

A walk through the cobblestone streets of Krems and Stein, especially after dark, is a real highlight. The tourist office has maps.

Getting There & Away

Car & Motorcycle From Vienna take the A22 north towards Stockerau, then take the S5 west to Krems. The journey takes about an hour.

Train Frequent daily trains connect the Wien Hauptbahnhof with Krems (€17.60, one hour).

Need to Know

- **Area Code** ☎02732
- **Location** 76km northwest of Vienna
- **Tourist Office** (☎02732-82 676; www.krems.info; Utzstrasse 1; ⏲9am-6pm Mon-Fri, 11am-6pm Sat, 11am-4pm Sun, shorter hours in winter)

SIGHTS

★FORUM FROHNER GALLERY

(Kunstmeile; www.kunsthalle.at; Minoritenplatz 4; adult/child €5/4; ⏲11am-7pm Tue-Sun) Part of Krems' Kunsthalle network, this contemporary white cube is named after the artist Adolf Frohner and is housed in the former Minorite monastery. It has an impressive calendar of conceptual work, both international and Austrian.

KUNSTHALLE KREMS GALLERY

(www.kunsthalle.at; Franz-Zeller-Platz 3; €10; ⏲10am-5pm Tue-Sun) The flagship of Krems' Kunstmeile, an eclectic collection of galleries and museums, the Kunsthalle has a program of changing exhibitions. These might be mid-19th-century landscapes or hardcore conceptual works, but are always well curated. Guided tours (€3) run on Sundays at 2pm.

KARIKATURMUSEUM MUSEUM

(www.karikaturmuseum.at; Steiner Landstrasse 3a; adult/child €10/3.50; ⏲10am-6pm) Austria's only caricature museum occupies a suitably tongue-in-cheek chunk of purpose-built architecture opposite the Kunsthalle. Changing exhibitions and a large permanent collection of caricatures of prominent

Austrian and international figures make for a fun diversion.

MUSEUM KREMS MUSEUM

(www.museumkrems.at; Körnermarkt 14; €5; ⌚11am-6pm Wed-Sun Apr & May, daily Jun-Oct) Housed in a former Dominican monastery, the town's museum has collections of religious and modern art, including works by Kremser Schmidt, who painted the frescoes in Pfarrkirche St Veit, as well as winemaking artefacts and a section on the famous Krems mustard.

PFARRKIRCHE ST VEIT CHURCH

(Pfarrplatz 5; ⌚dawn-dusk) Known as the 'Cathedral of the Wachau', the large baroque parish church boasts colourful frescoes by Martin Johann Schmidt, an 18th-century local artist who was also known as Kremser Schmidt and occupied a house from 1756 near the Linzer Tor in Stein. The baroque building is the work of Cipriano Biasino, who worked on several churches in the Wachau, including the abbey church at Stift Göttweig.

EATING

SCHWARZE KUCHL AUSTRIAN €

(www.schwarze-kuchl.at; Untere Landstrasse 8; mains €8-13; ⌚8.30am-7.30pm Mon-Fri, to 5pm Sat) For some good, honest local grub, head to this daytime tavern on the main

Krems an der Donau

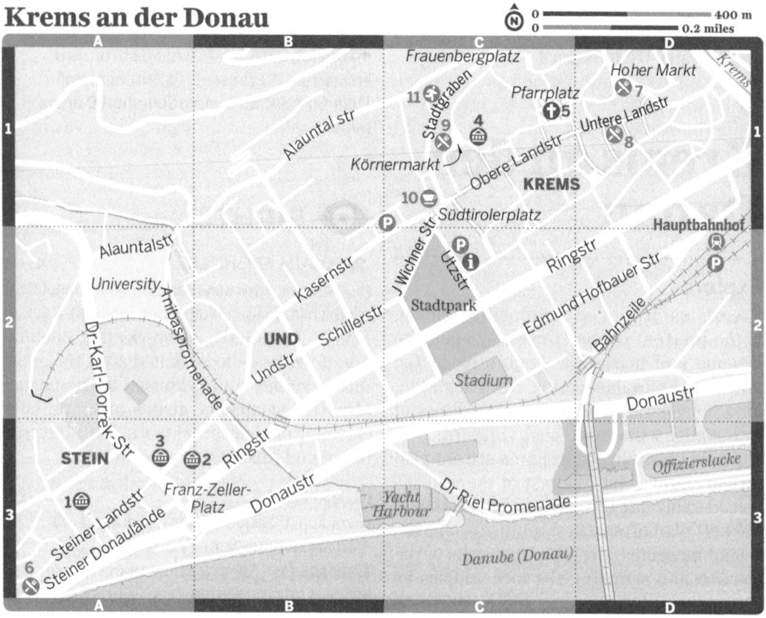

Krems an der Donau

Sights

1 Forum Frohner A3
2 Karikaturmuseum A3
3 Kunsthalle Krems A3
4 Museum Krems C1
5 Pfarrkirche St Veit C1

Eating

6 Blauenstein A3
7 Jell D1
8 Schwarze Kuchl D1
9 Zum Kaiser von Österreich C1

Drinking & Nightlife

10 Stadtcafe Ulrich C1
Weinstein .... (see 6)

Sports & Activities

11 Weingut der Stadt Krems C1

DRIVING & CYCLING TOUR: THE DANUBE VALLEY

Starting and ending in Krems, this 150km tour should take a full day. From the Krems-Stein roundabout in **Krems an der Donau** take the B3 southwest towards Spitz. About 3km from Krems-Stein you approach the small settlement of Unterloiben, where on the right you can see the **Franzosendenkmal** (French Monument), erected in 1805 to celebrate the victory of Austrian and Russian troops here over Napoleon. Shortly afterwards the lovely town of **Dürnstein**, 6km from Krems, comes into view with its blue-towered Chorherrenstift backed by Kuenringerburg, the castle where Richard the Lionheart was imprisoned in 1192.

The valley is punctuated by picturesque terraced vineyards as you enter the heart of the Wachau. In **Weissenkirchen**, 12km from Krems, you'll find a pretty fortified parish church on the hilltop. The Wachau Museum here houses work by artists of the Danube school. A couple of kilometres on, just after Wösendorf, you find the church of **St Michael**, in a hamlet with 13 houses. If the kids are along for this ride, now's the time to ask them to count the terracotta hares on the roof of the church (seven, in case they're not reading this!).

Some 17km from Krems, the pretty town of **Spitz** swings into view, surrounded by vineyards and lined with quiet, cobblestone streets. Some good trails lead across hills and to *Heurigen* (wine taverns) here (start from the church).

Turn right at Spitz onto the B217 (Ottenschläger Strasse). The terraced hill on your right is **1000-Eimer-Berg**, so-named for its reputed ability to yield 1000 buckets of wine each season. On your left, high above the valley opening, is the castle ruin **Burgruine Hinterhaus**. Continue along the B217 to the mill wheel and turn right towards **Burg Oberranna** (02713-8221; www.burg-oberranna.at; s/d €88/148; P), 6km west of Spitz in Mühldorf. Surrounded by woods, this castle and hotel overlooking the valley is furnished with period pieces and has a refreshing old-world feel.

From here, backtrack down to the B3 and continue the circuit. The valley opens up and on the left, across the Danube, you glimpse the ruins of Burg Aggstein.

Willendorf, located 21km from Krems, is where the 25,000-year-old Venus of Willendorf was discovered. It is today housed in the Naturhistorisches Museum in Vienna. Continuing along the B3, the majestic Stift Melk rises up across the river. There's some decent swimming in the backwaters here if you're game to dip into the Danube.

At Klein Pöchlarn, a sign indicates a turn-off on Artstettner Strasse (L7255): follow it for 5km to **Artstetten**, unusual for its many onion domes. From here, the minor road L7257 winds 6.5km through a sweeping green landscape to **Maria Taferl** high above the Danube Valley.

Head 6km down towards the B3. Turn left at the B3 towards Krems and follow the ramp veering off to the left and across the river at the Klein Pöchlarn bridge. Follow the road straight ahead to the B1 (Austria's longest road) and turn left onto this towards Melk. This first section along the south bank is uninteresting, but it soon improves. Unless the weather isn't playing along, across the river you can make out Artstetten in the distance, and shortly Stift Melk (p189) will rise up ahead in a golden shimmering heap.

From Stift Melk, a 7km detour leads south to the splendid Renaissance castle of Schloss Schallaburg (p189). To reach the castle from the abbey in Melk, follow the signs to the *Bahnhof* (train station) and Lindestrasse east, turn right into Hummelstrasse/Kirschengraben (L5340) and follow the signs to the castle.

Backtrack to the B33. Be careful to stay on the south side of the river. When you reach the corner of Abt-Karl-Strasse and Bahnhofstrasse, go right and right again at the river. Follow the B1 for 4km to **Schloss Schönbühel**, a 12th-century castle standing high on a rock some 5km northeast of Melk. Continue along this lovely stretch of the B33 in the direction of Krems. About 10km from Schloss Schönbühel the ruins of **Burg Aggstein** swing into view. This 12th-century hilltop castle was built by the Kuenringer family and now offers a grand vista of the Danube.

About 27km from Melk some pretty cliffs rise up above the road. From Mautern it's a detour of about 6km to **Stift Göttweig** (Göttweig Abbey; 02732-855 81-0; www.stiftgoettweig.at; Furth bei Göttweig; adult/child €8.50/5; 9am-6pm Jun-Sep, 10am-6pm Mar-May, Oct & Nov).

drag through town where you can enjoy veal goulash, apricot-filled pancakes and Waldviertel potato-and-beef hotpot *(Gröstl)* while warming your toes on the huge tiled oven.

BLAUENSTEIN AUSTRIAN €€
(☎0699 1930 788; www.blauenstein.at; Donaulände 56, Stein; mains €16.50-19.50, 4-course menu €42; ⊙5-11pm Thu-Mon, 11am-3pm Fri-Sun) Upstairs in the regional government building, this bright dining room does nicely modernised Austrian dishes with a sweet view over the Danube. There's also a regionally focused wine bar downstairs for a pre- or post-stroll glass.

JELL AUSTRIAN €€
(www.amon-jell.at; Hoher Markt 8-9; mains €13-23; ⊙10am-10.30pm Tue-Fri, to 2pm Sat & Sun) Occupying a gorgeous stone house, Jell is hard to beat for a rustic atmosphere and fine wine from its own vineyard. Its friendly staff also adds to a great regional experience; located just east of Pfarrkirche St Veit.

★ZUM KAISER VON ÖSTERREICH AUSTRIAN €€€
(☎0800 400 171 052; www.kaiser-von-oesterreich.at; Körnermarkt 9; 3-/4-/5-/6-course menu €45.50/49.50/59.50/69.50; ⊙6-11pm Tue-Sat) The 'Emperor of Austria' is one of Krems' most well-loved upmarket restaurants. Interiors recall a hunting lodge, which sets the scene for menus that are built around the region's bounty of game, from deer to pheasant to rabbit.

DRINKING & NIGHTLIFE

WEINSTEIN WINE BAR
(☎0664 1300 331; www.weinstein.at; Donaulände 56, Stein) A Danube-facing wine bar that has a very comprehensive line-up of local wines by the glass. The kitchen turns out good drinking food, say carpaccio in summer or chilli con carne in winter.

STADTCAFE ULRICH CAFE
(www.stadtcafe-ulrich.at; Südtirolerplatz 7; ⊙7am-11pm Mon-Thu, to midnight Sat, 9am-11pm Sun) Krems' busiest cafe is this elegantly high-ceilinged Viennese job next to the Steinertor (the medieval gateway into the Old Town).

SPORTS & ACTIVITIES

WEINGUT DER STADT KREMS WINE
(www.weingutstadtkrems.at; Stadtgraben 11; ⊙9am-noon & 1-5pm Mon-Fri, 9am-noon Sat) This city-owned vineyard yielding 200,000 bottles per year, with almost all Grüner Veltliner and riesling, offers a variety of wine for tasting and purchase.

Melk & Around

Explore

With its blockbuster abbey-fortress perched above the valley, Melk is a high point of any visit to the Danube Valley. Separated from the river by a stretch of woodland, this pretty town makes for an easy and rewarding day trip from Vienna. Combine a visit with nearby Renaissance-era Schloss Schallaburg, 6km south of town, and you have yourself a day packed with architectural interest.

Melk is one of the most popular destinations in Austria so you certainly won't be alone on its cobbled streets. It's also one of the few places in the Wachau that has a pulse in winter, making it a year-round option.

The Best...

- **Sight** Stift Melk
- **Place to Eat** Zum Fürsten
- **Exhibitions** Schloss Schallaburg

Getting There & Away

Car & Motorcycle The A1 motorway runs all the way west from Vienna to Melk. It's about a 90-minute journey.

Train Trains from Vienna's Hauptbahnhof and Westbahnhof (€17.60, one hour, up to two per hour) to Melk require a change in St Pölten.

Need to Know

- **Area Code** ☎02752
- **Location** 87km west of Vienna

➡**Tourist Office** (☎02752-511 60; www.stadt-melk.at; Kremser Strasse 5; ⏰9.30am-6pm Mon-Sat, to 4pm Sun Apr-Oct, 9am-5pm Mon-Thu, to 2.30pm Fri Nov-Mar)

SIGHTS

STIFT MELK ABBEY
(Benedictine Abbey of Melk; www.stiftmelk.at; Abt Berthold Dietmayr Strasse 1; adult/child €11/6, with guided tour €13/8; ⏰9am-5.30pm, tours 10.55am & 2.55pm May-Sep, tours only 11am & 2pm Nov-Mar) Of the many abbeys in Austria, Stift Melk is the most famous. Possibly Lower Austria's finest, the monastery church dominates the complex with its twin spires and high octagonal dome. The interior is baroque gone barmy, with regiments of smirking cherubs, gilt twirls and polished faux marble. The theatrical high-altar scene, depicting St Peter and St Paul (the church's two patron saints), is by Peter Widerin. Johann Michael Rottmayr created most of the ceiling paintings, including those in the dome.

Historically, Melk was of great importance to the Romans and later to the Babenbergs, who built a castle here. In 1089, the Babenberg margrave Leopold II donated the castle to Benedictine monks, who converted it into a fortified abbey. Fire destroyed the original edifice, which was completely baroque-ified between 1702 and 1738 according to plans by Jakob Prandtauer and his disciple, Josef Munggenast. It's claimed nine million bricks were used to create the 500 rooms – don't worry though, you don't have to visit them all! (Most of the complex is taken up by a school, monks' quarters and offices.)

Besides the monastery church, highlights include the Bibliothek (library) and the Marmorsaal (Marble Hall); both have amazing trompe l'oeil–painted tiers on the ceiling (by Paul Troger) to give the illusion of greater height, and ceilings are slightly curved to aid the effect. Eleven of the imperial rooms, where dignitaries (including Napoleon) stayed, are now used as a somewhat overcooked concept museum.

Before or after a tour of the main complex, take a spin around the Nordbastei where you'll discover some quirky temporary exhibitions, a viewing terrace and the Stift's gift shop.

A combined ticket with Schloss Schallaburg is €18. From around November to March, the monastery can only be visited by guided tour (11am and 2pm daily). Always phone or email ahead, even in summer, to ensure you get an English-language tour.

SCHLOSS SCHALLABURG PALACE
(☎02754-6317; www.schallaburg.at; Schallaburg 1; adult/child €11/3.50; ⏰9am-5pm Mon-Fri, to 6pm Sat & Sun Apr-early Nov) This palace is famous not only for its stunning architecture but also for the innovative exhibitions it houses, along with its stunning gardens. A wonderful curio are the 400 terracotta sculptures, completed between 1572 and 1573, the largest of which support the upper-storey arches of the palace. Yearly shows are thematically curated, and in recent years have focused on diverse cultural moments from The Beatles, Venice and Byzantium.

Combined tickets with Stift Melk cost €18. To reach Schallaburg, take the shuttle bus (€4) that leaves Melk train station at 10.40am, 1.15pm and 4.45pm.

EATING

ZUM FÜRSTEN INTERNATIONAL €
(☎02752-523 43; Rathausplatz 3; mains €4.50-10.50; ⏰10.30am-11pm) Right at the foot of the Stift, relax after a tour on faux velvet 1970s seating at this popular cafe serving pastas, strudel, chilli con carne and other international dishes.

ZUR POST AUSTRIAN €€
(☎02752-523 45; Linzer Strasse 1; mains €7.90-20; ⏰11.30am-10pm Mon-Sat; 🌿) This traditional and understated restaurant is in the hotel of the same name on Melk's main drag. Waldviertel carp, *Wiener Schnitzel,* Danube catfish and organic lamb grace the menu, which also features several vegetarian options.

Sleeping

Vienna's lodgings cover it all, from luxury establishments where chandeliers, antique furniture and original 19th-century oil paintings abound and statement-making design hotels at the cutting edge to inexpensive youth hostels. In between are homey, often family-run Pensionen (guesthouses), many traditional, and less ostentatious hotels, plus a smart range of apartments.

Reservations & Cancellations

It's wise to book ahead at all times. In the winter and autumn low and shoulder seasons (except for Christmas and New Year) a day or two is usually sufficient for most places, but for the best value, especially in the centre, a few weeks ahead is advisable. From around Easter to September you will need to book at least several weeks in advance, and some places in the centre are booked out a month or longer ahead. Most places are bookable online. Confirmed reservations in writing are binding, and cancellations within several days of expected arrival often involve a fee or full payment.

Hotels & Pensionen

Two stars Expect functional rooms starting around €50/90 a single/double close to the centre. It's often better to stay in a hostel.

Three stars Most hotels and *Pensionen* are in this category. Expect to pay about €70/130 for a single/double, less in winter or when booking online. Rooms should be clean, with a decent buffet breakfast, wi-fi, minibar, flat-screen TV and pleasant showers. Some have bathtubs.

Four & five stars Rooms in four-star hotels are generally larger than three-star rooms and should have sound insulation and contemporary or quality furnishing; some have wellness facilities. Five-star hotels have premium wellness facilities.

Hostels & Student Residences

Vienna has a smattering of *Jugendherbergen* (youth hostels), both private and hostels affiliated with Hostelling International (HI). In the former, no membership is required.

Apartment Rentals

The advantage of an apartment is that you have a kitchen and can save on food costs. Most central apartments cost from €120 per night.

The following websites are useful:

Apartment.at (www.apartment.at) A broad selection from a group of owners.

oh-vienna.com (www.oh-vienna.com) Many inexpensive options.

waytostay (www.waytostay.com) Online and telephone booking.

Chez Cliche (www.chezcliche.com) Eight uberstylish apartments, decorated with a mishmash of design pieces and flea-market finds. They're scattered across the city, from the Innere Stadt's backstreets to student-hub Alsergrund.

Lonely Planet's Top Choices

Grand Ferdinand Hotel (p194) dorms through to luxury suites with private champagne bars and Maseratis to rent.

Magdas (p196) Funky boutique hotel near the Prater run by refugees.

Grätzlhotel (p196) Slick, architect-designed boutique hotel/suites in formerly abandoned shops.

my MOjO vie (p195) Hostel with upbeat style.

DO & CO (p194) Sexiest hotel in the centre.

Best by Budget

€

Hotel am Brillantengrund (p195) Set around a sociable courtyard.

my MOjO vie (p195) Hostel with bright flair.

Hotel Drei Kronen (p194) Elegant *Pension* serving *Sekt* (sparkling wine) at breakfast.

€€

Hollmann Beletage (p193) Stylish with perks.

Boutiquehotel Stadthalle (p195) Cosy and eco-aware.

Spiess & Spiess (p195) Elegant, well-located pension.

Hotel Capricorno (p193) Shimmering interiors and canal-side balconies.

€€€

Grand Ferdinand Hotel (p194) With a rooftop infinity pool.

Radisson Blu Style Hotel (p193) Ultrastylish design.

Hotel Imperial (p194) Favourite for European royalty.

Best Classic Viennese Pensionen

Schweizer Pension (p193) Homey and won't break the budget.

Hotel Drei Kronen (p194) Old-fashioned flair in an art nouveau pension.

Angel's Place (p196) Heaven in the shape of a wine cellar-turned-guesthouse.

Best Design Hotels

Hotel Rathaus Wein & Design (p195) An oenologist's delight: minimalist-chic rooms themed by wine and vine.

Altstadt (p195) Razor-sharp design and original art bring this historic hotel bang up to date.

Magdas (p196) Retro-cool near the Prater.

Grätzlhotel (p196) By some of Vienna's top architects.

Ruby Sofie (p195) Inside a grand former concert hall.

Best Hostels

my MOjO vie (p195) Closest thing to a designer hostel, with everything from netbooks to musical instruments.

Grand Ferdinand Hotel (p194) Not only sumptuous rooms and suites but mahogany bunk beds too.

Wombat's (p196) Aussie charm and a lounge vibe.

NEED TO KNOW

Price Ranges

The following price ranges refer to a double with private bathroom:

€	less than €80
€€	€80 to €200
€€€	under €200

Check-in

Check-in is mostly at 2pm or 3pm. Earlier check-in is usually possible with advance notice. Check out is at 11am or noon.

Breakfast

Generally not included in the rate at higher-end hotels. An increasing number of midrange hotels don't automatically include it. Heading to a coffee house or cafe can be a better-value, more atmospheric option.

Parking

Very few establishments have their own parking on-site, though many have deals with parking garages nearby. Expect to pay between €15 and €35 for 24 hours.

Wi-fi

Almost always free, fast and reliable.

Where to Stay

NEIGHBOURHOOD	FOR	AGAINST
The Hofburg & Around	Central, close to the Hofburg, some accommodation close to MuseumsQuartier	High prices, less opportunity to interact with locals than some other neighbourhoods
Stephansdom & the Historic Centre	Quintessential Viennese architecture, close to key sights, bars and restaurants, great shopping, easy access to the entire city	More expensive, very popular, green spaces only on fringes
Karlsplatz & Around Naschmarkt	Proximity to Naschmarkt, good bars and restaurants, excellent transport connections, less expensive	More travel time is needed to get to sights from outlying areas
The Museum District & Neubau	Great local neighbourhood, especially closer to Ringstrasse, near museums, the Hofburg, bars and restaurants	Relatively low hotel density, dependence on trams in some parts
Alsergrund & the University District	Student atmosphere near the campuses, creative cafes and boutiques, good nightlife options, handful of good, inexpensive hotels	Transport to other districts often indirect unless near Ringstrasse
Schloss Belvedere to the Canal	Quiet and close to the palace	Few sights except Belvedere itself, limited restaurants and bars
Prater & East of the Danube	Increasingly hip, gentrifying areas, especially Leopoldstadt, good transport to centre and to the Prater, great markets, lots of outdoor activities	Limited sights except the Prater
Schloss Schönbrunn & Around	Some parts are close to Schönbrunn, others to the lively Brunnenmarkt eating and drinking area	Light on sights except for Schönbrunn, some sections along the Gürtel are seedy

The Hofburg & Around

STEIGENBERGER HOTEL HERRENHOF HOTEL €€

Map p246 (01-534 040; www.steigenberger.com; 01, Herrengasse 10; d €160-213, ste €509-709; ; Herrengasse) Decorated throughout in subtle aubergine hues, the 196-room Steigenberger Hotel Herrenhof offers style at great value. The 24- to 28-sq-metre superior rooms and 35-sq-metre deluxe rooms are complemented by free use of the two-storey wellness area with a sauna, steam bath and fully equipped gym. Corner deluxe rooms have extra-large windows. Its restaurant is well regarded.

PERTSCHY PALAIS HOTEL HOTEL €€

Map p246 (01-534 49-9; www.pertschy.com; 01, Habsburgergasse 5; s €91-148, d €125-183, f €153-228; ; Herrengasse, Stephansplatz) The baroque, 18th-century-built Palais Cavriani's quiet yet central location, just off the Graben, is hard to beat. Staff are exceedingly friendly, and children are warmly welcomed (toys for toddlers and high chairs for tots are available). Decorated in creams, royal-reds and golds, its 55 spacious, antique-furnished rooms have parquet floors. Family rooms have period fireplaces (alas, not in use).

★HOTEL SACHER HISTORIC HOTEL €€€

Map p246 (01-514 56 780; www.sacher.com; 01, Philharmonikerstrasse 4; d from €398, ste from €745; ; D, 1, 2, 71 Kärntner Ring/Oper, Karlsplatz) Stepping into the Hotel Sacher is like turning back the clocks 100 years. The lobby's dark-wood panelling, original oil paintings and deep red shades and heavy gold chandelier, are reminiscent of a fin de siècle bordello. The smallest rooms are surprisingly large and suites are truly palatial. Extras include a taste of the cafe's (p71) famous *Sacher Torte* on arrival.

RADISSON BLU STYLE HOTEL DESIGN HOTEL €€€

Map p246 (01-22 780 3214; www.radissonblu.com/stylehotel-vienna; 01, Herrengasse 12; d/ste from €170/290; ; Herrengasse) Although part of a global chain, this glamorous hotel is a contender for the title of 'most fashionable hotel address' in Vienna, with overtones of art nouveau and art deco in its snazzy contemporary decor, and amenities including Nespresso machines in all rooms. Breakfast costs €23 per person.

Stephansdom & the Historic Centre

★HOTEL CAPRICORNO HOTEL €€

Map p244 (01-533 31 04-0; www.schick-hotels.com/hotel-capricorno; 01, Schwedenplatz 3-4; s/d incl breakfast from €118/146; ; 1, 2, Schwedenplatz) Set behind an unpromising mid-20th-century facade, Hotel Capricorno was stunningly made over in 2015 in lustrous velveteens in zesty lime, orange, lemon and aubergine shades. Most of its 42 rooms have balconies (front rooms overlook the Danube Canal; rear rooms are quieter). On-site parking – rare for Vienna – is available for just €24 per day. It's a 10-minute walk from Stephansdom.

SCHWEIZER PENSION PENSION €€

Map p244 (01-533 81 56; www.schweizerpension.com; 01, Heinrichsgasse 2; incl breakfast d €81-130, tr €109-148; ; 1, Schottentor) Super-clean rooms at this pleasant little 11-room *Pension* aren't flush with the most up-to-date amenities but everything you'll find inside – from big, comfy beds to ornamental ceramic stoves – has a cosy, homey feel. Some rooms are low-allergy rooms; breakfast is organic. Singles with shared bathrooms cost €50 to €65, doubles €70 to €95. Tram to Salztorbrücke.

HOTEL AUSTRIA HOTEL €€

Map p244 (01-515 23; www.hotelaustria-wien.at; 01, Fleischmarkt 20; s €92-148, d €122-178, tr €152-208, q €174-230; ; 1, 2, Stephansplatz, Schwedenplatz) This elegant 46-room hotel offers some of the best value in the Innere Stadt. Cosy rooms come with mini bars and kettles for tea and coffee. Cheaper singles (€61 to €75) and doubles (€93 to €136) have private showers but share toilets. Bike rental costs €8. The 2nd-floor terrace stays open until 10pm. Cots and babysitting services are available.

HOLLMANN BELETAGE PENSION €€

Map p244 (01-961 19 60; www.hollmann-beletage.at; 01, Köllnerhofgasse 6; d €159-229, tr €179-279, q €199-300, ste from €390; ; 1, 2, Schwedenplatz) This minimalist establishment offers style and clean lines in its

25 rooms with natural wood floors, simple and classic furniture and designer lamps and door handles. A terrace and lounge where you can enjoy free snacks at 2pm are bonuses, as are the small hotel cinema and the free use of an iPad.

OPERA SUITES PENSION €€

Map p244 (☎01-512 93 10; www.operasuites.at; 01, Kärntner Strasse 47; d €155-170, apt from €168; 📶; 🚋D, 1, 2, 71, ⓊKarlsplatz) Located directly across from the famous Café Sacher (p71) and close to the major sights, Opera Suites offers comfortable standard and superior rooms (all with Nespresso coffee machines and mini bars), as well as apartments in the surrounding streets with kitchenettes. Continental breakfast costs €10. Tram to Kärntner Ring/Oper.

★GRAND FERDINAND HOTEL DESIGN HOTEL €€€

Map p244 (☎01-918 804 00; www.grandferdinand.com; 01, Schubertring 10-12; dm/d/ste from €30/180/500; ❄📶🏊; 🚋2, 71) An enormous taxidermied horse stands in the reception area of this ultrahip newcomer, which is shaking up Vienna's accommodation scene by offering parquet-floored dorms with mahogany bunks alongside richly coloured designer rooms with chaises longues and chandeliered suites with private champagne bars. Breakfast (€29) is served on the panoramic rooftop terrace, adjacent to the heated, open-air infinity pool.

★DO & CO DESIGN HOTEL €€€

Map p244 (☎01-241 88; www.docohotel.com; 01, Stephansplatz 12; d €249-289, ste €960-1550; @📶; ⓊStephansplatz) Up-close views of Stephansdom extend from higher-priced rooms at this swanky hotel, and all 43 rooms come with state-of-the-art entertainment systems and multicountry power sockets. Some have in-room Jacuzzis, but be aware that bathrooms (not toilets) have transparent glass walls. Cathedral views also unfold from the 6th-floor bar and 7th-floor rooftop restaurant and terrace. The breakfast buffet costs €29.

TOPAZZ VIENNA LUXURY HOTEL €€€

Map p244 (☎01-153 222 40; www.hoteltopazz.com; 01, Lichtensteg 3; d €259-359; ❄📶; ⓊStephansplatz) Luxurious furnishings in subtle green and grey hues at the 32-room Topazz are inspired by the Wiener Werkstätte period around the turn of the 20th century. Most of the deluxe and prestige rooms have large, padded porthole window seats; superior rooms have small balconies. Its sister hotel, Lamée Vienna, is across the street.

Karlsplatz & Around Naschmarkt

HOTEL DREI KRONEN PENSION €

Map p248 (☎01-587 32 89; www.hotel3kronen.at; 04, Schleifmühlegasse 25; s/d from €69/92; @📶; ⓊKettenbrückengasse) Within stumbling distance of the Naschmarkt (some rooms overlook it), this family-owned abode is one of Vienna's best-kept secrets. Palatial touches (shiny marble, polished brass, white-and-gold wallpaper) are distinctly Viennese, but nonetheless a casual feel prevails. Rooms are fitted with *Jugendstil* (Art Nouveau) furniture and art (including many prints by Gustav Klimt).

DAS TYROL HOTEL €€

Map p248 (☎01-587 54 15; www.das-tyrol.at; 06, Mariahilfer Strasse 15; s €109-229, d €149-259, studios €149-299; ❄@📶; ⓊMuseumsquartier) Design is the word at Das Tyrol. Done out in zesty yellow and green hues, the spacious rooms feature original artworks, such as Dieter Koch's playful Donald and Daisy Duck paintings, and Nespresso machines. Corner rooms have small balconies overlooking Mariahilfer Strasse; studios have kitchenettes. Breakfast, with eggs cooked to order and Prosecco, will keep you going all morning.

★HOTEL IMPERIAL HOTEL €€€

Map p248 (☎01-501 100; www.grandluxuryhotels.com; 01, Kärntner Ring 16; d/ste from €425/525; @📶; 🚋D, 1, 71 Karlsplatz, ⓊKarlsplatz) This rambling former palace, with all the marble and majesty of the Habsburg era, has service as polished as its crystal. Suites are filled with 19th-century paintings and genuine antique furniture (and come with butler service), while 4th- and 5th-floor rooms in Biedermeier style are far cosier and may come with a balcony. Breakfast costs €41.

The Museum District & Neubau

★MY MOJO VIE HOSTEL €

Map p252 (☎0676-551 11 55; www.mymojovie.at; 07, Kaiserstrasse 77; dm €24-28, d/tr/q with private bathroom €80/120/160, s/d/tr/q with shared bathroom €40/60/90/116; @; UBurggasse-Stadthalle) An old-fashioned cage lift rattles up to these design-focused backpacker digs. Everything you could wish for is here – well-equipped dorms with two power points per bed, a self-catering kitchen, netbooks for surfing, guidebooks for browsing and musical instruments for your own jam session. There's no air-con but fans are available in summer.

HOTEL AM BRILLANTENGRUND HOTEL €

Map p252 (☎01-523 36 62; www.brillantengrund.com; 07, Bandgasse 4; s/d/tr/q from €69/79/99/119; @; 49 Westbahnstrasse/Zieglergasse, UZieglergasse) In a lemon-yellow building set around a sociable courtyard strewn with potted palms, this community linchpin works with local artists and hosts regular exhibitions, along with DJs, live music and other events such as pop-up markets and shops. Parquet-floored rooms are simple but decorated with vintage furniture, which variously incorporate local artworks, funky wallpapers and retro light fittings. Breakfast included.

★HOTEL RATHAUS WEIN & DESIGN BOUTIQUE HOTEL €€

Map p252 (☎01-400 11 22; www.hotel-rathaus-wien.at; 08, Lange Gasse 13; s/d/tr/f/ste from €110/130/160/170/300; ; URathaus, Volkstheater) Each of the 39 minimalist-chic open-plan rooms at this boutique hotel is dedicated to an Austrian winemaker and the minibars are stocked with premium wines from the growers themselves. With clever backlighting, rooms reveal a razor-sharp eye for design, especially the opalescent ones with hybrid beds and bathtubs. Some rooms overlook the inner courtyard space.

BOUTIQUEHOTEL STADTHALLE HOTEL €€

Map p252 (☎01-982 42 72; www.hotelstadthalle.at; 15, Hackengasse 20; incl breakfast s €87-117, d €117-137, f €145-155; P; USchweglerstrasse) The world's first urban hotel with a zero-energy balance makes the most of solar power, rainwater collection and LED lighting and has a roof planted with fragrant lavender. Vivid shades of purple, pink and peach enliven the 79 vintage-meets-modern rooms, which are split over two buildings divided by an ivy-draped courtyard where organic breakfasts are served.

ALTSTADT PENSION €€

Map p252 (☎01-522 66 66; www.altstadt.at; 07, Kirchengasse 41; s €129-186, d €194-216, ste €199-427; ; UVolkstheater) Otto Ernst Wiesenthal has poured his passion and impeccable taste into creating one of Vienna's most outstanding guesthouses in Spittelberg. Design elements by Vitra and Philippe Starck merge seamlessly with original art from luminaries including Andy Warhol and Marcus Prachensky. The 45 individually decorated rooms have high ceilings, plenty of space and natural light. Children are charged by age (0-6/7-12/13-18 free/€20/40).

25HOURS HOTEL DESIGN HOTEL €€

Map p252 (☎01-521 51; www.25hours-hotels.com; 07, Lerchenfelder Strasse 1-3; d €160-190, ste €195-330; P; UVolkstheater) Decked out in bold colours, with big-top-style murals and pod-shaped rugs, the 217 Dreimeta-designed rooms here include 34 suites with kitchenettes. Top-whack suites come with terraces commanding grandstand views of the Hofburg. The Dachboden rooftop bar, Mermaid's Cave sauna area and free use of electro-bikes for whizzing about town make it a class act.

Schloss Belvedere to the Canal

SPIESS & SPIESS PENSION €€

Map p260 (☎01-714 85 05; www.spiess-vienna.at; 03, Hainburger Strasse 19; s €105-145, d €140-180; @; URochusgasse) The Spiess family goes out of its way to make you welcome at this elegant, well-positioned *Pension*. The spacious, crisp white rooms have been designed with care and utmost taste; the pricier ones come with fireplaces and balconies. Breakfast is a tempting smorgasbord of fresh fruit salad, bacon and eggs, cereals and pastries.

RUBY SOFIE BOUTIQUE HOTEL €€

Map p260 (☎01-361 96 60 60; www.ruby-hotels.com; 03, Marxergasse 17; d €74-119; UWien Mitte) 'Lean luxury' is the ethos of this slick boutique hotel occupying the Sofiensäle, a grand former concert hall. Interiors are minimal-stylish, the vibe laid-back, and the pared-down rooms come with oak floors and vintage furnishings, docking stations, in-room tablets and rain-showers. There's also a library, a bar that loans out a guitar, a yoga terrace and free bikes.

HOTEL PRINZ EUGEN HOTEL €€

Map p260 (☎01-505 17 41; http://prinz-eugen-vienna.hotel-rv.com; 04, Wiedner Gürtel 14; s €55-72, d €67-88; ❄@📶👪; ⓊSüdtiroler Platz) Though not as flash as the chandelier-lit marble lobby might suggest, this is nevertheless a sound pick, bang opposite the Hauptbahnhof and five minutes' walk from Belvedere. Rooms are dressed in plush fabrics, wood furnishings and muted tones, and those on higher floors look out across Vienna's rooftops. The huge buffet breakfast will keep you going most of the day.

Prater & East of the Danube

GAL APARTMENTS APARTMENT €

Map p258 (☎0650 561 19 42; www.apartmentsvienna.net; 02, Grosse Mohrengasse 29; apt d/tr/q €89/99/152; @📶👪; ⓊNestroyplatz, Taborstrasse) For a superb home away from home, check into these roomy apartments smack in the action of up-and-coming Leopoldstadt. Occupying a renovated Biedermeier house, the apartments are dressed in modern furniture and *Jugendstil*-inspired paintings. It's a short walk to the Karmelitermarkt, the Prater and the Augarten, and the subway whips you to the centre of town in less than 10 minutes.

★**GRÄTZLHOTEL** BOUTIQUE HOTEL €€

Map p258 (☎01-208 39 04; www.graetzlhotel.com; 02, Grosse Sperlgasse 6; d €119-189) Where electricians, lamp makers and bakers once plied a trade, the Grätzlhotel has injected new life into Leopoldstadt with ultra-cool interiors courtesy of some of Vienna's top architects. Just around the corner from Karmelitermarkt, the suites are minimalist and streamlined, with vintage lights and homely touches – kitchens with Nespresso makers, retro radios and Viennese Saint Charles Apotheke toiletries.

★**MAGDAS** BOUTIQUE HOTEL €€

Map p258 (☎01-720 02 88; www.magdas-hotel.at; 02, Laufbergergasse 2; d €70-150) How clever: the Magdas is a hotel making a social difference as here the staff who welcome guests are refugees. The former retirement home turned boutique hotel opened its doors in 2016 and hit the ground running. The rooms are retro cool, with one-of-a-kind murals, knitted cushions and upcycling. The pick of them have balconies overlooking the Prater, just around the corner.

HOTEL CAPRI HOTEL €€

Map p258 (☎01-214 84 04; www.hotelcapri.at; 02, Praterstrasse 44-46; s €75-105, d €109-149, tr €119-168, q €139-199; P📶👪; ⓊNestroyplatz) This midranger looks nondescript on the face of things, but its merits are many: it's five minutes' walk from Prater, two U-Bahn stops from Stephansplatz, and staff bend over backwards to please. Done up in pastel colours, rooms are streamlined and immaculate, all with flat-screen TVs and kettles. Breakfast is a wholesome spread of fruit, cereals, cold cuts and eggs.

Schloss Schönbrunn & Around

WOMBAT'S HOSTEL €

Map p262 (☎01-897 23 36; www.wombats-hostels.com; 15, Mariahilfer Strasse 137; dm €19-27, s €44-50, d €54-68; P@📶; ⓊWestbahnhof) For a dash of Aussie charm in Vienna, Wombat's is where savvy backpackers gravitate. The interior is a rainbow of colours, common areas include a bar, pool tables, music and comfy leather sofas, and the modern dorms have en suites. The relaxed staff hand you a drink and a useful city map on arrival, and bike hire can be arranged.

ANGEL'S PLACE GUESTHOUSE €

Map p262 (☎01-89 20 432; www.angelsplace-vienna.eu; 15, Weiglgasse 1; d €60-76, ste €100; 📶👪; ⓊSchönbrunn) A wine cellar has been converted into this cute guesthouse, in a workaday residential neighbourhood, a 10-minute stroll from Schloss Schönbrunn's gates. The warm-hued basement rooms are homey, with wood floors, bright textiles and original brick vaulting. There's a shared kitchen if you want to rustle up a snack; continental breakfast costs an extra €6.

Understand Vienna

Vienna Today

In 2016, Vienna topped the Mercer Quality of Living Survey for the seventh consecutive year, based on its economic and socio-cultural environment, health, pollution levels, public services and transportation. Despite political ripples affecting the country, the capital is becoming even more liveable thanks to new infrastructure and a commitment to becoming a 'smart city' integrating technological advancements with a green focus.

Best on Film

The Third Man (1949) Graham Greene's classic film noir set in postwar Vienna.

Amadeus (1984) Oscar-sweeping account of a fictionalised murder attempt on Mozart by a rival composer.

Before Sunrise (1995) Follows star-crossed lovers Ethan Hawke and Julie Delpy over one night in Vienna.

Letter from an Unknown Woman (1948) Unrequited love set in Vienna, underscoring the fragility of the human psyche.

Best in Print

The Piano Teacher (Elfriede Jelinek; 1983) By the Nobel Prize–winning author, about a repressed pianist and a sadomasochistic relationship.

The Road into the Open (Arthur Schnitzler; 1908) The story of an affair, with insights into Viennese society and culture in the early 20th century.

The World of Yesterday (Stefan Zweig; 1943) An autobiography of Zweig's life up to WWII, describing many well-known Viennese figures.

City of Ghosts (Shawn Kobb; 2015) Fast-paced thriller set in current-day Vienna following an American student caught up in a crime ring.

Local Politics

Vienna is a city-state, meaning the mayor doubles as the head of a state government. The capital has been governed by the Sozialdemokratischen Partei Österreichs (Social Democratic Party of Austria; SPÖ) and headed by an SPÖ mayor uninterrupted since 1945.

The SPÖ has also won an outright majority in state elections all but twice since 1945: in 1996, and again in the 2010 election, when the right-wing populist Freiheitliche Partei Österreichs (Freedom Party of Austria; FPÖ) took 25% of the vote. While the FPÖ used the misuse of asylum laws and assimilation of foreigners as populist issues to gain ground, the SPÖ wooed voters on its good record and longer-term infrastructure and quality of life issues, winning again in 2015 with 49% of the vote.

Today, under Bürgermeister and Landeshauptmann (mayor and governor) Dr Michael Häupl, the SPÖ governs Vienna in coalition with the Greens party, which picked up 10% of the 2015 vote. The next state elections will be held in 2020.

National Issues

At a national level, debate rages over the refugee crisis and its social and economic ramifications. Historically, Austria has a good track record of welcoming refugees and asylum seekers. When the crisis reached its borders in 2015, Austria initially expressed solidarity. At Vienna's Hauptbahnhof, a Train of Hope was established, with volunteers helping refugees. Austria accepted 90,000 asylum applications in 2015 – one of Europe's highest per capita.

By 2016, the tables were turning. No longer able to cope with the influx of migrants and struggling to successfully integrate and find jobs for them as unemployment continued to rise, the country capped the maximum number of migrants at 37,500. Following the first round of presidential elections in April 2016, it introduced a highly controversial bill to allow a 'state of emergency', permitting the rejection of the vast majority of refugees at borders should numbers surge. A 4km fence was erected on the Slovenian border, and further fences on the Hungarian and Italian (Brenner Pass) borders have been mooted. The UN and asylum experts have condemned such actions as flouting human rights laws.

Following the annulment by the constitutional court of the second round of the Austrian election in May 2016 due to voting irregularities, a re-run of the presidential election between left-wing, Green-backed, pro-European independent Dr Alexander Van der Bellen and far-right, Eurosceptic FPÖ member Norbert Hofer, took place on 4 December 2016. Van der Bellen won for a second time with a significantly increased majority. Meanwhile, inspiring initiatives in Vienna include a newly opened boutique hotel, Magdas, which is run by refugees.

Expanding City

Vienna has been the scene of some enormous infrastructure projects in recent years. A key opening was the new *Hauptbahnhof* (main train station) in 2015, part of a massive project transforming the formerly down-at-heel Südbahnhof area into the bright new Sonnwendviertel (Solstice Quarter), complete with some 5000 new apartments, shops and schools.

Rapid population growth is projected to continue for Vienna; by 2020, over €1.3 billion will be invested to ensure infrastructure such as drinking water supply, waste-water management and energy. An entirely new neighbourhood is also now under construction – in a departure from Vienna's historic profile, the futuristic, 240-hectare Aspern precinct (one of Europe's largest urban developments) is set on an artificial lake. It will combine industrial and office premises with contemporary apartments and form the new centre of Vienna's Donaustadt (22) district, served by the U-Bahn system.

The U-Bahn is also expanding: construction will begin in 2018 on the extension of the existing underground line U2 from Vienna's Rathaus (City Hall) station, and the first section of the new U5 line to Frankhplatz/Altes AKH.

Going Green

The goal of Vienna's ruling SPÖ party is to ensure optimal quality of life by minimising resource consumption. Strategies include an 80% reduction of CO2 emissions from 1990 levels (down from 3.1 tonnes per capita to 1 tonne), and for 50% of Vienna's gross energy consumption to originate from renewable sources such as solar and wind-turbine power. The target date for both is 2050, by which date diesel and petrol cars will be banned; a 15% reduction of motorised traffic is planned by 2030. Green spaces are planned to remain at over 50% of urban space within the city.

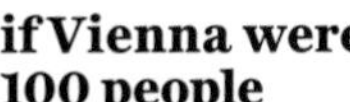

64 would be Austrian
14 would be other European
22 would be other

belief systems

(% of population)

population per sq km

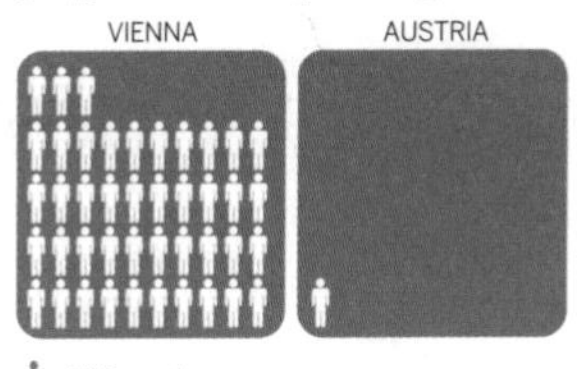

≈ 100 people

History

A key Roman outpost, then the hub of the Holy Roman Empire and the last bastion of the Occident against Ottoman Turks, Vienna experienced a creative explosion of high culture from the 18th century. Wars, the abolition of the monarchy, uprising and Austro-fascism followed before the city re-emerged in the mid-20th century as the capital of a modern Austrian state.

Early Vienna

The early history of Vienna dates back to the Palaeolithic age, around 35,000 years ago, evidence of which is the 25,000-year-old statuette called 'the Venus of Willendorf', which is today exhibited in the Naturhistorisches Museum.

Situated at a natural crossing of the Danube (Donau), it was probably an important trading post for the Celts when the Romans arrived around 15 BC. The Romans established Carnuntum as a provincial capital of Pannonia in AD 8, and around the same time created Vindobona, a second military camp that was located in what today is Vienna's Innere Stadt. A civil town flourished in the 3rd and 4th centuries, and around this time a visiting Roman Emperor, Probus, introduced vineyards to the hills of the Wienerwald (Vienna Woods). During this early period, Vindobona developed into a town of around 15,000 inhabitants and was important for trade and communication within the Roman Empire. Today, you can find remnants of this Roman town on Hoher Markt and Michaelerplatz.

The Holy Roman Empire grew out of the Frankish Reich, which was seen as the successor to the Roman Empire. It began life in 962 and finally collapsed in 1806, when Kaiser Franz II abdicated. Except for the period 1291–98, the Habsburgs ruled the empire from 1273.

The Babenberg Dynasty

In the year 976 a Bavarian Ostmark (Bavarian Eastern March) was established along the Danube River, and this gradually expanded to the north and east, lending greater importance to Vienna. The Eastern March was ruled by the Babenbergs, a wealthy Bavarian dynasty that held onto power until 1248. During their reign, the Babenbergs expanded their sphere of influence to include modern-day Lower Austria and Vienna, Styria and much of Upper Austria. In 1156, under the

TIMELINE

AD 8

Vindobona, the forerunner of Vienna's Innere Stadt, becomes part of the Roman province of Pannonia.

5th century

The Roman Empire collapses and the Romans are beaten back from Vindobona by invading Goth and Vandal tribes.

1137

Vienna is first documented as a city in the Treaty of Mautern, negotiated between the Babenbergs and the Bishops of Passau.

Babenberg monarch Heinrich II 'Jasmirogott', the Eastern March was elevated to a duchy (ie with its own duke and special rights) and Vienna became the capital. In 1221, two decades before the Babenberg dynasty died out, Vienna was granted its charter, achieving the status of a city.

Vienna of the 9th century consisted of a handful of Slavic and Avar tribal settlements, with the former Roman military road running through and Roman ruins, which served the Carolingian rulers as a basis for constructing a small fortress.

Habsburg Vienna: Late Middle Ages & Renaissance

The Babenbergs moved their residence to Vienna in the mid-12th century, setting the stage for Vienna to grow considerably. By the late 12th century it had become a significant trading capital, with links to Central and Western European capitals, Kiev (Ukraine) in the east and Venice in the south.

In 1273 Rudolf von Habsburg was elected king of the Romans (Rudolf I), ruling over the Holy Roman Empire and beginning the era of the Habsburgs. The dynasty would retain power until the 20th century.

In the 14th century, Vienna struggled under a string of natural disasters that made everyday life more difficult for many residents: first a plague of locusts in 1338; then the Black Death in 1349, which wiped out one-third of the city's population; followed by a devastating fire. Despite these setbacks, the centuries following the rise of the Habsburg dynasty gave Vienna a new scope of power. This was due in no small part to clever politicking on the part of monarchs – and even cleverer marriage alliances that catapulted this family of rulers to new heights.

In 1453 Friedrich III was elected Holy Roman Emperor; in 1469 he persuaded the pope to raise Vienna to a bishopric. Friedrich's ambition knew few bounds – his motto *'Austria est imperator orbi universo'* (AEIOU) made clear his view that the whole world was Austria's empire.

On the whole, the Habsburgs proved to be more adept at marriage than waging war. Maximilian I, the son of Friedrich III, acquired Burgundy through a clever marriage, while his son Philip the Handsome acquired Spain (and its overseas territories). The marriages of Maximilian's grandchildren brought the crowns of Bohemia and Hungary. This prompted the proverb, adapted from Ovid: 'Let others make war; you, fortunate Austria, marry!'

A ruler on the cusp of the Middle Ages and the Renaissance, Maximilian encouraged the teaching of humanism in Vienna's university and also founded the Vienna Boys' Choir.

When Richard the Lionheart was captured and held to ransom in 1192 while passing through Austria on his return from one of the Crusades, part of the ransom paid for his release was used to build a mint, which funded a new city wall on today's Ringstrasse.

Everyday Life

Everyday life in Vienna in the late Middle Ages and early Renaissance was far removed from the pomp and circumstance of its Habsburg rulers. Hoher Markt was not only the city's most important marketplace,

1155–56

Vienna becomes a residence of the Babenbergs; a new fortress is built on Am Hof and Babenberg's Margavate is elevated to Duchy.

1221

Vienna is granted its charter, achieving the status of a city.

1273–82

Otakar II hands the throne to a little-known count from Habichtsburg (read: Habsburg); Rudolf I of Habsburg resides in Vienna and the Habsburg dynasty begins.

1453

Friedrich III is elected Holy Roman Emperor. 16 years later he persuades the pope to raise Vienna to a bishopric.

it doubled as a site for Vienna's many public executions, undertaken for political as well as criminal activities; being beheaded or quartered was the usual method. At other sites around the city, convicted criminals were executed by being drowned in the Danube or burned alive.

Vienna built its first city wall around 1200 (funded by the ransom paid for the captured King Richard the Lionheart). Its main gates today live on as names along the city's Ringstrasse (Ring Road): Stubentor, Kärntner Tor, Schottentor and Rotenturmtor.

The first stone houses were erected around 1250, and the first mention of a public bath in Vienna dates to 1300. Fire and flooding were usual, and three earthquakes struck the city between 1267 and 1356.

Vienna's rapid growth led to the establishment of mendicant orders to feed the poor. These orders began arriving in Vienna in the mid-13th century, establishing monasteries and churches inside the city walls, such as the Minoritenkloster (Minoritenkirche), the Dominikanerkloster (later replaced by today's church) and an Augustine monastery that was later replaced by another in the Hofburg. These monasteries also cared for travellers and pilgrims.

In comparison with other European cities, Vienna was one of the most stable, largely thanks to privileges (*Ratswahlprivileg,* or the city council election privilege) introduced in 1396 that saw the city council divided up equally among patricians, merchants and tradesmen, creating a balance of interests.

Turks & Religious Troubles

The 16th and 17th centuries – a time in Vienna's history that included the high Renaissance and early baroque periods – were marked by Turkish attempts to take the capital; the Reformation and Thirty Years' War; a deadly plague; and, ultimately, an end to the Ottoman threat, paving the way for high baroque.

The era began badly when Karl V became Holy Roman Emperor and left the Austrian territories in the hands of his younger brother, Ferdinand I, a Spaniard by birth who didn't even speak German. An unpopular ruler, he soon had to deal with attacks from the Ottoman Turks who, having overrun the Balkans and Hungary, were on Vienna's doorstep by 1529. The city managed to defend itself under the leadership of Count Salm, but the 18-day siege highlighted glaring holes in Vienna's defences. Ferdinand moved his court to Vienna in 1533 (having spent most of his time elsewhere before then) and fortified the city's walls to include bastions, *ravelins* (star-shaped reinforcements of the outer wall) and ramparts, as well as a perimeter ditch, all of which followed the course of today's Ringstrasse. He rebuilt the Hofburg in the 1550s, adding the Schweizer Tor (Swiss Gate) you see today, with his own royal titles engraved on it.

From 1517, the year Martin Luther called for church reforms, the Reformation quickly spread to Austria. The nobility embraced it,

1520-30s

The Protestant Reformation spreads rapidly within Austria, and is embraced by the nobility. Ferdinand I defends the Catholic church.

1529

The first Turkish siege of Vienna takes place – but the Turks mysteriously retreat, leaving the city. Vienna survives and fortification of the city walls begins.

1670

The second expulsion of Jews is ordered by Leopold I; the financial strength of Vienna is severely weakened and Jews are soon invited back to the city.

1683

The Turks are repulsed at the gates of Vienna for the second time; Europe is free of the Ottoman threat and Vienna begins to re-establish itself as the Habsburgs' permanent residence.

and four of every five burghers became practising Protestants. After the Turkish siege of 1529, however, Ferdinand began purging Vienna of Protestantism. He invited the Jesuits to the city, one step in the Europe-wide Counter-Reformation that ultimately led to the Thirty Years' War (1618–48).

Towards the end of the 17th century Vienna suffered terribly. The expulsion of the Jews left its finances in a sorry state, and in 1679 the bubonic plague killed between 75,000 and 150,000. (The baroque Pestsäule was built shortly afterwards as a reminder of the epidemic.) In 1683, the city was once again besieged by the Turks. Vienna rebuffed this attack, however, and the removal of the Turkish threat helped lead the city to a new golden age.

The Golden Age of an Imperial City

After the Turks were beaten back from the gates of Vienna for the last time in 1683 and peace was restored, the path was clear for Vienna to experience a golden age of baroque culture and architecture

THE TURKS & VIENNA

The first of the Ottoman Empire's two great sieges of Vienna, in 1529, was undertaken by Suleiman the Magnificent, but the 18-day endeavour was not sufficient to break the resolve of the city. The Turkish sultan subsequently died at the Battle of Szigetvár in 1566, but his death was kept secret for several days in an attempt to preserve the morale of the army. This subterfuge worked – for a while. Messengers were led into the presence of the embalmed body, which was placed in a seated position on the throne, and unknowingly relayed their news to the corpse. The lack of the slightest acknowledgement of his minions by the sultan was interpreted as regal impassiveness.

At the head of the Turkish siege of 1683 was the general Kara Mustapha. Amid the 25,000 tents of the Ottoman army that surrounded Vienna he installed his 1500 concubines. These were guarded by 700 African eunuchs. Their luxurious quarters may have been set up in haste, but were still overtly opulent, with gushing fountains and regal baths.

Again, it was all to no avail. Mustapha failed to put garrisons on the Kahlenberg and was surprised by a quick attack from a German/Polish army rounded up by Leopold I, who had fled the city on news of the approaching Ottomans. Mustapha was pursued from the battlefield and defeated once again, at Gran. At Belgrade he was met by the emissary of the sultan. The price of failure was death, and Mustapha meekly accepted his fate. When the Austrian imperial army conquered Belgrade in 1718, Mustapha's head was dug up and brought back to Vienna in triumph, where it gathers dust in the vaults of the Wien Museum.

1740–90

The age of reform, influenced by the ideas of the Enlightenment, kicks into gear under the guidance of Empress Maria Theresia and her son Joseph II.

1805 & 1809

Napoleon occupies Vienna twice and removes the Holy Roman Emperor crown from the head of Franz II, who reinvents himself as Kaiser Franz I.

1815–48

The Metternich system, aimed at shoring up the monarchies of Austria, Russia and Prussia, ultimately begins the 19th-century middle-class revolution.

1857

City walls are demolished to make way for the creation of the monumental architecture today found along the Ringstrasse.

throughout the 18th century. During the reign of Karl VI, from 1711 to 1740, baroque architectural endeavours such as Schloss Belvedere, the Karlskirche and the Peterskirche transformed Vienna into a venerable imperial capital.

Vienna and the Jews, 1867–1938 by Steven Beller describes the role of Vienna's Jews in Viennese cultural and intellectual life.

By 1740 the Habsburg dynasty had failed to deliver a male heir, and Maria Theresia ascended the throne (the first and only female Habsburg to ever rule). She took up residence in Schloss Schönbrunn, which she enlarged from its original dimensions (which dated from 1700), gave a rococo style, and had painted in her favourite colour (the distinctive 'Schönbrunn yellow'). Although her rule was marred by wars – she was challenged by Prussia, whose star was on the rise, and by others who questioned the Pragmatic Sanction that gave her the right to the throne – Maria Theresia is widely regarded as the greatest of the Habsburg rulers. During her 40-year reign, Austria began to take on the forms of a modern state.

THE JEWS OF VIENNA

Historically, Vienna has had an ambivalent relationship with its Jewish population, who first settled in the city in 1194. By 1400 they numbered about 800, mostly living in the Jewish quarter centred on a synagogue on Judenplatz.

In 1420 the Habsburg ruler Albrecht V issued a pogrom against the Jews, who later drifted back into the city and prospered until the arrival of bigoted Leopold I and his even more bigoted wife, Margarita Teresa, who blamed her miscarriages on Jews. In 1670 Jews were expelled from the city and their synagogue destroyed, but this weakened the financial strength of Vienna, and the Jewish community was invited back.

The following centuries saw Jews thrive under relatively benign conditions and in the 19th century they were given equal civil rights and prospered in the fields of art and music. The darkest chapter in Vienna's Jewish history began on 12 March 1938 when the Nazis occupied Austria; with them came persecution and curtailment of Jewish civil rights. Businesses were confiscated (including some of Vienna's better-known coffee houses) and Jews were banned from public places; they were obliged to wear a Star of David and go by the names of 'Sara' and 'Israel'. Violence exploded on the night of 9 November 1938 with the November Pogrom, when synagogues and prayer houses were burned and 6500 Jews were arrested. Of the 180,000 Jews living in Vienna before the *Anschluss* (annexation), more than 100,000 managed to emigrate before the borders were closed in May 1939; another 65,000 died in ghettos or concentration camps. Only 6000 survived to see liberation by Allied troops.

Most survivors left afterwards. Today the city's Jewish population is approximately 7000 people, including many who immigrated from Eastern Europe and Russia. The website Jewish News from Austria (www.jewishnews.at) is an excellent resource on contemporary Jewish life in Vienna.

1866–67

Austria suffers defeat at the hands of Prussia (paving the way for a unified Germany without Austria) and is forced to create the dual Austro-Hungarian monarchy.

1873

Vienna hosts the World Fair, with the motto 'Culture and Education'; the event is marred by a cholera outbreak and the crash of the Vienna stock market.

1910–14

Vienna's population breaks the two million barrier, the largest it has ever been. The rise is mainly due to high immigration numbers, the majority of whom are Czechs.

1914–18

WWI rumbles through Europe and Vienna experiences a shortage of food and clothes. War-induced inflation destroys the savings of many middle-class Viennese.

The talented joined the wealthy and the great who frequented the opulent Schönbrunn palace during the reigns of Maria Theresia and the reform-minded Joseph II. A six-year-old Wolfgang Amadeus Mozart and his 10-year-old sister, Nannerl, performed in the palace's Spiegelsaal in 1762, while Joseph Haydn and other composers worked in the palace theatre. In the latter half of the 18th century (and beginning of the 19th) Vienna witnessed a blossoming musical scene never found in Europe before or since. During this time, Christoph Willibald Gluck, Haydn, Mozart, Ludwig van Beethoven and Franz Schubert all lived and worked in Vienna, producing some of their most memorable music.

When Napoleon occupied Vienna he established his headquarters in Schloss Schönbrunn, sleeping in what's known today as the Napoleonzimmer (Napoleon Room). In 1810 he married the daughter of Franz I, Marie Louise. A few years later, he demolished part of Vienna's city walls, creating space for Burggarten and Volksgarten.

Vienna in the Biedermeier Period

Napoleon swept across Europe in the early 19th century, triggering the end of the anachronistic Holy Roman Empire and the Kaiser who ruled it. The Habsburg Kaiser, Franz II, reinvented himself in 1804 as Franz I, Austria's first emperor, and formally dissolved the Holy Roman Empire two years later, following Napoleon's victory over Russian and Austrian troops in the Battle of Austerlitz (1805). Vienna was occupied twice by Napoleon (1805 and 1809), and the cost of war caused the economy to spiral into bankruptcy, from which Vienna took years to recover.

Following the defeat of Napoleon at the Battle of Waterloo in 1815, the European powers pieced together a post-Napoleonic Europe in the Congress of Vienna. The Congress was dominated by the skilful Austrian foreign minister, Klemens von Metternich. The period between the Congress of Vienna and 1848 – the year a middle-class revolution took hold of Europe – is known as the Biedermeier period. During this period Franz I and von Metternich presided over a period of repression that saw the middle classes retreat into private life to cultivate domestic music and a distinctive style of interior architecture, clothing and literature, known as Biedermeier from the word *bieder,* meaning 'staid' or 'stuffy'.

The lower classes suffered immensely, however: the Industrial Revolution created substandard working conditions, disease sometimes reached epidemic levels, and Vienna's water supply was completely inadequate.

Vienna in the Late 19th & Early 20th Century

The repressive mood of the Biedermeier period in first half of the 19th century in Vienna culminated in reaction and revolution among the middle classes, with calls for reform and, especially, freedom of expression.

1918

The Austrian Republic is declared on the steps of Vienna's Parlament (parliament); white and red are chosen as the colours of the nation's flag.

1919

The Treaty of St Germain is signed; the Social Democrats take control of the Vienna City Council, marking the beginning of a period known as Rotes Wien (Red Vienna).

1934

A series of skirmishes between right-wing and socialist forces, now known as the Austrian Civil War , breaks out in Vienna and other Austrian cities.

1938

Hitler invades Austria in the *Anschluss* (annexation) to Germany; he is greeted by 200,000 Viennese at Heldenplatz. Austria is officially wiped off the map of Europe.

In March 1848 the war minister was hanged from a lamppost. Von Metternich, who had been decisive in shaping the repressive Biedermeier period, fled to Britain and Emperor Ferdinand I abdicated, to be replaced by the 18-year-old Franz Josef I.

This liberal interlude was brief, however, and the army reimposed an absolute monarchy. In 1857 Franz Josef instigated the massive Ringstrasse developments around the Innere Stadt. In 1854 he married Elisabeth of Bavaria, affectionately nicknamed 'Sisi' by her subjects. The couple lived together in the Kaiserappartements of the Hofburg, which today house the Sisi Museum.

In the latter half of the 19th century and going into the 20th century, Vienna enjoyed a phase of rapid development. Massive improvements were made to infrastructure – trams were electrified, gasworks built and fledgling health and social policies instigated. Universal male suffrage was introduced in Austro-Hungarian lands in 1906 (women achieved suffrage in 1919 following the demise of the Habsburg dynasty). The city hosted the World Fair in 1873. Culturally, the period was one of Vienna's richest; these years produced Sigmund Freud, Gustav Klimt, Oskar Kokoschka, Gustav Mahler, Johannes Brahms, Egon

RED VIENNA

In the 1920s, Vienna was a model of social democratic municipal government, the most successful Europe has ever witnessed. The period is known as Rotes Wien, or Red Vienna.

The fall of the Habsburg Empire left a huge gap in the governing of Vienna. By popular demand the Social Democratic Workers' Party (SDAP) soon filled it, winning a resounding victory in the municipal elections in 1919. Over the next 14 years they embarked on an impressive series of social policies and municipal programs, particularly covering communal housing and health, aimed at improving the plight of the working class. Their greatest achievement was to tackle the severe housing problem Vienna faced after the war by creating massive housing complexes across the city. The plan was simple: provide apartments with running water, toilets and natural daylight, and housing estates with parkland and recreational areas. This policy not only gained admiration from within Austria but also won praise throughout Europe. Many of these colossal estates can still be seen in the city; the most celebrated, the Karl-Marx-Hof, was designed by Karl Ehn and originally contained an astounding 1600 apartments. Even so, Karl-Marx-Hof is by no means the biggest – Sandleitenhof in Ottakring and Friedrich-Engels-Hof in Brigittenau are both larger.

Guided tours of the main Red Vienna housing complexes are organised by the Architekturzentrum Wien (p116).

1938–39

In the Pogromnacht (Pogrom Night) of November 1938, Jewish businesses and homes are plundered and destroyed; 120,000 Jews leave Vienna over the next six months.

1945

WWII (1939–45) ends and a provisional government is established in Austria; Vienna is divided into four occupied quarters: American, British, Soviet Union and French.

1955

Austria regains its sovereignty as the Austrian State Treaty is signed at the Schloss Belvedere; over half a million Austrians take to the streets of the capital in celebration.

1972–88

The Donauinsel (Danube Island) is created to protect the city against flooding. Today it serves as one of the city's recreation areas, with parks, river beaches, trails and forest.

Schiele, Johann Strauss, as well as Otto Wagner, the most influential architect in fin de siècle Vienna and whose legacy is found throughout the city today.

Vienna: Capital of a Modern Republic

Vienna enjoyed enormous growth in the early 20th century, with its population reaching an all-time peak of over 2 million in 1910–14. The century, however, is marked by two cataclysmic wars – WWI (1914–18) and WWII (1939–45) – a 'Red Vienna' period in the 1920s, when left- and right-wing political forces clashed on Vienna's streets, the *Anschluss* (annexation) by Adolf Hitler that saw Vienna and the Austrian Republic as a whole become part of Hitler's Third Reich, liberation by the Soviet Union and occupation by the Allied powers, and finally the proclamation of Austria as a neutral, independent country in 1955. Most of these events are associated with one or more iconic features of the capital.

Vienna's neo-Gothic Rathaus is closely tied to the Social Democrats, who, following the collapse and abdication of the Habsburg monarchy in 1918, gained an absolute majority in all free elections from 1919 to 1996. The Palace of Justice, which was set on fire in 1927 by left-wing demonstrators following the controversial acquittal of members of the Frontkämpfervereinigung (a right-wing paramilitary group) on charges of assassination, perhaps best symbolises the political struggle of the era. This struggle culminated in several days of civil war in 1934. Hitler, who had departed Vienna many years before as a failed and disgruntled artist, returned to the city in triumph and held a huge rally at Heldenplatz (in the Hofburg) on 15 March 1938 in front of 200,000 ecstatic Viennese. A Holocaust memorial on Judenplatz is dedicated to the Jews who suffered under Nazism.

In March 1945, the Soviet Union liberated Vienna, today celebrated by the Russian Heroes' Monument on Schwarzenbergplatz, while Vienna's UNO-City, hosting the United Nations Office, best symbolises the city's post-WWII neutrality and evolution into a modern nation.

The Austrians: A Thousand Year Odyssey by Gordon Brook-Shepherd is a highly readable take on Austrian history.

1980

A third UN headquarters opens in Vienna as the headquarters for the International Atomic Energy Agency, the Office on Drugs & Crime, and other functions.

1986

Vienna ceases to be the capital of the surrounding *Bundesländ* of Niederösterreich (Lower Austria), replaced by Sankt Pölten.

1995

After resounding support from its populace and a referendum where 60% voted 'Yes' to joining, Austria enters the EU.

2016

Vienna tops the Mercer Quality of Living Survey – judged on factors such as economic and socio-cultural environment, public services and health – for the seventh consecutive year.

City of Music

With Mozart, Beethoven, Strauss and Schubert among its historical repertoire, Vienna is the world capital of opera and classical music. The rich musical legacy that flows through the city is evident everywhere, from buskers hammering out tunes on the streets to formal performances in one of the capital's renowned venues. Music also takes centre stage during festivals held throughout the year.

Habsburg Musical Tradition

The Habsburgs began patronising court musicians as far back as the 13th century, and by the 18th and 19th centuries they had created a centre for music that was unrivalled in the world. Many of the Habsburgs themselves were accomplished musicians. Leopold I (1640–1705) played violin; his granddaughter Maria Theresia (1717–80) played a respectable double bass; and her son Joseph II (1741–90) was a deft hand at the harpsichord.

Musical Masterpieces

Fifth Symphony in C Minor – Beethoven

Cradle Song, Op 49, No 4 – Brahms

The Creation – Haydn

The Magic Flute – Mozart

Hofmusik

Hofmusik (music of the royal court) had its beginnings in the Middle Ages when it developed as a form of music to accompany church Masses. From around 1300 a tradition of choirs with multiple voice parts established itself in Austria.

The Habsburgs adopted this tradition and, with the collapse of the Habsburg monarchy, the Austrian state took over the *Hofkapelle* (imperial chapel), which today includes members of Vienna's Philharmonic Orchestra, the Vienna State Opera and, above all, the young boys who traditionally provided the 'female' voice parts, the Wiener Sängerknaben – the Vienna Boys' Choir (p46). This tradition lives on with Sunday performances of the Vienna Boys' Choir in the Burgkapelle (p61) inside the Hofburg, and other venues.

Baroque Music

The first dedicated theatre for opera north of the Alps was built in Innsbruck in 1650, but opera was also playing a role in Vienna's cultural scene as early as the 1620s, capturing the hearts of the Habsburg rulers through its paraphernalia of excess – elaborate costumes and stage props, and performers who sang, danced and acted great dramas on stage.

Today the baroque era of music is most audible in performances of the works of two German masters of baroque church music, Johann Sebastian Bach (1685–1750) and Georg Friedrich Händel (1695–1759), performed in many of the churches around town.

Vienna's Philharmonic

An unmissable Viennese musical experience is a visit to the Vienna Philharmonic (www.wienerphilharmoniker.at), which performs mainly in the Grosser Saal of the Musikverein (p103). The Philharmonic has the privilege of choosing its conductors, whose ranks have included the likes of Gustav Mahler, Richard Strauss and Felix Weingartner. The instruments used by the Philharmonic generally follow pre-19th-century design and more accurately reflect the music that Mozart and Beethoven wrote.

COMPOSERS AT A GLANCE

Vienna and music go hand in hand. The following is a selection of composers who either came from Vienna or lived and worked in the capital.

Christoph Willibald Gluck (1714–87) Major works include *Orfeo* (1762) and *Alceste* (1767).

Wolfgang Amadeus Mozart (1756–91) Wrote some 626 pieces; among the greatest are *The Marriage of Figaro* (1786), *Don Giovanni* (1787), *Cosí fan Tutte* (1790) and *The Magic Flute* (1791). The Requiem Mass, apocryphally written for his own death, remains one of the most powerful works in the classical canon. Listen to Piano Concerto Nos 20 and 21, which comprise some of the best elements of Mozart: drama, comedy, intimacy and a whole heap of ingenuity in one easy-to-appreciate package.

Joseph Haydn (1732–1809) Wrote 108 symphonies, 68 string quartets, 47 piano sonatas and about 20 operas. His greatest works include Symphony No 102 in B-flat Major, the oratorios *The Creation* (1798) and *The Seasons* (1801), and six Masses written for Miklós II.

Ludwig van Beethoven (1770–1827) Studied briefly with Mozart in Vienna in 1787; he returned in late 1792. Beethoven produced a lot of chamber music up to the age of 32, when he became almost totally deaf and, ironically, began writing some of his best works, including the Symphony No 9 in D Minor, Symphony No 5 and his late string quartets.

Franz Schubert (1797–1828) Born and bred in Vienna, Schubert was a prolific composer whose best-known works are his last symphony (the Great C Major Symphony), his Mass in E-flat and the Unfinished Symphony.

The Strausses & the Waltz The early masters of the genre were Johann Strauss the Elder (1804–49) and Josef Lanner (1801–43). Johann Strauss the Younger (1825–99) composed over 400 waltzes, including Vienna's unofficial anthem, 'The Blue Danube' (1867) and 'Tales from the Vienna Woods' (1868).

Anton Bruckner (1824–96) Works include Symphony No 9, Symphony No 8 in C Minor and Mass in D Minor.

Johannes Brahms (1833–97) At the age of 29, Brahms moved to Vienna, where many of his works were performed by the Vienna Philharmonic. Best works include *Ein Deutsches Requiem*, his Violin Concerto and Symphony Nos 1 to 4.

Gustav Mahler (1860–1911) Known mainly for his nine symphonies; best works include *Das Lied von der Erde* (The Song of the Earth) and Symphony Nos 1, 5 and 9.

Second Vienna School Arnold Schönberg (1874–1951) founded the Second Vienna School of Music and developed theories on the 12-tone technique. His *Pieces for the Piano* Op 11 (1909) goes completely beyond the bounds of tonality. Viennese-born Alban Berg (1885–1935) and Anton Webern (1883–1945) also explored the 12-tone technique. At the first public performance of Berg's composition *Altenberg-Lieder*, the concert had to be cut short due to the audience's outraged reaction.

Vienna Classic

Wiener Klassik (Vienna Classic) dates back to the mid- and late 18th century and saw Vienna at the centre of a revolution that today defines the way we perceive classical music. Music moved away from the churches and royal courts into the salons and theatres of upper-middle-class society. The period is associated with great composers such as Wolfgang Amadeus Mozart (1756–91), Joseph Haydn (1732–1809), Ludwig van Beethoven (1770–1827) and Franz Schubert (1797–1828) – which later gave way to a new wave of classical composers in the 19th century, such as Franz Liszt (1811–86), Johannes Brahms (1833–97) and Anton Bruckner (1824–96).

The Klangforum Wien (www.klangforum.at), an ensemble of 24 artists from nine countries, is a unique collaboration between conductors and composers, who perform at various venues. See the website for current performances.

Contemporary Sounds

Vienna's impact on international jazz, rock or pop music is minimal, but it does have an interesting scene. Falco (1957–98), a household name for 1980s teenagers, reached the world stage with his hit 'Rock Me Amadeus', inspired by the film *Amadeus*.

Artists such as Kruder & Dorfmeister, Patrick Pulsinger and Erdem Tunakan have proved a powerful source for new electronic music. In the last few years the city's scene has experienced a revival, with old and new artists once again creating waves in the electronic genre. Tosca, a side project of Richard Dorfmeister, is well regarded; DJ Glow is known for his electro beats; the Vienna Scientists produce tidy house compilations; the Sofa Surfers' dub-hop tracks are often dark but well received; and the likes of Makossa & Megablast, Stereotype, Ill.Skillz, and Camo & Krooked are going from strength to strength.

Visual Arts & Architecture

Vienna is one of the world's most fascinating capitals when it comes to the visual arts and architecture. The Habsburg monarchs fostered and patronised the arts in grand style, leaving a rich legacy of fine historic paintings, sculptures and buildings. Complemented today by modern and contemporary works, they're visible at every turn when you walk through the city's streets.

Baroque & Rococo

Unwittingly, the Ottomans helped form much of Vienna's architectural make-up as seen today. The second Turkish siege was the major catalyst for architectural change; with the defeat of the old enemy (achieved with extensive help from German and Polish armies), the Habsburgs were freed from the threat of war from the east. Money and energy previously spent on defence was poured into urban redevelopment, resulting in a frenzy of building in the baroque period in the 17th and early 18th centuries.

Learning from the Italian model, Johann Bernhard Fischer von Erlach (1656–1723) developed a national style called Austrian baroque. This mirrored the exuberant ornamentation of Italian baroque with a few local quirks, such as coupling dynamic combinations of colour with undulating silhouettes. Johann Lukas von Hildebrandt (1668–1745), the other famous architect of the baroque era, was responsible for a number of buildings in the city centre.

Rococo, an elegant style incorporating pale colours and an exuberance of gold and silver, was all the rage in the 18th century. It was a great favourite with Maria Theresia, and Austrian rococo is sometimes referred to as late-baroque Theresien style.

Fresco painting in Austria dates back to the 11th century; the oldest secular murals in the capital, from 1398, are the Neidhart-Fresken. The dizzying heights of fresco painting, however, were reached during the baroque period, when Johann Michael Rottmayr (1654–1730), Daniel Gran (1694–1757) and Paul Troger (1698–1762) were active in Vienna and across the country.

Rottmayr was Austria's foremost baroque painter. He spent his early years as a court painter to the Habsburgs in Salzburg before moving to Vienna in 1696, where he became the favoured painter of the architect Fischer von Erlach. He worked on many of Fischer von Erlach's projects and is often compared to the Flemish painter Peter Paul Rubens, bringing together Italian and Flemish influences.

Like Rottmayr, the fresco painter Gran studied in Italy, but his style reined in most of the extravagant elements found in Rottmayr's work and offered a foretaste of neoclassicism – best illustrated in a magnificent ceiling fresco in the Nationalbibliothek.

Medieval & Earlier Architecture

Michaelerplatz (Roman ruins; p67)

Hoher Markt (Roman ruins; p79)

Ruprechtskirche (Romanesque; p80)

Stephansdom (Gothic; p76)

Maria am Gestade (Gothic; p79)

Michaelerkirche (Gothic; p67)

Museum Judenplatz (Jewry; p78)

Dom- & Diözesanmuseum (religious art; p77)

What to See

It's hard to turn a corner in the Innere Stadt without running into a baroque wall. Much of the Hofburg is a baroque showpiece; In der Burg square is surrounded on all sides by baroque wings, but its triumph is the Nationalbibliothek by Fischer von Erlach, whose Prunksaal (grand hall) was painted by Gran and is arguably one of the finest baroque interiors in Austria.

Herrengasse, running north from the Hofburg's Michaelertor, is lined with baroque splendour, including Palais Kinsky at No 4. The Peterskirche is the handiwork of Hildebrandt, with frescoes by Rottmayr, but its dark interior and oval nave is topped by Karlskirche, another of Erlach's designs with Rottmayr frescoes – this time with Byzantine touches. The highly esteemed Schloss Belvedere is also a Hildebrandt creation, which includes a large collection of masters from the baroque period, featuring works by Rottmayr, Troger, Franz Anton Maulbertsch (1724–96) and others.

Johann Michael Rottmayr's frescoes adorn the Karlskirche (where a lift/elevator ascends 70m into the cupola for a close-up view), the Peterskirche and, outside town, Stift Melk in the Danube Valley. A ceiling fresco he painted in Schloss Schönbrunn was lost during work on the palace in the 1740s.

Nicolas Pacassi is responsible for the masterful rococo styling at Schloss Schönbrunn, but the former royal residence is upstaged by its graceful baroque gardens.

The Habsburgs were generous patrons of the arts, and their unrivalled collection of baroque paintings from across Europe is displayed at the Kunsthistorisches Museum.

Sculpture's greatest period in Vienna was during the baroque years – the Providentia Fountain by George Raphael Donner and Balthasar Permoser's statue *Apotheosis of Prince Eugene* in the Unteres Belvedere are striking examples. The magnificent Pestsäule (1692) was designed by Erlach.

Neoclassical, Biedermeier & the Ringstrasse

From the 18th century (but culminating in the 19th), Viennese architects – like those all over Europe – turned to a host of neoclassical architectural styles.

The end of the Napoleonic wars and the ensuing celebration at the Congress of Vienna in 1815 ushered in the Biedermeier period (named after a satirical middle-class figure in a Munich paper). Viennese artists produced some extraordinary furniture during this period, often with clean lines and minimal fuss. Ferdinand Georg Waldmüller (1793–1865), whose evocative, idealised peasant scenes are captivating, is the period's best-known artist.

In the mid-19th century, Franz Josef I called for the fortifications to be demolished and replaced with a ring road lined with magnificent imperial buildings. Demolition of the old city walls began in 1857, and glorious buildings were created by architects such as Heinrich von Ferstel, Theophil von Hansen, Gottfried Semper, Karl von Hasenauer, Friedrich von Schmidt and Eduard van der Nüll. Some of the earlier buildings are Rundbogenstil (round-arched style, similar to neo-Roman) in style, but the typical design for the Ringstrasse is High Renaissance. This features rusticated lower storeys and columns and pilasters on the upper floors. Some of the more interesting ones stray from this standard, however; Greek Revival, neo-Gothic, neo-baroque and neo-rococo all play a part in the boulevard's architectural make-up.

Must-see Buildings

- *Stephansdom*
- *Schloss Belvedere*
- *Hofburg*
- *Schloss Schönbrunn*
- *Rathaus*

What to See

The Hofmobiliendepot has an extensive collection of Biedermeier furniture, and more can be seen in the Museum für Angewandte Kunst

(MAK). Ferdinand Georg Waldmüller's Biedermeier paintings hang in the Wien Museum and Oberes Belvedere and one of the few uniformly Biedermeier houses is the Geymüllerschlössel.

Taking a tram ride around the Ringstrasse provides a quick lesson in neoclassicism. High Renaissance can be seen in von Hansen's Palais Epstein, Gottfried Semper's Naturhistorisches Museum and von Hasenauer's Kunsthistorisches Museum.

Von Hansen also designed the Ring's Parlament, one of the last major Greek Revival works built in Europe. Von Ferstel's Votivkirche is a classic example of neo-Gothic, but the showiest building on the Ring, with its dripping spires and spun-sugar facades, is von Schmidt's unmissable Rathaus in Flemish-Gothic. The most notable neo-baroque example is van der Nüll's Staatsoper, though it's also worth having a look at Semper's Burgtheater.

While Franz Josef was emperor he had a new wing, the Neue Burg, added to the Hofburg. Gottfried Semper (1803–79) was instrumental in the planning of the Neue Burg and its museums, and the architect, von Hasenauer, stuck very closely to a traditional baroque look, though there are some 19th-century touches – a certain heavy bulkiness to the wing – that reveal it is actually neo-baroque.

Jugendstil & the Secession

Vienna's branch of the Europe-wide art nouveau movement, known as *Jugendstil* ('Youthful Style'), had its genesis from within the Akademie der Bildenden Künste (Academy of Fine Arts). The academy was a strong supporter of neoclassicism and wasn't interested in supporting any artists who wanted to branch out, so in 1897 a group of rebels, including Gustav Klimt (1862–1918), seceded. Architects such as Otto Wagner (1841–1918), Joseph Maria Olbrich (1867–1908) and Josef Hoffman (1870–1956) followed.

By the second decade of the 20th century, Wagner and others were moving towards a uniquely Viennese style, called Secession, which stripped away some of the more decorative aspects of *Jugendstil*. Olbrich designed the Secession Hall, the showpiece of the Secession, which was used to display other graphic and design works produced by the movement. The building is a physical representation of the movement's ideals, functionality and modernism, though it retains some striking decorative touches, such as the giant 'golden cabbage' on the roof.

Hoffman, who was inspired by the British Arts and Crafts movement led by William Morris, and also by the stunning art nouveau work of Glaswegian designer Charles Rennie Mackintosh, ultimately abandoned the flowing forms and bright colours of *Jugendstil* in 1901, becoming one of the earliest exponents of the Secession style. His greatest artistic influence in Vienna was in setting up the Wiener Werkstätte design studio in 1903, which included Klimt and Koloman Moser (1868–1918); they set out to break down the high-art/low-art distinction and bring *Jugendstil* into middle-class homes. In 1932 the WW closed, unable to compete with the cheap, mass-produced items being churned out by other companies.

No one embraced the sensualism of *Jugendstil* and Secessionism more than Klimt. Perhaps Vienna's most famous artist, Klimt was traditionally trained at the Akademie der Bildenden Künste but soon left to pursue his own colourful and distinctive, non-naturalistic style.

A contemporary of Klimt's, Egon Schiele (1890–1918) is considered to be one of the most notable early existentialists and expressionists. His gritty, confrontational paintings and works on paper created a huge

The Fin de Siècle Years

- *Klimt – Beethoven Frieze; The Kiss*
- *Loos – Loos Haus*
- *Schiele – Anything in the Leopold Museum*
- *Wagner – Kirche am Steinhof; Postsparkasse*

stir in the early 20th century. Alongside his sketches, he also produced many self-portraits and a few large, breathtaking painted canvases. The other major exponent of Viennese expressionism was playwright, poet and painter Oskar Kokoschka (1886–1980), whose sometimes turbulent works show his interest in psychoanalytic imagery and baroque-era religious symbolism.

Klimt protégé Egon Schiele attracted controversy: in 1911 he moved to Bohemia with his 17-year-old model and lover 'Wally' Neuzil but was driven out by offended locals. In 1912 he was detained for three weeks and later found guilty of corrupting minors with his erotic drawings and paintings.

The last notable Secessionist – and the one most violently opposed to ornamentation – was Czech-born, Vienna-based designer Adolf Loos (1870–1933). Up until 1909, Loos mainly designed interiors, but in the ensuing years he developed a passion for reinforced concrete and began designing houses with no external ornamentation. The result was a collection of incredibly flat, planar buildings with square windows that offended the royal elite no end. They are, however, key works in the history of modern architecture.

What to See

As well as 35 of Vienna's metro stations, Otto Wagner's works include the Stadtbahn Pavillons at Karlsplatz, and the Kirche am Steinhof, in the grounds of a psychiatric hospital.

A prolific painter, Klimt's works hang in many galleries around Vienna. His earlier, classical mural work can be viewed in the Kunsthistorisches Museum, while his later murals, in his own distinctive style, grace the walls of Secession, where you will find his famous *Beethoven Frieze,* and MAK. An impressive number of his earlier sketches are housed in the Leopold Museum, and his fully-fledged paintings are in the Leopold Museum, Wien Museum and Oberes Belvedere.

The largest collection of Schiele works in the world belongs to the Leopold Museum. More of his exceptional talent is on display at the Wien Museum, Albertina and Oberes Belvedere; Kokoschka can also be seen at the Oberes Belvedere and Leopold.

One of the most accessible designs of Loos' is the dim but glowing Loos American Bar, a place of heavy ceilings and boxy booths. Also worth a look are his public toilets on Graben. The Loos Haus is his most celebrated work. The Wien Museum provides a look into the personal world of Loos, with a reconstruction of a room from the archi-

OTTO WAGNER

Otto Wagner (1841–1918) was one of the most influential Viennese architects at the end of the 19th century (also known as the fin de siècle). He was trained in the classical tradition, and became a professor at the Akademie der Bildenden Künste. His early work was in keeping with his education, and he was responsible for some neo-Renaissance buildings along the Ringstrasse. But as the 20th century dawned he developed an art nouveau style, with flowing lines and decorative motifs. Wagner left the Academy to join the looser, more creative Secession movement in 1899 and attracted public criticism in the process – one of the reasons his creative designs for Vienna's Historical Museum were never adopted. In the 20th century, Wagner began to strip away the more decorative aspects of his designs, concentrating instead on presenting the functional features of buildings in a creative way.

The most accessible of Wagner's works are his metro stations, scattered along the network. The metro project, which lasted from 1894 to 1901, included 35 stations as well as bridges and viaducts. All of them feature green-painted iron, some neoclassical touches (such as columns) and curvy, all-capitals fin de siècle typefaces. The earlier stations, such as Hüttledorf-Hacking, show the cleaner lines of neoclassicism, while Karlsplatz, built in 1898, is a curvy, exuberant work of Secessionist gilding and luminous glass.

tect's own house. Pieces by the Wiener Werkstätte are on display at the MAK and can be bought from Woka (p91) and Altmann & Kühne (p91).

Modern Architecture

WWI not only brought an end to the Habsburg Empire, but also the heady fin de siècle years. Vienna's Social Democrat leaders set about a program of radical social reforms, earning the city the moniker 'Red Vienna'; one of their central themes was housing for the working class, best illustrated by Karl-Marx-Hof. Not everyone was pleased with the results – some of Vienna's leading architects, Adolf Loos included, criticised the government for failing to produce a unified aesthetic vision.

Since the late 1980s a handful of multicoloured, haphazard-looking structures have appeared in Vienna; these buildings were given a unique design treatment by maverick artist Friedensreich Hundertwasser (1928–2000). Hundertwasser felt that 'the straight line is Godless' and faithfully adhered to this principle in all his building projects, proclaiming that his uneven floors 'become a symphony, a melody for the feet, and bring back natural vibrations to man'. Although he complained that his more radical building projects were quashed by the authorities, he still transformed a number of council buildings with his unique style.

Hans Hollein (1934–2014) was one of Vienna's more influential architects since the 1960s. Works include Retti candle shop (Kohlmarkt 8–10); two jewellery stores designed for Schullin (Graben 26), which have been described as 'architectural Fabergés'; and Haas Haus, whose 'peeling' facade seems to reveal the curtain wall of glass below.

What to See

The municipality buildings of Red Vienna are scattered throughout the city. The most famous is Karl-Marx-Hof. Hundertwasserhaus attracts tourists by the busload, as does the nearby KunstHausWien, but Hundertwasser's coup d'état is the Fernwärme incinerator; opened in 1992, it's the most nonindustrial-looking heating plant you'll ever see.

Of the 21st-century architectural pieces, the MuseumsQuartier impresses the most, with its integration of the historic and the postmodern into the city's most popular space. On a 109-hectare site near Südtyroler Platz, Vienna's *Hauptbahnhof* is as large as the Josefstadt district and goes beyond its functional role as a station to form a city district in itself for 30,000 people, with some 5000 apartments, a large park, offices, schools and a kindergarten.

Contemporary Arts

Vienna has a thriving contemporary arts scene with a strong emphasis on confrontation, pushing boundaries and exploring new media – incorporating the artist into the art has a rich history in this city. Standing in stark contrast to the more self-consciously daring movements such as Actionism, Vienna's extensive Neue Wilde group emphasises traditional techniques and media.

One of Vienna's best-known contemporary artists, Arnulf Rainer (b 1929) worked during the 1950s with automatic painting (letting his hand draw without trying to control it). He later delved into Actionism, foot-painting, painting with chimpanzees and the creation of death masks.

Sculptor and photographer Erwin Wurm (b 1954) creates humorous large-scale works subverting everyday objects, such as bent yachts, flat cars and inverted houses.

The artist Eva Schlegel (b 1960) works in a number of media, exploring how associations are triggered by images. Some of her most powerful work has been photos of natural phenomena or candid street shots printed onto a chalky canvas then overlaid with layers of oil paint and lacquer.

Vienna in Print & on Film

Despite Vienna's renowned quality of life, Viennese writing and cinema is often bowed down by the weight of personal and national histories. Living under an autocratic empire, dealing with the end of the empire, the guilt of *Anschluss*, the horror of Nazism, the emotional legacy of WWII, neo-Nazism, misanthropy, religious upbringing and a real or imagined bleakness of life are all enduringly popular themes.

Literature

The best place to get an overview of Vienna's – and Austria's – literary past and present is at the Literaturmuseum (p81), which opened in 2015.

Top Books

The Play of the Eyes (Elias Canetti; 1985)

The Radetzky March (Joseph Roth; 1932)

The Third Man (Graham Greene; 1950)

Across (Peter Handke; 1986)

Measuring the World (Daniel Kehlmann; 2005)

19th to Mid-20th Century

Austria's literary tradition really took off around the end of the 19th century. Karl Kraus (1874–1936) was one of the period's major figures; his apocalyptic drama *Die Letzten Tage der Menschheit* (The Last Days of Mankind) employed a combination of reports, interviews and press extracts to tell its tale.

Peter Altenberg (1859–1919) was a drug addict, an alcoholic, a fan of young girls and a poet who depicted the bohemian lifestyle of Vienna. Whenever asked where he lived, he reputedly always gave the address of Café Central, where his papier-mâché figure still adorns the room today. Two of his collected works are *Evocations of Love* (1960) and *Telegrams of the Soul: Selected Prose of Peter Altenberg* (2005).

Robert Musil (1880–1942) was one of the most important 20th-century writers, but he achieved international recognition only after his death, when his major literary achievement about belle epoque Vienna, *Der Mann ohne Eigenschaften* (The Man Without Qualities), was – at seven volumes – still unfinished.

Stefan Zweig (1881–1942), another of the greatest writers in German, was born in Vienna. In his autobiography, *The World of Yesterday* (Die Welt von Gestern; 1942–3), he vividly describes the Vienna of the early 20th century. A poet, playwright, translator, paranoiac and pacifist, Zweig believed Nazism had been conceived specifically with him in mind; when he became convinced in 1942 that Hitler would take over the world, he killed himself in exile in Brazil.

Arthur Schnitzler (1862–1931), a friend of Sigmund Freud, was a prominent Jewish writer in Vienna's fin de siècle years. His play *Reigen* (Hands Around), set in 1900 against a Viennese backdrop, was described by Hitler as 'Jewish filth'; it gained considerable fame in the English-speaking world as Max Ophul's film *La Ronde*.

Joseph Roth (1894–1939), who was primarily a journalist, wrote about the concerns of Jews in exile and of Austrians uncertain of their identity at the end of the empire. His book *What I Saw: Reports from Berlin* is part of an upsurge of interest in this fascinating writer; his most famous works, *Radetzky March* and *The Emperor's Tomb*, are both gripping tales set in the declining Austro-Hungarian Empire.

Modern & Contemporary

Dutch-born Thomas Bernhard (1931–89) grew up and lived in Austria. He was obsessed with disintegration and death, and in later works like *Holzfällen: Eine Erregung* (Cutting Timber: An Irritation) turned to controversial attacks against social conventions and institutions. His novels are seamless (no chapters or paragraphs, few full stops) but surprisingly readable.

Peter Handke's (b 1942) postmodern, abstract output encompasses innovative and introspective prose works and stylistic plays. His book *The Goalie's Anxiety at the Penalty Kick* (1970) brought him acclaim; a film based on the book was directed by Wim Wenders. Handke's essay on the Balkan wars of the 1990s, *A Journey to the Rivers: Justice for Serbia* (1997), took an unpopular stance on Serbia and further cemented his reputation for controversy.

The provocative novelist Elfriede Jelinek (b 1946), winner of the Nobel Prize for Literature in 2004, dispenses with direct speech, indulges in strange flights of fancy and takes a very dim view of humanity. Her works are highly controversial, often disturbingly pornographic, and either loved or hated by critics. Jelinek's *Women as Lovers* (1994) and *The Piano Teacher* (1983) are two of her most acclaimed works. Her controversial *Greed* (2000) focuses on gender and the relationships between men and women.

Wolf Haas (b 1960) is well known for his dark-humoured crime novels featuring Detective Simon Brenner, several of which are set in Vienna. Three have been made into films, including the Vienna-set *Komm, süsser Tod* (Come, Sweet Death; 1998); the film was released in 2000.

The most successful of the contemporary writers is arguably Munich-born, Vienna-raised Daniel Kehlmann (b 1975), who achieved national and international acclaim with his *Measuring the World,* based on the lives of Alexander von Humboldt and Carl Friedrich Gauss. A film based on the book was released in 2012, directed by the idiosyncratic German director and actor Detlev Buck.

Many Viennese authors are also playwrights – perhaps the Viennese fondness for the avant-garde encourages the crossing of artistic boundaries. Schnitzler, Bernhard, Jelinek and Handke have all had their plays performed at the premier playhouse in Austria, Vienna's Burgtheater.

Cinema

The Austrian film industry is lively and productive, turning out Cannes Film Festival–sweepers like Michael Haneke, whose *The Piano Teacher* (2001, based on the novel by Jelinek), *Funny Games* (2008), *The White Ribbon* (2009) and *Amour* (2012) have all picked up prizes at Cannes. *Amour* also won the Academy Award for Best Foreign Film.

A healthy serving of government arts funding keeps the film industry thriving, as does the Viennese passion for a trip to the *Kino* (cinema). Home-grown films are showcased at the Metro Kinokulturhaus (p89), opened in 2015 and part of the national film archive. Local, independent films are as well attended as blockbusters by Graz-boy-made-good, Arnie Schwarzenegger. The annual Viennale (p46) festival draws experimental and fringe films from all over Europe, while art-house cinemas like the gorgeous *Jugendstil* **Breitenseer Lichtspiele** (www.bsl-wien.at; 14, Breitenseer Strasse 21; tickets adult/child €8.50/7; U Hütteldorfer Strasse) keep the Viennese proud of their rich cinematic history.

That history has turned out several big Hollywood names. Director Fritz Lang made the legendary *Metropolis* (1926), the story of a society enslaved by technology, and *The Last Will of Dr Mabuse* (1932), during which an incarcerated madman spouts Nazi doctrine. Billy Wilder, writer and director of massive hits like *Some Like it Hot, The Apartment* and *Sunset Boulevard*, was Viennese, though he moved to the US early in his career. Hedy Lamarr – Hollywood glamour girl and inventor of submarine guidance systems (and technology still used in wi-fi and GPS) – was also born in Vienna. Klaus Maria Brandauer, star of *Out of*

Africa and *Mephisto*, is another native. Vienna itself has been the star of movies such as *The Third Man* (1949), *The Night Porter* (1974), *Amadeus* (1984) and *Before Sunrise* (1995).

Documentary-maker Ulrich Seidl has made *Jesus, You Know* (2003), following six Viennese Catholics as they visit their church for prayer, and *Animal Love* (1995), an investigation of Viennese suburbanites who have abandoned human company for that of pets. Lately he has branched into features with *Dog Days* (2001). Jessica Hausner has earned a strong reputation by directing films such as *Lovely Rita* (2001), the story of a suburban girl who kills her parents in cold blood, and *Lourdes* (2009), which is about an atheistic woman with multiple sclerosis who makes a pilgrimage to Lourdes.

Vienna's oldest theatres that still exist include the Burgtheater, founded in 1741, the two *Vorstädte* theatres, Theater in der Josefstadt (1788) and Theater an der Wien (1801), and the Volkstheater (1889).

The Third Man

Sir Alexander Korda asked English author Graham Greene to write a film about the four-power occupation of postwar Vienna. Greene flew to Vienna in 1948 and searched with increasing desperation for inspiration. Nothing came to mind until, with his departure imminent, Greene had lunch with a British intelligence officer who told him about the underground police who patrolled the huge network of sewers beneath the city, and the black-market trade in penicillin. Greene put the two ideas together and created his story.

Shot in Vienna in the same year, the film perfectly captures the atmosphere of postwar Vienna using an excellent play of shadow and light. The plot is simple but gripping: Holly Martins, an out-of-work writer played by Joseph Cotton, travels to Vienna at the request of his old schoolmate Harry Lime (played superbly by Orson Welles), only to find him dead under mysterious circumstances. Doubts over the death drag Martins into the black-market penicillin racket and the path of the multinational forces controlling Vienna. Accompanying the first-rate script, camera work and acting is a mesmerising soundtrack. After filming one night, director Carol Reed was dining at a *Heuriger* (wine tavern) and fell under the spell of Anton Karas' zither playing. Although Karas could neither read nor write music, Reed flew him to London to record the soundtrack. His bouncing, staggering 'Harry Lime Theme' dominated the film, became a chart hit and earned Karas a fortune.

The Third Man was an instant success, and has aged with grace and style. It won first prize at Cannes in 1949 and the Academy Award for Best Camera for a Black and White Movie in 1950, and was selected by the British Film Institute as 'favourite British film of the 20th century' in 1999. For years, the Burg Kino (p103) has screened the film on a weekly basis.

The film's popularity has spawned the Third Man Private Collection (p96). True aficionados may want to take the Third Man Tour (p28) in English. It covers all the main locations used in the film, including a glimpse of the underground sewers, home to 2.5 million rats.

Important figures in the modern era of Austrian theatre were the playwright Franz Grillparzer (1791–1872), Johann Nestroy (1801–62) and Ferdinand Raimund (1790–1836), whose works include *Der Alpenkönig und Der Menchenfiend* (The King of the Alps and the Misanthrope).

Theatre

The roots of theatre in Vienna date back to religious liturgies and passion plays of the mid- and late Middle Ages. Baroque operas staged from the late 16th century were very much influenced by Italian styles, and under Habsburg monarchs such as Ferdinand III and Karl VI, baroque theatre of the royal court rose to its zenith. In 1741 Maria Theresia paved the way for a broad theatre audience when she had a hall used for playing the tennis-like game *jeu de paume* converted into the original Burgtheater on Michaelerplatz. This later moved to the Ringstrasse into the premises of today's Burgtheater.

Survival Guide

Transport

ARRIVING IN VIENNA

Vienna sits at the crossroads of Western and Eastern Europe, and has excellent air, road and rail connections to both regions, as well as services further afield.

Children aged under six travel free on public transport; from ages six to 15 they generally pay half-price. Children 14 years and under travel free on the CAT service to/from Vienna International Airport.

Flights, cars and tours can be booked online at lonelyplanet.com/bookings.

Air

Vienna International Airport

Located 19km southwest of the city centre, **Vienna International Airport** (VIE; ☎01-700 722 233; www.viennaairport.com; 📶) operates services worldwide. Facilities include restaurants and bars, banks and ATMs, money-exchange counters, supermarkets, a post office, car-hire agencies and two left-luggage counters open 5.30am to 11pm (per 24 hours €4 to €8; maximum six-month storage). Bike boxes (€35) and baggage wrapping (per item €12) are available.

TRAIN

The **City Airport Train** (CAT; www.cityairporttrain.com; single/return €11/19) departs from Vienna International Airport every 30 minutes from 6.09am to 11.30pm, and from Wien-Mitte train station every 30 minutes from 5.36am to 11.06pm. Journey time is 15 minutes.

The S7 (www.oebb.at) suburban train (€4.40, 25 minutes) does the same journey to/from the airport. It runs from 4.48am to 12.18am from the airport to Wien-Mitte, and from 4.19am to 11.49pm from Wien-Mitte to the airport.

BUS

Vienna Airport Lines (☎01-700 732 300; www.postbus.at; ⊙8am-7.30pm Mon-Sat) has three services connecting different parts of Vienna with the airport. The most central is the **Vienna Airport Lines bus stop** (Map p244) at Morzinplatz/Schwedenplatz (bus 1185; one way/return €8/13, 20 minutes), running via the Wien-Mitte train station.

TAXI

A taxi to/from the airport costs between €25 and €50. The yellow **Taxi 40100** (☎01-401 00; www.taxi40100.at) in the arrival hall (near the bookshop) has a fixed airport rate of €36. **C&K Airport Service** (☎01-444 44; www.cundk.at) has rates starting at €33.

CLIMATE CHANGE & TRAVEL

Every form of transport that relies on carbon-based fuel generates CO_2, the main cause of human-induced climate change. Modern travel is dependent on aeroplanes, which might use less fuel per kilometre per person than most cars but travel much greater distances. The altitude at which aircraft emit gases (including CO_2) and particles also contributes to their climate change impact. Many websites offer 'carbon calculators' that allow people to estimate the carbon emissions generated by their journey and, for those who wish to do so, to offset the impact of the greenhouse gases emitted with contributions to portfolios of climate-friendly initiatives throughout the world. Lonely Planet offsets the carbon footprint of all staff and author travel.

VIENNA'S NEW HAUPTBAHNHOF

With its diamond-shaped translucent glass-and-steel roof, Vienna's new *Hauptbahnhof* (main train station) is an architectural triumph. Opened in December 2015, it was designed and built by acclaimed Austrian firm Strabag. Up to 1000 trains per day carrying some 145,000 passengers now pass through the station, which also has 84 shops, bars and restaurants, parking for 600 cars, three bike garages, electric bike–charging points, and two **Citybike Wien** (Vienna City Bike; www.citybikewien.at; 1st/2nd/3rd hr free/€1/2, per hr thereafter €4) bike-share-scheme rental stations.

Airport Bratislava (Letisko)

Bratislava, Slovakia's capital, is only 60km east of Vienna, and **Airport Bratislava** (BTS; ☎02-3303 3353; www.bts.aero; Ivanská cesta), serving Bratislava, makes a feasible alternative to flying into Austria.

BUS

Slovaklines (www.slovaklines.sk) in conjunction with Eurolines (www.eurolines.com) runs buses between Airport Bratislava and Vienna International Airport and on to Südtiroler Platz at Vienna's *Hauptbahnhof* (one way/return €7.50/13, one hour, up to two per hour).

Buses leave outside the Airport Bratislava arrival hall between 8.30am and 9.35pm daily, and from Südtiroler Platz at Vienna's *Hauptbahnhof* from 8.30am and 9.35pm daily.

You can also take bus 61 to the centre of Bratislava and pick up a frequent train from Bratislava train station to Vienna.

Boat

The Danube is a traffic-free access route for arrivals and departures from Vienna. Eastern Europe is the main destination; **Twin City Liner** (Map p244; ☎01-904 88 80; www.twincityliner.com; 01, Schwedenplatz; one-way adult €20-35; 1, 2, U Schwedenplatz) connects Vienna with Bratislava in 1½ hours, while its sister company **DDSG Blue Danube Schiffahrt** (Map p258; ☎01-588 80; www.ddsg-blue-danube.at; 02, Handelskai 265, Reichsbrücke; one-way €99-109, return €125; ⌚9am-5pm Mon-Fri, 10am-4pm Sat & Sun, closed Sat & Sun Nov-Feb) links Budapest with Vienna from mid-May to September, departing Vienna Wednesday, Friday and Sunday, departing Budapest Tuesday, Thursday and Saturday. DDSG tickets may also be obtained or picked up at Twin City Liner.

Slovakian ferry company **LOD** (Map p258; ☎in Slovakia 421 2 529 32 226; www.lod.sk; Schiffstation Reichsbrücke, Handelskai 265 (Vienna departure point); one-way/return €20/29; ⌚late Apr-early Oct) runs hydrofoils between Bratislava and Vienna (1½ hours) five to seven days per week from late April to early October. The season can vary depending on weather conditions.

Bus

Eurolines (☎0900 128 712; www.eurolines.at; 03, Erdbergstrasse 200; ⌚office 8am-6pm; U Erdberg) has basically tied up the bus routes connecting Austria with the rest of Europe. Its main terminal is at the U3 U-Bahn station Erdberg but some buses stop at the U6 and U1 U-Bahn and train station Praterstern, and at Südtiroler Platz by Vienna's *Hauptbahnhof*.

Car & Motorcycle

Bordering eight countries (Czech Republic, Hungary, Germany, Slovakia, Slovenia, Italy, Switzerland and Liechtenstein), Austria is easily reached by road. If you're bringing your own vehicle, you'll need a Motorway Vingette (toll sticker). For 10 days/two months it costs €8.80/25.70 per car; €5.50/12.90 per motorcycle. Buy it at petrol stations in neighbouring countries before entering Austria. More information is available at www.austria.info.

Train

Austria's train network is a dense web reaching the country's far-flung corners. The system is fast, efficient, frequent and well used. Österreiche Bundesbahn (ÖBB; www.oebb.at) is the main operator, and has information offices at all of Vienna's main train stations. Tickets can be purchased online, at ticket offices or train-station ticket machines. Long-distance train tickets can be purchased onboard but incur a €3 service charge. Tickets for local, regional and intercity trains must be purchased before boarding.

Wien Hauptbahnhof

Vienna's main train station, the Wien Hauptbahnhof, 3km south of Stephansdom, handles all international trains as well as trains from all of Austria's provincial capitals, and many local and regional trains.

S-Bahn S-Bahn lines S1, S2 and S3 connect Wien Hauptbahnhof with Wien Meidling, Wien-Mitte and Praterstern.

U-Bahn U1 serves Karlsplatz and Stephansplatz.

Tram 0 to Praterstern, 18 to Westbahnhof and Burggasse/Stadthalle. Tram D connects Hauptbahnhof-Ost with the Ringstrasse.

Bus 13A runs through Vienna's *Vorstädte* (inner suburbs) Margareten, Mariahilf, Neubau and Josefstadt, all between the Ringstrasse and the Gürtel.

Wien Meidling

All western and southwestern regional trains, including services to Graz, stop at Wien Meidling before continuing to the *Hauptbahnhof*.

S-Bahn S1, S2 and S3 connect Wien Meidling with the *Hauptbahnhof*, Wien-Mitte and Praterstern.

U-Bahn U6 (Wien Meidling/Philadelphiabrücke) serves the Westbahnhof and the Gürtel stations.

Wien Westbahnhof

Primarily a commuter station serving Vienna's outer suburbs, Westbahnhof is also the terminus for the Westbahn (https://westbahn.at) intercity service to/from Salzburg via Linz.

U-Bahn U6 runs along the Gürtel, U3 to Stephansplatz via Herrengasse.

GETTING AROUND VIENNA

Vienna's comprehensive and unified public transport network is one of the most efficient in Europe. Flat-fare tickets are valid for trains, trams, buses, the underground (U-Bahn) and the S-Bahn regional trains. Services are frequent and you rarely have to wait more than 10 minutes.

Transport maps are posted in all U-Bahn stations and at many bus and tram stops. Free maps are available from **Wiener Linien** (☎01-7909-100; www.wienerlinien.at), located in nine U-Bahn stations. The Karlsplatz, Stephansplatz and Westbahnhof information offices are open 6.30am to 6.30pm Monday to Friday and 8.30am to 4pm Saturday and Sunday. Those at Schottentor, Praterstern, Floridsdorf, Philadelphiabrücke and Erdberg are closed at weekends.

Bicycle

Vienna is a fabulous place to get around by bike. Bicycles can be carried free of charge on carriages marked with a bike symbol on the S-Bahn and U-Bahn from 9am to 3pm and after 6.30pm Monday to Friday, after 9am Saturday and all day Sunday. It's not possible to take bikes on trams or buses. The city also runs the **Citybike Wien** (Vienna City Bike; www.citybikewien.at; 1st/2nd/3rd hr free/€1/2, per hr thereafter €4) shared-bike program, with bike stands scattered throughout the city.

Bus

Bus connections can be useful for outlying parts of town or for travellers with limited physical mobility.

Regular buses 13A runs north–south through the *Vorstädte* between *Hauptbahnhof* and Alser Strasse. 2A connects Schwarzenbergplatz, Stephansplatz, Schwedenplatz and Michaelerplatz. 3A connects Börsenplatz and Schottentor with Stephansplatz and Stubentor. Most lines run from 5am to midnight, with fewer (sometimes nonexistent) services on weekends.

Night buses *Nightline* routes cover much of the city and run every half-hour from 12.30am to 5am. Note that on early Saturday and Sunday mornings (ie after midnight Friday and Saturday) the U-Bahn runs all night. Schwedenplatz, Schot-

TICKETS & PASSES

Tickets and passes for **Wiener Linien** (☎01-7909-100; www.wienerlinien.at) services (U-Bahn, trams and buses) can be purchased at U-Bahn stations and on trams and buses, in a *Tabakladen* (*Trafik;* tobacco kiosk), as well as from a few staffed ticket offices.

Single Ticket *(Einzelfahrschein)* €2.20; good for one journey, with line changes; costs €2.30 if purchased on trams and buses (correct change required).

24-/48-/72-hour Tickets *(24-/48-/72-Stundenkarten)* €7.60, €13.30 and €16.50 respectively. Require validation.

Eight-day Ticket *(8-Tage-Klimakarte)* €38.40; valid for eight days, not necessarily consecutive; validate the card as and when you need it.

Weekly Ticket *(Wochenkarte)* €16.20; valid Monday to Sunday only (ie tickets purchased on a Friday are still only valid to the Sunday).

Senior Citizens Over 60s can buy a €2.80 ticket valid for two trips; enquire at transport information offices.

tentor and Kärntner Ring/Oper are stopping points for many night bus services; look for buses and bus stops marked with an 'N'. All transport tickets are valid for *Nightline* services. N25 runs around the Ringstrasse then via Schwedenplatz, Leopoldstadt to Kagraner Platz and beyond on weekdays.

Car & Motorcycle

You may consider hiring a car to see some of the outer sights but in Vienna itself it's best to stick with the excellent public transport system.

Hire

All the big car-hire names have desks in the *Hauptbahnhof* and Vienna International Airport; some also have branches in the city.

Austrian car-hire company **Megadrive** (☎05-010 541 20; www.megadrive.at; 03, Erdbergstrasse 202; per day from €30; ⏲7am-7pm Mon-Fri, 8am-2pm Sat, 8am-1pm Sun; Ⓤ Erdberg) is situated adjacent to the Eurolines bus terminal.

Taxi

Taxis are reliable and relatively cheap by Western European standards. City journeys are metered; the minimum charge is roughly €3.80 from 6am to 11pm Monday to Saturday and €4.30 any other time, plus a per kilometre fee of €1.42. A telephone reservation costs an additional €2.80. A tip of 10% is expected. Taxis are easily found at train stations and taxi stands all over the city. To order one, contact **Taxi 40100** (☎01-401 00; www.taxi40100.at) or **Willkommen Taxi** (☎01-60 160; www.taxi60160.at). These accept common credit and debit cards (check before hopping in, though).

Tram

There's something romantic about travelling by tram, even though they're slower than the U-Bahn. Vienna's tram network is extensive, with 29 lines, and it's the perfect way to view the city on the cheap. Trams are either numbered or lettered (eg 1, 2, D) and cover the city centre and some suburbs. Services run from 5.15am to 11.45pm.

Train

U-Bahn

The U-Bahn is a quick, efficient and inexpensive way of getting around the city. There are five lines: U1 to U4 and U6 (there is currently no U5; construction starts in 2018). Stations have lifts as well as escalators. Platforms have timetable information and signs showing the exits and nearby facilities. The U-Bahn runs from 5am to midnight Monday to Thursday and continuously from Friday through to Sunday night.

U-Bahn and tram services get you close to most sights, especially in the centre and fringing *Vorstadt* areas (ie between the Ringstrasse and Gürtel).

S-Bahn

S-Bahn trains, designated by a number preceded by an 'S', operate 10 lines from train stations and service the suburbs or satellite towns. Trains run from 4.30am to 1.10am. If you're travelling outside of Vienna, and outside of the ticket zone, you'll probably have to purchase an extension on your standard Vienna transport ticket or buy a ticket from a machine at the station; check on maps posted in train stations.

Directory A–Z

Discount Cards

Vienna Card (*Die Wien-Karte;* 48/72 hours €21.90/24.90) Unlimited travel on the public transport system (including night buses) and hundreds of discounts at selected museums, cafes, *Heurigen* (wine taverns), restaurants and shops across the city, and on guided tours and the City Airport Train (CAT). The discount usually amounts to 5% to 25% off the normal price. Purchased at **Tourist Info Wien** (Map p246; ☎01-245 55; www.wien.info; 01, Albertinaplatz; ⏰9am-7pm; 📶; 🚊D, 1, 2, 71 Kärntner Ring/Oper, Ⓤ Stephansplatz), the city's main tourist office, the **Airport Information Office** (⏰7am-10pm) and many concierge desks at the top hotels.

Emergency

In case of emergency, the general number for ambulance, fire and police is 112.

Ambulance *(Rettung)*	☎144
Fire *(Feuerwehr)*	☎122
Police *(Polizei)*	☎133

PRACTICALITIES

Newspapers & Magazines Newspapers remain very popular in Vienna and English-language papers are widely available. Many coffee houses have a good selection of daily UK newspapers.

Smoking Smoking has officially been banned in public places since 2009; however, cafes, restaurants and bars have been exempt from this law. In 2015 laws were passed to ban smoking in all restaurants and cafes from May 2018, in line with EU legislation. In the meantime, most restaurants are nonsmoking, but some allow smoking after 10pm, while large bars often have separate smoking and nonsmoking areas, and small ones are invariably smoking. Cafes and coffee houses are mostly nonsmoking or have separate areas.

Weights & Measures Austria uses the metric system.

Electricity

230V/50Hz

Gay & Lesbian Travellers

Vienna is increasingly tolerant towards gay and lesbian locals and visitors (more so than the rest of Austria), and the country legalised civil same-sex partnerships (though not marriage) in 2010. A sign of the capital's openness is its traffic lights, which have male-male and female-female pairings (with love hearts in between) on its pedestrian walk signals, in addition to male-female couplings.

Hang-outs

Mariahilf (6th district) and Margareten (5th district), fanning out around the Naschmarkt, have a higher than average concentration of gay and lesbian bars.

Festivals & Events

Headlining events on the gay and lesbian calendar include the **Regenbogen Parade** (Rainbow Parade; www.hosiwien.at/regenbogenparade; ⏲mid-Jun), the **Life Ball** (http://lifeball.org; ⏲mid-May; 🚋D, 1, 2 Rathaus, Ⓤ Rathaus), and **Identities** (www.identities.at; ⏲mid-Jun odd-numbered years; Ⓤ Kettenbrückengasse), Vienna's Queer Film Festival.

Information

Vienna's main point for gay and lesbian information, **Die Villa** (Map p248; ☎01-586 8150; http://dievilla.at; 06, Linke Wienzeile 102; ⏲hours vary; Ⓤ Pilgramgasse), has advice and information on what's on offer in the city. The tourist office website www.wien.info/en/vienna-for/gay-lesbian has extensive information on the scene.

Other resources include the following:

Gay in Wien (www.gayin.wien)

Gayboy (www.gayboy.at)

Gay Guide (www.gayguide.me)

Gaynet (www.gaynet.at)

Vienna Pride (www.viennapride.at)

Wiener Antidiskriminierungsstelle (www.queer.wien.at) Also has information for transgender locals and visitors.

Internet Access

Virtually all hostels and hotels in Vienna offer free wi-fi, called WLAN (pronounced vee-lan) in German. Many cafes, coffee houses and bars also offer free wi-fi; check locations at www.freewave.at/en/hotspots.

The city has more than 400 free hotspots, which are mapped on www.wien.gv.at/stadtplan. Search for 'wien.at Public WLAN', accept the terms of use and connect.

Alternatively, if your phone is unlocked, you can purchase a pre-paid SIM card with a data allowance from phone shops, kiosks and *tabakladen* (tobacconists).

Insurance

Comprehensive travel insurance to cover theft, loss and medical problems is highly recommended.

Worldwide travel insurance is available at www.lonelyplanet.com/travel-insurance. You can buy, extend and claim online anytime – even if you're already on the road.

Money

Austria's currency is the euro, which is divided into 100 cents. There are coins for one, two, five, 10, 20 and 50 cents, and €1 and €2. Notes come in denominations of €5, €10, €20, €50, €100, €200 and €500.

For the latest exchange rates, check out www.xe.com. Note that travellers cheques are no longer commonly exchanged in Austria.

ATMs

Bankomats (ATMs), which accept credit cards and debit cards such as Maestro, are never very far away in Vienna – just look for a neon sign with two green and blue stripes sticking out from a bank facade. *Bankomats* can also be found in the main train stations and at the airport.

Changing Money

Banks are the best places to exchange cash, but it pays to shop around as exchange rates and commission charges can vary a little between them. Typically, there's a charge of about 3% on currency exchange, with a minimum charge, so it's best to exchange larger amounts at one time.

There are plenty of exchange offices in the Innere Stadt, particularly around Stephansplatz and on Kärntner Strasse. Commission charges are around the same here as at banks, but quite often their exchange rates are uncompetitive.

It's cheaper to use debit cards in ATMs than changing money.

Credit Cards

Visa, EuroCard and MasterCard are more widely accepted than American Express and Diners Club, although a surprising number of shops and restaurants refuse to accept any credit cards at all. Boutiques, high-end shops and restaurants will usually accept cards, though, and the same applies for hotels. Train tickets can be usually bought by credit card in main stations, but not all non-European cards will work – ask your bank for advice before you leave.

Opening Hours

Many restaurants, bars, entertainment venues and smaller shops shut in July/August.

Banks 8am or 9am to 3pm Monday to Friday, to 5.30pm on Thursday. Smaller branches close for lunch.

Post offices 8am to noon and 2pm to 6pm Monday to Friday; some also open Saturday morning. The **main post office** (Map p244; www.post.

at; 01, Fleischmarkt 19; ⏲7am-10pm Mon-Fri, 9am-10pm Sat & Sun; 🚊1, 2, ⓊSchwedenplatz) has extended hours.

Pubs & clubs Vary.

Restaurants Generally 11am to 2pm and 6pm to 10pm or 11pm.

Shops Usually 9am to 6.30pm Monday to Friday (some to 9pm Thursday or Friday) and until 5pm Saturday.

Supermarkets All close Sunday.

Public Holidays

The only establishments remaining open on holidays are bars, cafes and restaurants. Museums are usually open except for New Year's Day, Christmas Day and sometimes May Day. The big school break is July and August; most families go away during this time, so you'll find the city is quieter, but the downside is that a high percentage of restaurants and entertainment venues close.

New Year's Day (Neujahr) 1 January

Epiphany (Heilige Drei Könige) 6 January

Easter Monday (Ostermontag) March or April

Labour Day (Tag der Arbeit) 1 May

Ascension Day (Christi Himmelfahrt) Sixth Thursday after Easter

Whit Monday (Pfingstmontag) Sixth Monday after Easter

Corpus Christi (Fronleichnam) Second Thursday after Pentecost

Assumption (Maria Himmelfahrt) 15 August

National Day (Nationalfeiertag) 26 October

All Saints' Day (Allerheiligen) 1 November

Immaculate Conception (Mariä Empfängnis) 8 December

Christmas Eve (Heiligabend) 24 December; everything closed afternoon

Christmas Day (Christfest) 25 December

St Stephen's Day (Stephanitag) 26 December

Telephone

Country code Austria's country code is ☎0043.

Area code Vienna's area code is ☎01. When calling from overseas drop the zero in the Vienna code.

Roaming Network works on GSM 1800 and is compatible with GSM 900 phones. US mobile phones (cell phones) will only work here if they are at least tri-band. Japanese phones need to be quad-band (world phone).

Prepaid SIM cards Phone shops, kiosks and *Tabakladen* (tabacconists) sell prepaid SIM cards for phone calls and data. To use one, your phone needs to be unlocked.

Data roaming Make sure the data transfer capability is deactivated while you are roaming. Austria has lots of wi-fi hotspots which can be used for surfing on smart phones with wi-fi capability.

Time

Austria is on Central European time, one hour ahead of GMT/UTC. Clocks go forward one hour on the last Saturday night in March and back again on the last Saturday night in October.

Note that in German *halb* is used to indicate the half-hour before the hour, hence *halb acht* (half-eight) means 7.30, not 8.30.

Toilets

- Large shopping centres have facilities that are free to use.
- Facilities at U-Bahn stations and public places marked by a 'WC' sign usually incur a small charge (around €0.50).
- Museums reliably have good, clean facilities.
- At cafes and bars, facilities are only for paying customers; ask first or consider investing in a coffee.

Tourist Information

Tourist Info Wien (Map p246; ☎01-245 55; www.wien.info; 01, Albertinaplatz; ⏲9am-7pm; 📶; 🚊D, 1, 2, 71 Kärntner Ring/Oper, ⓊStephansplatz) Vienna's main tourist office, with a ticket agency, hotel booking service, free maps and every brochure under the sun.

Airport Information Office (⏲7am-10pm) Full services, with maps, Vienna Card and walk-in hotel booking. Located in the Vienna International Airport arrival hall.

Jugendinfo (Vienna Youth Information; Map p248; ☎01-4000 84 100; www.wienxtra.at/jugendinfo; 01, Babenbergerstrasse 1; ⏲2-7pm Mon-Wed, 1-6pm Thu-Sat; 🚊D, 1, 2, 71 Burgring, ⓊMuseumsquartier) Offers various reduced-priced event tickets for 14 to 26 year olds. Staff can tell you about events around town.

Rathaus Information Office (Map p252; ☎01-525 50; www.wien.gv.at; 01, Rathaus; ⏲8am-6pm Mon-Fri; 🚊D, 1, 2 Rathaus, ⓊRathaus) City Hall provides information on social, cultural and practical matters, and is geared as much to residents as to tourists. There's a useful info-screen.

Travellers with Disabilities

Vienna is increasingly well geared for people with disabilities *(Behinderte)*. Ramps are common (though by no means ubiquitous). Most U-Bahn stations have wheelchair lifts. All U-Bahn stations have guiding strips for the blind. All buses these days have ramps (the driver will assist) and tilt technology, and most of the trams in service have low-floor access allowing entry in a wheelchair; this will rise to 100% of trams in 2017. Traffic lights 'bleep' to indicate when pedestrians can safely cross the road.

Tourist Info Wien (left) can give advice and information. Its detailed booklet *Accessible Vienna*, in German or English, provides information on hotels and restaurants with disabled access, plus addresses of hospitals, medical-equipment shops, parking places, toilets and much more. It's available for download at www.wien.info/en/travel-info/accessible-vienna.

Download Lonely Planet's free Accessible Travel guide from http://lptravel.to/AccessibleTravel.

Organisations

Bizeps (Map p258; ☎01-523 89 21; www.bizeps.at; 02, Schönngasse 15-17, Vienna; Ⓤ Messe-Prater) A centre providing support and self-help for people with disabilities. Located two blocks north of Messe-Prater U-Bahn station.

Visas

Visas for stays of up to 90 days are not required for citizens of the EU, the EEA (European Economic Area) and Switzerland, much of Eastern Europe, Israel, USA, Canada, the majority of Central and South American nations, Japan, Malaysia, Singapore, Australia or New Zealand. All other nationalities, including nationals of China, Russia and South Africa, require a visa.

The Federal Ministry for Europe, Integration & Foreign Affairs (www.bmeia.gv.at) website has a list of Austrian embassies where you can apply. For some nationals a biometric passport is required.

Austria is part of the Schengen Agreement, which includes all EU states (minus Britain and Ireland) and a handful of European countries including Switzerland. In general, a visa issued by one Schengen country is good for all the other member countries.

Language

German is the national language of Austria. It belongs to the West Germanic language family and has around 100 million speakers worldwide.

German is easy for English speakers to pronounce because almost all of its sounds are also found in English. If you read our coloured pronunciation guides as if they were English, you should be understood just fine. Note that kh sounds like the 'ch' in 'Bach' or in the Scottish *loch* (pronounced at the back of the throat), r is also pronounced at the back of the throat, zh is pronounced as the 's' in 'measure', and ü as the 'ee' in 'see' but with rounded lips. The stressed syllables are indicated with italics in our pronunciation guides. The markers 'pol' and 'inf' indicate polite and informal forms.

BASICS

Hello.	*Guten Tag./ Servus.*	*goo*·ten tahk/ *zer*·vus
Goodbye.	*Auf Wiedersehen.*	owf *vee*·der·zay·en
Bye.	*Tschüss./ Tschau.*	chüs/ chow
Yes.	*Ja.*	yah
No.	*Nein.*	nain
Please.	*Bitte.*	*bi*·te
Thank you.	*Danke.*	*dang*·ke
You're welcome.	*Bitte.*	*bi*·te
Excuse me.	*Entschuldigung.*	ent·*shul*·di·gung
Sorry.	*Entschuldigung.*	ent·*shul*·di·gung

WANT MORE?

For in-depth language information and handy phrases, check out Lonely Planet's *German phrasebook*. You'll find it at **shop.lonelyplanet.com**, or you can buy Lonely Planet's iPhone phrasebooks at the Apple App Store.

How are you?
Wie geht es Ihnen/dir? (pol/inf) — vee gayt es *ee*·nen/deer

Fine. And you?
Danke, gut. — *dang*·ke goot
Und Ihnen/dir? (pol/inf) — unt *ee*·nen/deer

What's your name?
Wie ist Ihr Name? (pol) — vee ist eer *nah*·me
Wie heißt du? (inf) — vee haist doo

My name is ...
Mein Name ist ... (pol) — main *nah*·me ist ...
Ich heiße ... (inf) — ikh *hai*·se ...

Do you speak English?
Sprechen Sie Englisch? (pol) — *shpre*·khen zee *eng*·lish
Sprichst du Englisch? (inf) — shprikhst doo *eng*·lish

I don't understand.
Ich verstehe nicht. — ikh fer·*shtay*·e nikht

ACCOMMODATION

guesthouse	*Pension*	pahng·*zyawn*
hotel	*Hotel*	ho·*tel*
inn	*Gasthof*	*gast*·hawf
youth hostel	*Jugendherberge*	*yoo*·gent·her·ber·ge

Do you have a ... room?	*Haben Sie ein ...?*	*hah*·ben zee ain ...
double	*Doppelzimmer*	*do*·pel·tsi·mer
single	*Einzelzimmer*	*ain*·tsel·tsi·mer

How much is it per ...?	*Wie viel kostet es pro ...?*	vee feel *kos*·tet es praw ...
night	*Nacht*	nakht
person	*Person*	per·*zawn*

Is breakfast included?
Ist das Frühstück inklusive? — ist das *frü*·shtük in·kloo·*zee*·ve

DIRECTIONS

Where's ...?
Wo ist ...? vaw ist ...

What's the address?
Wie ist die Adresse? vee ist dee a·*dre*·se

How far is it?
Wie weit ist es? vee vait ist es

Can you show me (on the map)?
Können Sie es mir (auf der Karte) zeigen? *ker*·nen zee es meer (owf dair *kar*·te) *tsai*·gen

How can I get there?
Wie kann ich da hinkommen? vee kan ikh dah *hin*·ko·men

EATING & DRINKING

I'd like to reserve a table for ... *Ich möchte einen Tisch für ... reservieren.* ikh *merkh*·te *ai*·nen tish für ... re·zer·*vee*·ren

(eight) o'clock *(acht) Uhr* (akht) oor

(two) people *(zwei) Personen* (tsvai) per·*zaw*·nen

I'd like the menu, please.
Ich hätte gern die Speisekarte, bitte. ikh *he*·te gern dee *shpai*·ze·kar·te *bi*·te

What would you recommend?
Was empfehlen Sie? vas emp·*fay*·len zee

I'm a vegetarian.
Ich bin Vegetarier/ Vegetarierin. (m/f) ikh bin ve·ge·*tah*·ri·er/ ve·ge·*tah*·ri·e·rin

That was delicious.
Das hat hervorragend geschmeckt. das hat her·*fawr*·rah·gent ge·*shmekt*

Cheers!
Prost! prawst

Please bring the bill.
Bitte bringen Sie die Rechnung. *bi*·te *bring*·en zee dee *rekh*·nung

Key Words

bar (pub)	*Kneipe*	*knai*·pe
bottle	*Flasche*	*fla*·she
breakfast	*Frühstück*	*frü*·shtük
cold	*kalt*	kalt
cup	*Tasse*	*ta*·se
desserts	*Nachspeisen*	*nahkh*·shpai·zen
dinner	*Abendessen*	*ah*·bent·e·sen
drink list	*Getränkekarte*	ge·*treng*·ke·kar·te
fork	*Gabel*	*gah*·bel
glass	*Glas*	glahs
hot (warm)	*warm*	warm
knife	*Messer*	*me*·ser
lunch	*Mittagessen*	*mi*·tahk·e·sen
market	*Markt*	markt
plate	*Teller*	*te*·ler
restaurant	*Restaurant*	res·to·*rahng*
spoon	*Löffel*	*ler*·fel
with/without	*mit/ohne*	mit/*aw*·ne

NUMBERS

1	*eins*	ains
2	*zwei*	tsvai
3	*drei*	drai
4	*vier*	feer
5	*fünf*	fünf
6	*sechs*	zeks
7	*sieben*	*zee*·ben
8	*acht*	akht
9	*neun*	noyn
10	*zehn*	tsayn
20	*zwanzig*	*tsvan*·tsikh
30	*dreißig*	*drai*·tsikh
40	*vierzig*	*feer*·tsikh
50	*fünfzig*	*fünf*·tsikh
60	*sechzig*	*zekh*·tsikh
70	*siebzig*	*zeep*·tsikh
80	*achtzig*	*akht*·tsikh
90	*neunzig*	*noyn*·tsikh
100	*hundert*	*hun*·dert
1000	*tausend*	*tow*·sent

Meat & Fish

beef	*Rindfleisch*	*rint*·flaish
carp	*Karpfen*	*karp*·fen
fish	*Fisch*	fish
herring	*Hering*	*hay*·ring
lamb	*Lammfleisch*	*lam*·flaish
meat	*Fleisch*	flaish
pork	*Schweinefleisch*	*shvai*·ne·flaish
poultry	*Geflügelfleisch*	ge·*flü*·gel·flaish
salmon	*Lachs*	laks
sausage	*Wurst*	vurst
seafood	*Meeresfrüchte*	*mair*·res·frükh·te
shellfish	*Schaltiere*	*shahl*·tee·re
trout	*Forelle*	fo·*re*·le
veal	*Kalbfleisch*	*kalp*·flaish

Fruit & Vegetables

apple	*Apfel*	*ap*·fel
banana	*Banane*	ba·*nah*·ne
bean	*Bohne*	*baw*·ne
cabbage	*Kraut*	krowt
capsicum	*Paprika*	*pap*·ri·kah
carrot	*Mohrrübe*	*mawr*·rü·be
cucumber	*Gurke*	*gur*·ke
grapes	*Weintrauben*	*vain*·trow·ben
lemon	*Zitrone*	tsi·*traw*·ne
lentil	*Linse*	*lin*·ze
lettuce	*Kopfsalat*	*kopf*·za·laht
mushroom	*Pilz*	pilts
nuts	*Nüsse*	*nü*·se
onion	*Zwiebel*	*tsvee*·bel
orange	*Orange*	o·*rahng*·zhe
pea	*Erbse*	*erp*·se
plum	*Pflaume*	*pflow*·me
potato	*Kartoffel*	kar·*to*·fel
spinach	*Spinat*	shpi·*naht*
strawberry	*Erdbeere*	*ert*·bair·re
tomato	*Tomate*	to·*mah*·te
watermelon	*Wasser-melone*	*va*·ser·me·*law*·ne

Other

bread	*Brot*	brawt
cheese	*Käse*	*kay*·ze
egg/eggs	*Ei/Eier*	ai/*ai*·er
honey	*Honig*	*haw*·nikh
jam	*Marmelade*	mar·me·*lah*·de
pasta	*Nudeln*	*noo*·deln
pepper	*Pfeffer*	*pfe*·fer
rice	*Reis*	rais
salt	*Salz*	zalts
soup	*Suppe*	*zu*·pe
sugar	*Zucker*	*tsu*·ker

Drinks

beer	*Bier*	beer
coffee	*Kaffee*	*ka*·fay
juice	*Saft*	zaft
milk	*Milch*	milkh
orange juice	*Orangensaft*	o·*rang*·zhen·zaft
red wine	*Rotwein*	*rawt*·vain
tea	*Tee*	tay
water	*Wasser*	*va*·ser
white wine	*Weißwein*	*vais*·vain

EMERGENCIES

Help!	*Hilfe!*	*hil*·fe
Go away!	*Gehen Sie weg!*	*gay*·en zee vek

Call the police!
Rufen Sie die Polizei! — roo·fen zee dee po·li·*tsai*

Call a doctor!
Rufen Sie einen Arzt! — roo·fen zee *ai*·nen artst

Where are the toilets?
Wo ist die Toilette? — vo ist dee to·a·*le*·te

I'm lost.
Ich habe mich verirrt. — ikh *hah*·be mikh fer·*irt*

I'm sick.
Ich bin krank. — ikh bin krangk

I'm allergic to ...
Ich bin allergisch gegen ... — ikh bin a·*lair*·gish *gay*·gen ...

SHOPPING & SERVICES

I'd like to buy ...
Ich möchte ... kaufen. — ikh *merkh*·te ... *kow*·fen

Can I look at it?
Können Sie es mir zeigen? — *ker*·nen zee es meer *tsai*·gen

How much is this?
Wie viel kostet das? — vee feel *kos*·tet das

That's too expensive.
Das ist zu teuer. — das ist tsoo *toy*·er

There's a mistake in the bill.
Da ist ein Fehler in der Rechnung. — dah ist ain *fay*·ler in dair *rekh*·nung

ATM	*Geldautomat*	*gelt*·ow·to·maht
post office	*Postamt*	*post*·amt
tourist office	*Fremden-verkehrsbüro*	*frem*·den·fer·kairs·bü·raw

SIGNS

Ausgang	Exit
Damen	Women
Eingang	Entrance
Geschlossen	Closed
Herren	Men
Offen	Open
Toiletten (WC)	Toilets
Verboten	Prohibited

TIME & DATES

What time is it?
Wie spät ist es? — vee shpayt ist es

It's (10) o'clock.
Es ist (zehn) Uhr. — es ist (tsayn) oor

At what time?
Um wie viel Uhr? — um vee feel oor

At ...
Um ... — um ...

morning	*Morgen*	*mor*·gen
afternoon	*Nachmittag*	*nahkh*·mi·tahk
evening	*Abend*	*ah*·bent
yesterday	*gestern*	*ges*·tern
today	*heute*	*hoy*·te
tomorrow	*morgen*	*mor*·gen

Monday	*Montag*	*mawn*·tahk
Tuesday	*Dienstag*	*deens*·tahk
Wednesday	*Mittwoch*	*mit*·vokh
Thursday	*Donnerstag*	*do*·ners·tahk
Friday	*Freitag*	*frai*·tahk
Saturday	*Samstag*	*zams*·tahk
Sunday	*Sonntag*	*zon*·tahk

TRANSPORT

boat	*Boot*	bawt
bus	*Bus*	bus
metro	*U-Bahn*	*oo*·bahn
plane	*Flugzeug*	*flook*·tsoyk
train	*Zug*	tsook

At what time's the ... bus?	*Wann fährt der ... Bus?*	van fairt dair... bus
first	*erste*	*ers*·te
last	*letzte*	*lets*·te
next	*nächste*	*naykhs*·te

A ... to (Linz).	*Eine ... nach (Linz).*	*ai*·ne ... nahkh (lins)
1st-/2nd-class ticket	*Fahrkarte erster/ zweiter Klasse*	*fahr*·kar·te *ers*·ter/ *tsvai*·ter *kla*·se
one-way ticket	*einfache Fahrkarte*	*ain*·fa·khe *fahr*·kar·te
return ticket	*Rückfahrkarte*	*rük*·fahr·kar·te

Does it stop at ...?
Hält es in ...? — helt es in ...

What station is this?
Welcher Bahnhof ist das? — *vel*·kher *bahn*·hawf ist das

QUESTION WORDS

What?	*Was?*	vas
When?	*Wann?*	van
Where?	*Wo?*	vaw
Who?	*Wer?*	vair
Why?	*Warum?*	va·*rum*

What's the next stop?
Welches ist der nächste Halt? — *vel*·khes ist dair *naykh*·ste halt

I want to get off here.
Ich möchte hier aussteigen. — ikh *merkh*·te heer *ows*·shtai·gen

Please tell me when we get to ....
Könnten Sie mir bitte sagen, wann wir in ... ankommen? — *kern*·ten zee meer *bi*·te *zah*·gen van veer in ... *an*·ko·men

Please take me to (this address).
Bitte bringen Sie mich zu (dieser Adresse). — *bi*·te *bring*·en zee mikh tsoo (*dee*·zer a·*dre*·se)

platform	*Bahnsteig*	*bahn*·shtaik
ticket office	*Fahrkarten-verkauf*	*fahr*·kar·ten·fer·kowf
timetable	*Fahrplan*	*fahr*·plan

I'd like to hire a ...	*Ich möchte ein ... mieten.*	ikh *merkh*·te ain ... *mee*·ten
bicycle	*Fahrrad*	*fahr*·raht
car	*Auto*	*ow*·to

How much is it per ...?	*Wie viel kostet es pro ...?*	vee feel *kos*·tet es praw ...
day	*Tag*	tahk
week	*Woche*	*vo*·khe

bicycle pump	*Fahrradpumpe*	*fahr*·raht·pum·pe
child seat	*Kindersitz*	*kin*·der·zits
helmet	*Helm*	helm
petrol	*Benzin*	ben·*tseen*

Does this road go to ...?
Führt diese Straße nach ...? — fürt *dee*·ze *shtrah*·se nahkh ...

Can I park here?
Kann ich hier parken? — kan ikh heer *par*·ken

Where's a petrol station?
Wo ist eine Tankstelle? — vaw ist *ai*·ne *tangk*·shte·le

I need a mechanic.
Ich brauche einen Mechaniker. — ikh *brow*·khe *ai*·nen me·*khah*·ni·ker

Are there cycling paths?
Gibt es Fahrradwege? — geept es *fahr*·raht·vay·ge

Behind the Scenes

SEND US YOUR FEEDBACK

We love to hear from travellers – your comments keep us on our toes and help make our books better. Our well-travelled team reads every word on what you loved or loathed about this book. Although we cannot reply individually to your submissions, we always guarantee that your feedback goes straight to the appropriate authors, in time for the next edition. Each person who sends us information is thanked in the next edition – the most useful submissions are rewarded with a selection of digital PDF chapters.

Visit **lonelyplanet.com/contact** to submit your updates and suggestions or to ask for help. Our award-winning website also features inspirational travel stories, news and discussions.

Note: We may edit, reproduce and incorporate your comments in Lonely Planet products such as guidebooks, websites and digital products, so let us know if you don't want your comments reproduced or your name acknowledged. For a copy of our privacy policy visit lonelyplanet.com/privacy.

OUR READERS

Many thanks to the travellers who used the last edition and wrote to us with helpful hints, useful advice and interesting anecdotes:

Alessandra Furlan, Anita Wimmer, Charlotte Brennan, David Mabb, Donald Kilgore, Gaybrielle Gordon, Georgia Alexander, Jeff Angermann, Joanna Durst, Jonathan Hales, Jürgen Alphonsus, Laura Herring, Leonard Eichel, Mark Meyrick, Markus Husa, Mikkel Wrang, Thomas Myrin, Vicki Munro, Warren Mak

WRITER THANKS

Catherine Le Nevez

Vielen Dank first and foremost to Julian, and to my co-authors Kerry Christiani and Donna Wheeler, as well as all the locals and fellow travellers in Vienna for insights, information and good times. Huge thanks too to Destination Editors Helen Elfer and Dan Fahey, and everyone at LP. As ever, *merci encore* to my parents, brother, *belle-sœur* and *neveu*.

Kerry Christiani

A heartfelt *Dankeschön* goes out to all the wonderful people I met on my travels, not least Maggie Ritson, Shane Pearce in St Anton, and Chiara and Karin Juchem in Vienna. Thanks also go to all the pros who made the road to research smoother: Wilma Himmelfreundpointner, Martina Trumer, Helena Hartlauer, Bettina Jamy-Stowasser and many more. Finally, a big thank you to Eugene Quinn of Vienna's Space and Place for creative ideas and inspiration.

Donna Wheeler

In Austria, gratitude goes to Anja Cervenka, Ingo Dietrich, Stephanie Tscheppe-Eselböck and Andrea and Alexander Almásy, with special mentions to the incredibly welcoming and fascinating Peter and Sabine Eichinger as well as Birgit Enge and Ingrid Enge for your kindness and local insights. Big thanks also to the best ever travel companion Joe Guario, and to Justin Westover, Gwen Jamois and Laura Lot for quality Paris R&R.

ACKNOWLEDGEMENTS

Climate map data adapted from Peel MC, Finlayson BL & McMahon TA (2007) 'Updated World Map of the Köppen-Geiger Climate Classification', Hydrology and Earth System Sciences, 11, 163344.

Cover photograph: Stephansdom, Religious Images/UIG/Getty ©

THIS BOOK

This 8th edition of Lonely Planet's *Vienna* guidebook was researched and written by Catherine Le Nevez, Kerry Christiani and Donna Wheeler. The previous edition was written by Anthony Haywood, Kerry Christiani and Marc Di Duca. This guidebook was produced by the following:

Destination Editors Helen Elfer, Daniel Fahey
Product Editor Kate James
Senior Cartographer Anthony Phelan
Book Designers Clara Monitto, Michael Buick
Assisting Editors Andrea Dobbin, Carly Hall, Ali Lemer, Anne Mulvaney, Christopher Pitts
Cover Researcher Naomi Parker
Thanks to Cheree Broughton, Jennifer Carey, Neill Coen, Daniel Corbett, Jane Grisman, Andi Jones, Claire Naylor, Karyn Noble, Martine Power, Tony Wheeler

Index

See also separate subindexes for:

Sights 000
Map Pages **000**
Photo Pages **000**

Sights 000
Map Pages **000**
Photo Pages **000**

DRINKING & NIGHTLIFE

ENTERTAINMENT

SHOPPING

SLEEPING

SPORTS & ACTIVITIES

Vienna Maps

Sights

- Beach
- Bird Sanctuary
- Buddhist
- Castle/Palace
- Christian
- Confucian
- Hindu
- Islamic
- Jain
- Jewish
- Monument
- Museum/Gallery/Historic Building
- Ruin
- Shinto
- Sikh
- Taoist
- Winery/Vineyard
- Zoo/Wildlife Sanctuary
- Other Sight

Activities, Courses & Tours

- Bodysurfing
- Diving
- Canoeing/Kayaking
- Course/Tour
- Sento Hot Baths/Onsen
- Skiing
- Snorkelling
- Surfing
- Swimming/Pool
- Walking
- Windsurfing
- Other Activity

Sleeping

- Sleeping
- Camping

Eating

- Eating

Drinking & Nightlife

- Drinking & Nightlife
- Cafe

Entertainment

- Entertainment

Shopping

- Shopping

Information

- Bank
- Embassy/Consulate
- Hospital/Medical
- Internet
- Police
- Post Office
- Telephone
- Toilet
- Tourist Information
- Other Information

Geographic

- Beach
- Gate
- Hut/Shelter
- Lighthouse
- Lookout
- Mountain/Volcano
- Oasis
- Park
- Pass
- Picnic Area
- Waterfall

Population

- Capital (National)
- Capital (State/Province)
- City/Large Town
- Town/Village

Transport

- Airport
- Border crossing
- Bus
- Cable car/Funicular
- Cycling
- Ferry
- Metro station
- Monorail
- Parking
- Petrol station
- S-Bahn/Subway station
- Taxi
- T-bane/Tunnelbana station
- Train station/Railway
- Tram
- Tube station
- U-Bahn/Underground station
- Other Transport

Note: Not all symbols displayed above appear on the maps in this book

Routes

- Tollway
- Freeway
- Primary
- Secondary
- Tertiary
- Lane
- Unsealed road
- Road under construction
- Plaza/Mall
- Steps
- Tunnel
- Pedestrian overpass
- Walking Tour
- Walking Tour detour
- Path/Walking Trail

Boundaries

- International
- State/Province
- Disputed
- Regional/Suburb
- Marine Park
- Cliff
- Wall

Hydrography

- River, Creek
- Intermittent River
- Canal
- Water
- Dry/Salt/Intermittent Lake
- Reef

Areas

- Airport/Runway
- Beach/Desert
- Cemetery (Christian)
- Cemetery (Other)
- Glacier
- Mudflat
- Park/Forest
- Sight (Building)
- Sportsground
- Swamp/Mangrove

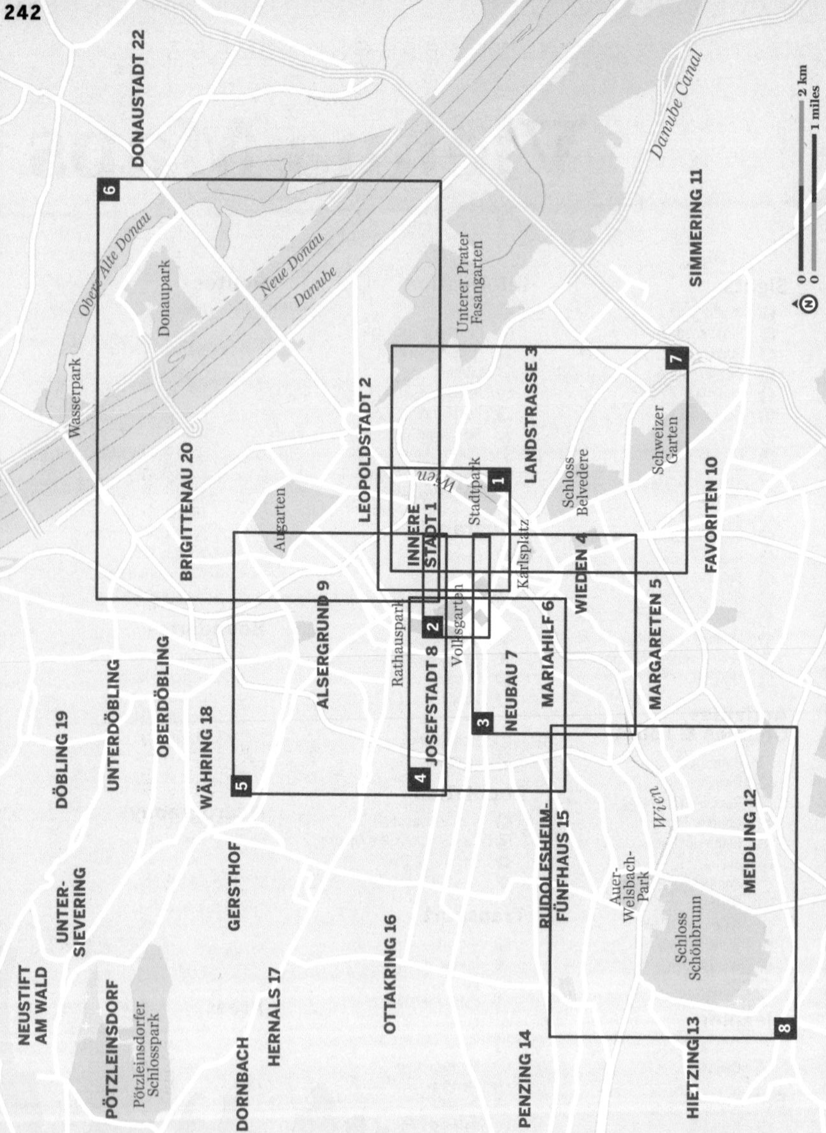
DONAUSTADT 22
Danube Canal
SIMMERING 11
2 km
1 miles
Obere Alte Donau
Donaupark
Neue Donau
Danube
Unterer Prater
Fasangarten
Wasserpark
LEOPOLDSTADT 2
LANDSTRASSE 3
Schweizer Garten
Schloss Belvedere
Wien
Stadtpark
BRIGITTENAU 20
Augarten
INNERE STADT 1
Karlsplatz
FAVORITEN 10
WIEDEN 4
MARGARETEN 5
ALSERGRUND 9
Rathauspark
Volksgarten
MARIAHILF 6
NEUBAU 7
JOSEFSTADT 8
DÖBLING 19
UNTERDÖBLING
OBERDÖBLING
WÄHRING 18
Wien
MEIDLING 12
RUDOLFSHEIM-FÜNFHAUS 15
Auer-Welsbach-Park
Schloss Schönbrunn
UNTER-SIEVERING
GERSTHOF
OTTAKRING 16
NEUSTIFT AM WALD
PÖTZLEINSDORF
Pötzleinsdorfer Schlosspark
DORNBACH
HERNALS 17
PENZING 14
HIETZING 13
1
2
3
4
5
6
7
8

MAP INDEX

STEPHANSDOM & THE HISTORIC CENTRE *Map on p244*

Top Sights (p76)

1 Haus der Musik C7
2 Stephansdom C5

Sights (p78)

3 Am Hof A3
4 Ankeruhr D3
5 Archiv des Österreichischen Widerstands C3
Cathedral Pummerin (see 2)
Cathedral South Tower (see 2)
6 Dom- & Diözesanmuseum D4
7 Dominikanerkirche E4
8 Dr-Ignaz-Seipel-Platz E4
Fleischmarkt (see 10)
9 Franziskanerkirche D6
Graben (see 20)
10 Griechenkirche zur Heiligen Dreifaltigkeit E3
11 Holocaust-Denkmal B3
12 Kirche Am Hof B3
13 Literaturmuseum C6
14 Maria am Gestade B2
Monument to the Victims of Fascism (see 15)
15 Morzinplatz D2
16 Mozarthaus Vienna D5
17 Museum Judenplatz B3
18 Neidhart-Fresken C3
19 Österreichische Akademie der Wissenschaften E4
20 Pestsäule B5
21 Peterskirche B4
22 Postsparkasse F4
23 Römer Museum C3
24 Ruprechtskirche D3
25 Stadttempel D3
Stephansdom Katakomben (see 2)
26 Uhren Museum B3

Eating (p85)

27 Artner D6
28 Beim Czaak E4
29 Brezl Gwölb B3
30 Café Korb C4
31 Donuteria C7
32 Figlmüller D4
33 Figlmüller D4
34 Fratelli D4
35 Griechenbeisl E3
36 Hidden Kitchen B2
37 Huth Gastwirtschaft D7
38 Maschu Maschu D3
39 Motto am Fluss E3
40 Plachutta E5
41 Restaurant Bauer E4
42 Tian D6
43 Wrenkh C4
44 Xpedit F3
45 Zanoni & Zanoni D4
46 Zum Schwarzen Kameel B4

Drinking & Nightlife (p87)

47 1516 Brewing Company C7
48 Café Prückel F5
49 Diglas D5
50 Enrico Panigl E4
51 Flanagan's D7
52 Haas & Haas D5
53 Kaffee Alt Wien E4
54 Kleines Café D6
55 Kruger's American Bar C7
56 Sky Bar C6
57 Vinogin E4
58 Vinothek W-Einkehr E3
Vis-à-vis (see 33)
59 Why Not? B2
60 Zwölf Apostelkeller D4

Entertainment (p89)

61 Gartenbaukino E6
62 Jazzland D2
63 Kammeroper E4
64 Metro Kinokulturhaus C6
65 Porgy & Bess E6

Shopping (p90)

66 Altmann & Kühne C5
67 Art Up C4
68 Atelier Naske C3
69 Das Neue Schwarz C4
70 Herzilein E5
71 Kiss Kiss Bang Bang D7
72 Manner C4
73 Runway B4
74 Schau Schau D4
75 So Austria D4
76 Unger und Klein C2
77 Wald & Wiese E5
78 Wein & Co C4
79 Wiener Rosenmanufaktur E4
80 Woka D5

Sports & Activities (p91)

81 Badeschiff G3

Sleeping (p193)

82 DO & CO C5
83 Grand Ferdinand Hotel D8
84 Hollmann Beletage D4
85 Hotel Austria E4
86 Hotel Capricorno E3
87 Opera Suites C7
88 Schweizer Pension B2
89 Topazz Vienna D4

STEPHANSDOM & THE HISTORIC CENTRE

Key on p243

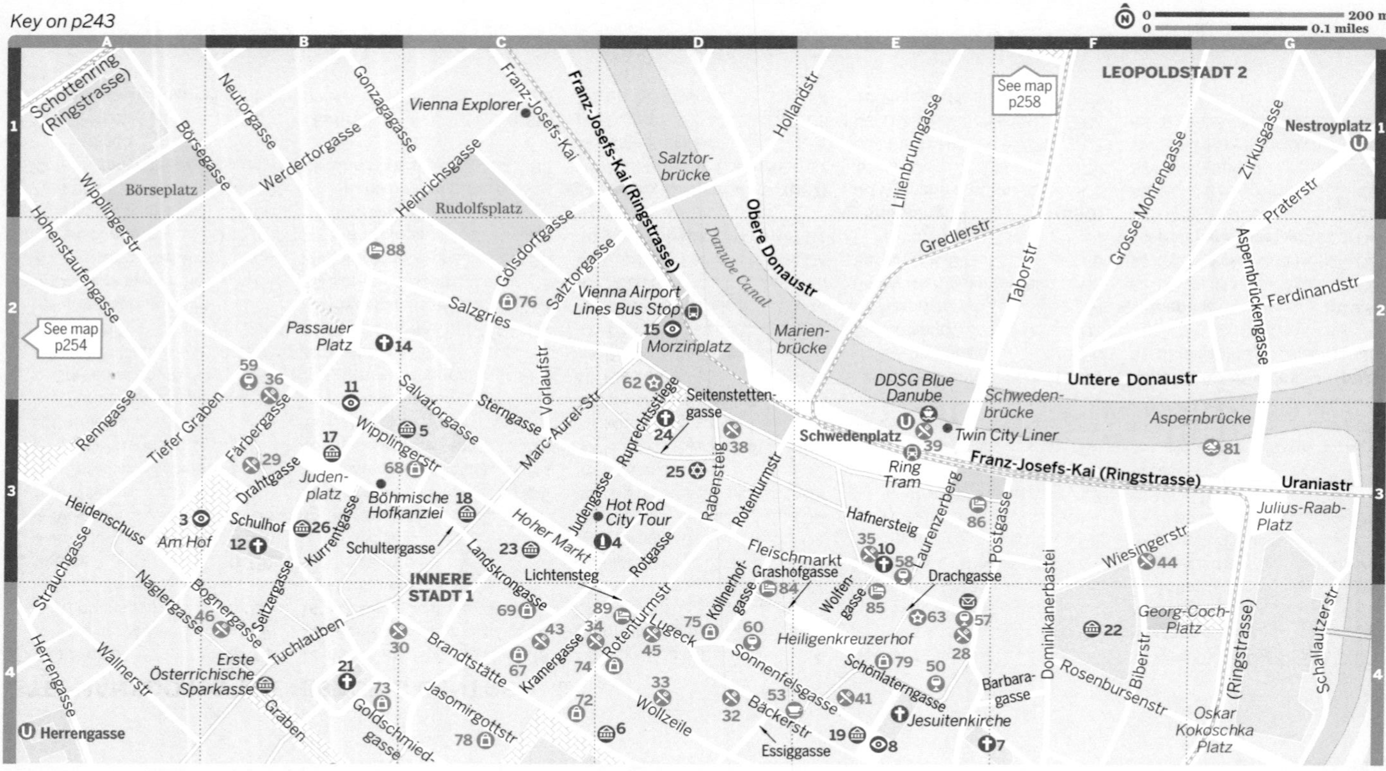

STEPHANSDOM & THE HISTORIC CENTRE

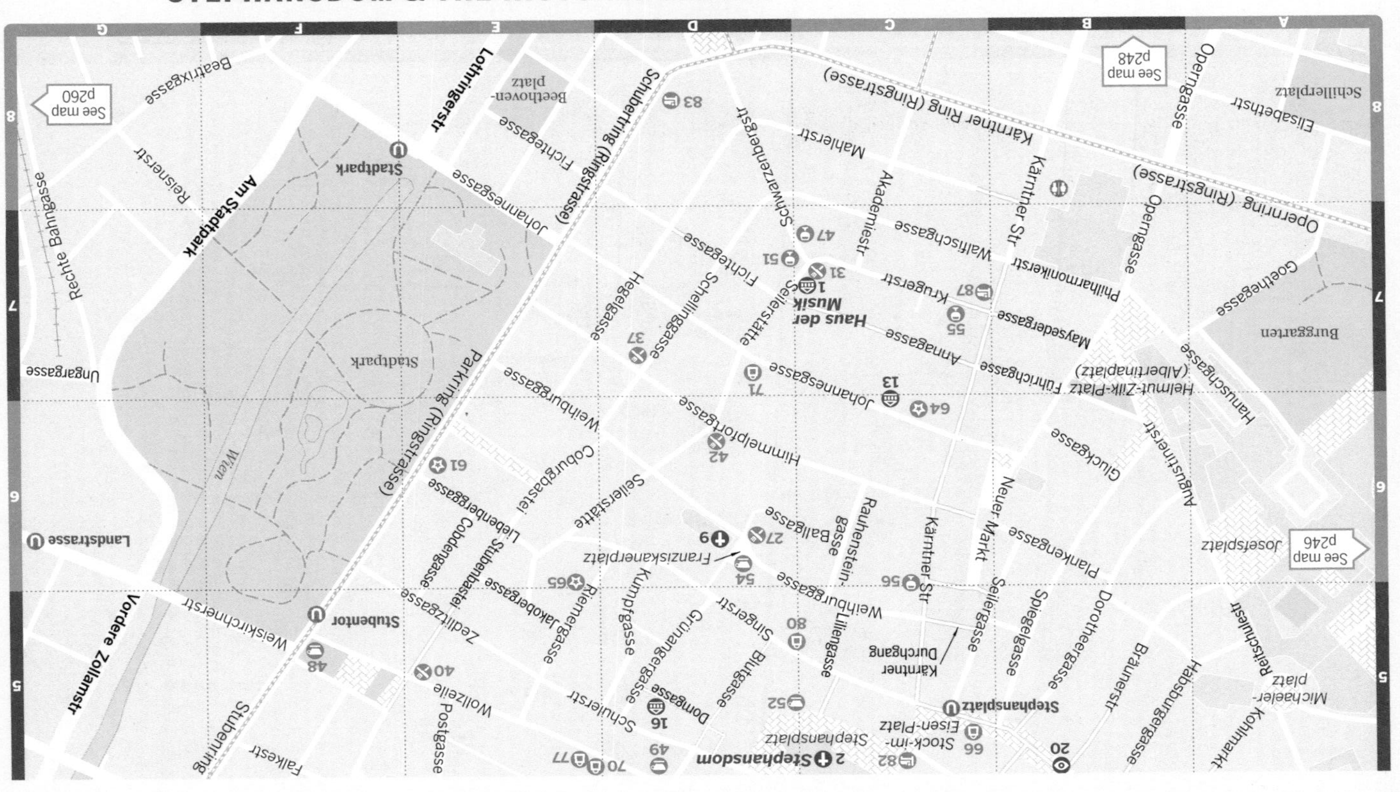

THE HOFBURG & AROUND

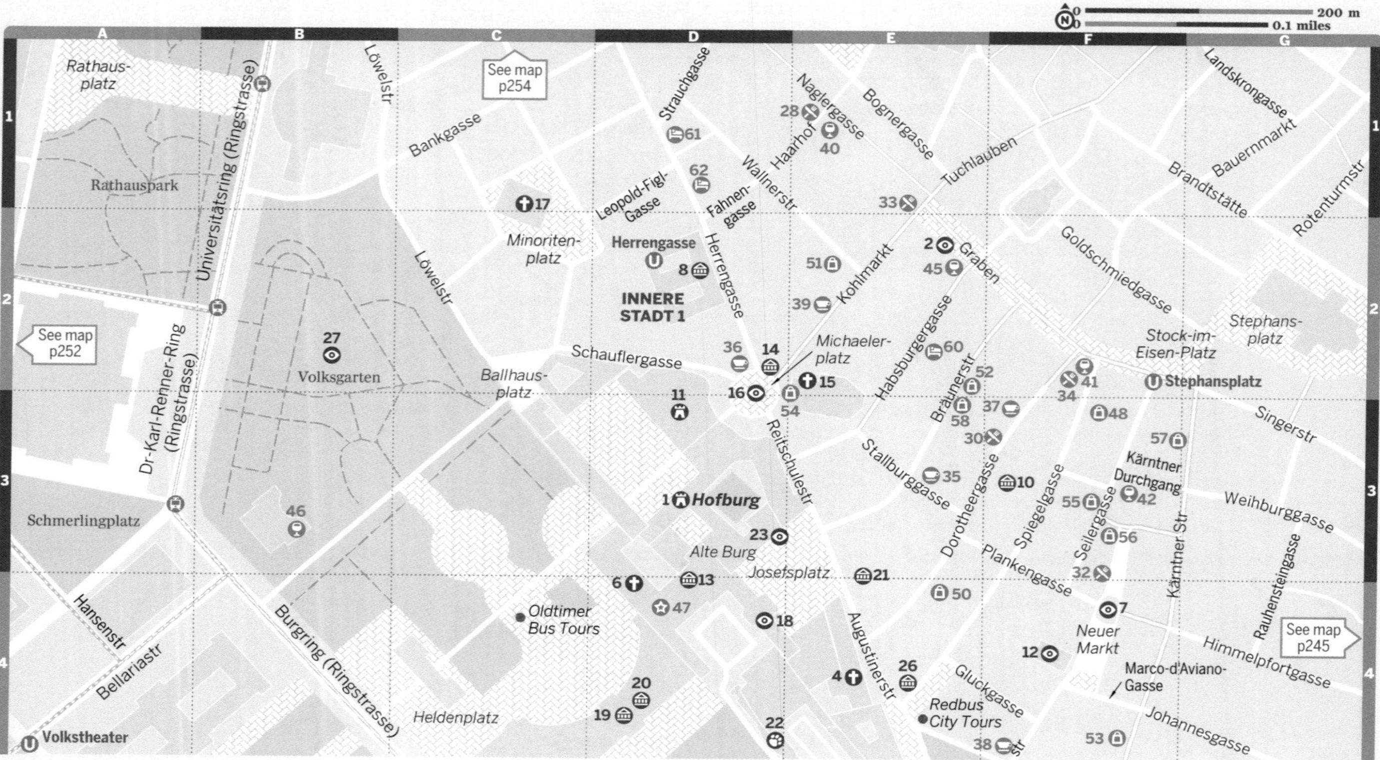

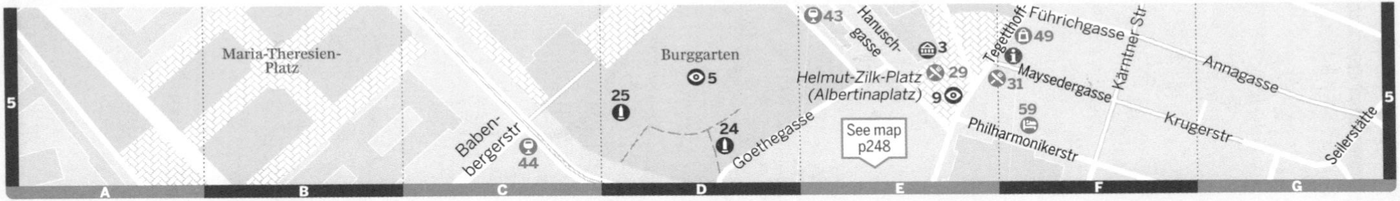

Top Sights (p60)
1 Hofburg D3

Sights (p66)
2 Adolf Loos' Public Toilets E2
3 Albertina E5
4 Augustinerkirche E4
5 Burggarten D5
6 Burgkapelle D4
7 Donnerbrunnen F4
Esperanto-museum .... (see 8)
8 Globenmuseum D2
9 Helmut-Zilk-Platz E5
10 Jüdisches Museum F3
11 Kaiserappartements D3
12 Kaisergruft F4
13 Kaiserliche Schatzkammer D4
Kapuziner-kirche .... (see 12)
14 Loos Haus D2
15 Michaelerkirche E2
16 Michaelerplatz Roman Ruins D2
17 Minoritenkirche C1
Monument Against War & Fascism .... (see 9)
18 Nationalbibliothek Prunksaal D4
19 Neue Burg Museums D4
20 Papyrusmuseum D4
21 Phantastenmuseum Wien E3
22 Schmetterlinghaus D4
Silberkammer .... (see 11)
Sisi Museum .... (see 11)
23 Spanish Riding School D3
24 Statue of Franz Josef D5
25 Statue of Mozart D5
26 TheaterMuseum E4
27 Volksgarten B2

Eating (p69)
28 Bierhof E1
29 Bitzinger Würstelstand am Albertinaplatz E5
30 Blue Mustard F3
31 Café Mozart E5
32 Le Bol F3
33 Meinl's Restaurant E1
Restaurant Herrlich .... (see 62)
34 Trześniewski F2

Drinking & Nightlife (p70)
35 Café Bräunerhof E3
36 Café Griensteidl D2
37 Café Leopold Hawelka F3
Café Sacher .... (see 59)
38 Café Tirolerhof F4
39 Demel E2
40 Esterházykeller E1
41 Fledermaus F2
42 Loos American Bar F3
Meinl's Weinbar .... (see 33)
Palffy Club .... (see 21)
43 Palmenhaus E5
44 Passage C5
45 Villon E2
46 Volksgarten ClubDiskothek B3

Entertainment (p72)
Burgkapelle Vienna Boys' Choir Tickets .... (see 6)
47 Hofburg Concert Halls D4
Österreichisches Filmmuseum .... (see 3)

Shopping (p72)
48 Augarten Wien F3
49 Bonbons Anzinger F5
50 Dorotheum E4
51 Freytag & Berndt E2
52 Gmundner E2
53 J&L Lobmeyr Vienna F4
54 Loden-Plankl E2
Meinl am Graben .... (see 33)
55 Mühlbauer F3
56 Oberlaa F3
57 Österreichische Werkstätten F3
58 Steiff E3

Sleeping (p193)
59 Hotel Sacher F5
60 Pertschy Palais Hotel E2
61 Radisson Blu Style Hotel D1
62 Steigenberger Hotel Herrenhof D1

Key on p250

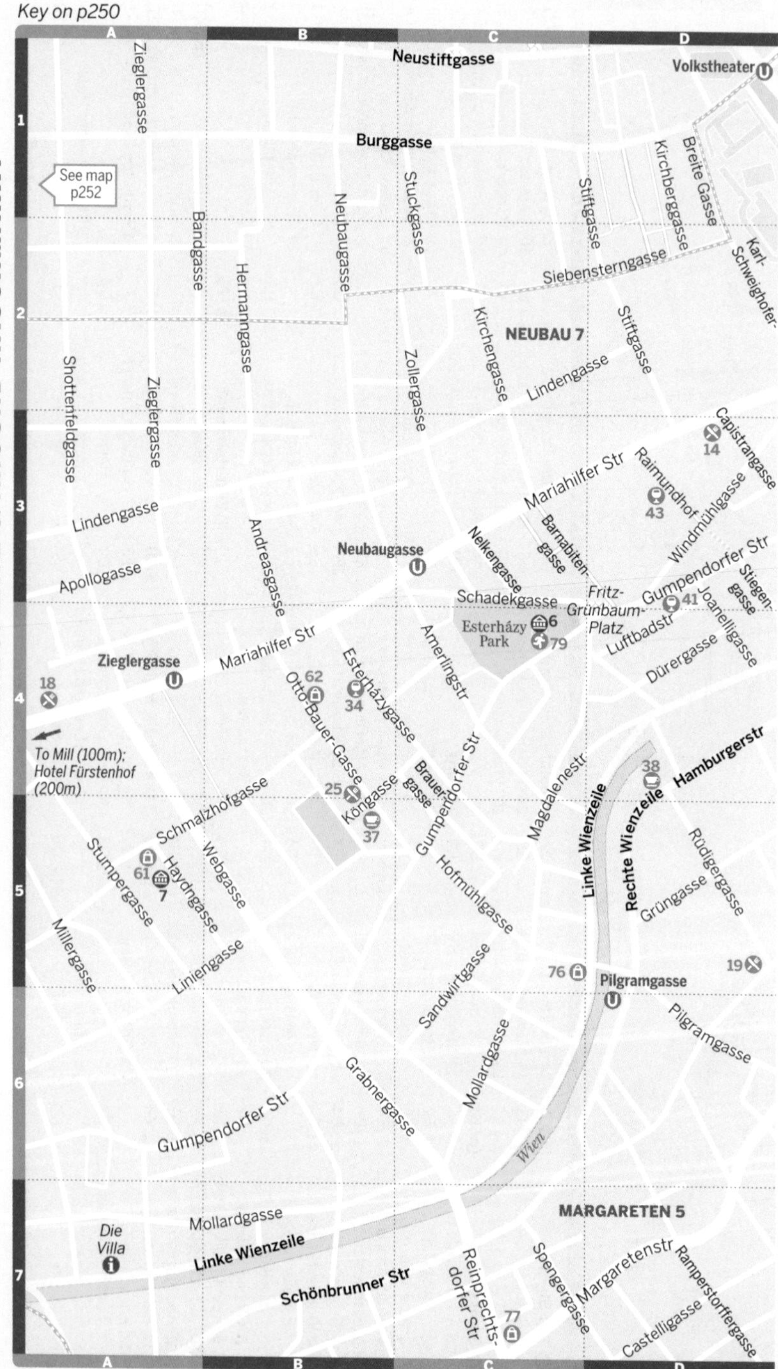
KARLSPLATZ & AROUND NASCHMARKT
A
B
C
D
1
2
3
4
5
6
7
Neustiftgasse
Volkstheater
Zieglergasse
Burggasse
See map p252
Bandgasse
Hermanngasse
Neubaugasse
Stuckgasse
Stiftgasse
Kirchberggasse
Breite Gasse
Siebensterngasse
Karl-Schweighofer-
Kirchengasse
NEUBAU 7
Zollergasse
Stiftgasse
Shottenfeldgasse
Zieglergasse
Lindengasse
Capistrangasse
14
Mariahilfer Str
Raimundhof
43
Windmühlgasse
Lindengasse
Andreasgasse
Neubaugasse
Nelkengasse
Barnabitengasse
Gumpendorfer Str
Stiegengasse
Apollogasse
Schadekgasse
Fritz-Grünbaum-Platz
41
Joanelligasse
Esterházy Park
6
79
Luftbadstr
Zieglergasse
Mariahilfer Str
Amerlingstr
Dürergasse
18
62
34
Esterházygasse
Otto-Bauer-Gasse
To Mill (100m); Hotel Fürstenhof (200m)
Gumpendorfer Str
Brauergasse
Magdalenestr
38
Hamburgerstr
25
Köngasse
37
Schmalzhofgasse
Linke Wienzeile
Rechte Wienzeile
Rüdigergasse
61
7
Haydngasse
Webgasse
Stumpergasse
Hofmühlgasse
Grüngasse
Millergasse
Liniengasse
Sandwirtgasse
76
Pilgramgasse
19
Pilgramgasse
Mollardgasse
Grabnergasse
Gumpendorfer Str
Wien
MARGARETEN 5
Mollardgasse
Die Villa
Linke Wienzeile
Schönbrunner Str
Reinprechtsdorfer Str
Spengergasse
Margaretenstr
Ramperstorffergasse
77
Castelligasse

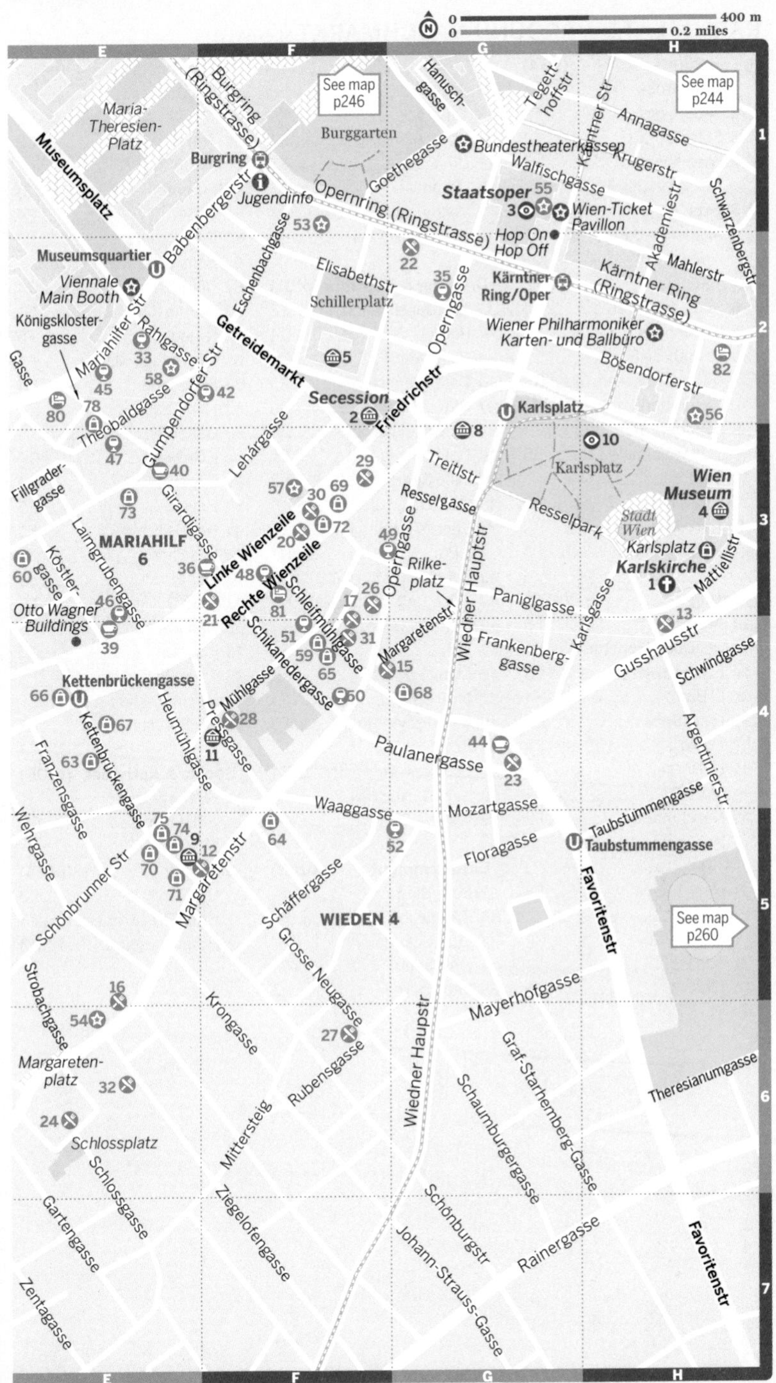

0 400 m
0 0.2 miles
See map p246
See map p244
See map p260
Maria-Theresien-Platz
Museumsplatz
Burgring (Ringstrasse)
Burgring
Jugendinfo
Burggarten
Goethegasse
Bundestheaterkassen
Staatsoper
Wien-Ticket Pavillon
Hop On Hop Off
Opernring (Ringstrasse)
Kärntner Ring/Oper
Kärntner Ring (Ringstrasse)
Wiener Philharmoniker Karten- und Ballbüro
Museumsquartier
Viennale Main Booth
Babenbergerstr
Eschenbachgasse
Elisabethstr
Schillerplatz
Getreidemarkt
Secession
Friedrichstr
Karlsplatz
Wien Museum
Karlskirche
MARIAHILF 6
WIEDEN 4
Linke Wienzeile
Rechte Wienzeile
Otto Wagner Buildings
Kettenbrückengasse
Taubstummengasse
Wiedner Hauptstr
Favoritenstr
Margaretenplatz
Schlossplatz

KARLSPLATZ & AROUND NASCHMARKT *Map on p248*

Top Sights (p94)

1 Karlskirche H3
2 Secession F2
3 Staatsoper G1
4 Wien Museum H3

Sights (p96)

5 Akademie der Bildenden Künste F2
6 Haus des Meeres C4
7 Haydnhaus A5
8 Kunsthalle Project Space G3
Naschmarkt (see 20)
9 Schubert Sterbewohnung E5
10 Stadtbahn Pavillons H3
11 Third Man Private Collection F4

Eating (p98)

12 Aromat F5
13 Delicious Monster H4
14 Eis Greissler D3
15 El Burro F4
16 Haas Beisl E5
17 Kojiro F4
18 Le Burger A4
19 Motto D5
20 Naschmarkt F3
Naschmarkt Deli (see 21)
21 Neni F3
22 Said the Butcher to the Cow G2
23 Santos G4
24 Silberwirt E6
25 Steman B4
26 Süssi F3
27 Tancredi F6
28 Ubl F4
29 Umar F3
30 Urbanek F3
31 Vollpension F4
32 Zum Alten Fassl E6

Drinking & Nightlife (p101)

33 Aux Gazelles E2
34 Barfly's Club B4
35 Bier & Bierli G2
36 Café Drechsler F3
37 Café Jelinek B5
38 Café Rüdigerhof D4
39 Café Savoy E4
40 Café Sperl E3
Club U (see 10)
41 Ebert's Cocktail Bar D3
42 Felixx F2
43 Juice Deli D3
44 Kaffee Fabrik G4
45 Lutz E2
46 Mango Bar E3
47 Mon Ami E3
48 Rafael's Vinothek F3
49 Roxy F3
50 Schikaneder F4
51 Sekt Comptoir F4
52 Wieden Bräu G5

Entertainment (p103)

53 Burg Kino F1
54 Filmcasino E6
55 Info unter den Arkaden G1
56 Musikverein H2
Schikaneder (see 50)
Staatsoper (see 3)
57 Theater an der Wien F3
58 Top Kino E2

Shopping (p103)

59 Babettes F4
60 Beer Lovers E3
61 Blühendes Konfekt A5
62 Die Schwalbe B4
63 Dörthe Kaufmann E4
64 feinedinge F5
65 Flo Vintage Mode F4
66 Flohmarkt E4
67 Fruth E4
68 Gabarage Upcycling Design G4
69 Gegenbauer F3
70 Helene E5
71 Henzls Ernte E5
72 Käseland F3
73 Lichterloh E3
74 Mein Design E5
75 Näherei Apfel E5
76 Rave Up C5
77 Thum Schinkenmanufaktur C7
78 We Bandits E2

Sports & Activities (p106)

79 Kletteranlage Flakturm C4

Sleeping (p194)

80 Das Tyrol E2
81 Hotel Drei Kronen F3
82 Hotel Imperial H2

MUSEUM DISTRICT & NEUBAU *Map on p252*

Top Sights (p109)

1 Kunsthistorisches Museum H4
2 MuseumsQuartier G4
3 Naturhistorisches Museum G4
4 Rathaus G1

Sights (p119)

5 Architekturzentrum Wien G4
6 Burgtheater H1
7 Hauptbücherei Wien B5
8 Hofmobiliendepot D6
9 Justizpalast G3
10 Kunsthalle Wien G4
11 Leopold Museum G4
12 MUMOK G4
13 Palais Epstein G3
14 Zoom G5

Eating (p120)

15 Amerlingbeisl F4
16 Die Burgermacher F4
17 Figar F5
18 Gaumenspiel D4
19 Glacis Beisl G4
20 Gradwohl D7
21 Halle G4
22 Kantine G4
23 Konoba D3
24 Liebling E6
25 Maschu Maschu II E6
26 Pizzeria-Osteria Da Giovanni F4
27 Pure Living Bakery D4
28 St Josef E5
29 Tart'a Tata E5
30 Tian Bistro F4
Vestibül ...... (see 6)

Drinking & Nightlife (p122)

31 Brickmakers Pub & Kitchen D5
Café Leopold ...... (see 11)
Café Oben ...... (see 7)
Dachboden ...... (see 60)
32 Donau G5
33 Europa E6
34 Frauencafé E3
Le Troquet ...... (see 17)
Rote Bar ...... (see 40)
35 Siebensternbräu F5
36 Wirr D4

Entertainment (p125)

Burgtheater ...... (see 6)
37 Dschungel Wien G4
38 Tanzquartier Wien G5
39 Vienna's English Theatre F2
40 Volkstheater G3

Shopping (p126)

41 Art Point E5
42 Das Möbel F4
43 Die Werkbank G4
44 Dirndlherz D3
45 Elke Freytag F5
46 Göttin des Glücks E5
47 Holzer Galerie F5
48 Ina Kent E5
49 Motmot E4
50 Mühlbauer E5
51 Park E5
52 Rathausplatz Christkindlmarkt G1
53 S/GHT E5
54 Schauraum E5
55 Schmuckladen E4
56 Schokov F5
57 Spittelberg Christkindlmarkt F4
58 Wiener Konfektion F5

Sports & Activities (p126)

59 Wiener Eistraum G1

Sleeping (p195)

60 25hours Hotel F3
61 Altstadt E4
62 Boutiquehotel Stadthalle A6
63 Hotel am Brillantengrund D5
64 Hotel Rathaus Wein & Design E3
65 my MOjO vie B4

Key on p251

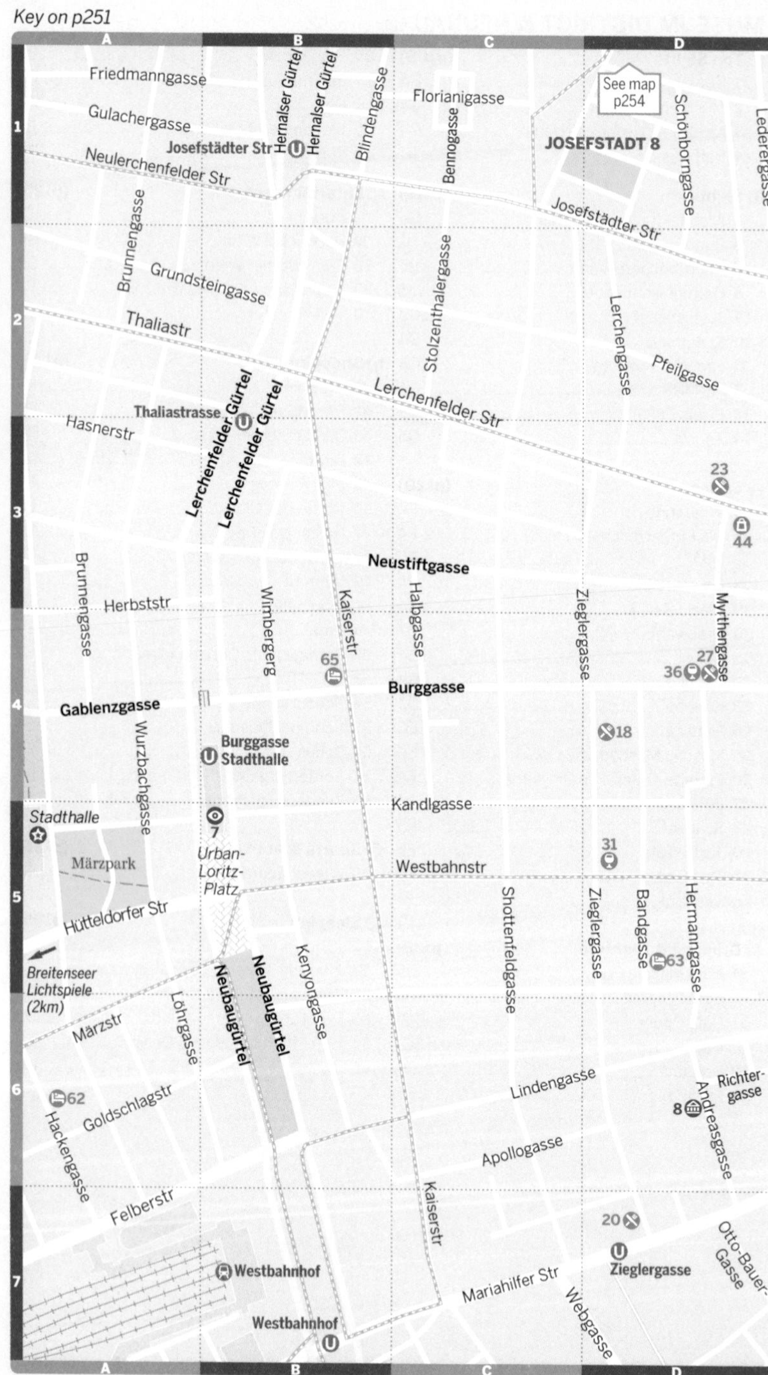

A
B
C
D
1
2
3
4
5
6
7
Friedmanngasse
Gulachergasse
Josefstädter Str
Hernalser Gürtel
Hernalser Gürtel
Blindengasse
Florianigasse
Bennogasse
See map p254
JOSEFSTADT 8
Schönborngasse
Lederergasse
Neulerchenfelder Str
Josefstädter Str
Brunnengasse
Grundsteingasse
Stolzenthalergasse
Thaliastr
Lerchengasse
Pfeilgasse
Lerchenfelder Str
Thaliastrasse
Lerchenfelder Gürtel
Lerchenfelder Gürtel
Hasnerstr
23
44
Neustiftgasse
Brunnengasse
Herbststr
Wimberggasse
Kaiserstr
Halbgasse
Zieglergasse
Myrthengasse
65
27
36
Burggasse
Gablenzgasse
18
Wurzbachgasse
Burggasse Stadthalle
Kandlgasse
Stadthalle
7
Märzpark
Urban-Loritz-Platz
31
Westbahnstr
Hütteldorfer Str
Shottenfeldgasse
Zieglergasse
Bandgasse
Hermanngasse
63
Breitenseer Lichtspiele (2km)
Neubaugürtel
Neubaugürtel
Kenyongasse
Märzstr
Löhrgasse
Lindengasse
Richtergasse
62
Goldschlagstr
8
Andreasgasse
Hackengasse
Apollogasse
Felberstr
Kaiserstr
20
Otto-Bauer-Gasse
Westbahnhof
Zieglergasse
Mariahilfer Str
Webgasse
Westbahnhof

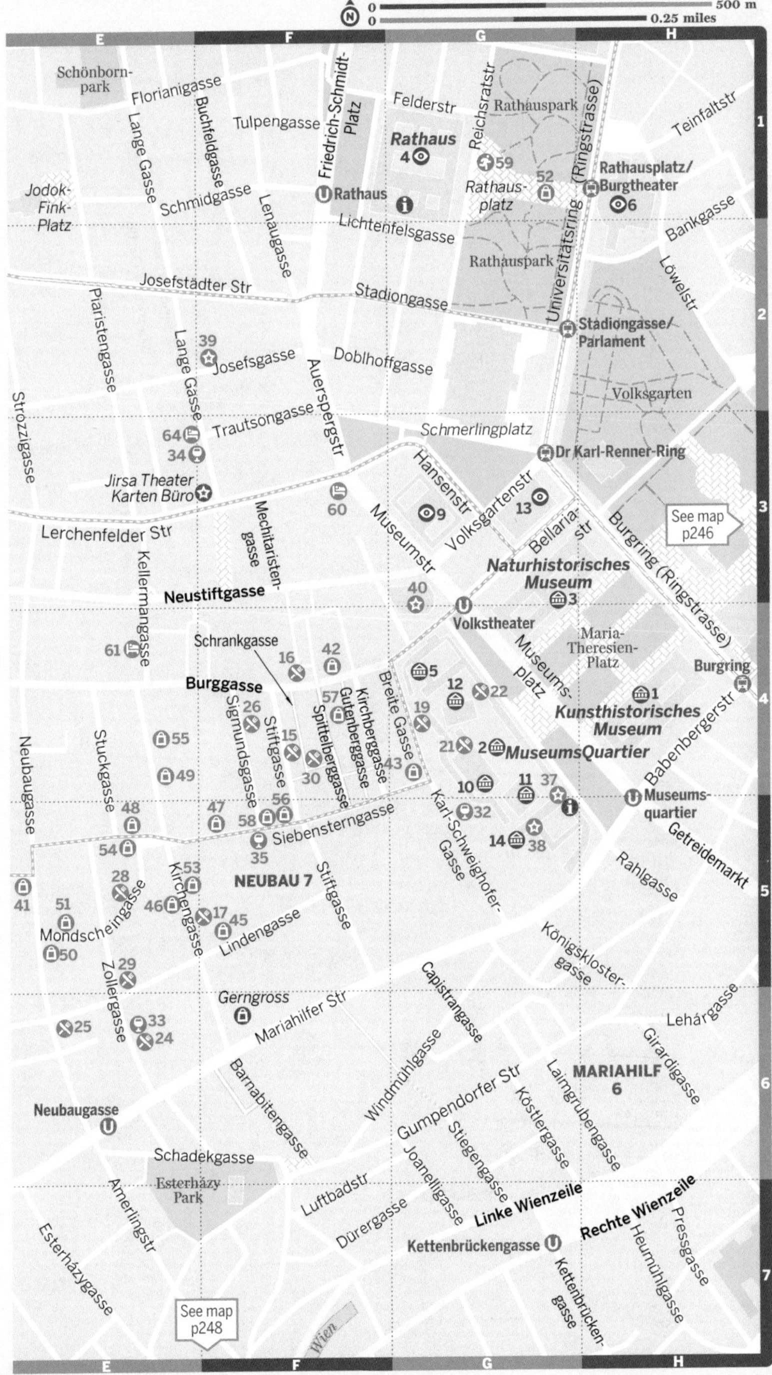

Schönbornpark
Florianigasse
Lange Gasse
Buchfeldgasse
Tulpengasse
Friedrich-Schmidt-Platz
Felderstr
Rathaus
Reichsratstr
Rathauspark
Universitätsring (Ringstrasse)
Teinfaltstr
Rathausplatz/Burgtheater
Jodok-Fink-Platz
Schmidgasse
Lenaugasse
Rathausplatz
Lichtenfelsgasse
Bankgasse
Löwelstr
Josefstädter Str
Stadiongasse
Piaristengasse
Stadiongasse/Parlament
Josefsgasse
Doblhoffgasse
Auerspergstr
Volksgarten
Strozzigasse
Trautsongasse
Schmerlingplatz
Dr Karl-Renner-Ring
Jirsa Theater Karten Büro
Hansenstr
Volksgartenstr
Mechitaristengasse
Museumstr
Bellariastr
Burgring (Ringstrasse)
See map p246
Lerchenfelder Str
Kellermangasse
Naturhistorisches Museum
Neustiftgasse
Volkstheater
Maria-Theresien-Platz
Schrankgasse
Museumsplatz
Burgring
Burggasse
Breite Gasse
Kirchberggasse
Gutenberggasse
Spittelberggasse
Sigmundsgasse
Stiftgasse
Kunsthistorisches Museum
Babenbergerstr
Stuckgasse
MuseumsQuartier
Neubaugasse
Museumsquartier
Karl-Schweighofer-Gasse
Siebensterngasse
Getreidemarkt
Rahlgasse
NEUBAU 7
Kirchengasse
Mondscheingasse
Lindengasse
Königsklostergasse
Zollergasse
Capistrangasse
Gerngross
Mariahilfer Str
Lehárgasse
Girardigasse
Barnabitengasse
Windmühlgasse
Gumpendorfer Str
Köstlergasse
Laimgrubengasse
MARIAHILF 6
Neubaugasse
Stiegengasse
Joanelligasse
Schadekgasse
Esterházy Park
Amerlingstr
Luftbadstr
Linke Wienzeile
Rechte Wienzeile
Dürergasse
Kettenbrückengasse
Heumühlgasse
Pressgasse
Esterházygasse
Kettenbrückengasse
See map p248
Wien
0 500 m
0 0.25 miles
E F G H
1 2 3 4 5 6 7

Key on p256

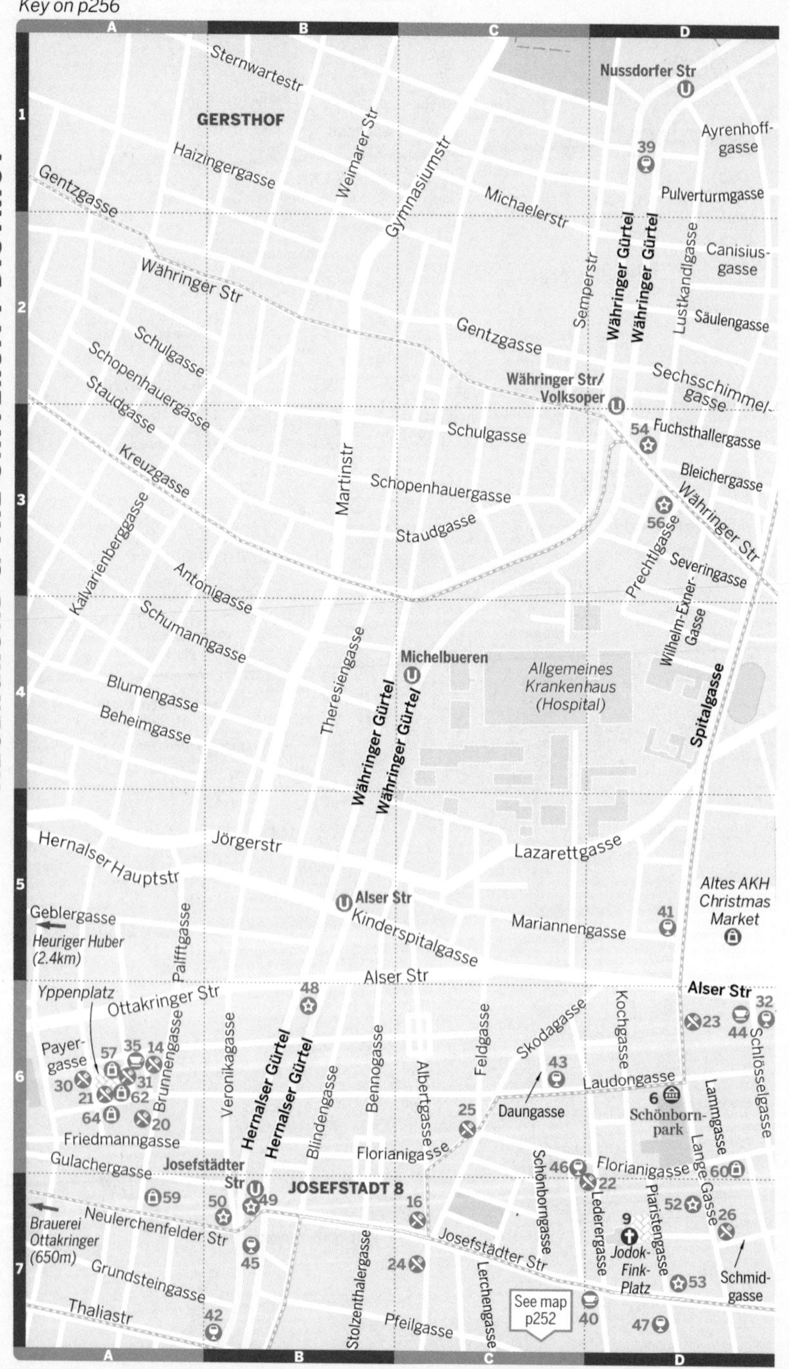
A
B
C
D
1
2
3
4
5
6
7
GERSTHOF
Sternwartestr
Nussdorfer Str
Ayrenhoff-gasse
39
Haizingergasse
Weimarer Str
Gymnasiumstr
Gentzgasse
Michaelerstr
Pulverturmgasse
Canisius-gasse
Währinger Gürtel
Währinger Gürtel
Semperstr
Lustkandlgasse
Währinger Str
Säulengasse
Gentzgasse
Schulgasse
Schopenhauergasse
Währinger Str/ Volksoper
Sechsschimmel-gasse
Staudgasse
Schulgasse
54
Fuchsthallergasse
Kreuzgasse
Martinstr
Schopenhauergasse
Bleichergasse
Währinger Str
56
Staudgasse
Kalvarienberggasse
Antonigasse
Prechtlgasse
Severingasse
Schumanngasse
Wilhelm-Exner-Gasse
Michelbueren
Allgemeines Krankenhaus (Hospital)
Blumengasse
Theresiengasse
Beheimgasse
Währinger Gürtel
Währinger Gürtel
Spitalgasse
Hernalser Hauptstr
Jörgerstr
Lazarettgasse
Altes AKH Christmas Market
Alser Str
Geblergasse
Heuriger Huber (2.4km)
Kinderspitalgasse
Mariannengasse
41
Palffygasse
Alser Str
Yppenplatz
Ottakringer Str
48
Alser Str
32
Payer-gasse
57
35
14
Brunnengasse
Veronikagasse
Hernalser Gürtel
Hernalser Gürtel
Bennogasse
Albertgasse
Feldgasse
Skodagasse
Kochgasse
23
44
Schlösselgasse
30
31
21
62
64
20
Blindengasse
43
Laudongasse
6
Schönborn-park
Lammgasse
25
Daungasse
Friedmanngasse
Florianigasse
Gulachergasse
Josefstädter Str
Schönborngasse
46
Florianigasse
Lange Gasse
60
JOSEFSTADT 8
22
59
50
49
16
Lederergasse
Piaristengasse
52
Brauerei Ottakringer (650m)
Neulerchenfelder Str
26
9
45
Josefstädter Str
Jodok-Fink-Platz
24
Stolzenthalergasse
Lerchengasse
53
Schmid-gasse
Grundsteingasse
See map p252
42
Thaliastr
Pfeilgasse
40
47

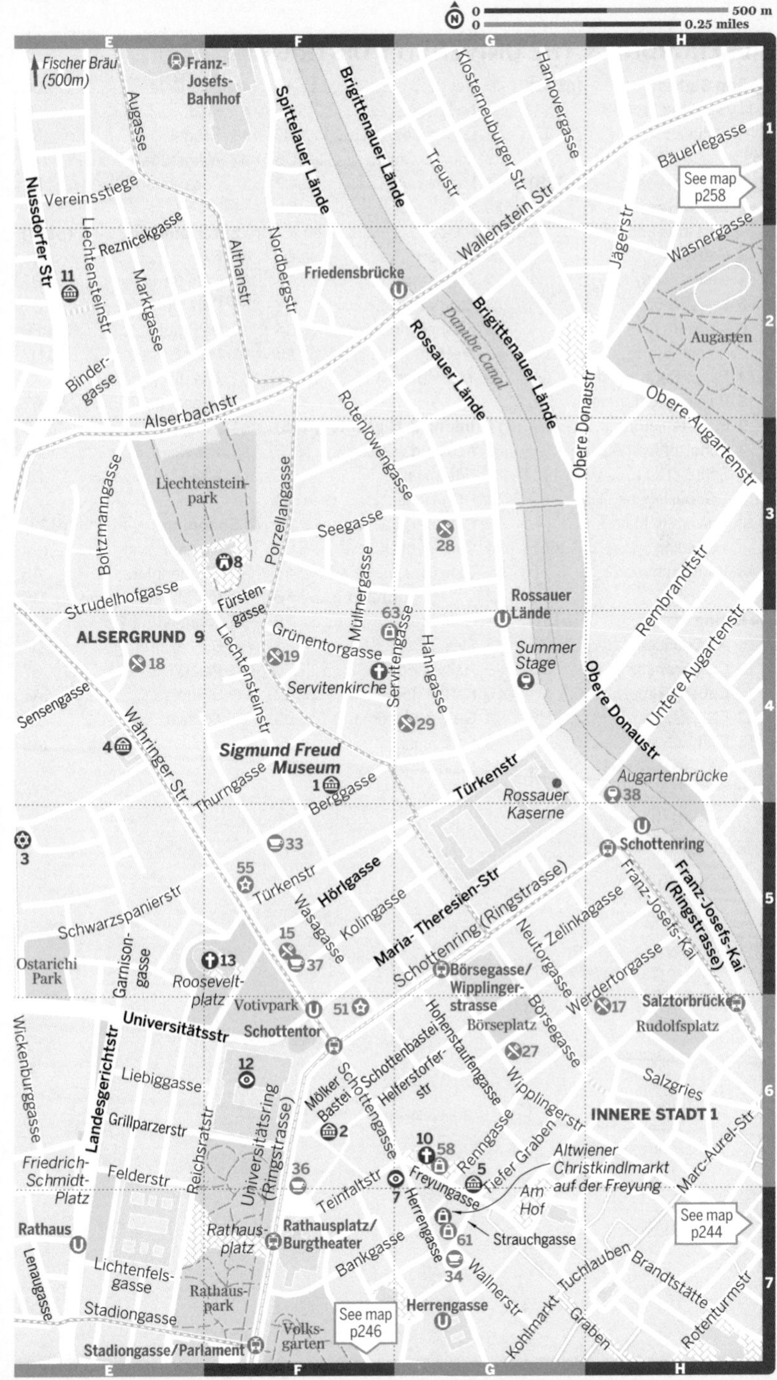

ALSERGRUND & THE UNIVERSITY DISTRICT
0 500 m
0 0.25 miles
Fischer Bräu (500m)
Franz-Josefs-Bahnhof
Augasse
Spittelauer Lände
Brigittenauer Lände
Klosterneuburger Str
Hannovergasse
Treustr
Bäuerlegasse
See map p258
Nussdorfer Str
Vereinsstiege
Lichtensteinstr
Reznicekgasse
Althanstr
Nordbergstr
Wallenstein Str
Jägerstr
Wasnergasse
Friedensbrücke
Marktgasse
Rossauer Lände
Danube Canal
Augarten
Bindergasse
Alserbachstr
Rotenlöwengasse
Obere Donaustr
Obere Augartenstr
Boltzmanngasse
Liechtensteinpark
Porzellangasse
Seegasse
Müllnergasse
Strudelhofgasse
Fürstengasse
Rossauer Lände
Rembrandtstr
ALSERGRUND 9
Grünentorgasse
Servitengasse
Hahngasse
Summer Stage
Liechtensteinstr
Servitenkirche
Untere Augartenstr
Sensengasse
Währinger Str
Sigmund Freud Museum
Türkenstr
Augartenbrücke
Thurngasse
Berggasse
Rossauer Kaserne
Schottenring
Hörlgasse
Maria-Theresien-Str
Schottenring (Ringstrasse)
Franz-Josefs-Kai (Ringstrasse)
Türkenstr
Wasagasse
Kolingasse
Zelinkagasse
Schwarzspanierstr
Franz-Josefs-Kai
Neutorgasse
Ostarichi Park
Garnisongasse
Roosevelt-platz
Börsegasse/Wipplinger-strasse
Werdertorgasse
Votivpark
Salztorbrücke
Rudolfsplatz
Universitätsstr
Schottentor
Börseplatz
Börsegasse
Hohenstaufengasse
Wickenburggasse
Landesgerichtstr
Liebiggasse
Schottenbastei
Helferstorferstr
Salzgries
Mölker Bastei
Schottengasse
Wipplingerstr
INNERE STADT 1
Grillparzerstr
Reichsratstr
Universitätsring (Ringstrasse)
Renngasse
Tiefer Graben
Marc-Aurel-Str
Friedrich-Schmidt-Platz
Felderstr
Altwiener Christkindlmarkt auf der Freyung
Teinfaltstr
Freyungasse
Am Hof
Herrengasse
Rathaus
Rathausplatz
Rathausplatz/Burgtheater
Strauchgasse
See map p244
Lenaugasse
Lichtenfelsgasse
Bankgasse
Wallnerstr
Tuchlauben
Brandstätte
Rathauspark
Kohlmarkt
Graben
Rotenturmstr
Stadiongasse
See map p246
Herrengasse
Volksgarten
Stadiongasse/Parlament
E
F
G
H
1
2
3
4
5
6
7
1
2
3
4
5
7
8
10
11
12
13
15
17
18
19
27
28
29
33
34
36
37
38
51
55
58
61
63

ALSERGRUND & THE UNIVERSITY DISTRICT *Map on p254*

Top Sights (p130)

1 Sigmund Freud Museum ...F4

Sights (p129)

2 Beethoven Pasqualatihaus...F6
3 Bethaus...E5
4 Josephinum...E4
5 Kunstforum...G6
6 Museum für Volkskunde...D6
7 Palais Daun-Kinsky...G6
8 Palais Liechtenstein...F3
9 Piaristenkirche...D7
10 Schottenkirche...G6
11 Schubert Geburtshaus...E2
12 University Main Building...F6
13 Votivkirche...F5

Eating (p131)

14 An-Do Fisch...A6
15 Café Français...F5
16 Café Hummel...C7
17 EN...H6
18 Flein...E4
19 Gasthaus Wickerl...F4
20 Kent...A6
21 La Salvia...A6
22 La Tavolozza...D7
23 Leones Gelato...D6
24 Mamamon...C7
25 Punks...C6
Rasouli...(see 35)
26 Schnattl...D7
27 Soupkultur...G6
28 Stomach...G3
29 Suppenwirtschaft...G4
30 Wetter...A6
31 Yppenplatz 4...A6

Drinking & Nightlife (p135)

32 Achtundzwanzig...D6
Botanical Gardens...(see 37)
33 Café Berg...F5
34 Café Central...G7
35 Café Cl...A6
36 Café Landtmann...F6
37 Café Stein...F5
38 Flex...H4
39 Halbestadt Bar...D1
40 KaffeeModul...D7
41 Lane & Merriman's...D5
42 Loft...B7
43 Mas!...C6
44 POC Cafe...D6
45 Rhiz...B7
46 Tunnel...C6
47 Weinstube Josefstadt...D7

Entertainment (p137)

48 B72...B6
49 Café Carina...B7
50 Café Concerto...B7
51 De France...F6
52 Miles Smiles...D7
53 Theater in der Josefstadt...D7
54 Volksoper...D3
55 Votivkino...F5
56 WUK...D3

Shopping (p138)

57 Bauernmarkt Yppenplatz...A6
58 Bio-Markt Freyung...G6
59 Brunnenmarkt...A7
60 Die Höllerei...D6
61 Palais Ferstel...G7
62 Staud's...A6
63 Xocolat...F4
64 Y5...A6

PRATER & EAST OF THE DANUBE *Map on p258*

Key on p257

PRATER & EAST OF THE DANUBE

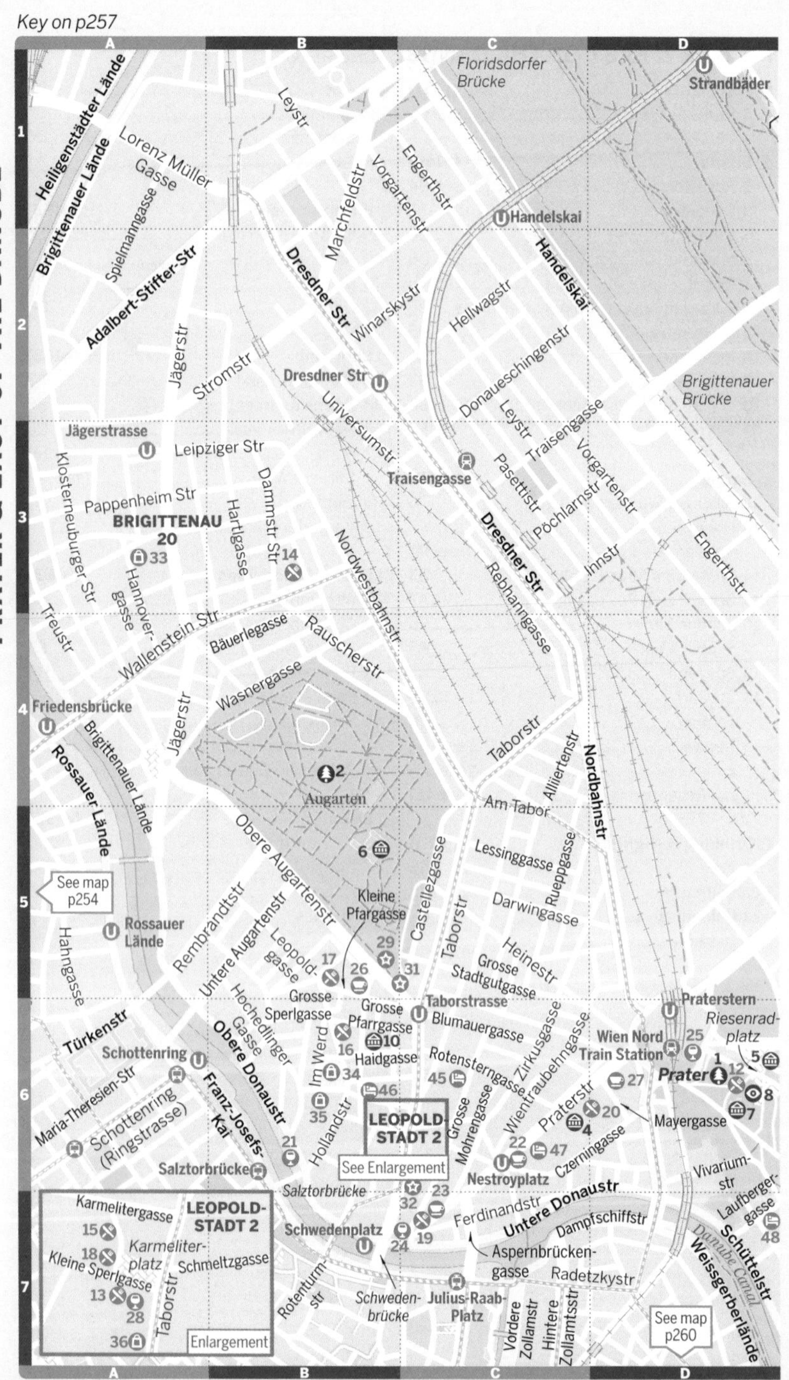

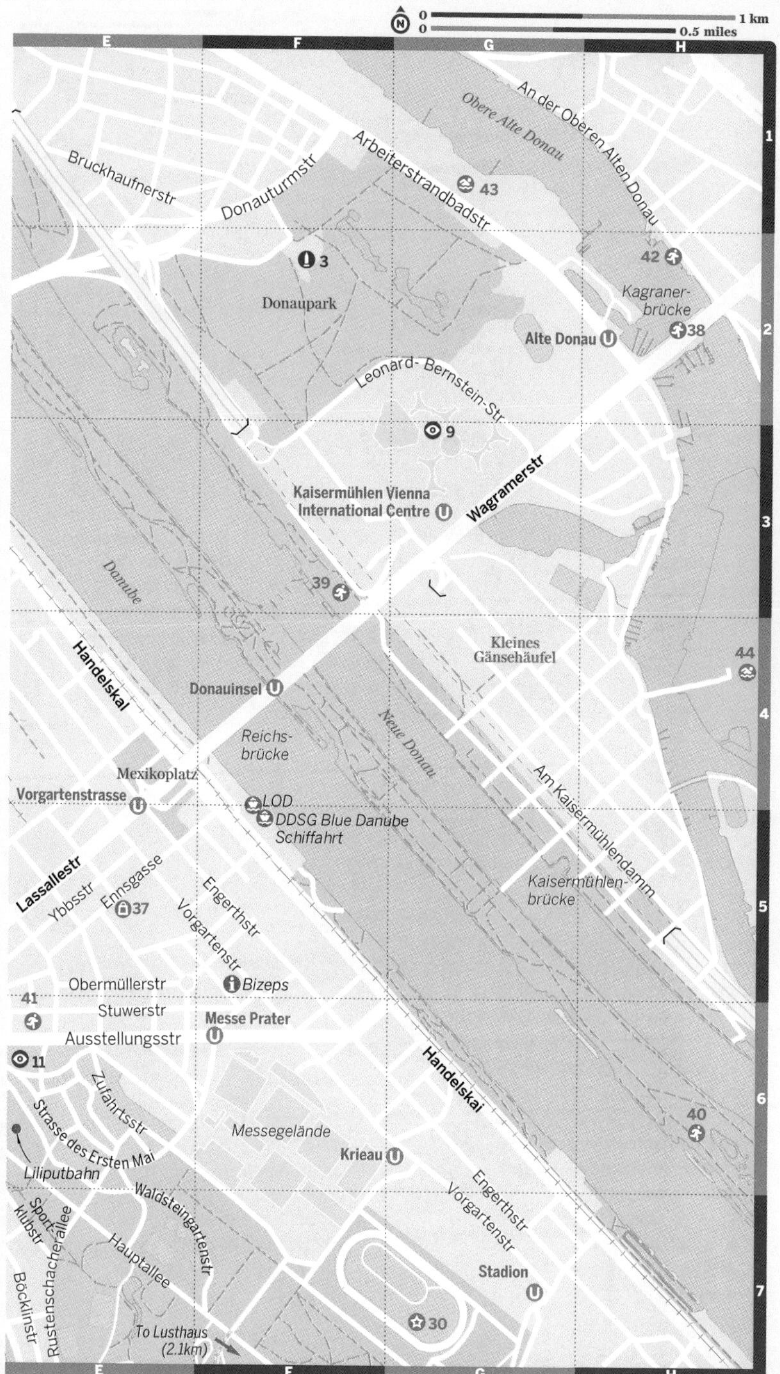

0
1 km
0
0.5 miles
E
F
G
H
1
2
3
4
5
6
7
PRATER & EAST OF THE DANUBE
Obere Alte Donau
An der Oberen Alten Donau
Arbeiterstrandbadstr
Bruckhaufnerstr
Donauturmstr
43
3
Donaupark
42
Kagraner-
brücke
38
Alte Donau
Leonard- Bernstein-Str
9
Kaisermühlen Vienna
International Centre
Wagramerstr
Danube
39
Kleines
Gänsehäufel
44
Handelskai
Donauinsel
Reichs-
brücke
Neue Donau
Mexikoplatz
Am Kaisermühlendamm
Vorgartenstrasse
LOD
DDSG Blue Danube
Schiffahrt
Lassallestr
Ybbsstr
Ennsgasse
37
Engerthstr
Vorgartenstr
Kaisermühlen-
brücke
Obermüllerstr
Bizeps
41
Stuwerstr
Messe Prater
Ausstellungsstr
11
Handelskai
Zufahrtsstr
Strasse des Ersten Mai
Liliputbahn
Messegelände
Krieau
40
Waldsteingartenstr
Sport-
klubstr
Rustenschacherallee
Hauptallee
Engerthstr
Vorgartenstr
Stadion
Böcklinstr
To Lusthaus
(2.1km)
30

SCHLOSS BELVEDERE TO THE CANAL

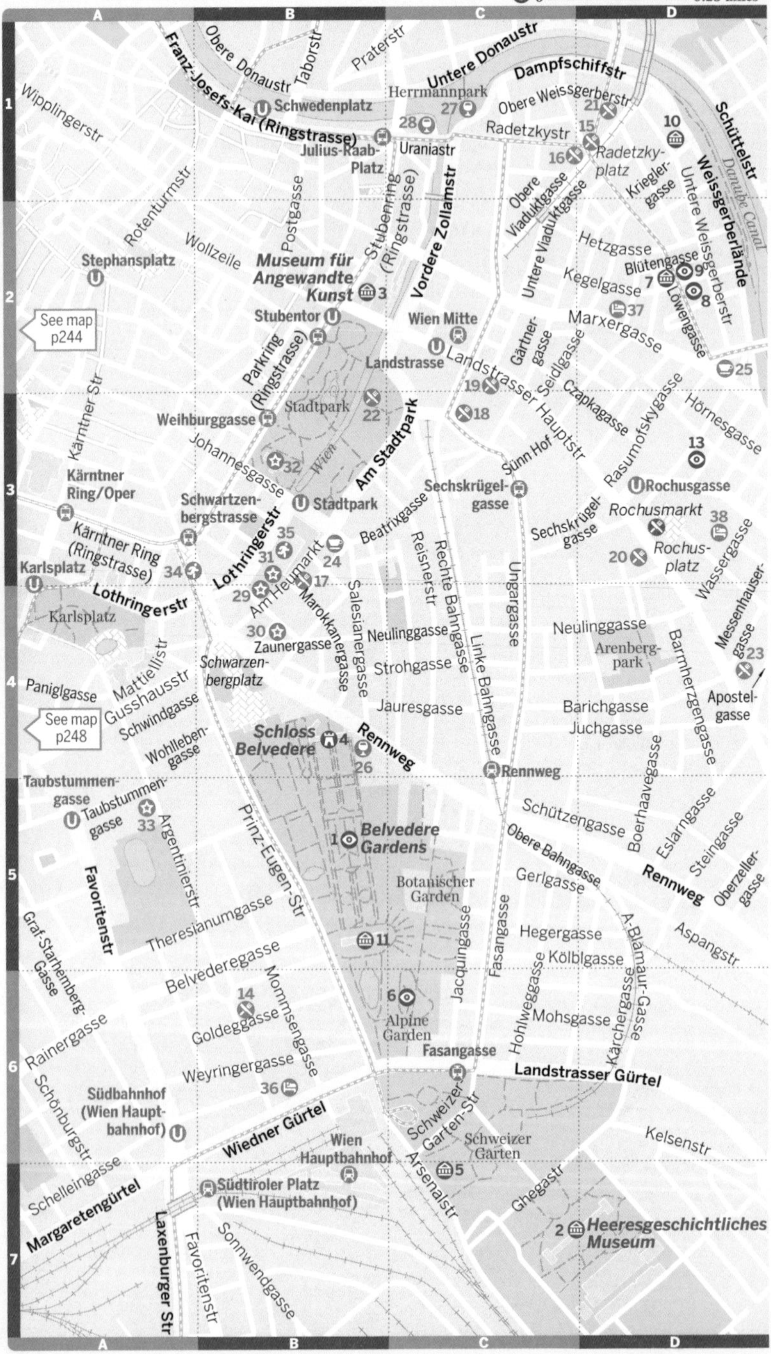

0 500 m
0 0.25 miles

A B C D

1 2 3 4 5 6 7

Franz-Josefs-Kai (Ringstrasse)
Obere Donaustr
Taborstr
Praterstr
Untere Donaustr
Dampfschiffstr
Herrmannpark
27
Obere Weissgerberstr
21
Schüttelstr
10
Wipplingerstr
Schwedenplatz
28
Radetzkystr
15
Julius-Raab-Platz
Uraniastr
16
Radetzkyplatz
Krieglergasse
Weissgerberlände
Untere Weissgerberstr
Danube Canal
Rotenturmstr
Postgasse
Stubenring (Ringstrasse)
Vordere Zollamstr
Obere Viaduktgasse
Untere Viaduktgasse
Hetzgasse
Wollzeile
Stephansplatz
Museum für Angewandte Kunst
3
Blütengasse
7
9
8
Kegelgasse
Löwengasse
37
Stubentor
Wien Mitte
Marxergasse

See map p244

Parkring (Ringstrasse)
Landstrasse
Gärtnergasse
Seidlgasse
25
Kärntner Str
Landstrasser Hauptstr
19
Czapkagasse
Rasumofskygasse
Hörnesgasse
Stadtpark
22
18
Weihburggasse
Am Stadtpark
Sünn Hof
13
Johannesgasse
Wien
32
Sechskrügelgasse
Rochusgasse
Kärntner Ring/Oper
Schwartzenbergstrasse
Stadtpark
Sechskrügelgasse
Rochusmarkt
38
Kärntner Ring (Ringstrasse)
35
Beatrixgasse
Lothringerstr
31
24
Reisnerstr
Rechte Bahngasse
Ungargasse
20
Rochusplatz
Wassergasse
Karlsplatz
34
Am Heumarkt
17
Lothringerstr
29
Marokkanergasse
Salesianergasse
Messenhausergasse
Karlsplatz
30
Neulinggasse
Neulinggasse
Zaunergasse
Arenbergpark
Barmherzgengasse
23
Mattiellistr
Schwarzenbergplatz
Strohgasse
Linke Bahngasse
Paniglgasse
Gusshausstr
Apostelgasse
Schwindgasse
Jauresgasse
Barichgasse

See map p248

Wohllebengasse
Schloss Belvedere
4
Rennweg
Juchgasse
26
Boerhaavegasse
Rennweg
Taubstummengasse
Taubstummengasse
33
Argentinierstr
Prinz-Eugen-Str
Schützengasse
Eslarngasse
Steingasse
1
Belvedere Gardens
Obere Bahngasse
Favoritenstr
Rennweg
Oberzellergasse
Botanischer Garden
Gerlgasse
Graf-Starhemberg-Gasse
Theresianumgasse
A-Blamaur-Gasse
Aspangstr
11
Jacquingasse
Fasangasse
Hegergasse
Belvederegasse
Mommsengasse
Kölblgasse
14
6
Alpine Garden
Hohlweggasse
Mohsgasse
Kärchergasse
Goldeggasse
Fasangasse
Rainergasse
Weyringergasse
Landstrasser Gürtel
36
Schönburgstr
Südbahnhof (Wien Hauptbahnhof)
Schweizer-Garten-Str
Wiedner Gürtel
Schweizer Garten
Kelsenstr
Wien Hauptbahnhof
5
Schelleingasse
Südtiroler Platz (Wien Hauptbahnhof)
Arsenalstr
Ghegastr
Margaretengürtel
2
Heeresgeschichtliches Museum
Laxenburger Str
Favoritenstr
Sonnwendgasse

Top Sights **(p141)**
1 Belvedere Gardens ... B5
2 Heeresgeschichtliches Museum ... C7
3 Museum für Angewandte Kunst ... B2
4 Schloss Belvedere ... B4

Sights **(p150)**
5 21er Haus ... C7
6 Alpengarten ... C6
7 Fälschermuseum ... D2
8 Hundertwasserhaus ... D2
9 Kalke Village ... D2
10 KunstHausWien ... D1
11 Oberes Belvedere ... B5
12 St Marxer Friedhof ... E7
Unteres Belvedere ... (see 4)
13 Wittgensteinhaus ... D3

Eating **(p151)**
14 Café Goldegg ... B6
15 Cafe Menta ... D1
16 Gasthaus Wild ... C1
17 Gmoakeller ... B3
18 Hidden Kitchen Park ... C3
19 Joseph Brot ... C2
20 Lingenhel ... D3
Meierei im Stadtpark . (see 22)
21 Restaurant Indus ... D1
22 Steirereck im Stadtpark ... B3
23 That's Amore ... D4

Drinking & Nightlife **(p152)**
24 Café am Heumarkt ... B3
25 Café Zartl ... D2
26 Salm Bräu ... B4
27 Strandbar Herrmann ... C1
28 Urania ... C1

Entertainment **(p152)**
29 Akademietheater ... B4
30 Arnold Schönberg Center ... B4
31 Konzerthaus ... B3
32 Kursalon ... B3
33 Radiokulturhaus ... A5

Sports & Activities **(p154)**
34 3 City Wave ... A3
35 Wiener Eislaufverein ... B3

Sleeping **(p195)**
36 Hotel Prinz Eugen ... B6
37 Ruby Sofie ... D2
38 Spiess & Spiess ... D3

SCHLOSS SCHÖNBRUNN & AROUND

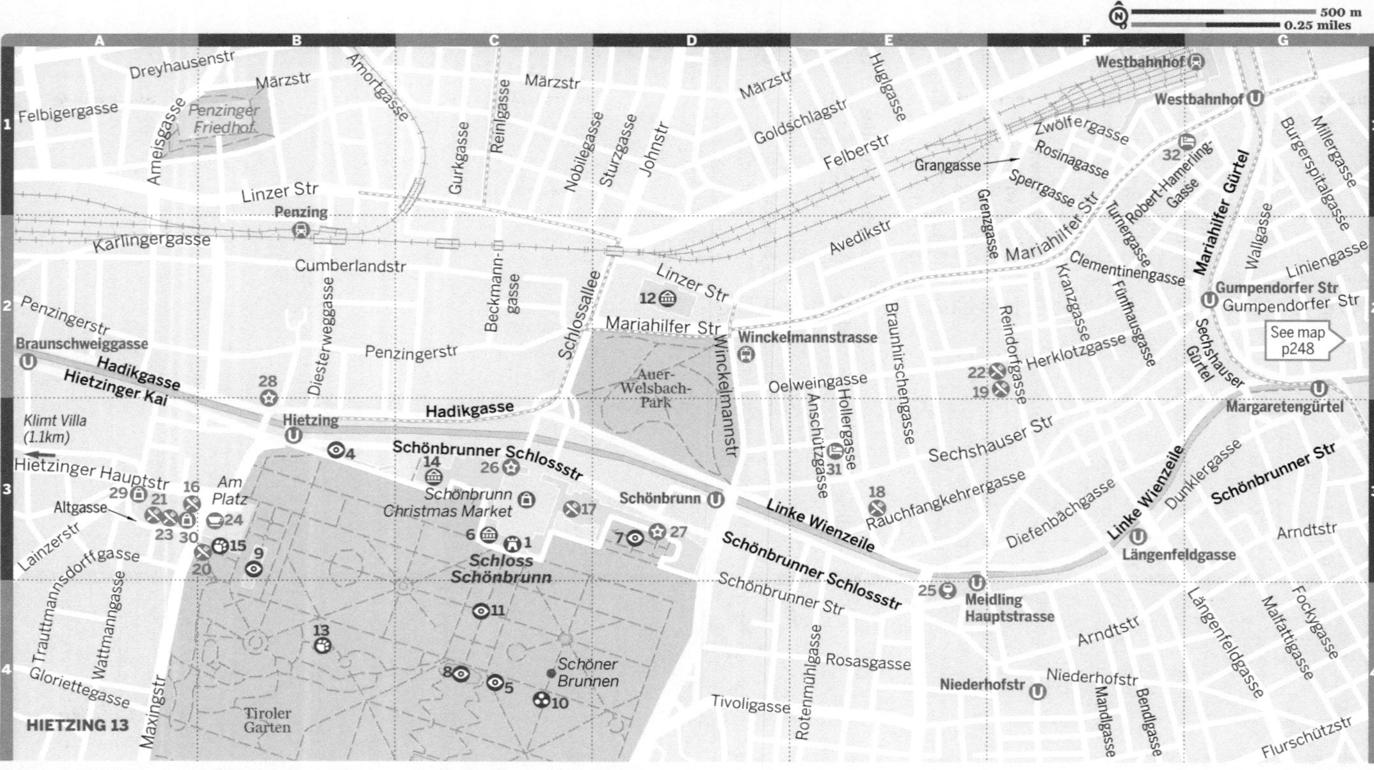

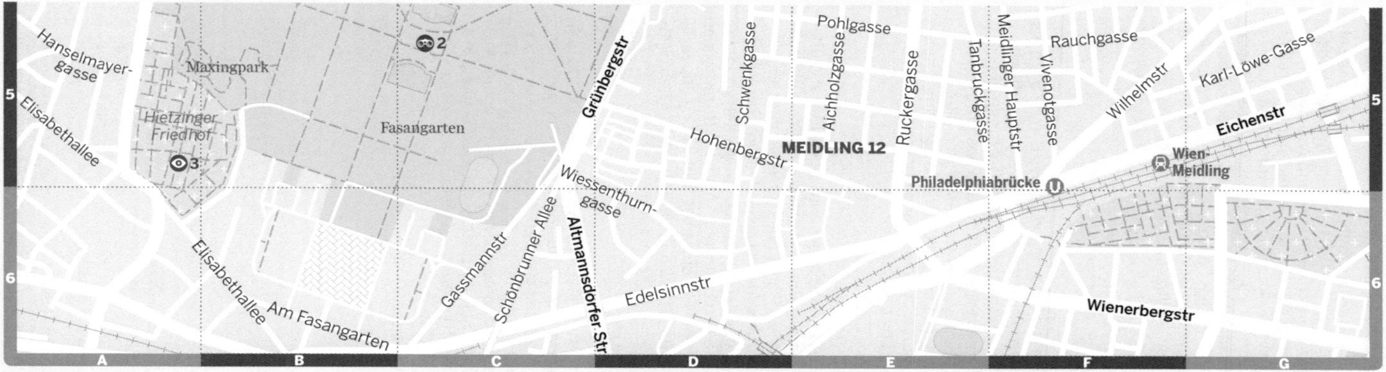

Top Sights (p167)
1 Schloss Schönbrunn ... C3

Sights (p171)
2 Gloriette ... C5
3 Hietzinger Friedhof ... A5
4 Hofpavillon Hietzing ... B3
5 Irrgarten ... C4
6 Kindermuseum ... C3
7 Kronprinzengarten ... D3
8 Neptunbrunnen ... C4
9 Palmenhaus ... B3
10 Roman Ruins ... C4
11 Schloss Schönbrunn Gardens ... C4
12 Technisches Museum ... D2
13 Tiergarten ... B4
14 Wagenburg ... C3
15 Wüstenhaus ... B3

Eating (p172)
16 Brandauers Schlossbräu ... A3
17 Hofbackstube Schönbrunn ... C3
18 Hollerei ... E3
19 Mafiosi ... F2
20 Maxing Stüberl ... B3
21 Pure Living Bakery ... A3
22 Quell ... F2
23 Waldemar ... A3

Drinking & Nightlife (p173)
24 Aida ... B3
Café Gloriette ... (see 2)
25 U4 ... E4

Entertainment (p174)
26 Marionetten Theater ... C3
27 Orangery ... D3
28 Reigen ... B3

Shopping (p174)
29 1130Wein ... A3
30 Gold n' Guitars ... A3

Sleeping (p196)
31 Angel's Place ... E3
32 Wombat's ... G1

Our Story

A beat-up old car, a few dollars in the pocket and a sense of adventure. In 1972 that's all Tony and Maureen Wheeler needed for the trip of a lifetime – across Europe and Asia overland to Australia. It took several months, and at the end – broke but inspired – they sat at their kitchen table writing and stapling together their first travel guide, *Across Asia on the Cheap*. Within a week they'd sold 1500 copies. Lonely Planet was born.

Today, Lonely Planet has offices in Franklin, London, Melbourne, Oakland, Dublin, Beijing and Delhi, with more than 600 staff and writers. We share Tony's belief that 'a great guidebook should do three things: inform, educate and amuse'.

Our Writers

Catherine Le Nevez

Catherine's wanderlust kicked in when she roadtripped across Europe from her Parisian base aged four, and she's been hitting the road at every opportunity since, travelling to around 60 countries and completing her Doctorate of Creative Arts in Writing, Masters in Professional Writing, and postgrad qualifications in editing and publishing along the way. Over the past dozen-plus years she's written scores of Lonely Planet guides and articles covering Paris, France, Europe and far beyond. Her work has also appeared in numerous online and print publications. Topping Catherine's list of travel tips is to travel without any expectations.

Kerry Christiani

Kerry is an award-winning travel writer, photographer and Lonely Planet author, specialising in central and southern Europe. Based in Wales, she has authored and co-authored more than a dozen Lonely Planet titles. An adventure addict, she loves mountains, cold places and true wilderness. She features her latest work at www.its-a-small-world.com and tweets @kerrychristiani. Kerry's insatiable wanderlust has taken her to all seven continents – from the frozen wilderness of Antarctica to the Australian outback – and shows no sign of waning. Her writing appears regularly in publications like *Adventure Travel* magazine and she is a *Telegraph Travel* expert for Austria and Wales.

Donna Wheeler

Donna has written guidebooks for Lonely Planet for 10 years, including the *Italy, Norway, Belgium, Africa, Tunisia, Algeria, France, Austria* and *Melbourne* titles. She is the author of *Paris Precincts*, a curated photographic guide to the city's best bars, restaurants and shops, and is reporter for Italian contemporary art publisher My Art Guides. Donna's work on contemporary art, architecture and design, food, wine, wilderness areas and cultural history also can be found in a variety of other publications. She became a travel writer after various careers as a commissioning editor, creative director, digital producer and content strategist.

Published by Lonely Planet Global Limited
CRN 554153
8th edition – May 2017
ISBN 978 1 78657 438 1

10 9 8 7 6 5 4 3 2 1
Printed in Singapore